WRITER'S RESOURCES:
From Paragraph to Essay

Julie Robitaille and Robert Connelly

Writer's Resources:

From Parapraph to Essay

Julie Robitaille and Robert Connelly

THOMSON
HEINLE

Australia • Canada • Mexico • Singapore • Spain • United Kingdom • United States

THOMSON
HEINLE

Writer's Resources: From Paragraph to Essay
Julie Robitaille and Robert Connelly

Publisher: Michael Rosenberg
Acquisitions Editor: Stephen Dalphin
Production Editor: Michael Burggren
Marketing Manager: Ken Kasee
Manufacturing Coordinator: Mary Beth Hennebury

Compositor: Argosy
Project Manager: Argosy
Illustrator: Argosy
Cover/Text Designer: Chris Twitchell/Amy Adams
Printer: Quebecor World

For permission to use material from this text or product contact us:

Tel	1-800-730-2214
Fax	1-800-730-2215
Web	www.thomsonrights.com

ISBN: 0-15-504995-x

Library of Congress Cataloging-in-Publication Data

Robitaille, Julie.
    Writer's Resources : From Paragraph to Essay / by Julie Robitaille & Robert Connelly
        p. cm.
Includes index.
    ISBN 0-15-504995-X (alk. paper)
    1. English language—Rhetoric.   2. Report writing.
I. Connelly, Robert, 1952-   II. Title.
    PE1408 .R6379 2002
    808' .042—dc21

                                        2002070072

International Division List

ASIA (excluding India)
Thomson Learning
60 Albert Street #15-01
Albert Complex
Singapore 189969

AUSTRALIA/NEW ZEALAND
Nelson/Thomson Learning
102 Dodds Street
South Melbourne
Victoria 3205 Australia

CANADA
Nelson/Thomson Learning
1120 Birchmount Road
Scarborough, Ontario
Canada M1K 5G4

LATIN AMERICA
Thomson Learning
Seneca, 53
Colonio Polanco
11560 México D.F. México

SPAIN
Thomson Learning
Calle Magallanes, 25
28015-Madrid
España

UK/EUROPE/MIDDLE EAST
Thomson Learning
Berkshire House
168-173 High Holborn
London, WC1V 7AA, United Kingdom

Table of Contents

Part VII

Preface

Writer's Resources is an outgrowth of our twenty years of experience teaching beginning college students in the classroom and in the writing center. In addition to being teachers, we are both actively committed to the writing life. Our personal experience as writers and our professional experience as teachers have taught us that writing is one of the most difficult yet most significant activities we can engage in as human beings. Writing helps us know what we think, and, as a result, it helps us to know who we are. It also helps us interact with others and participate in our community.

The writing classroom is changing just as our culture and the demographics of our student population are changing. Beginning college writers need more than the basics of instruction in order to succeed. We support the notion that the classroom is a learning community in which the diversity of the class is embraced and celebrated through the writing of its members. We plant the seeds for this learning community with our own peer models who accompany students on the journey through this textbook. The four peers provide examples of their journals, their writing process, their paragraphs, and their essays. They also encourage the kind of supportive learning environment that student writers need in order to feel comfortable taking the risks necessary to become better writers.

About the Text

Writer's Resources provides the support that students need to develop into successful writers. The resources to which the title refers include instruction in basic skills and forms of writing, numerous peer and professional models of good writing, and an explanation of the writing process.

Our approach to teaching adult learners is pragmatic. We break down rules and concepts into manageable pieces that allow students to focus on one concept at a time and to build understanding and mastery incrementally. Concepts are presented in simple, clear language, supported with numerous examples, and reinforced by frequent practice exercises that allow students to apply what they have learned. Our approach to the forms of writing—paragraphs, essays, and rhetorical patterns—is to begin with one or more peer examples and then to break the form down into its component parts, with illustrations from various sources.

Organization

Part I: Getting Started

Chapter 1, "Finding Your Voice," foregrounds the relationship between writing and empowerment, introduces the concept of the writer's voice, and introduces the four student peers (Alicia, Tony, Beth, and Dan) who share their writing throughout the text. The chapter ends with an assignment in which students introduce themselves to their classmates and instructor by telling the story of how they came to college. The four student peers share their introductory essays as examples.

Chapter 2, "Using Journals," provides an introduction to both writers' and readers' journals, sample professional and peer journals, and suggested journal topics.

Part II: The Writing Process

The writing process chapters are intended as an overview of a process that will be used, reinforced, and developed throughout the text. We illustrate the writing process by using a single example—Beth's "Ready for the Junk Heap, " about the disadvantages of her car—so that students can follow the process from beginning to end with one accessible topic.

In order to accommodate instruction at both the paragraph and essay level, the writing process has been divided into three chapters. Chapter 3, "First Steps," covers narrowing the topic, determining the writing context, formulating a main idea, and generating supporting ideas. Chapter 4, "Writing a Paragraph," and Chapter 5, "Writing an Essay," cover the specific demands of organizing ideas, drafting, revising, and editing at the paragraph and essay levels. Instructors who focus on paragraph-length writing would assign Chapters 3 and 4, and instructors who begin with the essay would assign Chapters 3 and 5. The transition from paragraph- to essay-length writing is facilitated here, as elsewhere in the text, by the development of a single topic as both a paragraph and an essay.

After each step in the process, students can apply what they have learned by responding to writing process prompts to develop their own topic. A complete set of prompts is available at the end of Chapters 4 and 5 so that students can easily refer back to them for future assignments.

Part III: The Structure of the Paragraph

Chapter 6, "The Paragraph," introduces students to the parts of the paragraph. The peer models offer a number of examples of paragraphs written on topics students can relate to. Each part of the paragraph is broken down into basic concepts with examples and exercises. The instruction is intended to show students how to construct well-developed paragraphs. For example, we stress the use of specific details that directly relate to the topic sentence. Examples and exercises help students grasp this vital concept in the process of composing paragraphs.

This material is coordinated with the paragraph lesson on the CD-ROM that accompanies *Writer's Resources*. There, students can interact with the paragraph examples in order to identify the use of concepts discussed in the text. In addition, the peer models comment on the process they used to write their paragraphs. Related Readings provides links to numerous additional peer examples, and the Begin Writing prompt that accompanies Writing Topics summons a template in the word processor that guides students through paragraph developments.

Part IV: The Structure of the Essay

Chapter 7 defines and explores the parts of the essay. The sample essays are amplifications of paragraphs students were introduced to in Chapter 6. Particular attention is paid to the learning process students must undergo in moving from paragraph to essay writing. Concepts include a detailed presentation on how to provide background information, formulate thesis statements, develop effective body paragraphs, conclude an essay, and avoid common pitfalls.

The CD-ROM provides audio and graphic illustration of the concepts in the text, allows students to explore essay examples, and provides links to numerous additional peer examples.

Part V: Rhetorical Patterns

The eleven rhetorical pattern lessons are designed to be used at either the paragraph or the essay level and to be thorough and flexible enough to accommodate a variety of instructional approaches. For each pattern, students are given a definition, a sample student paragraph and essay on one topic, and sample thesis statements and outlines (both blank templates and the outlines of the student models used in the example are provided). They can also review transitions that are common for the pattern, tips on developing a paper in that pattern, and pitfalls to be avoided. Students can then select a writing topic and develop their paragraph or essay using writing process prompts tailored to each pattern. We imagine that students would read and discuss the lesson and any peer or professional models before writing their own paragraph or essay.

The CD-ROM allows students to explore elements of the paragraph and essay example, lists links to additional peer examples, and provides practice ordering jumbled paragraphs and essay outlines. Most significantly, the Begin Writing prompt with the writing topics summons a template in the word processor that guides students in the development of their writing and includes paragraph and essay outline templates. Students can save or print the files they create to share with classmates and/or turn in.

Part VI: Writing Elements and Skills

Rather than lodging instruction on grammar, punctuation, and stylistic issues (such as word choice and sentence variety) within chapters on the paragraph or essay, we have separated them into the twenty-one chapters of Part VI so that instructors can introduce topics in the order they feel is most appropriate for their students. Because it would be impossible to cover all of these chapters in one semester, we intend instructors and students to select those chapters that fit their individual needs.

The organization of the skills and concepts chapters lends itself to presentation in class and to independent review. Instructors may wish to cover certain topics in class and assign others for students to review independently, and students who want help with topics such as spelling can find abundant resources for independent review and practice.

The CD-ROM provides additional scored practices (more than two thousand items) and the advantage of multimedia technology to reinforce skill acquisition. Brief practices (of three to five items) follow the introduction of each concept. Various formats are used for practices, including drag and drop, hear and write, click to identify, multiple choice, and fill in the blank. Writing Practices ask students to respond to a question or topic or create their own sentences in the word processor (which is summoned when they click *Begin Writing*). The practices' difficulty level builds throughout lessons, culminating in ten-item Practice Sets, Review Exercises, and/or Editing Practices that test all the concepts introduced in a lesson. Students receive feedback and scores on all practices.

Part VII: Readings

The professional essays are intended to serve as models of good writing and as springboards for discussion and writing. The readings are drawn from a wide range of popular periodicals. We have tried to gather an eclectic mix of "traditional" and "new" readings that will appeal to a variety of interests and reading levels.

The Special Topics section that appears before each reading highlights composition strategies used by professional writers. Topics include introduction and conclusion strategies, use of rhetorical patterns, use of sources and tag phrases, and thematic relationships between essays.

Marginal glosses of words, names, and events are provided to aid students' understanding of words in context and to improve their understanding of the essay as a whole. Because we have found that students are unfamiliar with many of the words and references they encounter in essays, we have tried to err on the side of inclusion rather than exclusion. The professional essays are followed by comprehension questions, discussion questions, and suggestions for writing topics.

Features

Student Models

Adult learners perform best if given concrete models of the writing they are asked to complete. "Show; don't tell" is an axiom not just for fiction writers, but also for writing instructors. The peer models are a powerful vehicle for demonstrating the process of writing and the products that students can produce. These models also help students understand how readers come to know writers through their writing.

Focus on Writing Process

The writing process is introduced in Part II, discussed further in Parts III and IV, and reinforced in each rhetorical pattern lesson of Part V (where writing process prompts are tailored to each pattern).

Transition from Paragraph to Essay

The transition from paragraph to essay is facilitated by paragraph- and essay-level models of the same topic in Parts II through V.

Flexibility

In combination with *Writer's Resources* CD-ROM, the text lends itself to use in a variety of classroom settings, including the traditional classroom, the computerized classroom, and the distance class. The CD-ROM provides an individualized, interactive learning experience.

Unlike many texts, *Writer's Resources* does not dictate the order or sequence in which topics are introduced. Although we imagine most users will begin with Chapter 1, "Finding Your Voice," instructors may select the chapters that fit the topics they teach in the sequence they deem most appropriate. Some instructors might assign chapters from several parts of the book simultaneously. For example, Chapter 23, "Word Choice," could used be in conjunction with Chapter 8, "Description." Numerous suggestions for such pairings are available in the instructors' manual.

Supplements

Writer's Resources CD-ROM

The CD-ROM offers the advantage of multimedia technology used to reinforce skill acquisition and provides more than two thousand additional scored practices. The use of color, graphics, animation, and audio in the lessons helps focus student attention and appeals to a variety of learning styles. The audio in animations reinforces but does not repeat the text on screen, and students are free to pause, stop, and replay animations. The CD enables students to review skills and concepts independently.

Writer's Resources On-line Testing Program

Writer's Resources On-line Testing, available in both Web-CT and Blackboard platforms, allows instructors to measure and keep track of student progress in skill acquisition without having to grade or record tests. The testing program makes testing available to students twenty-four hours a day, seven days a week through the Internet.

The program includes **pretests** that diagnose students' proficiency in a given areas, **skill tests** that measure students' understanding of a skill after review and instruction, and **post-tests** that measure students' retention of skills at the end of a term. Instructors determine the skills to include in the testing sequence and the passing score for tests. Items are scored at the end of the test, and students receive detailed feedback on each incorrect item.

Instructors' Manual

In addition to providing the answers to exercises in the text, the instructors' manual contains chapter-by-chapter suggestions for implementing the material, sample syllabi, additional paragraphs and essays by the student peers, additional professional readings, and additional proofreading tests and resources.

Acknowledgements

We wish to thank the countless people who have been instrumental in the inception, development, and review of *Writer's Resources* text and CD-ROM. First, thanks to Carol Wada, developmental acquisitions editor at Harcourt, who first conceived of this project and whose drive and determination kept it on track for many years. Thanks also to the people at Interactive Technologies who helped develop and execute our ideas, especially Joni Craner and Nancy Tassler. Claire Brantley, our interim editor, kept the project going during some rough times and was a joy to work with. We appreciate Earl McPeek and Steve Dalphin for their confidence and guidance, and we're grateful to our developmental editor, Jill Johnson, for her hard work, common sense, and grace.

We also wish to thank the many College Prep instructors and Writing Lab staff at Santa Fe Community College who have inspired, contributed to, and collaborated in the development of our ideas.

Julie would like to thank her husband, Steve Robitaille, and her two sons, Jean Paul and Jordan, for their support and patience. Bob wishes to acknowledge his mentor, Gary Steele, and to thank his significant other, Claudia Munnis, for her support.

About the Authors

Bob Connelly counts writing as one of his favorite activities. After receiving his B.A. from the University of Florida, Bob spent time living and studying in northern Europe and then attended the University of Chicago, where he received an M.A. in English literature. He has been teaching writing for more than twenty years at Santa Fe Community College in Gainesville, Florida. In addition to writing textbooks, he has written a novel entitled *Hollywood*, which is as yet unpublished. In his spare time, Bob competes in triathlons and practices meditation.

Julie Robitaille has struggled all her life to create meaning with language. She received a B.A. in English from Emory University, an M.A. in English literature from the University of North Carolina at Chapel Hill, and an M.A. in creative writing from the University of Florida. For twenty years, she has directed the Writing Lab at Santa Fe Community College in Gainesville, Florida. In addition to teaching and writing textbooks, she also writes short stories, novels, and screenplays. She lives in Gainesville with her husband, Steve, and their two sons, Jean Paul and Jordan.

To the Student

Writing helps us know ourselves. We believe that writing helps all of us engage more fully with the world around us. As a process in which we formulate our thoughts and opinions and communicate them to others, writing helps us know ourselves and connect with our community. Writing well is one of the truly essential skills of a college-educated person.

In our experience, students come into a beginning writing course filled with a mixture of hope and fear. We all know that writing is not an easy activity. It takes courage and determination to sit down to face a blank sheet of paper. We don't always look forward to the comments of our readers, especially when they are English teachers. Yet writing classes in college are consistently ranked as some of the most popular classes for college freshmen. Students report that they enjoy the engagement with classmates and the sense of community that they develop, and most students find the exchange of ideas in a writing class stimulating.

We have guided more than twenty thousand students through the material you will use this term. Through our experience, we have developed a set of principles that we would like to share with you as you begin your writing course.

Learning to write well is important. Good writing is a tool that empowers you—it can enable you to succeed in school and, as a result, get and keep a good job. Becoming comfortable with the writing process can also help you figure out what you think. Once you know what your thoughts and beliefs are, you can share them with others and perhaps convince those people to share or at least understand your point of view.

Given clear models and enough practice, everyone can learn to write well. One of the best ways to learn is to see clear examples of what you are asked to do. Therefore, we have provided four student peers to share their work throughout the book. Their paragraphs and essays may not be as sophisticated as the professional essays generally seen in textbooks, but they do show you what you can attain. All of you can learn to write as clearly and as persuasively as the peer writers do, especially when you learn to take ownership of your writing, care about what you say, and work to communicate your ideas clearly.

The more you practice, the better you get. Another key factor in learning to write well is practice. Like anything else—learning to play basketball, for example—the more you practice, the better you get. Developing the skill of writing is like developing any skill. It takes a combination of isolated drills to develop certain muscles and performance practice to hone the skill of writing. You can't learn to write simply by doing drills on individual skills, any more than you can learn to play basketball by practicing shooting free throws. But that practice at the free-throw line can certainly help your performance when you are under pressure. And given the number of states that are requiring exit testing from writing classes, performing under pressure is the name of the game. The more you work with and manipulate language, just like the more you handle a ball, the more adept and coordinated you will become.

Attitude counts. As in any sport, how you think about your performance matters. You wouldn't stand much of a chance of improving if every time you took a shot at the basket you told yourself, "I'm never going to make it." You have to believe in yourself and you have to think positively. You have to imagine yourself doing well if you are going to improve your chances of making the shot.

Being a student is one of the most difficult jobs in the world. Every day you are confronted with what you don't know. Learning can be hard on the ego. Please remember that you have our respect for having the courage to become a student and better yourself through higher learning.

Having a coach helps. Your instructor will use *Writer's Resources* as a tool to help you learn to write well. It's important that you develop a good relationship with your instructor because he or she will coach you through the process of becoming a better writer. You have to listen to your coach if you are going to improve your performance. Coaches give you feedback not to make you feel bad but to help you improve. If you don't know what you are doing wrong, how can you possibly improve?

Teammates can help too. The four student models (Beth, Tony, Alicia, and Dan) who share their work and experience with you are the beginnings of your learning community. You will enjoy your writing class more and get more out of it if you connect with the other members in it. Your classmates and your instructor can help you succeed in the course in numerous ways, from helping you generate ideas for your writing to giving you feedback on your writing.

Use the tools. You may use the CD-ROM that accompanies *Writer's Resources* as an added resource. The CD includes lots of practice on skills, animated demonstrations of concepts, and hundreds of paragraphs and essays to learn from.

Every adventure starts with the first steps. We hope that you will enjoy the learning process you are now beginning. Again, we encourage you to get to know your instructor and the members of your class. It's important that you identify time in your busy schedule when you will work on this writing course. Most experienced college students set up a weekly schedule of classes, work, and times for homework, and they stick to that schedule throughout the term. Good luck, and may you succeed in meeting your goals and living your dream!

Part I

Getting Started

Tony Anderson   Alicia Martinez   Dan Tribble   Beth Kamiski

The Student Peers

Chapter 1
Finding Your Voice

Why Write?

Let's start with the most basic question: Why bother learning to write well?

Many students feel that new technology will decrease or even eliminate the need to study writing. In fact, new technology and new ways of communicating through e-mail and discussion boards make the ability to write well more important in the twenty-first century than ever before. Few people have time to edit their e-mails carefully, and no one pauses in the middle of an Internet chat session to look up how to use an apostrophe or comma correctly. However, these forms of communication represent us to our peers and often to our supervisors. It is through our writing that people form opinions of us and of our ability to communicate clearly.

Learning to write well is important because it gives you power. Writing well enables you to accomplish your goals, whether those goals include being successful in school, getting and keeping a good job, or simply expressing your ideas clearly. We each see the world differently, and language is the way we communicate who we are and how we see the world. Learning to use language effectively may not be easy, but it can help you share your vision of the world with others.

Here is what four student peers who have already taken this course have to say about why writing is important to them.

In this chapter, we introduce the concept of **voice**, and we introduce to you the four student peers, **Alicia**, **Tony**, **Dan**, and **Beth**, who share their writing throughout the text.

Group

ALICIA: I never used to think being able to write well was particularly important or useful. Then I got to college, and classes started moving a lot faster, and all of a sudden it's sink or swim, and without writing skills, I felt like I was sinking.

TONY: Writing is important to me because it can help me get what I want in life. With the economy changing, I'm going to need a degree if I want a decent job. There's no question about how important writing is if you want to succeed in school. It's not just what you know but also how well you can communicate it that counts. Most classes require writing, whether it's essays or reviews or lab reports. Being able to write well will make taking your classes easier, and it will help you get better grades. And employers are going to look at your transcripts to see if you have the communication skills and work habits they are looking for.

DAN: I can vouch for how important writing skills are on the job. I'm interested in designing Web pages, and I know I'm going to need writing skills for that. The last thing a company wants to see is an error on a Web page that the whole world is going to see. There's no question that the work world is getting more and more competitive, and employers are looking for people who have strong communication and interpersonal skills. Technology is changing the way we work, and in my experience, computers have made writing skills more important rather than less important. Today people use e-mail instead of the phone, and most e-mails are done in one draft, so you'd better know how to write or you're going to embarrass yourself. In all the jobs I've held, I've never had a secretary to prepare anything for me. I had to write all kinds of things on the job—letters to customers, memos, reports, fliers, bids, proposals, even ads, so I can tell you, the ability to write well is the key to success in most jobs.

BETH: To me, writing is important, not because it will help me on the job, but because I use it day-to-day and because writing helps me figure out what I'm feeling and thinking. For years, I've kept a journal in which I record everything from my kids' first step to my thoughts and feelings and experiences. Writing in my journal has helped me through some rough times, especially when I got divorced. In that way, writing enriches my life. Also, I use writing more and more in my personal life, whether it's writing an e-mail to a friend or chatting on the Internet. Being able to express my thoughts and feelings clearly is important to me because it helps define who I am, and to me that's what it's all about. 99

Spotlight on People

You don't have to be a professional writer to see the impact your writing can have. Lots of people use writing to draw attention to issues they think are important. Here is one example of a student who has done just that.

Shoshana Nisbet

To draw attention to the difficulties of negotiating the campus in a wheelchair, Shoshana Nisbett sent a humorous e-mail to several prominent officials at her community college. Shoshana chose to use humor to make her point, and she succeeded in getting the attention of the school officials, who each responded to her e-mail, enabling her to open a dialogue about the difficulties she faces daily in order to attend classes. A few short weeks later, she was taking a group of school officials on a tour of the campus. Why was the tour so successful? In part because Shoshana had them all ride in wheelchairs so they could experience firsthand the difficulties of negotiating closed doors and bumpy sidewalks. Shoshana says, "I wanted to raise awareness, and I think I managed to do that."

Make Yourself Heard

E-mail us stories of how you have used writing to draw attention to a problem, to voice your opinion, or to get something done. Also, e-mail us with ideas on things you'd like to see included in this textbook, with accounts of how you've used the textbook successfully, and of course, with any errors you've found in the textbook. You may contact us by sending an email to: writersresources@heinle.com.

Discussion Idea
Writing Topic

1. Why do you think writing is or is not important?

2. How have you or someone you know used writing to make a difference?

3. Does the widespread use of e-mail and Internet chat-rooms make writing more or less important than it once was? Explain.

4. What kind of writing do you do frequently? What do you enjoy or not enjoy about the writing you do in your everyday life?

Voice

What Is Voice?

Each of us has had different experiences, and those experiences have helped shape who we are and how we see the world. A writer's ability to communicate his or her personality and vision of the world in writing is called voice. Voice is something you probably haven't heard much about in your other English classes, but it has to do with expressing in your writing your ideas, views, and even something of your personality.

Developing your voice in writing doesn't mean writing the way you speak. It means learning to use language effectively to communicate your unique vision of the world. It enables each individual to become a spokesperson for his or her personal or cultural perspective on life.

Voice is one of the ingredients that makes a personal essay interesting and engaging. One of the pleasures of reading personal essays is getting to know the writer and coming to see the world as he or she does. We tend to respond more positively to writing that comes from a real person than we do to writing that is faceless or general. Of course, voice is most appropriate in personal essays. It usually would not be appropriate on a history exam or in a factual report. You will get lots of experience with both personal and academic writing as you read and work through the exercises in *Writer's Resources*.

Developing Voice

Writing in a journal is one of the best ways to develop your voice.

One of the most fundamental pieces of advice professional writers give aspiring writers is "Write about what you know." That same advice holds true for you, whether or not you aspire to write for a living; practice writing in your journal about things that interest you, that you know about, and that you care about, and you'll be working toward developing your voice. Think about what makes you unique, what experiences you've had that others haven't had.

Reading good writing is another way to develop awareness of voice.

Being aware of the voices of other writers is a good way to develop your own voice. As you read professional and student essays in *Writer's Resources* and elsewhere, think about how a sense of the writer's personality comes through in the writing. The four student peers, introduced below, are good examples of voice because they write about topics that interest or concern them, topics that come from their worlds. After a while, you will probably be able to guess which one of them wrote each paragraph and essay that you read.

Meet the Peers

We'd like to introduce the four student peers who share their advice, their experiences, and their writing with you throughout *Writer's Resources*. Because one of the best ways to learn how to write is to see clear models, Beth, Tony, Alicia, and Dan share their journals, their writing process, their paragraphs, and their essays. They are not professional writers, and that's the point. We'd like you to see examples of writing that you can produce. We believe all of you can learn to write as clearly as the student peers, especially if you care about what you say and how clearly you say it.

One of the best ways to learn is from other people. To get to know the peers, read the following essays, which they wrote to introduce themselves to their instructor and classmates. The peers are only the beginnings of your learning community. You should also get to know your classmates; they can help you succeed in the course by helping you generate ideas, by sharing their writing, and by giving you feedback on your writing.

Beth Kamiski

Age: 28

Hometown: Minneapolis, Minnesota

Family: Two children— Kyle, 8, and Kristi, 5

Hobbies: Raising two kids

Work experience: Sales clerk in camera shop and a video store

Major: Nursing

A Second Chance

This isn't my first time in college. Since my parents expected me to go to college after graduation, I never really gave it much thought. I just went. Unfortunately, it was the first time I ever had any freedom, and school was nowhere near the top of my list of priorities. I made a lot of choices that didn't help me do well in school, but I don't like to view anything as a mistake. They are just character-building exercises to me. Before I bombed out of college, though, I met a nice guy, and we decided to get married. My parents were disappointed about my decision to drop out of college, but they didn't pressure me or disown me.

After I got married, I worked in a video store for a while and then in a camera store. I didn't like either job because I had to work long hours, often evenings and weekends, and there was nothing particularly exciting about the work I was doing. It wasn't hard for me to decide to stop working when I got pregnant. I was lucky that my husband's salary made it possible for me to stay home and raise my son Kyle and my daughter Kristi. Unfortunately, nothing lasts forever, and my marriage was destined not to last either. One day my husband came home and informed me that he was in love with someone else and that he wanted a divorce.

After the divorce, I had to go back to work, but the cost of day care for two kids just about canceled out my paycheck. Every night I came home exhausted from standing on my feet all day, and I had to fix dinner, take care of the house, and play with the kids. The more exhausted I was, the more depressed I got. I knew something had to change. Even though my ex-husband was helping with child support, there was no way I could support my family on the salary I was making. I was working a dead-end job and was just barely making ends meet.

That's when my parents stepped in and suggested I go back to school. My dad offered to help with tuition, and my mom offered to look after the kids when I needed study time. Their support and encouragement helped me make up my mind to give college a try. I have to confess that I'm scared to death because I've been out of school for so long, and I'm not sure I'm smart enough for college. Now that I've started classes I'm at least relieved to find out I'm not the only older student in the class. Everyone seems friendly, and I know I'm going to give it my best shot. I still sometimes hear that little voice in my head saying, "Forget it, you're not smart enough to be here," but I'm trying to shut that part of me up. I know going to college is important to my future and to my children's future, and I'm determined to work hard and see how far I can go. I wish I had woken up in high school and realized how important an education was, but it's never too late, and at least I realize it now.

Influences

My mother never pushed me to go to college, not because she doesn't love me, but because she doesn't view college as a necessity. No one in my family has ever gone to college, and even though my mom doesn't have a degree, that has never stood in her way. She has managed to support her family through her work as a beautician. I'm proud of my mom because even though we were never rich, we always had what we needed, and my sister and I always had the latest hairstyles for every school function. For lots of kids in my high school, it wasn't cool to study. Most of my friends thought more about clothes and cars and sports than about making anything out of themselves after high school. The three things that helped me be different were watching my mom struggle, my ninth-grade English teacher, and my work experience.

Watching my mother struggle to support three kids helped me decide I wanted something better out of life. I love and respect my mom deeply for all the work she has done for us, but I don't want to have to work as hard as she has had to. She had us kids when she was young, so she never had a chance to go to college or get a better job. I want to have a family too someday, but I want to wait until I'm out of college before I think about settling down and having kids. Lots of the girls I knew got pregnant in high school, but I knew I wanted something different. I don't want to have to struggle to make ends meet. I don't want to have to stand on my feet all day like my mother does, or have to worry about the car breaking down and not being able to fix it. I want a job that will give me a good salary and give me respect for what I do. I also want to do something that will challenge me to do my best and will allow me to use my special talents.

Another big influence on my decision to go to college was Susan Singleton, my ninth- and tenth-grade English teacher. In my first year in high school, when I felt lost, Mrs. Singleton took an interest in me and encouraged me to get involved in school activities as a way to meet people and develop my interests. I joined the Environmental Club and a student service organization. Not only did joining those clubs help me fit in and make friends, but the clubs also got me involved in school and community service projects like recycling aluminum cans, cleaning up parks, and helping needy families during the holidays. The next year Mrs. Singleton encouraged me to join Chain Reaction, a youth leadership organization, which gave me the opportunity to become a volunteer tutor and mentor to younger children. Mrs. Singleton helped me learn that getting involved and helping others is a good way to help myself and others. She taught me to have high expectations of myself and to always do my best. She encouraged me to get serious about school and aim for college. Thanks to her encouragement, I stayed involved in school and school activities. I was a representative to student council, I was a cheerleader, and I was a member of the National Honor Society.

When I was a junior in high school, I got a job at Sophisticated You, a women's clothing store in the mall, and my work experience also helped

Alicia Martinez

Age: 19

Hometown: Just south of Los Angeles, California

Family: Mother and two sisters

Work Experience: Three years of experience as a sales associate at Sophisticated You, a clothing store in the Valley View Mall

Major: Business

encourage me to come to college. I went to work because I knew my mother couldn't afford to send me to college, and even if I were lucky enough to get a scholarship, I knew I would need money to live on. Sophisticated You was the perfect place for me because the manager was willing to work around my school hours. Another reason the job was perfect is that I love nice clothes, and the employee discount allowed me to buy some really smart clothes for my mom to pay her back for all she has done for me. As soon as I started working, I discovered I was good at sales. I had a knack for showing customers clothes that would flatter them, and my manager saw my potential and encouraged me. She said I had an eye for fashion and for color, and she used me as a model in two local fashion shows, which was great experience for me. The longer I worked, the more interested I was in the business. My manager recognized my ambition and encouraged me to learn all the parts of the business, from bookkeeping and advertising to customer relations. By the time I was a senior, she was letting me design the front window displays, and as soon as I graduated from high school, she made me assistant manager.

Because I worked twenty hours a week through my junior and senior years, I didn't have time to party or get in trouble. I don't regret missing out on parties because working helped me discover something that I am good at and helped me save the money I needed to start school. After three years working in retail sales, I still like what I do and I know I'm good at it, but I also know I don't want to be a salesperson the rest of my life. Someday I'd like to be a fashion buyer for a large retail organization, or I'd like to own my own store. Either way, I know I need a degree to make my dreams come true.

I'm in college because I know I can be successful if I try hard enough. I want to set a good example for my younger brother and sister, and I want to make something of myself and, I hope, make enough money so that my mother won't have to stand on her feet all day when she's fifty years old, and my sisters won't have to work as hard as I will to put themselves through school. If I live at home and keep working twenty hours a week, I should be able to get my degree in fashion design and marketing in two years. Then I'll decide if I want to go on for a four-year degree in business or marketing.

My Road to College

In high school I was an average student. I got mostly Bs and Cs. The crowd I hung out with wasn't serious about school, and we mostly just hung out together playing music and having a good time. Because I didn't have any definite plans for my future, I mostly drifted. As a result, when I graduated, I didn't have the grades or the scores to get into college, but I didn't have any other plans either. I knew that if I got a job waiting tables and continued to hang out with my high school friends, I'd end up in trouble. They were serious partyers and none of them wanted to do anything but hang out and have a good time. I knew that I had to get out of town if I was going to make anything of myself. I had always wanted to travel, and the Army offered me the opportunity to do just that.

My tour of duty in the Army fulfilled my desire to see the world and helped me to grow up. My first duty assignment was in Berlin, Germany. During my two-and-a-half-year stay, I had the chance to visit many European countries and to learn firsthand about different cultures and people. My stay in Germany was the most exciting experience in my life. Not only did I have a chance to visit places I'd seen in magazines, but also the Army helped me believe in myself and my own abilities. I attained the rank of sergeant and was progressing quickly in my career. Unfortunately, the advantages were not without a price. My job was demanding both physically and emotionally, and I often had to work sixty-hour weeks.

When my tour of duty was over, I volunteered for a duty assignment with the 82nd Airborne Division. I spent my second tour in Fort Bragg, North Carolina, and in Panama. Even though I benefited from and enjoyed my time in the Army, I decided not to reenlist for a third tour. I had gained what I could from the Army, and it was time to move on. I couldn't advance very far without a degree, but the Army helped me gain valuable work experience and confidence in my abilities. I knew I was able to take responsibility, I had a good head on my shoulders, and I could achieve almost anything if I set my mind to it. After six years in the military, I felt I had developed the discipline and work habits to be successful in school, and I decided to give college a try.

Unfortunately, my family didn't have the confidence in me that I did. Maybe they remembered too well some of my high school behaviors such as skipping school. My parents both said I was crazy to give up a successful career in the military to go back to school. They seem convinced that I'll bomb out of school and end up on the streets. All I can do is show them they are wrong. The one person in my family who supports my decision is my sister, who manages a restaurant in Atlanta. She believes in me and supports my decision one hundred percent.

When I first decided to return to school, I thought I wanted to major in one of the medical technology fields. Now I think I want to do something to help kids who have trouble believing in themselves just as I did. Maybe I should be a teacher or a counselor so that I can reach kids before it's too late and they make decisions that can ruin their lives forever. Right now, I don't know which career I'll end up in, but I know that I'm going to make it. Even if no one else in the world believes in me, I'm going to make it.

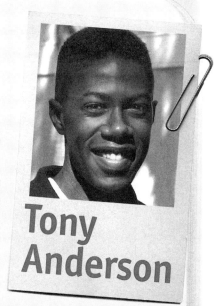

Tony Anderson

Age: 25

Hometown: Atlanta, Georgia

Family: Mother, father, and two sisters

Work Experience: U.S. Marines, bike mechanic, camp counselor

Major: Psychology

Dan Tribble

Age: 35

Hometown: Upstate New York

Family: Wife and two kids

Hobbies: Building model planes, hunting and fishing, listening to baseball

Work experience: Mostly retail (electronics)

Major: Something to do with computers

Career Change

The idea of going to college never crossed my mind when I was in high school. I was mostly interested in girls and racing cars. When I graduated, I took a job working construction because that was about the best job available in my hometown. Unfortunately, in New York construction can be pretty seasonal work because a lot of it dries up in the winter. I worked construction for five years, and I learned skills that have come in handy plenty of times since. I've helped my in-laws rebuild their front porch and add a deck, and I've added two rooms to our house. However, once I got married and we had a baby, I realized that construction was too physically demanding and too irregular to depend on in the long run.

I took a job in an auto parts store and worked there for five years, but chances for promotion were limited. When I had a chance to move to an electronics store, I did. After only a year with the company, I was promoted to assistant manager, but I was assistant manager for three years, and there wasn't any place to go from there. My manager was only a few years older than I was, and he was not about to take another job or retire anytime soon, especially since I was doing most of the work and he was getting most of the credit. It was clear to me that no matter how good I was at what I did, without a degree I wouldn't be able to advance the way I wanted to.

In my years in retail, I saw computers take over inventory, bookkeeping, and sales. I knew firsthand just how dependent businesses were on the computers running properly. I could see the potential for someone in computer programming or repair because people are going to become more and more dependent on computers in the future. Leaving a secure job, even one with limited potential, was a big risk. But I knew if I was ever going to make a change in my life, it had better be while I was still young enough to do it.

Luckily, my family was supportive of my decision to return to school. We had a family conference and discussed the good and bad points of my going back to school, and they all encouraged me to go for it. My wife has a good job at a bank, so her salary can cover our expenses while I'm in school. We'll have to give up our once-a-year vacation at the beach, and there won't be any new cars in the picture anytime soon, but in the long run, it will be worth it. My kids understand that money will be tight for a while, but they are willing to make sacrifices, and it's good for them to learn to economize and live on a budget.

Now that I've started classes, I realize it won't be as easy as I imagined. At first I was angry that I had to take two college prep classes (writing and reading) because it would take me that much longer to get my degree. However, when I thought about it, I calmed down. I'm not really surprised that I need prep English because I was never good in English in high school, and I'm sure I will need writing skills if I am going to be successful in business. Second, I want to set a good example for my children, and I know I've developed good work habits in my fifteen years of experience in the workforce. I'm going to give college my best shot, and I am hopeful it will make a difference in my life.

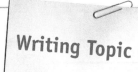
Writing Topic

Write a two-page paper in which you tell the story of how you came to college. What were you like in high school? Who were your friends? What were you doing outside of school? What issues or ideas were you thinking about? Was there a particular person (parent, teacher, counselor, minister) who encouraged or discouraged you from attending college? Did your family expect you to go to college? Did you think college was a good idea for you? Why or why not? If you worked or went into the military before attending college, what were your experiences like? How did they help make up your mind to attend college?

Chapter 2
Using Journals

What Is a Writer's Journal?

The word *journal* comes from the French word meaning "daily." As the name implies, journal writing is daily writing. The purpose of a journal is to explore and experiment with ideas, feelings, and experiences. A journal is personal writing, and it can serve different purposes for different people. Some writers like to write about their ideas and feelings; others like to write about external events. In a writing class, one of the purposes of a journal may be to help develop your voice or to experiment with the various writing strategies you've discussed in class or seen in a reading.

If you've never done it before, writing in a journal may seem awkward at first, but the more you do it—and we recommend writing two or three times a week, if not every day—the more you'll get the hang of it, and hopefully the more you'll enjoy it. Writing regularly in a journal offers a number of benefits.

Here is what the four student peers have to say about how they've used journals.

In this chapter, we discuss the uses of a writer's journal and reader's journal and give professional and peer examples of each.

Group

> **BETH:** I started keeping a journal when my kids were little. I'd write down the funny things they said and did. My journal was a way of recording their growth, and a way of hanging on to the memories. Then when I went through my divorce, my journal changed to being focused on feelings, and writing became my way of figuring out how I felt.
>
> **TONY:** I never kept a journal before this class, but I think it's one of those habits that is going to stick. I've learned that by writing in my journal, I figure out what I think. I start writing about something that happened or something that's been on my mind, and by the time I'm finished with the entry, I have a pretty good idea what I think. Writing in my journal definitely helps me process feelings and ideas. That's helped me learn to start on papers a little earlier than I used to. Most of the papers I turned in in high school should have been journal entries because I figured out what I wanted to say by the time I finished. Now I'm learning to do a second draft so that I start out knowing what I want to say and I can work on saying it, which is hard enough.
>
> **ALICIA:** Writing in a journal definitely helps me figure out what I think and what I want to say. Every time I write a paper, I sit down and write a journal on the topic. I use my journal to try out ideas; some of them turn into papers and some don't.
>
> **DAN:** I like the journal because I don't get graded on errors. The journal also helps me figure out the readings. I try to do a journal entry on each of the assigned readings—I just let myself think out loud on paper, and the interesting thing is that when I go to class the next day, I find I have a lot more to say than I would have otherwise. I'm usually pretty quiet in class, but keeping a reader's journal helps me have something to contribute.

Related Readings

Your instructor may ask you to read one or more of the following professional and peer journal selections. These selections are intended to show you how various professional and student writers use a journal to explore and develop ideas.

Professional Journals
Anne Frank, excerpt from *Diary of a Young Girl*

Saturday, 20 June, 1942

Dear Kitty,

I'll start straight away. It is so peaceful at the moment, Mummy and Daddy are out and Margot has gone to play ping-pong with some friends. I've been playing ping-pong a lot myself lately. We ping-pongers are very partial to an ice cream, especially in summer, when one gets warm at the game, so we usually finish up with a visit to the nearest ice-cream shop, Delphi or Oasis, where Jews are allowed. We've given up scrounging for extra pocket money. Oasis is usually full and among our large circle of friends we always manage to find some kindhearted gentleman or boy friend, who presents us with more ice cream than we could devour in a week.

I expect you will be rather surprised at the fact that I should talk of boy friends at my age. Alas, one simply can't seem to avoid it at our school. As soon as a boy asks if he may bicycle home with me and we get into conversation, nine out of ten times I can be sure that he will fall head over heels in love immediately and simply won't allow me out of his sight. After a while it cools down of course, especially as I take little notice of ardent[1] looks and pedal blithely[2] on.

If it gets so far that they begin about "asking Father" I swerve slightly on my bicycle, my satchel falls, the young man is bound to get off and hand it to me, by which time I have introduced a new topic of conversation.

These are the most innocent types; you get some who blow kisses or try to get hold of your arm, but then they are definitely knocking at the wrong door. I get off my bicycle and refuse to go further in their company, or I pretend to be insulted and tell them in no uncertain terms to clear off.

There, the foundation of our friendship is laid, till tomorrow!

Yours, Anne

[1] passionate

[2] lightheartedly

Wednesday, 8 July, 1942

Dear Kitty,

Years seem to have passed between Sunday and now. So much has happened, it is just as if the whole world had turned upside down. But I am still alive, Kitty, and that is the main thing, Daddy says.

Yes, I'm still alive. Indeed, but don't ask where or how. You wouldn't understand a word, so I will begin by telling you what happened on Sunday afternoon. At three o'clock (Harry had just gone, but was coming back later) someone rang the front doorbell. I was lying lazily reading a book on the veranda in the sunshine, so didn't hear it. A bit later, Margot appeared at the kitchen door looking very excited. "The S.S. have sent a call-up notice for Daddy," she whispered. "Mummy has gone to see Mr. Van Daan already." (Van Daan is a friend who works with Daddy in the business.) It was a great shock to me, a call-up; everyone knows what that means. I picture concentration camps and lonely cells—should we allow him to be doomed to this? "Of course he won't go," declared Margot, while we waited together. "Mummy has gone to the Van Daans to discuss whether we should move into our hiding place tomorrow. The Van Daans are going with us, so we shall be seven in all." Silence. We couldn't talk any more, thinking about Daddy, who, little knowing what was going on, was visiting some old people in the Joodse Invalide; waiting for Mummy, the heat and suspense, all made us very overawed[3] and silent.

³ quieted by awe

Suddenly the bell rang again. "That is Harry," I said. "Don't open the door." Margot held me back, but it was not necessary as we heard Mummy and Mr. Van Daan downstairs, talking to Harry, then they came in and closed the door behind them. Each time the bell went, Margot or I had to creep softly down to see if it was Daddy, not opening the door to anyone else.

Margot and I were sent out of the room. Van Daan wanted to talk to Mummy alone. When we were alone together in our bedroom, Margot told me that the call-up was not for Daddy, but for her. I was more frightened than ever and began to cry. Margot is sixteen; would they really take girls of that age away alone? But thank goodness she won't go, Mummy said so herself; that must be what Daddy meant when he talked about us going into hiding.

Into hiding—where would we go, in a town or the country, in a house or a cottage, when, how, where . . . ?

⁴ necessary to survival

These were questions I was not allowed to ask, but I couldn't get them out of my mind. Margot and I began to pack some of our most vital[4] belongings into a school satchel. The first thing I put in was this diary, then hair curlers, handkerchiefs, schoolbooks, a comb, old letters; I put in the craziest things with the idea that we were going into hiding. But I'm not sorry, memories mean more to me than dresses. At five o'clock Daddy finally arrived, and we phoned Mr. Koophuis to ask if he could come around in the evening. Van Daan went and fetched Miep. Miep has been in the business with Daddy since 1933 and has become a close friend, likewise her brand-new husband, Henk. Miep came and took some shoes, dresses, coats, underwear, and stockings away in her bag, promising to return in the evening. Then silence fell on the house; not one of us felt like eating anything, it was still hot and everything was very strange. We let our large upstairs room to a certain Mr. Goudsmit, a divorced man in his thirties, who appeared to have nothing to do on this particular evening; we simply could not get rid of him without being rude; he hung about until ten o'clock. At eleven o'clock Miep and Henk Van Santen arrived. Once again, shoes, stockings, books, and underclothes disappeared into Miep's bag and Henk's deep pockets, and at eleven-thirty they too disappeared. I was dog-tired and although I knew that it would be my last night in my own bed, I fell asleep immediately and didn't wake up until Mummy called me at five-thirty the next morning. Luckily it was not so hot as Sunday; warm rain fell steadily all day. We put on heaps of clothes as if we were going to the North Pole, the sole reason being to take clothes with us. No Jew in our situation would have dreamed of going out with a suitcase full of clothing. I had on two vests, three pairs of pants, a dress, on top of that a skirt, jacket, summer coat, two pairs of stockings, lace-up shoes, woolly cap, scarf, and still more; I was nearly stifled before we started, but no one inquired about that.

Margot filled her satchel with schoolbooks, fetched her bicycle, and rode off behind Miep into the unknown, as far as I was concerned. You see I still didn't know where our secret hiding place was to be. At seven-thirty the door closed behind us. Mootje, my little cat, was the only creature to whom I said farewell. She would have a good home with the neighbors. This was all written in a letter addressed to Mr. Goudsmit.

There was one pound of meat in the kitchen for the cat, breakfast things lying on the table, stripped beds, all giving the impression that we had left helter-skelter. But we didn't care about impressions, we only wanted to get away, only escape and arrive safely, nothing else. Continued tomorrow.

Yours, Anne.

---

1. Who is Anne Frank addressing in her journal? That is, who is "you"?

2. What are her concerns in the first entry?

3. What are her concerns in the second entry?

4. What preparations do Anne and her family make to go into hiding? What does she choose to take with her?

5. How would you describe Anne Frank? What details reveal her personality?

Discussion Idea
Writing Topic

Professional Journals
May Sarton, from *Journal of a Solitude*

September 15th

BEGIN HERE. It is raining. I look out on the maple, where a few leaves have turned yellow, and listen to Punch, the parrot, talking to himself and to the rain ticking gently against the windows. I am here alone for the first time in weeks, to take up my "real" life again at last. That is what is strange—that

¹ dry, barren

² curved in on itself

³ atmosphere
⁴ incapable, not good enough

⁵ not repentant, stubborn

⁶ spiritual pain
⁷ the center of life, the womb

⁸ unbreakable, strict
⁹ uproar

friends, even passionate love, are not my real life unless there is time alone in which to explore and to discover what is happening or has happened. Without the interruptions, nourishing and maddening, this life would become arid[1]. Yet I taste it fully only when I am alone here and "the house and I resume old conversations."

On my desk, small pink roses. Strange how often the autumn roses look sad, fade quickly, frost-browned at the edges! But these are lovely, bright, singing pink. On the mantel, in the Japanese jar, two sprays of white lilies, recurved[2], maroon pollen on the stamens, and a branch of peony leaves turned a strange pinkish-brown. It is an elegant bouquet; shibui, the Japanese would call it. When I am alone the flowers are really seen; I can pay attention to them. They are felt as presences. Without them I would die. Why do I say that? Partly because they change before my eyes. They live and die in a few days; they keep me closely in touch with process, with growth, and also with dying. I am floated on their moments.

The ambiance[3] here is order and beauty. That is what frightens me when I am first alone again. I feel inadequate[4]. I have made an open place, a place for meditation. What if I cannot find myself inside it?

I think of these pages as a way of doing that. For a long time now, every meeting with another human being has been a collision. I feel too much, sense too much, am exhausted by the reverberations after even the simplest conversation. But the deep collision is and has been with my unregenerate[5], tormenting, and tormented self. I have written every poem, every novel, for the same purpose—to find out what I think, to know where I stand. I am unable to become what I see. I feel like an inadequate machine, a machine that breaks down at crucial moments, grinds to a dreadful halt, "won't go," or, even worse, explodes in some innocent person's face.

Plant Dreaming Deep has brought me many friends of the work (and also, harder to respond to, people who think they have found in me an intimate friend). But I have begun to realize that, without my own intention, that book gives a false view. The anguish[6] of my life here—its rages—is hardly mentioned. Now I hope to break through into rough rocky depths, to the matrix[7] itself. There is violence there and anger never resolved. I live alone, perhaps for no good reason, for the reason that I am an impossible creature, set apart by a temperament I have never learned to use as it could be used, thrown off by a word, a glance, a rainy day, or one drink too many. My need to be alone is balanced against my fear of what will happen when suddenly I enter the huge empty silence if I cannot find support there. I go up to Heaven and down to Hell in an hour and keep alive only by imposing upon myself inexorable[8] routines. I write too many letters and too few poems. It may be outwardly silent here but in the back of my mind is a clamor[9] of human voices, too many needs, hopes, fears. I hardly ever sit still without being haunted by the "undone" and the "unsent." I often feel exhausted, but it is not my work that tires (work is a rest); it is the effort of pushing away the lives and needs of others before I can come to the work with any freshness and zest.

1. Why does May Sarton enjoy being alone?

2. What do you think she means by taking up her "real" life?

3. Why does she not mind it that flowers wither and die before her eyes?

4. Sarton says she has written all her poems and novels in order to find out what she thinks. Does that seem an accurate description of what you do when you write?

5. What does Sarton fear in sitting down to write or in being alone?

Professional Journals
Florida Scott-Maxwell, from *The Measure of My Days*

Age puzzles me. I thought it was a quiet time. My seventies were interesting, and fairly serene[1], but my eighties are passionate. I grow more intense as I age. To my own surprise I burst out with hot conviction. Only a few years ago I enjoyed my tranquillity, now I am so disturbed by the outer world and by human quality in general, that I want to put things right as though I still owed a debt to life. I must calm down. I am far too frail[2] to indulge[3] in moral fervor[4].

Old people are not protected from life by engagements, or pleasures, or duties; we are open to our own sentience[5]; we cannot get away from it, and it is too much. We should ward[6] off the problematic[7], and above all the insoluble[8]. These are far, far too much, but it is just these that attract us. Our one safety is to draw in, and enjoy the simple and immediate. We should rest within our own confines[9]. It may be dull, restricted, but it can be satisfying within our own walls. I feel most real when alone, even most alive when alone. Better to say that the liveliness of companionship and the liveliness of solitude differ, and the latter is never as exhausting as the former. When I am with other people I try to find them, or try to find a point in myself from which to make a bridge to them, or I walk on the egg-shells of affection trying not to hurt or misjudge. All this is very tiring, but love at any age takes everything you got.

What fun it is to generalize in the privacy of a notebook. It is as I imagine waltzing on ice might be. A great delicious sweep in one direction, taking you your full strength, and then with no trouble at all, an equally delicious sweep in the opposite direction. My notebook does not help me think, but it eases my crabbed[10] heart.

I love my family for many reasons; for what I see them to be, for the loveliness they have been, for the good I know in them. I love their essence, their "could be," and all this in spite of knowing their faults as well. I love the individual life in them that I saw when in bud. I have spent

[1] calm, peaceful, unclouded

[2] fragile

[3] to give oneself up to

[4] passion

[5] awareness, consciousness

[6] to protect against, fend off

[7] associated with problems

[8] unsolvable

[9] boundaries

[10] pinched, tight

[11] stilled, without wind

[12] deepest feelings, as in "hurt to the quick"

[13] literally, the state of bearing fruit; realization, fulfillment

[14] pushed

[15] literally, separating the wheat from the chaff; the process of separating what is of value from what can be discarded

much of my life watching it unfold, enchanted and anxious. At times it has seemed like frail craft shaking out sails. I have feared for it when it was becalmed[11], when it was in danger, and when I knew nothing, nothing. I have felt respect, even reverence, for I have seen it meet tragedy and gain nobility. I have watched it win its prizes and I have learned the hard truth a mother learns slowly, that the quick[12] of intimacy she has known becomes hope for loved strangers.

A mother's love for her children, even her inability to let them be, is because she is under a painful law that the life that passed through her must be brought to fruition[13]. Even when she swallows it whole she is only acting like any frightened mother cat eating its young to keep it safe. It is not easy to give closeness and freedom, safety plus danger.

No matter how old a mother is she watches her middle-aged children for signs of improvement. It could not be otherwise for she is impelled[14] to know that the seeds of value sown in her have been winnowed.[15] She never outgrows the burden of love, and to the end she carries the weight of hope for those she bore. Oddly, very oddly, she is forever surprised and even faintly wronged that her sons and daughters are just people, for many mothers hope and half expect that their new-born child will make the world better, will somehow be a redeemer. Perhaps they are right, and they can believe that the rare quality they glimpsed in the child is active in the burdened adult.

[16] inability to be corrected

Age is truly a time of heroic helplessness. One is confronted by one's own incorrigibility.[16] I am always saying to myself, "Look at you, and after a lifetime of trying." I still have the vices that I have known and struggled with—well it seems like since birth. Many of them are modified, but not much. I can neither order nor command the hubbub of my mind. Or is it my nervous sensibility? This is not the effect of age; age only defines one's boundaries. Life has changed me greatly, it has improved me greatly, but it has also left me practically the same. I cannot spell, I am overcritical, egocentric[17] and vulnerable. I cannot be simple. In my effort to be clear I become complicated. I know my faults so well that I pay them small heed.[18] They are stronger than I am. They are me.

[17] centered on oneself, selfish

[18] attention

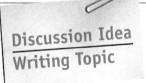

Discussion Idea Writing Topic

1. Compare Florida Scott-Maxwell's journal with May Sarton's. How are the two women alike? Compare their voices, their feelings about being alone, and the distinctions they draw between company and solitude.

2. "[A]ge only defines one's boundaries. Life has changed me greatly, it has improved me greatly, but it has also left me practically the same." Respond to Scott-Maxwell's assertion about the effects of age. In what ways are you the same as you were when you were younger? In what ways have you changed?

Princess Diana

I remember my parents talking about how they can remember where they were when they heard that President Kennedy had been shot. How much it marked them. It was like a blow that froze that moment in time so that they'll never forget it.

I had never had an experience like that until the morning that I heard Princess Diana had been killed in a car accident in Paris. It's strange because I didn't exactly consider Diana a hero, and I certainly wasn't one of her followers, but I remember how devastated I felt when I heard she was dead. I started seeing her as a human being for the first time and realizing what a hard life she'd had, at least in some ways. I realized how much I would miss the image of her shy smile. Her image was so familiar it was almost like losing someone you knew. And I felt so sorry for her boys. It made me start thinking about my two kids and what would happen to them if I died, how terrible it would be for them to grow up without a mother. It made me want to hold them all the tighter and appreciate what we have—this life together—instead of complaining about what we don't have. It's those brushes with mortality that make you appreciate life all over again.

An Experience of Discrimination

Early this semester I went in to apply for a job waiting tables at The Courtyards, a retirement home. Amy, a friend in my algebra class, told me about the job. Her manager had said they were short-staffed and needed additional help desperately. I figured it would be the perfect job for me because I've had experience waiting tables. I could use some extra money, and it sounded like I'd only need to work on weekends, so it wouldn't interfere with my schoolwork.

I wore a starched shirt and a tie to school that day because I know how important first impressions can be. As I was crossing campus, two African-American girls were walking toward me, and they laughed out loud as we passed and made comments like "Who does he think he is." It's frustrating when members of your own race put you down for trying.

When I got to The Courtyards, I asked the man at the front desk to speak with whoever was doing the hiring for wait staff, and he disappeared into the back looking none too happy. I've seen that look before, and I could tell right away that he wasn't happy about a black male applying for the job. He came back out a few minutes later with an application, and said, "We're not hiring right now, but if you're welcome to leave an application." I knew he was lying. I knew the only reason they weren't interested in me was the color of my skin. I looked him straight in the eye and said, "I can tell there wouldn't be much point." If they don't want me, it's their loss. I would have been perfect for the job, but if they have attitudes like that, I wouldn't want to work there anyway.

Suggested Journal Topics

1. If this is your first semester in school, discuss your first impressions of your college or university. What do you think of the classes, teachers, students, campus, work load, and so on? If this is not your first semester in school, discuss your experiences in school last term. What sorts of difficulty or success did you encounter? What do you plan to do differently this semester?

2. Discuss the differences between your experience of high school and college.

3. Describe in detail one room in your house or apartment. Use all five senses (taste, touch, hearing, smell, and sight) and discuss the room's significance, its history, and its meaning to you.

4. Describe someone you know well, perhaps a friend or close member of your family. Try to capture the person's appearance, mannerisms, and personality.

5. Consider your past experience with writing. What has given you the most problems? What do you think you need to do to improve your writing?

6. Describe an outdoor place that you particularly liked as a child (park, river, beach, tree house, or playground).

7. Describe the place you have lived that you liked the best.

8. Examine the similarities and differences between yourself and a parent.

9. Define the role you played in your family (caretaker, peacemaker, troublemaker, etc.)

10. Analyze how a TV show portrays someone of your gender, age, and race. How does that character behave? What are his or her values? How is he or she different from other characters on the show? What values are being endorsed? What message is being communicated?

What Is a Reader's Journal?

We all have a little voice in our heads that comments on what we are reading. The voice might make comments such as "I like this," "I don't get it," "No way, I don't buy that," or "That reminds me of . . ." Keeping a reader's journal is a way of harnessing and exploring that little voice in your head.

The purpose of a reader's journal is to allow the reader to respond to the ideas encountered in reading. The reader's journal engages the reader in a dialogue with what the writer says (content) and how the writer says it (form).

One use for a reader's journal is to explore what you like and don't like about the essays you read, what seems effective and what doesn't. Think about the strategies the writer uses and how you might use similar strategies in your own writing. Another advantage of a journal is that you can come up with ideas that you might develop in a paper. As you read, ask yourself what connections you can make to your own experiences. Often such ideas can be expanded and developed into an essay of your own.

Questions to Ask about Readings

1. How does the writer begin the essay? Does the writer begin with a story or something personal or give background on the subject?

2. How does the writer get your attention and interest?

3. How does the writer help you see the scene he or she is describing?

4. What sorts of language and images does he or she use?

5. How does the writer help you understand his or her ideas?

6. Does the writer use examples? Does he or she use comparison/contrast or other traditional rhetorical patterns? Rhetorical patterns (discussed in Part V) are traditional methods of structuring speech or writing in order to communicate effectively. They include example, narration, definition, description, process analysis, comparison/contrast, cause/effect, classification, and division.

7. How does the writer end the essay?

8. Who do you think the writer perceives as the audience (the intended reader of the work)? How would this perception affect the way the essay was written?

9. If you had written about the same subject, what would you have done differently?

Peer Reader's Journal Selections

Here are example reader's journal entries from the four student peers. Beth, Dan, Tony, and Alicia are responding to professional essays contained in *Writer's Resources*. You may be asked to respond to the professional or student essays in a similar fashion. These examples are intended to help you understand how to use a reader's journal.

PEER
EXAMPLE

Tony

On Excerpt from *Journal of a Solitude* by May Sarton

That May Sarton sounds like a tough old bird. I hear a lot of anger and restlessness in her voice. I liked her honesty in admitting her fears of being inadequate and her willingness to confront what lies inside—including the violence and unresolved anger. She mentions meditation, which got me interested because I meditate. Writing seems to be a form of meditation for her. It makes her confront herself. She seems to reach peace through turmoil or conflict, through an exploration of the depths of self. In some ways she is trying to reach the same goal as I am in meditating.

I practice mindfulness meditation. The idea is to observe the self with equanimity. My teacher stresses letting the thoughts come and go without taking the mind road and being swept away in thoughts. You just observe what the mind is doing without preferring one thought over another. Sarton sounds like she is always getting swept away by thoughts or interactions with other people. I wonder what she'd say to my teacher. He is Korean and has sat in silence for a year at a time. Nothing seems to bother him. He laughs a lot. I don't see May Sarton laughing much. I wonder what she'd say when he asked her one of his simple questions like "Who are you?"

Hmm. If I were her maybe I'd reply, "I'm the spray of pink on the mantle, catching my breath." Yes, she'd like that answer because she seems to live in her flowers and lose herself observing them.

PEER
EXAMPLE

Beth

On "Why White Lies Hurt" by Grace Bennett (p. 460)

This article really hit home with me because it's about a situation I deal with almost daily. Sometimes, like the mothers in the article, I find myself giving in to the constant pressure to buy my kids things. If they're in a bad mood or had a bad day at school, I find myself trying to make them happy by buying them things. It's as if we've all bought into the idea that happiness is having things, which it isn't. And of course, trying to appease them by buying them things doesn't work, or not for long. No sooner have I gotten them the new toy or the special drink than they are unhappy about something else.

The article made me realize that I'm contributing to the problem by avoiding the real issue that is upsetting them. I have to keep reminding myself that as their mother it is my role to help them learn to deal with disappointment and frustration instead of helping them learn how to ignore it or cover it up by buying things. So, I'm making myself a promise to help them talk about what is bothering them next time instead of trying to make them happy with "things."

PEER
EXAMPLE

On "Not in Our Town" by Edwin Dobb (p. 465)

When I read "Not in Our Town," I thought of it as an isolated incident. But since then, it seems like I've heard one news story after another about similar things happening all over the country. It's scary because people who commit hate crimes hate anyone who is not like them. All kinds of groups are the targets—gays, blacks, Jews, foreigners. It made me realize I could be the target next. The more I think about the article, the more I'm grateful I read it because it made me realize you can't sit by and do nothing when a hate crime occurs in your city. You have to take action or speak out against hatred and prejudice because you or someone you love could be the next target. It's sad that so many people are filled with hate, and I wish we could do more to help people learn to understand each other and respect each other's differences.

PEER
EXAMPLE

On "What's Your Emotional IQ?" by Daniel Goleman (p. 480)

Reading this article was like turning on a light for me. It validated what I've always felt but never heard from anyone else before. Happy people are smart, no matter what their position in life may be. My dad was happy and was smart, and I respect him as much as I respect any president or public figure in our culture. And yet because he is a farmer and never went to college and doesn't make a ton of money, our culture doesn't think of him smart or successful. We seem to label people who have money as smart and successful, and we label people who don't have money as failures because if you were smart you'd have money, or so the reasoning goes. But I don't buy it and I never have. My mom's brother is rich—he lives in a big house and drives a fancy car and his kids go to the best schools, but I've never thought of him as happy, and if I had to choose today who I'd rather be like, my dad or him, there'd be no question that I would choose my dad because my dad is happy with himself. He's proud of the choices he's made, he loves his family, and he is involved in and respected in his community. He has what the author calls emotional intelligence. He lives according to his principles, and that seems like something we should respect a man for.

Writing Topic

Write a reader's journal entry on one of the professional journals in this chapter or one of the professional readings in Part VII.

Part II

The Writing Process

Introduction

Most beginning writers assume that good writers have some magic 'folder' in their brains that they can open when they are given a writing assignment and pull out a completed 'A' paper without having to agonize or struggle to produce it. Nothing is further from the truth. Writing is difficult for everyone because writing involves first figuring out what you think, and once that hurdle is overcome, writing means figuring out how to communicate your ideas effectively. That task is difficult for everyone. Even for the best writers, it takes time and effort to figure out what they think or want to say, and then it takes more time, effort, and skill to figure out how to express their ideas effectively.

The good news is that over the years, successful writers have worked to share their writing process—how they go about coming up with ideas, organizing ideas, and producing a finished product. The writing process described here and in other textbooks is the product of their efforts. At first, this process may seem time-consuming, unnecessary, and even cumbersome. The truth is that good writers do the work necessary to develop a successful piece of writing.

It may help to think of writing as a process like any other— like baking bread or building a house. When you see the finished product— a loaf of bread or a house or an 'A' paper, it's hard to imagine all the steps that went into producing it. But good writing is the product of a process, and you won't succeed if you ignore important steps in the process any more than a recipe would succeed if you left out ingredients or a construction project would succeed if you started nailing boards together without a blueprint to follow. Unfortunately, many beginning writers are either unaware of the process that is necessary to produce good writing or they are too impatient to follow the steps of the process successfully.

The three chapters on the writing process describe the steps good writers follow to develop a piece of writing from the time they get an assignment until the time they turn in the final draft. These steps are **narrowing the topic, examining the writing context, generating ideas, organizing ideas, drafting, revising,** and **editing.** Some of these steps may only take a few minutes; others may take an hour or more. In addition, you may have to repeat certain steps at different stages of the process. For example, you may find that you need to generate more ideas once you start organizing your writing, or you may need to generate additional ideas to get your reader interested in your topic or to conclude your essay.

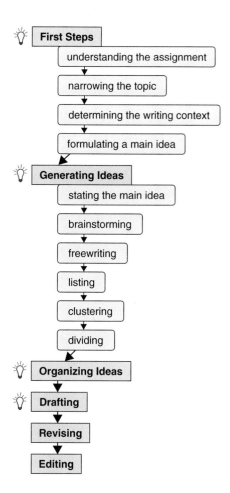

Writing in class

You may wonder how you can follow the steps of writing process if you are asked to produce a finished piece of writing in a fifty-minute class? Once you become familiar with the steps of the process, you will find that you can adapt them to use even when you are writing under time pressure. Rather than abandoning the process, good writers adapt the process to fit the time available. You may spend five to ten minutes generating ideas, five to ten minutes organizing your ideas, thirty to forty minutes composing your writing, and five to ten minutes proof-reading. Even though you spend less time on each step, following the steps helps to guarantee a better finished product.

Because every writing situation is different, you will end up tailoring the process to fit the topic, the situation, and your preferences. Although the process is similar for any length assignment, most of you will be working on either a paragraph or an essay, so after the initial steps described in "First Steps," we've separated the process into "Writing a Paragraph" and "Writing an Essay" in order to better address the unique needs of the two forms. The writing process chapters are intended as an overview of the process, and not as detailed instruction on the structure or form of a paragraph or essay. The chapters entitled "The Paragraph" and "The Essay" analyze in detail the parts of the paragraph and essay and provide practice exercises and multiple student examples.

The purpose of the Writing Process chapters is to give you an overview of a process that you will practice many more times in the future—we hope with every writing assignment you complete. We suggest that you try to read these chapters and complete the process of developing your assignment from topic to finished draft in a relatively short period of time. Don't get bogged down with what you don't know—details about how to write the perfect topic sentence or thesis or how to construct the perfect map or outline. That's not the point here. The point is for you to get a 'feel' for what it is like to use a process to complete a writing assignment. Do your best to complete each step in the writing process.

Because you will best learn the writing process by trying it out and practicing it, we provide Writing Practice after each step in the process. In Writing Practice, we suggest that you develop a topic you have been assigned or have chosen. Alternatively, your instructor may choose to have you review the entire writing process before you begin working on your own topic. The Writing Process Prompts are available at the end of "Writing a Paragraph" and "Writing an Essay" so that you can access them easily to complete future assignments.

We illustrate the writing process by using a single example, Beth's "Ready for the Junk Heap" about the disadvantages of her car so that you can follow the process from beginning to end with a single coherent topic.

Chapter 3
First Steps

The biggest mistake most beginning writers make is to start writing on the topic they have been given without doing the leg work (mind work in this case) necessary to ensure a successful outcome. Nothing is worse than getting halfway through an assignment only to find out that your writing is off topic, too general, or not adequately developed. Don't jump the gun!

Experienced writers know that before they can begin writing they have to examine the topic carefully to make sure they understand what is being asked. They must then narrow the topic; determine the writing context (which includes deciding on purpose, audience, and tone); formulate a main idea; and, finally, generate supports for developing the topic successfully. We illustrate these first steps of the writing process by following one of the student peers, Beth, as she tackles an assignment. The topic she has been given, "modes of transportation," is a very general one, and she demonstrates both individual and group brainstorming techniques to narrow her topic. Beth also tries out each of the techniques for generating ideas in order to illustrate how the techniques differ. We suggest that you follow her example and try each of the techniques with your own topic so that you get a "feel" for each method.

In this chapter, we describe the first steps in the writing process:

- **Understanding the Assignment**

- **Narrowing the Topic**
  Using a narrowing tree
  Brainstorming

- **Determining the Writing Context**
  Purpose
  Audience
  Tone

- **Generating Ideas**
  Brainstorming
  Freewriting
  Listing
  Clustering
  Dividing

Understanding the Assignment

It's important that you understand your assignment before you begin writing because each college assignment is likely to have different requirements.

First, make sure you are clear on requirements such as

- Due date.

- Length.

- Format of paper.

- Topic restrictions.

Next, make sure you understand the vocabulary of the assignment. Understanding the following words, commonly used in assignments, will help you focus your writing:

Analyze: Examine one or more of the parts of a topic.

Compare: Examine the similarities and differences in two topics, with the emphasis on similarities.

Contrast: Examine the differences in two topics.

Discuss: Present various sides of, focus on, or explain one topic.

Explain: Make clear, give the reasons for, or analyze a topic in a step-by-step fashion.

Prove: Provide evidence to persuade the reader that a statement is true.

Summarize: Restate the main points of an issue or article in a shortened form.

WRITING PRACTICE 1   Determine the following for your topic:

Assignment: _____

Length: _____

Due date: _____

Narrowing the Topic

Depending on your assignment, your first step may be to narrow the topic. If you are given a general topic such as "education" or "computerization," you will want to narrow the topic to a subject you can develop in a paragraph or short essay.

Using a Narrowing Tree

Use a **narrowing tree** to divide a general topic or subject into more specific parts until you find a specific topic of interest.

> My instructor gave us a general topic—modes of transportation—and asked us to narrow it before we went any further.

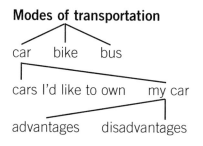

Modes of transportation

car   bike   bus

cars I'd like to own   my car

advantages   disadvantages

I started by thinking of different modes of transportation, but with two kids, I never ride a bike or take the bus, so I quickly focused on cars. From there I daydreamed briefly about the kind of car I'd like to own (dream on), and then turned my attention to the car I'm stuck with, an ancient Plymouth station wagon. It wasn't hard to decide I'd have plenty to say if I focused on the specific topic of the disadvantages of my car.

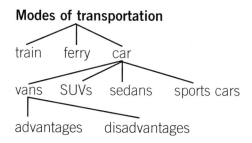

Modes of transportation

train   ferry   car

vans   SUVs   sedans   sports cars

advantages   disadvantages

Different people will narrow the same topic in different ways. The important thing is to arrive at a specific topic you are interested in or have knowledge about and that you can develop in the assignment you are given.

Brainstorming

Another way to narrow a general topic is to work **individually** or **in a group** to **brainstorm** a more specific topic. Working alone, you can narrow a topic by thinking of the aspects of the topic or of specific examples and writing down all the ideas that come to mind. Similarly, two or more people can help narrow a topic together. Each individual contributes his or her ideas, which in turn stimulate other ideas. In the world of work, groups often brainstorm creative solutions to problems.

Beth

> Modes of transportation, let's see. What do I know about transportation? I haven't taken the bus in years because I've had a car since I got out of high school. My car is a pain right now because it's such a junker—it's always breaking down and I can't depend on it. I guess I could write about the disadvantages of my mode of transportation, my car.

Group

> **TONY:** So we need to narrow the topic, "modes of transportation." Any ideas?
>
> **ALICIA:** Well, there's mass transit—trains and boats and planes.
>
> **TONY:** I used to take MARTA to school, and the service was pretty good, so I suppose I could write about using the metro. How about the rest of you? (Silence)
>
> OK, so we need to narrow to something we can all write about, something that we know more about.
>
> **BETH:** Why not focus on the form of transportation each of us uses, the advantages or disadvantages of however we get around. For me that would be my car, and it won't be hard for me to decide to write about disadvantages because something is always going wrong with it.
>
> **ALICIA:** I ride the bus. There are advantages because it's cheap, but there are disadvantages too because it takes so long, so I don't know which I would focus on.
>
> **BETH:** You might make a list of advantages and disadvantages and see which seems stronger.
>
> **TONY:** I ride a bike most of the time, so I wouldn't have any trouble coming up with reasons and details about why I like it. Or I could try to persuade students to ride their bikes safely by wearing helmets and obeying traffic laws.
>
> **DAN:** There are lots of ways to narrow "bikes." I just read this article in the newspaper about expanding the city's bike paths and making the city more bike-friendly to encourage more people to use bikes. I could write something trying to persuade the city to improve bike lanes.

> **BETH:** Alicia, if you're focusing on the bus and you decide you want to write about disadvantages, you could direct it toward the bus company or the city to try to make them improve the service.
>
> **ALICIA:** Good idea! As a student rider, I've got lots of suggestions for improvements.
>
> **BETH:** Does everyone have a narrowed topic? I'm doing the disadvantages of my car. Dan, what did you decide on?
>
> **DAN:** I'm going to try to convince the city to improve bike paths.
>
> **TONY:** And I'm going to focus on the advantages of bikes for students.
>
> **ALICIA:** I'm going to do something about improving bus service for students.

Use either a narrowing tree or group or individual brainstorming to narrow your topic to one that can be developed to fit the length of your assignment.   **WRITING PRACTICE 2**

Determining the Writing Context

Determining the writing context means examining your purpose in writing, your audience, and the tone you wish to use. As the writer, you have lots of options to choose from in how to present your ideas.

Ask yourself questions such as these:

- Do you want to inform your readers or persuade them?

- Is your audience predetermined or can you choose who you want your readers to be?

- Do you want this to be a serious piece or a humorous one?

Purpose

Your purpose includes why you are writing, what your goals are, and what you hope to accomplish. Understanding your purpose will help you determine what to include and what to leave out of your writing and will help you shape your topic sentence or thesis. The purpose of most college writing is to inform, to persuade, or to entertain.

If your topic is "a restaurant" and your purpose is to inform, you might provide factual information on a particular restaurant such as name, location, type of food, hours of operation, and prices.

EXAMPLE

Purpose:
to inform

Ernesto's Restaurant

Ernesto's Restaurant, located at 2100 South University Avenue, specializes in Mexican food. Some of the most popular dishes are fajitas, burritos, chimichangas, and chiles rellenos, and the prices for entries range from four to six dollars. Ernesto's also offers a children's menu (priced two to three dollars) with items such as chicken bites, hamburgers, and grilled cheese sandwiches. The restaurant is decorated with tropical plants and travel posters of Mexico. The atmosphere is casual, and the clientele is mostly students and families.

If your purpose instead is to persuade, you might wish to convince your audience that the restaurant you have chosen is a good or bad place to go. You might include much of the same information, but you would also include details that slant the information as either positive or negative. Notice in the following example how the favorable adjectives and adverbs help persuade the reader that this is a good restaurant.

EXAMPLE

Purpose:
to persuade

A Great Mexican Restaurant

Ernesto's Restaurant, located at 2100 South University Avenue, offers superb Mexican cuisine. Ernesto's specializes in authentic south-of-the-border dishes such as sizzling fajitas, ample burritos, succulent chimichangas, and flavorful chiles rellenos. The portions are large and delivered to the table piping hot. All entrées are reasonably priced, between four and six dollars. In addition, the kids' menu, priced between two and three dollars, offers traditional kid favorites such as chicken bites, hamburgers, and grilled cheese sandwiches. The restaurant is tastefully decorated with lush tropical plants and travel posters of exotic Mexican locations; mariachi music completes the atmosphere. Ernesto's casual atmosphere makes it a popular spot with both students and families. Word of mouth has quickly spread about this great dining establishment.

Audience

Your audience is the reader or readers with whom you are communicating. We tend to be more aware of audience when we speak than when we write because the audience for the spoken word is right in front of us. We make decisions unconsciously about what to say and how to say it, tailoring our statements to the person or group to whom we are speaking. Although we have plenty of experience in choosing words for an audience, we sometimes forget this intuitive knowledge when it comes to writing—which we usually do alone rather than face to face with our audience.

Good writers tailor what they have to say and how they say it to fit what they know about their audience. Keep in mind your audience's interests, concerns, values, educational backgrounds, and attitudes in determining what information to include and how to present it.

PEER EXAMPLE

> " Here's a paragraph on bikes that I am directing toward students. Determining my audience helped me narrow my topic and helped me pick the supports I would use, for example cost and convenience. "

Free Wheeling

Riding my bike to school is a great alternative to driving a car. First, the purchase price of my brand-new, top-of-the-line touring bike, $800, was well within my budget compared to the thousands I would have had to spend to purchase even a dilapidated secondhand car. Second, my bike saves me money every day on maintenance costs because I don't have to pay for insurance, repairs, or gas. It's also convenient to ride my bike because I don't have to purchase a parking decal or spend twenty minutes hunting for a parking place; I can park my bike next to my class and not have to fight the homicidal crowds in the parking lot. Next, riding my bike is a great form of exercise since it provides a cardiovascular workout, burns fat, and tones my muscles at once. Lastly, riding my bike is enjoyable because it puts me in touch with the beauty of nature in a way that I never would be if I were shut up inside a car with the windows rolled up. Riding my bike benefits me and benefits the environment, and that makes me feel good.

PEER EXAMPLE

> " Here's my paragraph that began with the same general topic of bikes, but the selection of the city as my audience helped me narrow my focus and build an argument that would appeal to the interests and concerns of city officials, for example, improving safety, saving money, and attracting new businesses. "

The Advantages of Bike Paths

The city should strive to improve its bike paths. By constructing more bike paths, the city could reduce the number of bike-related injuries and fatalities, thereby improving the health and safety of its citizens. Improved bike paths would encourage more citizens to bike to and from work, and fewer cars on the road would help reduce congestion and reduce the amount of money the city spends on road widening projects and road maintenance. In addition, the construction of bike paths and greenways encourages citizens to get out and appreciate their neighbors and their community, thus improving the overall livability of a city. A city with bike paths is also attractive to new businesses looking for a pleasant environment for their workers. Moreover, bike paths and greenways can help revitalize downtown businesses by encouraging use without increasing the need for parking places. Bike paths are an economical way to improve safety, stimulate business, and keep voters happy.

Exercise 1

Directions: Suppose that you have been given the topic "technological training for employees" and that your purpose is to persuade your audience of its importance. From each list of ten items below, select the five strongest ones that you think would be appropriate for the given audience. In other words, which five items would be most likely to persuade the given audience that technological training is important?

Audience 1: Business managers

1. more stable society
2. higher potential employee salaries
3. reduced cost of prisons
4. increased competitiveness
5. more stable workforce
6. increased profits
7. increased product innovation
8. greater employee accountability
9. greater chance of being hired
10. reduced cost of social services

Audience 2: Educators

1. more stable society
2. higher potential employee salaries
3. increased enrollment
4. increased competitiveness
5. reduced cost of social services
6. increased profits
7. reduced cost of prisons
8. education relevant to workplace
9. greater chance of student being hired
10. ease of adjustment to workplace

Audience 3: Government

1. more stable society
2. reduced cost of prisons
3. lower crime rate
4. reduced cost of social services
5. ease of adjustment to workplace
6. increased profits
7. increased enrollment
8. more stable workforce
9. more competitive salary negotiations
10. greater efficiency on job

Audience 4: Students

1. more stable society
2. higher potential salary
3. increased enrollment
4. greater chance of being hired
5. ease of adjustment to workplace
6. increased profits
7. reduced cost of prisons
8. lower crime rate
9. better salary negotiations
10. greater efficiency on job

Tone

Tone means the writer's attitude toward the subject or audience. We tend to be more aware of tone when we are speaking or listening to other people than when we are writing. Their tone of voice tells us a lot about their meaning. For example, if someone says, "Nice weather," in the middle of a blizzard, we know he or she is being sarcastic. Tone can range from serious to sarcastic, or from angry to humorous.

Writers should consider the effect their tone will have on the intended audience. Tones that could be described as dismissive, condescending, demeaning, insensitive, or strident are not likely to be well received by an audience.

Serious tone example:

The following is a fairly straightforward description of how to carve a jack-o'-lantern. The paragraph makes the process seem pretty easy if you follow the instructions given. Compare the tone of this paragraph to the tone of the next paragraph on the very same subject.

How to Carve a Jack-o'-Lantern

The process of carving a jack-o'-lantern is a relatively simple one. The first step is selecting and preparing the perfect pumpkin. Choose a deep orange, uniformly shaped fruit that fits the look you have in mind. Then cut a hole in the top of the pumpkin large enough to fit your hand through and remove the seeds. The next step, creating a design for your pumpkin, is the most artistically challenging. I recommend experimenting on a sheet of paper until you are satisfied with your design. Once you have perfected your design, transfer it to the surface of the pumpkin by tracing the outline with a pencil or a knife, making sure that the design is imprinted on the pumpkin. The final step, actually carving the pumpkin, requires a steady hand and lots of patience. Insert the knife along your design line and use a sawing motion to cut away the sections to be removed. When you are finished, place a lighted candle inside the pumpkin, and stand back and admire your masterpiece.

Sarcastic tone example:

Does the following paragraph prove that carving a jack-o'-lantern is relatively easy? No. In fact, it proves that the exact opposite is true. It makes carving a jack-o'-lantern sound like an impossible job. The tone is ironic or sarcastic, which means it is proving the exact opposite of what it says it's proving.

Easy as Pie

The process of carving a jack-o'-lantern is a relatively simple one. The first step is selecting the perfect pumpkin from the hundreds you will find piled in small mountains outside of most grocery stores. While you're at it, you might want to bring home a couple dozen extras in case your first few prototypes have design flaws. The next step, creating a design for your pumpkin, is the most artistically challenging. Do you want your pumpkin to look like Minnie Mouse or an M. C. Escher print? You should probably experiment on a sheet of paper until you are satisfied with your design—that is, unless you want to have a few hundred ruined pumpkins littering your kitchen. Next comes the simple task of transferring your two-dimensional design to the irregular, curved surface of the pumpkin. For this step, I strongly recommend a degree in design engineering. Before you begin the final step of actually carving the pumpkin, you may want to take out an insurance policy that covers severed fingers. To execute your design, simply insert the knife into the rock-hard pumpkin and carve away the sections to be removed. What could be easier? When you are finished, have friends and family come admire your work, and assure them there was nothing to it.

Formulating a Main Idea

Once you have determined your purpose, audience, and tone, try to formulate a main idea about your narrowed topic. Think about the direction you might be heading or what you might write about. Stating a **tentative** main idea will help you generate ideas about your narrowed topic more effectively. Once you finish generating ideas, you will formulate a new main idea statement based on the ideas you have generated.

PEER EXAMPLE

Determining the Writing Concept

Beth

Decide on your purpose, audience, and tone; then formulate a tentative main idea.

Purpose: To persuade

Audience: Students like myself

Tone: Serious

Tentative main idea: My car has lots of disadvantages.

> I am directing my paper to other students like myself, parents who are struggling to make ends meet while they go to school and who don't have the money to buy a new car if and when they want one. My tone will be serious, and I have tried to state my main idea as clearly and simply as I could.

Exercise 2

Read each paragraph and then select the audience, purpose, and tone from the list that follows.

A. Technological training for employees is important. In order to remain competitive, businesses need to ensure that employees are on the cutting edge of technological advancements. Rather than hiring new employees to fill this ever-changing need for expertise in current technology, employers should supply technological training for current employees. Promoting increased technological skills among employees would help increase innovation and productivity, which would in turn help businesses remain competitive in the marketplace. Helping an employee develop new skills not only helps a business remain competitive but also helps the employee feel more secure in his position and in

continues

continued

his value to the company. This sense of security will help improve employee morale and loyalty. Countless studies have shown that satisfied workers tend to change jobs less frequently and tend to be more productive. A stable workforce saves the business money; therefore, it is in a business's best interest to invest in technological training for its employees.

Audience	Purpose	Tone
Employees	Persuade	Serious
Employers	Entertain	Humorous
Government	Inform	Sarcastic
College instructors		

B. Remaining abreast of current technological innovations is important in order to prepare students for the demands of the job world. Technology is revolutionizing the workplace, and job candidates who are familiar with current technology have an advantage when looking for jobs. Familiarizing students with the technology they will be expected to use on the job therefore gives them an advantage. For example, engineering instructors who fail to teach students how to use AutoCAD fail to prepare them for the reality of a work world in which they will be expected to use AutoCAD to design structures. Similarly, graphic designers who do not know how to use the latest graphics software and accountants who do not know how to use spreadsheets and accounting programs are at a disadvantage in the workplace. Technological training is an essential part of the discipline specific knowledge that instructors have a responsibility to teach their students.

Audience	Purpose	Tone
College students	Persuade	Serious
College instructors	Entertain	Humorous
Government	Inform	Sarcastic

For the topic you narrowed in Writing Practice 2, decide on your pur-   **WRITING PRACTICE 3**
pose, audience, and tone, and then formulate a tentative main idea.

Purpose: _____

Audience: _____

Tone:_____

Tentative main idea: _____

_____

Generating Supporting Ideas

Generating supporting ideas is an important stage in the writing
process because it helps you think of enough ideas or specific details to
develop your topic. If you've never consciously tried to write down
ideas before you begin writing the assignment itself, this stage in the
process may seem a bit artificial at first, but the more you practice generating supporting ideas with one of the techniques we show you, the
more natural and useful it will seem. All of the techniques we demonstrate help you focus on your topic in different ways—and focusing on
your topic is the key, because once you start thinking about your topic,
you will start getting ideas. Don't worry about whether those ideas will
be useful in the long run or not; just jot them down as they pop into
your head. At this stage in the writing process, your job is to come up
with as many ideas and images as possible. You can evaluate them later.

We suggest that you begin by trying each of the techniques
described here. You may find that some work better for you than others, or that some feel more natural than others. As a general rule, if you
try one technique and don't come up with enough ideas, try another.
Some techniques work with one topic, and other techniques are more
successful with a different topic.

Brainstorming

As with brainstorming to narrow the topic, in brainstorming to
generate supporting ideas, you allow as many ideas as possible to pop
into your head. One idea leads to another, and you write down anything
that comes to mind related to the topic. Brainstorming is like priming
a pump; once the ideas start coming, they come faster and faster. Again,
brainstorming to generate ideas can be done individually or in a group.

Individual brainstorming: One person can generate supporting
ideas on a narrowed topic by focusing on the topic and writing down
all the ideas that come to mind. Don't worry about spelling, punctua-

tion, or grammar at this point. Most people get ideas about their topic by visualizing the topic or picturing it in their minds. Try to be aware of all the senses—sight, hearing, taste, smell, and touch. Imagine what the person, place, or thing looks like. Imagine you are in the scene. Imagine you are walking through it or experiencing it.

PEER EXAMPLE

Brainstorming

Beth

" Here's an example of my brainstorming ideas on the topic of the disadvantages of my car. I tried to picture my car and the experience of driving it and I wrote down everything that came to mind. The more I focused on my car, the more ideas I came up with. "

Topic: Disadvantages of my unreliable car

Ugly

Unreliable

always breaking down

stuck in the rain or on the way home

safety

towing

mechanic

what's wrong with it?

how much will it cost?

Embarrassing my kids

I wish I could afford a new car.

Group brainstorming: Two or more people can help each other generate ideas by brainstorming together. The group focuses on each individual's narrowed topic and tentative main idea statement, and everyone contributes as many ideas as possible. One person's ideas might stimulate other ideas, and before you know it, the group has generated enough ideas to get the writer started. The group then focuses on another writer's tentative main idea statement next, and so on. We suggest you take notes as the group helps you brainstorm ideas. When it comes to generating ideas, two heads are definitely better than one.

BETH: Here's how we helped Tony generate ideas to support his narrowed topic on transportation.

TONY: My narrowed topic is the advantages of riding a bike for students. This should be easy.

BETH: OK, what are some advantages of bikes for students?

Details:

cost	**DAN:** Bikes are cheap. You can buy a good one for a couple hundred bucks.
purchase ($100–$400)	**TONY:** A really good one would cost more than that, but you can buy a good used bike for around a hundred.
Maintenance (no gas, no insurance, no expense repairs)	**BETH:** And it can't cost much to maintain a bike. There's no gas or insurance. You could do most repairs yourself.
convenience no parking decal saves times	**DAN:** And you don't have to pay for a parking decal, or get to school a half hour before your class to get a parking place.
help environment no pollution use less gas	**ALICIA:** How about it also helps the environment. You're not using gas or polluting.
saves metal	**BETH:** Or using all the natural resources it takes to make a car. Anything else?
Exercise stay fit	**TONY:** It's good exercise. Riding helps keep me in shape.
no gym membership	**ALICIA:** There you go; you can save on the cost of membership at a gym.
Enjoyable see trees and flowers	**BETH:** I imagine it must also be kind of enjoyable, at least on nice days. You're out in nature and you can see trees and flowers and things better than people can in cars. So what do you have so far, Tony?

> **TONY:** I've got that they're inexpensive, good for the environment, good exercise, and enjoyable. I think I can make two supports out of cost because I can say they're inexpensive to purchase and inexpensive to maintain. Hey, thanks for all your help in brainstorming supports for my topic.

Freewriting

Freewriting is another way of generating ideas where you focus on the topic and write down everything that comes to mind, no matter how important or unimportant. Write as much and as fast as you can, without worrying about spelling or grammar.

PEER EXAMPLE

Free Writing

> As I freewrote about the disadvantages of my car, I wrote everything that came to mind when I thought about my car. I didn't worry about writing correctly, so there are fragments and grammar errors in my freewriting. The important thing is to get ideas on paper without stopping to think about or be distracted by what is correct or incorrect.

I hate my car. Always afraid of breaking down and being late for work and then not being able to pay to get it towed or get it fixed. I hate dealing with mechanics and never knowing whether to trust what they're telling me about what is wrong with the car and what needs to be fixed. The worst part is the fear of being stranded on the road by myself or with one of the kids, and these days it's not paranoia, but a realistic fear. The kids would say, you worry for nothing mom. For them the worst part is the way the car looks, rusted fenders and scratched paint, not shiny and new like most of their friends parents cars.

Listing

Another way to generate ideas is listing. Don't worry about trying to write in sentences; just list words or phrases that come to mind when you focus on your topic. Focus on your topic by visualizing it, and write a list of everything that comes to mind. Try to see the topic in your mind's eye and be aware of all the senses—sight, hearing, taste, smell, touch.

Listing

Beth

> Here is an example of the list I came up with for the topic "the disadvantages of my car."

—breaking down—late for work

—Mr. Rains angry at me and not believing my car broke down

—then having to deal with the car

—towing it

—the cost, and where to take it

—which garage to trust—who to believe when I don't know if it's the ignition or a hose

—fear of being stranded

—long dark road home

—afraid of crazy person

—kids embarrassed when I drop them off at school

—they want new car

—I can't afford the payments

Clustering

Clustering is a visual representation of ideas. Because you cluster related ideas together, clustering begins the process of grouping or organizing your ideas. Many writers begin by freewriting or listing and then cluster those ideas into related groups that generate further ideas. When you cluster, you write down words or images you associate with your topic. These words may be parts of your topic. Then cluster related ideas together by drawing lines between them.

PEER
EXAMPLE

Beth

> ❝ I seemed to have three major complaints about my car: how unreliable it is, how expensive it is, and how terrible it looks. Once I came up with those three areas, I was able to generate specific details or problems I'd had in each of those areas. ❞

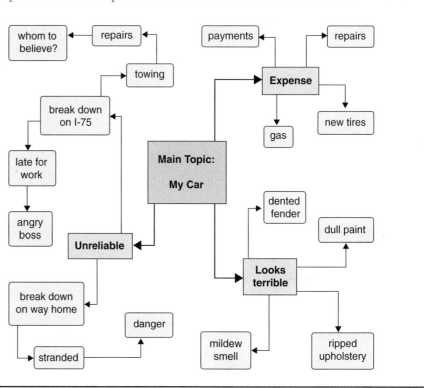

Dividing

Dividing generates ideas by breaking the topic into its component parts. Use the journalistic questions of **who, what, where, when, why,** and **how** in order to divide a topic.

Ask yourself, "What are the parts of my topic?" One technique is to imagine yourself in your topic—at school, on the job, playing a sport—and move through the event or the experience chronologically. What happens first, second, third? What issues do you have to face at each moment of the task or situation? Dividing a topic is useful in building supports for your main idea.

Once you have divided a topic into its component parts, you will be able to generate specific ideas about each part. Focus on each part and think of specifics that will support your point of view about your topic.

Beth

> Here's an example of how I divided the topic "car" into its component parts. Let's see, what are the typical parts of a car? There's appearance, what it looks like. There's performance, how it handles and accelerates and parks; there's reliability, whether you can count on it not to leave you stranded; there's cost, for me that would be the cost of repairs; then there's the cost of insurance and gas and maintenance like oil changes. There's also safety. That gives me enough areas to start developing.

Appearance

Performance

Reliability

Cost

Maintenance

Safety

Here are the complete writing process prompts for the initial steps in the writing process. You may wish to consult the prompts each time you develop an assignment until the process becomes second nature.

Writing Process Prompts

1. **Understanding the assignment**

   Assignment: _____

   Length: _____

   Due date: _____

If necessary, use a narrowing tree or brainstorming to narrow your topic to a subject that interests you and that you can develop in the length of paper you have been assigned. You may find it helpful to use scratch paper.

Narrowed topic: _____

2. **Determining the writing context and formulating a main idea**

   Decide on your purpose, audience, and tone.

   Purpose: _____

   Audience: _____

   Tone: _____

   Tentative main idea: _____

3. **Generating supporting ideas**

   Generate ideas by brainstorming, freewriting, listing, clustering, or dividing. You may find it helpful to use scratch paper.

   _____

   _____

   _____

   _____

   _____

   _____

   _____

   _____

   _____

   _____

   _____

   _____

   _____

   _____

   _____

   _____

   _____

   _____

   _____

   _____

   _____

   _____

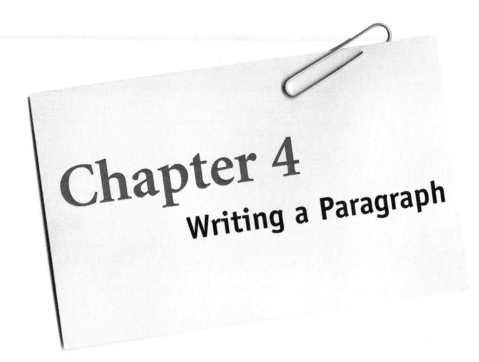

Chapter 4
Writing a Paragraph

This chapter will lead you through the process of **organizing, drafting**, **revising**, and **editing** a **paragraph**. It is intended as an overview of the writing process for a paragraph and not as detailed instruction on the parts of the paragraph. Chapter 6, "The Paragraph," analyzes each part of the paragraph in detail and provides practice exercises and multiple student examples. In this chapter we use one example, Beth's paragraph "Ready for the Junk Heap" to illustrate the steps of the writing process. Because the best way to learn the writing process is to practice it, we suggest that for each step of the process, you respond to the prompt in Writing Practice to develop a topic you have chosen or been assigned.

Stating the Main Idea

The main idea of a paragraph is expressed in a **topic sentence**. In this sentence you state simply and clearly the main point of your paragraph.

Before you began generating supporting ideas, you formulated a tentative main idea, the point you thought your paragraph would be about. Take a look at the ideas you generated through brainstorming, freewriting, listing, clustering, or dividing. Did you stick with your original main idea, or did you change it as you generated supporting ideas? You may find that you narrowed your focus or changed your focus slightly. Examine your original main idea statement to see if it fits the ideas you generated or if you need to restate your main idea.

As you formulate and refine your main idea statement, keep your assignment, audience, purpose, and tone in mind. Make sure your main idea statement is appropriate for the length and type of assignment you are completing and for the audience to whom you are directing your writing. Make sure your topic sentence indicates

The steps in the writing process described in **Writing a Paragraph** are

- **Stating the Main Idea**

- **Organizing Supporting Ideas**
  Mapping
  Outlining

- **Drafting**

- **Revising**
  Peer Feedback
  Instructor Feedback
  Self-Evaluation

- **Editing**

53

your purpose, whether it is to inform, persuade, or entertain. Also, make sure your topic sentence matches your desired tone, whether it is serious, sarcastic, or humorous.

WRITING PRACTICE 1   Revise your tentative topic sentence.

Turning a Discussion Question into a Topic Sentence

Many college writing assignments are given in the form of discussion questions. A discussion question can often be turned into a topic sentence.

 **EXAMPLE**

Assignment: Analyze the effects of Hurricane Andrew.

Topic Sentence: Hurricane Andrew devastated South Florida.

OR

There were two primary effects of Hurricane Andrew.

Organizing Supporting Ideas

Organizing your ideas before you start writing is an important step in creating a successful paragraph. Using a **map** or **outline** can help you plan your supports so that you don't leave out important supports or wander away from your main idea. Some writers like to use a map because it shows supporting ideas on one line. Others are familiar with the outline form and prefer it. What matters is that you find a way to plan and organize your ideas before you start writing.

As you work on creating a map or outline for your paragraph, you may find that you haven't generated enough ideas to support your topic sentence adequately. If so, use one of the generating techniques described in Chapter 3 to generate additional ideas and details to support your main idea.

Mapping

A paragraph map is like a road map; it shows you how to get from point A to point B without getting lost. A map can take many forms, but in it you plan and order your supporting ideas and details. A map takes only a few minutes to complete, and yet it can make the difference between a well-organized paragraph and a disorganized one.

A basic paragraph map consists of a topic sentence, a list of supports in the order they will be presented, and a list of the specific details that will be used to develop each area of support. A more detailed map may contain an indication of the reasoning behind each support or a statement of how or why your supports relate to the topic sentence. Making your reasoning explicit ensures that both you and the reader clearly understand how your supporting ideas relate to your topic sentence.

Area of Support	Specific Details	Relation to Topic Sentence
1.		
2.		
3.		

 I started my map by placing my topic sentence at the top and listing my areas of support in the order I plan to use them.

Topic sentence: My car has lots of disadvantages for me.

Area of Support

1. reliability
2. expenses
3. appearance

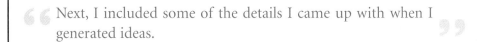 Next, I included some of the details I came up with when I generated ideas.

Area of Support	Specific Details
1. reliability	breakdowns
2. expenses	tires, brakes, headlights, gas
3. appearance	dented door rusted fender

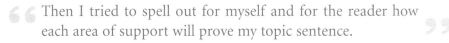 Then I tried to spell out for myself and for the reader how each area of support will prove my topic sentence.

Area of Support	Specific Details	Relation to Topic Sentence
1. reliability	breakdowns	anxiety, safety
2. expenses	tires, brakes, headlights, gas	hard on budget
3. appearance	dented door rusted fender	kids embarrassed

Outlining

An outline is a formal structure that helps you organize support topics and subtopics. Outline form is broken down into main headings (I, II, III, IV); support headings (A, B, C); and details (1, 2, 3). Use as many main headings, support headings, and details as you need to develop your topic. However, each heading that is broken down should have at least two subheadings. For example, if you have an A, you need a B; if you have a 1, you need a 2. Remember that the number of main topics, supporting ideas, and details is up to you and will vary depending on the ideas you have generated.

Many students find it difficult to outline a paragraph because outline form is somewhat rigid. You should adapt the form presented here to fit the ideas you are presenting. The form will help you incorporate both specific details and a relation to the topic sentence if one is appropriate.

Paragraph Outline

Topic sentence:
    I. Support #1
      A. Specifics
      B. Relation
   II. Support #2
      A. Specifics
      B. Relation
  III. Support #3
      A. Specifics
      B. Relation
  IV. Support #4
      A. Specifics
      B. Relation

Beth

Topic sentence: My car has a lot of disadvantages for me.
I. Reliability
   A. Breakdowns, noises
   B. Safety
II. Cost
   A. Tires, brakes, gas
   B. Hard on budget
III. Appearance
   A. Dented door, rusted fender
   B. Kids embarrassed

WRITING PRACTICE 2

1. Examine the ideas you have generated and revise your tentative topic sentence.

2. Select your strongest supporting ideas and place them in the map or outline template in the order you would like to use them. Do more brainstorming if you do not have enough supports to develop your topic sentence.

3. Generate specific details for each of your supports.

4. You may wish to state how each support relates to or proves the topic sentence.

Map Template
Topic sentence: _____

Area of Support	Specific Details	Relation to Topic Sentence
1. _____	_____	_____
_____	_____	_____
2. _____	_____	_____
_____	_____	_____
3. _____	_____	_____
_____	_____	_____
4. _____	_____	_____
_____	_____	_____
5. _____	_____	_____
_____	_____	_____

Outline Template

Topic sentence: _____

   I. Support #1 _____

      A. Specifics _____

      B. Relation _____

  II. Support #2 _____

      A. Specifics _____

      B. Relation _____

 III. Support #3 _____

      A. Specifics _____

      B. Relation _____

 IV. Support #4 _____

      A. Specifics _____

      B. Relation _____

Drafting

Once you have organized your ideas, you're ready to write a first draft. To write a first draft, you follow your map or outline, putting your ideas into sentences. In a first draft, you focus on presenting your ideas as clearly as possible, without worrying about mechanical errors such as spelling.

PEER EXAMPLE

Draft

Beth

66 I wrote a draft of my paragraph by writing a sentence or two for each area of support on my map. 99

Topic sentence: My car has lots of disadvantages for me.

Area of Support	Specific Details	Relation to Topic Sentence
1. reliability	breakdowns	anxiety, safety

Draft: I'm constantly afraid of breaking down on the interstate on the way to school or on the long dark road home at night. Because it's always making strange noises, I feel like I can't rely on it to get me where I'm going safely. These days breaking down could mean more than being late for work and getting yelled at by the boss; it could mean never showing up for work, period.

Area of Support	Specific Details	Relation to Topic Sentence
2. expenses	tires, brakes, headlights, gas	hard on budget

Draft: My car is a constant drain on my budget because I'm always having to repair the lights or brakes, and gas is expensive too.

Area of Support	Specific Details	Relation to Topic Sentence
3. appearance	dented door rusted fender	kids embarrassed

Draft: Worst of all, my car looks so bad with its dented door and rusted fender that my kids are embarrassed to be seen in it.

Write a draft of your paragraph by creating a sentence or sentences for each area of supports on your map or outline. Incorporate your specific details and, where appropriate, the relation to the topic sentence.

WRITING PRACTICE 3

Revising

Revising is the process of examining the content and organization of your writing to see how they could be improved. Whenever possible, it's a good idea to let someone else read your first draft and give you feedback on what works and what doesn't work, what is and isn't clear. If you can't get feedback, use the Paragraph Revision Checklist on page 62 to help you revise your own writing. In revising, you focus on developing and clarifying your ideas. You may decide you need more supporting details, or you may decide to delete details that don't relate to your topic sentence.

When you revise, you also work on polishing the presentation of your ideas. You may want to consider using precise language and appropriate vocabulary. The more specific your writing, the better. Therefore, you want to avoid general nouns such as *people* and *things*, and avoid weak verbs such as *is/are, has/have, does/do.* It's much more effective to use specific, concrete nouns and active verbs. Chapter 23, "Word Choice," provides instruction on improving your word choice.

Polishing your writing may also mean improving your sentence structure. It's a good idea to vary the length and pattern of your sentences. Try to alternate long and short sentences, and try to use a variety of sentence types. For example, use some compound and some complex sentences (see Chapter 31, "Sentence Variety"). Writing, like music, depends on rhythm, and varying the rhythm of your sentences can help you both convey your ideas effectively and keep the reader's attention.

Peer Feedback

Your peers can give you a good idea of what is and isn't working in your draft. If anything in your draft isn't clear to a reader, you will probably want to go back and reexamine or revise it. Listen carefully to the comments of your peer reviewers, but remember that in the end you are the one who decides what to include or not include in your paper. If questions about the assignment or mechanical errors arise, consult your instructor or use the chapters in Part VI, "Writing Elements and Skills." If you aren't sure whether your reviewer was right to say you need a comma before an *and* in your paragraph, look it up in Chapter 32, "Commas."

Note to peer reviewers: When giving feedback on someone else's paragraph, remember that you are trying to help the writer communicate his or her ideas as clearly and effectively as possible. It won't help the writer to be polite and say only that everything is fine, especially if you have trouble following the meaning or the logic of the paragraph. It's your responsibility to pay careful attention as you read or listen to your classmate's draft and then to be as helpful as possible. The questionnaire below can help you let the writer know where you have trouble following the ideas or logic in the paragraph.

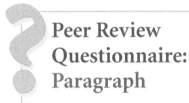

Peer Review Questionnaire: Paragraph

Directions: Read the paragraph carefully and answer the following questions as specifically as possible. Remember, your goal is to help your peer improve his or her paragraph.

1. Is the topic sentence clear? Restate it in your own words.

   _____

   _____

2. Does the paragraph adequately explain or develop the topic sentence? List the areas of support used.

   _____

   _____

   _____

   _____

3. Does the order of supports seem logical? _____

4. Is there enough information or support to develop the topic sentence? What additional information or supporting ideas could the writer have included?

_____

_____

_____

_____

_____

5. What did you like most about the paragraph?

_____

_____

_____

_____

6. What seemed most unclear about the paragraph?

_____

_____

_____

_____

7. Did you notice mechanical errors in the paragraph? If so, please list.

_____

_____

_____

_____

Instructor Feedback

Whenever possible, get feedback on the draft of your paragraph from your instructor. You may have an opportunity to submit a draft for review, or you may be able to use your instructor's office hours to get feedback. Instructors generally comment on the strength or weakness of the content and structure of a piece of writing. They may or may not mark errors or list the types of errors they've noticed in your paragraph. Know your instructor's grading symbols (the marks he or she uses to indicate mechanical errors in your writing). If you don't understand your instructor's comments (whether verbal or written), ask him or her to explain. Both seeking feedback on your draft and making sure that you understand it show your instructor that you are serious about improving your writing.

Self-Evaluation

If peer or instructor feedback isn't available, or if you prefer self-evaluation, you can use the Paragraph Revision Checklist below to get ideas on how to revise your paragraph. First, it's a good idea to give yourself some distance from what you've written by putting your paragraph aside for as long as you can before coming back to revise it. You may be able to put it aside for an hour or two, or overnight, but if you're writing an in-class paper, you may only have a minute or two before you need to start revising. However much time you have, getting some distance from your ideas will help you spot problems more easily. In revising, you should read your paragraph as critically as possible, looking for areas that could be improved.

Paragraph Revision Checklist

1. **Form**

   Title: Are the major words (including the first and last words) capitalized?

   Does the title reveal the topic and slant of the paragraph?

   Does it catch the reader's attention?

   Is the first sentence indented?

   Does the paragraph have the required number of sentences?

   Does the paragraph have the required organizational pattern?

2. **Topic Sentence**

   Does the topic sentence fit the assignment?

   Is it appropriate for the intended audience and purpose?

   Is the main idea clear?

3. **Support**

   Is there enough support (three to five supports, depending on the assignment) to explain or prove your topic sentence?

   Does each support clearly relate to or develop the topic sentence?

   Are there enough specific details, facts, and examples to convince the reader?

   Are any supports repeated?

Does anything in the paragraph not relate to the main idea?

Is the relationship between support sentences clear?

Are there clear transitions within and between sentences?

Is the order of supports clear and logical?

Are the sentences varied in length and structure?

Is appropriate vocabulary used?

Is the language clear and precise? (Are there strong verbs, specific nouns, and colorful adjectives and adverbs?)

4. **Conclusion**

Does the conclusion tie together the paragraph?

Does it introduce any new ideas or arguments that might confuse the reader?

PEER
EXAMPLE

Original Draft: *Identify make/year*   Revision

                                        Review topic sentence guidelines

I hate (my car) (because) its a pain. Its so unreliable. I'm constantly   *Review its/it's*   Beth
afraid of breaking down on the interstate on the way to school or on the
long dark road home at night. Because it's always making strange noises,
I feel like I can't rely on it to get me where I'm going safely. These days
breaking down could mean more than being late for work and getting
yelled at by the boss; it could mean never showing up for work, period.
My car is a constant drain on my budget because I'm always having to   *Add specific*
repair the lights or brakes, and gas is expensive too. Worst of all, my car   *details*
looks so bad with its dented door and rusted fender that my kids are
embarrassed to be seen in it.

> ❝ Here's a revision of my paragraph on the disadvantages of my
> car. I tried to respond to my instructor's comments by adding
> more specific detail and further explaining the drawbacks of
> my car. ❞

Revision: (Changes are italicized)

My car, a 1990 Plymouth sedan, has lots of disadvantages. I'm constantly afraid of breaking down on the interstate on the way to school or
on the long dark road home at night. Because it's always making strange
noises, I feel like I can't rely on it to get me where I'm going safely. These
days breaking down could mean more than being late for work and getting yelled at by the boss; it could mean never showing up for work *at all.*
Not only is my car unreliable, but it's a constant drain on my budget. *In*

the last two months, I've had to fix the brakes, buy new tires, and replace a headlight. Even when my car isn't eating up money in repairs, it costs me between thirty and fifty dollars a week to cover insurance, maintenance, and gasoline. My dinosaur of a car only gets twelve miles to the gallon and burns a quart of oil a week, so I'm always pumping money into it. Worst of all, my kids are embarrassed to be seen in our car *because of the dented door, rusted fender, and the trunk tied down with a bungee cord. Maybe it's time to start shopping for a late-model used car.*

WRITING PRACTICE 4   Revise your paragraph. If possible, get feedback on your paragraph from peers or your instructor. If your peers or instructor are not available to give feedback, analyze the strengths and weaknesses of your paragraph using the paragraph revision checklist on page 62.

Editing

One of the most important skills in writing is editing. All too often, writers receive low grades on their work because they have neglected to edit carefully. No one intends to turn a paragraph in with errors, but finding errors takes time and attention to detail.

Using an editing checklist like the one below can help you catch and correct errors in your English. When you edit, you should read your paragraph five or six times, focusing on one type of error each time—fragments, verb errors, comma errors, spelling errors, and so on—paying particular attention to errors you have had trouble with in the past.

One reason it is so hard to spot errors is that we tend to read what we *intended* to write down rather than what is actually on the page. A technique that you might want to try is reading your paragraph backward, starting at the bottom and moving to the top. Reading backward forces you to focus on the words rather than on the content.

Another technique that may be helpful is called tracking. Tracking means using a pencil to point to each word as you read it. Tracking can help slow your reading down and help you focus on one word at a time.

All of these techniques are intended to help you find errors so that you can correct them before you turn in your paragraph.

As you learn about the following skills, add them to your editing checklist.

1. Check for run-ons and fragments. Is there one complete sentence between every two periods? (Identify the subject and the verb, and make sure the word group expresses a complete thought.)

2. Check every verb. Do subjects and verbs agree? Is proper verb tense used? Be sure to check the problem phrases such as *there is/there are* and pay attention to singular subjects such as *everyone.*

3. Use the dictionary or computer spell check to catch capitalization errors and misspellings. Remember, however, that the spell check will not catch errors with problem words such as *there/their.*

4. Remember your personal list of errors. Check your writing for any of these errors.

5. Check for apostrophes in contractions and possessives.

6. Check commas.

7. Check pronouns. Do they agree with their antecedents? Is the reference clear?

8. Look for any missing words or letters by reading the writing slowly from the last sentence to the first.

9. Check for parallelism in pairs, series, and comparisons.

10. Check for dangling and misplaced modifiers.

11. Check semicolon and colon use.

Beth edits the first half of her paragraph for the errors on her personal error list. This type of editing would typically come after the basic steps outlined above.

PEER
EXAMPLE

Editing

My car, a 1990 Plymouth sedan, has lots of disadvantages. I'm constantly afraid of breaking down on the interstate on the way to school or on the long dark road home at night. Because it's always making strange noises, I feel like I can't rely on it to get me where I'm going safely. These days breaking down could mean more ~~then~~ *than* being late for work and getting yelled at by the boss, it could mean never showing up for work at all. Not only is my car unreliable, but it's a constant drain on my budget. In the last two months, I've had to fix the brakes, buy new tires, and replace a headlight. Even when my car isn't eating up money in repairs, it costs me between thirty and fifty dollars a week to cover insurance, maintenance, and gasoline. My dinosaur of a car only gets twelve miles to the gallon and burns a quart of oil a week, so I'm always pumping money into it. Worst of all, my kids are embarrassed to be seen in our car because of the dented door, rusted fender, and the trunk tied down with a bungee cord. Maybe it's time to start shopping for a late-model used car.

WRITING PRACTICE 5   Use the Editing Checklist above to proofread your paragraph for errors.

Paragraph Writing Process Prompts

The following prompts will guide you in writing paragraphs. You may wish to consult these prompts each time you write a paragraph until the process becomes second nature.

1. **Understanding the assignment**

   Assignment: _____

   Length: _____

   Due date: _____

   If necessary, use a narrowing tree or brainstorming to narrow your topic to a subject that interests you and that you can develop in the length of paper you have been assigned. You may find it helpful to use scratch paper.

   Narrowed topic: _____

   _____

   _____

2. Determining the writing context

Decide on your purpose, audience, and tone. Then choose a tentative main idea.

Purpose: _____

Audience: _____

Tone: _____

Tentative main idea: _____

3. Generating ideas

Generate ideas by brainstorming, freewriting, listing, clustering, or dividing. You may find it helpful to use scratch paper. Come up with as many ideas as possible. Keep your purpose and audience in mind as you generate ideas to support your topic sentence.

_____

_____

_____

_____

_____

4. Organizing ideas

1. Examine the ideas you have generated and revise your tentative topic sentence.

2. Select your strongest support ideas and place them in the map or outline template in the order you would like to use them. Do more brainstorming if you do not have enough supports to develop your topic sentence.

3. Generate specific details for each of your supports.

4. You may wish to state how each support relates to or proves the topic sentence.

Map Template

Topic sentence: _____

Relation to Area of Support	Specific Details	Topic Sentence
1. _____	_____	_____
_____	_____	_____
2. _____	_____	_____
_____	_____	_____
3. _____	_____	_____
_____	_____	_____
4. _____	_____	_____
_____	_____	_____
5. _____	_____	_____
_____	_____	_____

Outline Template

Topic sentence:_____

    I. Support #1 _____

       A. Specifics_____

       B. Relation _____

    II. Support #2 _____

       A. Specifics_____

       B. Relation _____

   III. Support #3 _____

       A. Specifics_____

       B. Relation _____

   IV. Support #4 _____

       A. Specifics_____

       B. Relation _____

5. Drafting

Write a draft of the paragraph by creating a sentence or sentences for each area of support on your map or outline. Incorporate your specific details and, where appropriate, the relation to the topic sentence.

6. Revising

If possible, get feedback on your paragraph from peers or your instructor. If feedback is not available, analyze the strengths and weaknesses of your paragraph using the Paragraph Revision Checklist on page 62.

Getting the Paragraph Back

Contrary to popular belief, the process isn't over when you get your graded paper back from your instructor. Part of the process of improving your writing is learning from your mistakes. The last thing most students want to do when they get back a paper is pay attention to the errors that have been marked, but figuring out what you did wrong is the key to improving your performance. Just as in sports, you need to listen to your coach if you hope to play your best. Think of your instructor's marks and comments as a way of helping you improve.

First, you need to make sure you understand the errors your instructor has marked. If you don't understand the marks, ask your instructor to explain them. Next, you need to know how to correct the errors. One way to do this is to look up each one in Part VI, "Writing Elements and Skills." Detailed instruction and practices are available for the common grammar and punctuation errors.

Next, record the errors your instructor has marked in your paragraph on a **personal error list**. This will help you keep track of the types of errors you have made so that you can avoid repeating them. Although it may take several minutes to record errors on your personal error list, learning to correct past errors is the best way to avoid making those same errors again. A template for your personal error list is available in the appendix at the end of this book. Your completed personal error list also serves as a great way to review before a test or before an in-class writing. Simply take your error list out and review it for a few minutes before you begin writing. That way your past errors are fresh in your mind and you are less likely to repeat them.

EXAMPLE

Sample
Error List

Error	Explanation/Rule	Correction
1. recieved	spelling	received
2. use to go	spelling	used to go
3. alot	spelling	a lot
4. Always being late for class.	I am always late for class.	fragment

Chapter 5
Writing an Essay

This chapter will lead you through the process of **organizing**, **drafting**, **revising**, and **editing** an **essay**. It is intended as an overview of the writing process for an essay and not as detailed instruction on the parts of the essay. Chapter 7, "The Essay," analyzes each part of the essay in detail and provides practice exercises and multiple examples. In this chapter we use one example, Beth's essay "Ready for the Junk Heap," to illustrate the steps of the writing process. Because the best way to learn the writing process is to practice it, we suggest that for each step of the process, you respond to the prompt in Writing Practice to develop a topic you have chosen or been assigned.

Stating the Main Idea

Once you have generated ideas, you can examine them to determine your main idea. In a paragraph the main idea is stated in a topic sentence, but in an essay, the main idea statement is generally called a **thesis**. The thesis is the main point your writing will communicate. Everything in your essay should support your thesis statement.

Before you began generating supporting ideas, you formulated a tentative main idea, the point you thought your essay would be about. Take a look at the ideas you generated through brainstorming, freewriting, listing, clustering, or dividing. Did you stick with your original thesis, or did your main idea change as you generated ideas? You may find that you narrowed your focus or changed your focus slightly. Examine your original main idea statement to see if it fits the ideas you generated or if you need to restate it.

As you formulate and refine your thesis statement, keep in mind your assignment, audience, purpose, and tone. Make sure that your main idea statement is appropriate for the length and type of assignment you

The steps in the writing process described in **Writing an Essay** are

- **Stating the Main Idea**

- **Outlining the Essay**
  Using Outline Form
  Creating an Outline
  Generating More Ideas

- **Drafting**
  Drafting Body
    Paragraphs
  Drafting the
    Introduction and
    Conclusion

- **Revising**
  Peer Feedback
  Instructor Feedback
  Self-Evaluation

- **Editing**

are completing and for the audience to whom you are directing your writing. Make sure your thesis statement indicates your purpose, whether it is to inform, persuade, or entertain. Also, make sure your thesis statement matches the tone you plan to use in your essay, whether it is serious, sarcastic, or humorous.

You may want to use a **blueprinted thesis**, which is a thesis that includes the main areas of support in the order you will introduce them and thus acts as a blueprint for the essay.

PEER EXAMPLE

Blueprinted Thesis

> " A blueprinted thesis for my essay would include the main supports I intend to develop. They should be listed in the same order I plan to introduce them in the body of my essay. "

Blueprinted thesis: My car has lots of disadvantages because it is unreliable, expensive, and unattractive.

WRITING PRACTICE 1   Revise your tentative thesis.

Outlining the Essay

Once you have formulated a tentative thesis, you must begin organizing your ideas to illustrate, support, or prove your main idea. If you don't organize your ideas before you start writing, your writing will have a tendency to wander. Because an essay is more complex than a paragraph, we recommend using a formal outline. The outline of your essay is like the framework of a house; without it, the house won't stand, and without a plan or outline, your essay won't hold together. In planning or outlining your ideas, you decide which supports you will use to illustrate or prove your thesis. You also decide the order of your supports and what details will develop each support.

Using Outline Form

An essay outline contains a thesis statement and an outline of the body or support paragraphs. Introductions and conclusions are included on the outline but generally are not specified or explained. (Many students prefer to generate ideas for the introduction and conclusion after they have written a draft of the body paragraphs.)

Outlines can be done in phrases or complete sentences, depending on your instructor's preference. If you instructor requires you to turn in your outline, you will want to check your outline for spelling errors. Otherwise, do not be overly concerned at this point about mechanics (spelling, punctuation, etc.); you will check for correctness later, at the editing stage.

Outline form

An outline is a formal structure that helps you organize support topics and subtopics.

Outline form is broken down into main headings (I, II, III, IV);

support headings (A, B, C);

and details (1, 2, 3).

Use as many headings, support headings, and details as you need to develop your topic. However, each heading that is broken down should have at least two subheadings. For example, if you have an A, you need a B; if you have a 1, you need a 2. Remember that the number of main topics, supporting ideas, and details is up to you and will vary depending on the ideas you have generated.

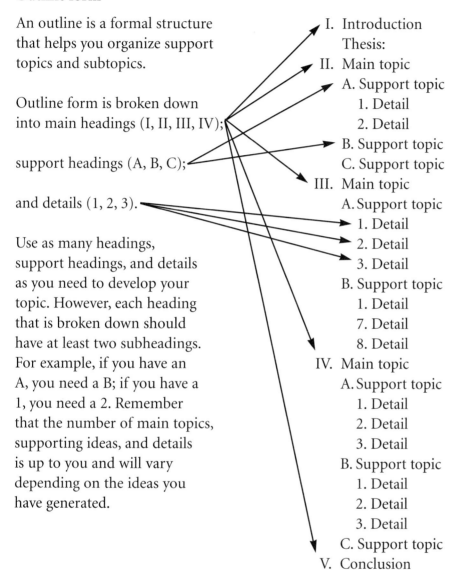

I. Introduction
   Thesis:
II. Main topic
   A. Support topic
      1. Detail
      2. Detail
   B. Support topic
   C. Support topic
III. Main topic
   A. Support topic
      1. Detail
      2. Detail
      3. Detail
   B. Support topic
      1. Detail
      7. Detail
      8. Detail
IV. Main topic
   A. Support topic
      1. Detail
      2. Detail
      3. Detail
   B. Support topic
      1. Detail
      2. Detail
      3. Detail
   C. Support topic
V. Conclusion

Beth

Phrase
Outline

I. Introduction
   Thesis: My car has a lot of disadvantages.
II. Reliability
   A. Breaks down
      1. On dark road home
      2. In rain
   B. Makes noises
   C. Safety issue
III. Expenses
   A. Repairs
      1. Brakes
      2. Ignition
      3. Air conditioner
   B. Maintenance
      1. Oil changes
      2. Tires
      3. Gas
IV. Appearance
   A. Exterior
      1. Rust
      2. Dents
      3. Trunk
   B. Interior
      1. Upholstery ripped
      2. Carpet stained
      3. Headliner falling down
   C. Embarrassment
V. Conclusion

Beth

Sentence
Outline

I. Introduction
   Thesis: My car has a lot of disadvantages.
II. The biggest problem with my car is that it's not reliable.
   A. Because it's always making strange noises, I feel like I can't rely on it to get me where I'm going safely.
   B. Last week, I broke down in a rainstorm, and as a result, I got to work soaked and late, and got yelled at by my boss.
   C. I'm constantly afraid of breaking down in places where it would be not only an inconvenience, but downright dangerous—on the interstate or on the long dark road home at night. These days breaking down could mean more than being late for work; it could mean never showing up for work at all.

III. Not only is my car unreliable, but it is also a constant drain on my budget.
    A. In the last two months, I've had to fix the brakes and replace the ignition. Now the air conditioner has given out, and I can't afford the $700 it will cost to repair it.
    B. Even when my car isn't eating up money in repairs, it costs me between thirty and fifty dollars a week to cover maintenance costs such as insurance, oil changes, and tune-ups.
    C. My dinosaur of a car only gets twelve miles to a gallon and burns a quart of oil a week, so I'm always pumping money into it.
    D. Sometimes I wonder how a car this worthless can be so expensive. I might as well be making payments on a car I can rely on.
IV. Worst of all, my kids are embarrassed to be seen in our car because it looks so terrible.
    A. Exterior
        1. The once shiny paint is now dull and bleached from road salt and there are patches of rust around the wheel wells and fenders.
        2. There is a dent in the passenger door that someone left while I was grocery shopping last year, and ever since another student hit my car in the school parking lot, the trunk latch hasn't worked and I've had to tie it down with a bungee cord.
    B. The interior of my car is no better than the exterior. The upholstery and carpet are stained from years of carrying around two kids and a dog and the headliner is coming loose in several places.
    C. Who can blame my kids for not wanting their friends to ride in such a car?
V. Conclusion

Creating an Outline

1. Begin by filling in your thesis.

2. Next, select the main ideas you will use to support your thesis. Remember that you will develop one main idea in each body paragraph of the essay.

3. Generate additional ideas if you don't have enough main ideas to support your thesis.

4. Using the Outline Template found on page 76, write a tentative topic sentence for each body paragraph (next to each Roman numeral.)

5. Generate ideas to develop each body paragraph.

6. Decide which supports to use and the order in which to present them. Add them to your outline.

7. Revise your thesis statement to fit the ideas you will develop in the essay. If you intend to use a blueprinted thesis (one that includes the main areas of support), you should list the areas of support in the order you will introduce them in the essay.

Generating More Ideas

As you work on creating an outline for your essay, you will probably find that you need to generate additional ideas to support your thesis or to support the topic sentences of your body paragraphs. Generate ideas by brainstorming, freewriting, listing, clustering, or dividing (see Chapter 3)—whichever seems most appropriate for the topic you have selected and/or you feel most comfortable with. You should understand that generating additional ideas is a normal part of several stages of the writing process.

WRITING PRACTICE 2   Create a phrase or sentence outline for the topic you are developing using the steps on page 75.

 EXAMPLE

Essay Outline Template
(*Note:* You can add as many main topics, support topics, and specific supports as necessary.)

   I. Introduction

     Thesis: _____

  II. Main topic _____

    A. Support topic _____

    B. Support topic _____

    C. Support topic _____

 III. Main topic _____

    A. Support topic _____

    B. Support topic _____

    C. Support topic _____

 IV. Main topic _____

    A. Support topic _____

    B. Support topic _____

    C. Support topic _____

  V. Conclusion _____

Drafting

Many writers find it easiest first to draft the body paragraphs, and then to go back and write an introduction and conclusion that seem appropriate. Others prefer to draft the introduction first. Either way, you will probably find that you need to generate additional ideas for your body and introduction.

Drafting Body Paragraphs

Writing a first draft is easy if you have a well-developed outline. If you've done a phrase outline, all you need to do is to write a sentence or two for each area of support on your outline. If you've done a sentence outline, transfer your sentences into paragraphs. Write one body paragraph at a time, incorporating the information from your outline into your paragraph.

PEER EXAMPLE

Draft of Body Paragraph

 In writing my first draft, I focused on trying to get as much information from my outline into my sentences as possible. I wanted to get it all out on paper so I could evaluate what I had and what I needed.

Map:

II. The biggest problem with my car is that it is unreliable.
   A. Strange noises
   B. Break down in rain
   C. Fear, safety issue

The biggest problem with my car is that it's unreliable. Because it's always making strange noises, I feel like I can't rely on it to get me where I'm going safely. Last week I broke down in a rainstorm, and I got to work soaking wet and late, and got yelled at by my boss. I'm constantly afraid of breaking down in places where it would be not only an inconvenience, but downright dangerous—on the interstate or on the long dark road home at night. These days breaking down could mean more than being late for work; it could mean never showing up for work at all. At some point I have to start asking myself how much my safety and peace of mind are worth.

Drafting the Introduction

The introduction to an essay should get the reader interested in the topic, provide background information about the topic, and state the thesis of the essay.

The introduction is the most important part of the essay because it establishes the reader's attitude toward the topic and toward the writer. An interesting introduction will make the reader want to read the rest of the essay. Essays generally don't begin immediately with the thesis. Instead, they start gradually by getting the reader ready for the thesis. Background information, like background music in a movie, gets the reader in the mood to read the essay.

Chapter 7, "The Essay," provides specific techniques and examples that can be used to get the reader's attention and provide background information.

PEER EXAMPLE

Draft of Introduction

Beth

❝ Since my paper is personal, I decided to introduce myself and establish how important a car is to me. A car is a necessity to most people nowadays, so readers should be able to identify with me. ❞

My car is indispensable to me. I'm a single mother of two children and I live ten miles out of town. I also work twenty hours a week and I'm taking classes at the community college. Without a car, I'd be lost. Lots of the kids I see at school have new cars, but I don't see how they can afford them. I know I can't even though nothing would make me or my kids happier than owning a new car. My car has lots of disadvantages because its unreliable, costs me too much for repairs, and its appearance.

Drafting the Conclusion

When you have finished the introduction and body, read through your draft before writing the conclusion. Some writers like to generate ideas for the introduction and conclusion together so that the introduction and conclusion serve as bookends that hold the essay together. Whichever way you choose, spend a few minutes thinking through how you want to end your essay before you begin writing.

The purpose of the conclusion is to bring the essay to a close. The length of the conclusion depends on the length and complexity of the essay.

These two techniques are most common for conclusions:

- Refer back to the story, problem, question, or quote that began the introduction.

- Emphasize the important points: remind the reader of the essay's thesis and how its major details are developed.

PEER
EXAMPLE

Draft of
Conclusion

> Since my essay is about me, perhaps my conclusion should refer back to me and to what I've concluded as a result of writing the paper, which is that I desperately need a new car.

My car is a junker. Even though I hate the thought of spending the money, I guess it's about time to start looking for a later model used car. I'll have to work more hours to make the payments, but it'll be worth it to have a car that I'll feel safe in. I'd also like a car that won't cost and arm and a leg in repairs and that my kids won't be embarrassed to be seen in.

Body

Write a draft for each of your body paragraphs, incorporating the information from your outline into your sentences. Focus on communicating your main ideas as clearly as possible.

Introduction

Use a technique such as brainstorming, freewriting, listing, clustering, or dividing to generate ideas for your introduction. How can you get your reader's attention? Can you think of a story or anecdote to dramatize the point of your essay? What background information does the reader need to understand your thesis?

Conclusion

Generate ideas for your conclusion. Can you refer back to something in your introduction to conclude your paper? Can you emphasize or restate the main points of your essay?

WRITING PRACTICE 3

Revising

Revising is the process of examining the content and organization of your writing to see how they could be improved. Whenever possible, it's a good idea to let someone else read your first draft and give you feedback on what works and what doesn't work, what is and isn't clear. If you can't get feedback, use the Essay Revision Checklist on page 000 to help you revise your own writing. In revising, you focus on developing and clarifying your ideas. You may decide you need more supporting details, or you may decide to delete details that don't relate to your main idea.

When you revise, you also work on polishing the presentation of your ideas. You may want to consider using precise language, active verbs, and appropriate vocabulary and transitions. The more specific your writing, the better. Therefore, you should try to avoid general nouns such as *people* and *things*, and avoid weak verbs such as *is/are*, *has/have,* and *does/do.* It's much more effective to use specific, concrete nouns and active verbs. Chapter 23, "Word Choice," provides instruction on improving your word choice.

Polishing your writing may also mean improving your sentence structure. It's a good idea to vary the length and pattern of your sentences. Try to alternate long and short sentences, and try to use a variety of sentence types. For example, use some compound and some complex sentences (see Chapter 31, "Sentence Variety"). Writing, like music, depends on rhythm, and varying the rhythm of your sentences can help you both convey your ideas effectively and keep the reader's attention.

Peer Feedback

Your peers can give you a good idea of what is and isn't working in your draft. If anything in your draft isn't clear to a reader, you will probably want to go back and reexamine or revise it. Listen carefully to the comments of your peer reviewers, but remember that in the end you are the one who decides what to include or not include in your paper. If questions about the assignment or mechanical errors arise, consult your instructor or use the chapters in Part VI, "Writing Elements and Skills." If you aren't sure whether your reviewer was right to say you need a comma before an *and* in your essay, look it up in Chapter 32, "Commas."

Note to peer reviewers: When giving feedback on someone else's essay, remember that you are trying to help the writer communicate his or her ideas as clearly and effectively as possible. It won't help the writer to be polite and say only that everything is fine, especially if you have trouble following the meaning or the logic of the essay. It's your responsibility to pay careful attention as you read or listen to your classmate's draft and then to be as helpful as possible. The questionnaire below can help you let the writer know where you have trouble following the ideas or logic in the essay.

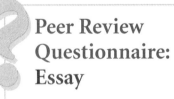

Peer Review Questionnaire: Essay

Directions: Read the essay carefully and answer the following questions as specifically as possible. Remember your goal is to help your peer improve his or her essay. Wherever possible, provide suggestions for improvement.

1. Is the introduction well developed? _____

   Interesting? _____

2. Is the thesis clear? _____

   Restate it in your own words. _____

   _____

   _____

3. For each body paragraph, indicate whether or not there is a clear topic sentence that supports the thesis. Restate the main idea in your own words.

   T. S. #1 _____

   _____

   T. S. #2 _____

   _____

   T. S. #3 _____

   _____

   T. S. #4 _____

   _____

4. Are body paragraphs well developed? _____

5. Can you think of additional information or supporting ideas the writer could have included?

   _____

   _____

   _____

6. Does the essay develop in a logical order? _____

7. Does the essay adequately develop the thesis? _____

8. What did you like most about the essay?

   _____

   _____

   _____

9. What seemed most unclear about the essay?

   _____

   _____

   _____

10. What mechanical errors did you notice in the essay?

    _____

    _____

    _____

    _____

Instructor Feedback

Whenever possible, get feedback on the draft of your essay from your instructor. You may have an opportunity to submit a draft for review or you may be able to use your instructor's office hours to get feedback. Instructors generally comment on the strength or weakness of the content and structure of a piece of writing. They may or may not mark errors or list the types of errors they've noticed in your essay. Know your instructor's grading symbols (the marks he or she uses to indicate mechanical errors in your writing). If you don't understand your instructor's comments (whether verbal or written), ask him or her to explain. Both seeking feedback on your draft and making sure that you understand it show your instructor that you are serious about improving your writing.

Self-Evaluation

If peer or instructor feedback isn't available, or of you prefer self-evaluation, you can use the Essay Revision Checklist below to get ideas on how to revise your essay. First, it's a good idea to give yourself some distance from what you've written by putting your essay aside for as long as you can before coming back to revise it. You may be able to put it aside for an hour or two, or overnight, but if you're writing an in-class paper, you may have only a minute or two before you need to start revising. However much time you have, getting some distance from your ideas will help you spot problems more easily. In revising, you should read your essay as critically as possible, looking for areas that could be improved.

Essay Revision Checklist

1. Introduction

Is the background information interesting? Does it engage the reader?

Does it prepare the reader for the thesis?

Does the introduction provide a logical progression toward the thesis?

Does it focus on, provide background for, or lead into the thesis?

Is the introduction adequately developed?

Thesis:

Is the thesis a clear statement of the main idea of the essay?

Does it fit the assignment?

2. Body Paragraphs

Organization:

If there is a blueprinted thesis, do the body paragraphs develop points in the same order as they are listed in the thesis?

Even if the thesis is not a blueprint, do the body paragraphs follow a logical order?

Is the relationship between paragraphs clear?

Are appropriate transitions used between paragraphs?

Topic Sentences:

Is each topic sentence clear? Does it make one point that supports the thesis?

Supports:

Are there enough supports (three to five supports, depending on the assignment) to explain or prove the topic sentences?

Does each support sentence clearly develop the topic sentence?

Do any supports wander away from the topic?

Are any supports repeated?

Is the relationship between support sentences clear?

Are there clear transitions between sentences?

Is there enough specific detail in each sentence to convince the reader?

Is the order of supports clear and logical?

Are the sentences varied in length and structure?

Is the vocabulary appropriate?

Is the language clear and precise? (Are there strong verbs, specific nouns, and colorful adjectives and adverbs?)

3. Conclusion

Does the conclusion summarize or tie together the essay?

Does it relate back to the hook or story used in the introduction?

Does it introduce any new ideas or arguments that would confuse the reader?

4. **Entire essay**

Does the essay make sense?

Does the essay develop in a logical order?

Does the essay adequately develop the thesis?

Does the essay deliver everything promised in the thesis?

Does the essay repeat itself?

PEER EXAMPLE

Beth

Draft

My car is indispensable to me. I'm a single mother of two children and I live ten miles out of town. I also work twenty hours a week, and I'm taking classes at the community college. Without a car, I'd be lost. Lots of the kids I see at school have new cars, but I don't see how they can afford them. I know I can't even though nothing would make me or my kids happier than owning a new car. My car has lots of disadvantages because its unreliable, costs me too much for repairs, and its appearance.

The biggest problem with my car is that it's unreliable. Because it's always making strange noises, I feel like I can't rely on it to get me where I'm going safely. Last week I broke down in a rainstorm, and I got to work soaking wet and late, and got yelled at by my boss. I'm constantly afraid of breaking down in places where it would not only be an inconvenience, but downright dangerous on the interstate or on the long dark road home at night. These days breaking down could mean more than being late for work; it could mean never showing up for work at all. At some point I have to start asking myself how much my safety and peace of mind are worth.

Next, my car is expensive. In the last two months, I've had to fix the brakes and replace the ignition. Now the air conditioner has given out, and I can't afford the $700 it will cost to repair it. Even when my car isn't eating up money in repairs, it costs me a lot to cover maintenance. My car only gets twelve miles to a gallon and burns a quart of oil a week, so it's expensive. Sometimes I wonder how a car this worthless can be so expensive.

My car's appearance is pathetic. There are patches of rust around the wheel wells and fenders. There is a dent in the passenger door that someone left while I was grocery shopping last year. Ever since another student hit my car in the school parking lot, the trunk latch hasn't worked, and I've had to tie it down with a bungee cord. Also, the upholstery and carpet are stained from years of carrying around two kids and a dog and the headliner is coming loose in several places. Who can blame my kids for not wanting their friends to ride in such a car?

My car is about ready for the junk pile. Even though I hate the thought of spending the money, I guess it's about time to start looking for a later model used car. I'll have to work more hours to make the payments, but it'll be worth it to have a car that I'll feel safe in. I'd also like a car that won't cost and arm and a leg in repairs and that my kids won't be embarrassed to be seen in.

Beth

> In revising my essay, I eliminated material that didn't seem to fit, added new material, and improved the parallelism of my thesis. I also tried to add more specific detail and added transitions to relate ideas within and between the paragraphs.

Ready for the Junk Heap

Because of the way most people live today, cars are no longer luxuries but necessities. I'm a single mother of two *active* children, and I live ten miles out of town. I also work twenty hours a week and take classes at the community college. *Needless to say*, without a car, I'd be lost. *Unfortunately, my car is no longer as reliable as it once was, and the older it gets, the more of a cause of anxiety and concern it becomes. It was originally a wedding present from my folks ten years ago, but now that my husband and I are divorced, it's an unhappy reminder of the past. But that's just the beginning of the drawbacks to my old clunker of a car.* My car has lots of disadvantages because it is *unreliable, expensive, and unattractive.*

The biggest problem with my car is that it is unreliable. Because it is always making strange noises, I feel like I can't rely on it to get me where I'm going safely. Last week, I broke down in a rainstorm, and *as a result,* I got to work *soaked* and late, and got yelled at by my boss. I'm constantly afraid of breaking down in places where it would *be not only an* inconvenience, but *also* downright dangerous—on the interstate or on the long dark road home at night. These days breaking down could mean more than being late for work; it could mean never showing up for work at all. At some point I have to start asking myself how much my safety and peace of mind are worth.

Not only is my car unreliable, but it is a constant drain on my budget. In the last two months, I've had to fix the brakes and replace the ignition. Now the air conditioner has given out, and I can't afford the $700 it will cost to repair it. Even when my car isn't eating up money in repairs, it costs me between thirty and fifty dollars a week to cover maintenance *costs such as insurance, oil changes, and tune-ups.* My *dinosaur of a car* only gets twelve miles to a gallon and burns a quart of oil a week, *so I'm always pumping money into it.* Sometimes I wonder how a car this worthless can be so expensive. *I might as well be making payments on a car I can rely on.*

Worst of all, my kids are embarrassed to be seen in our car because it looks so terrible. *The once-shiny paint is now dull and bleached from road salt* and there are patches of rust around the wheel wells and fenders. There is a dent in the passenger door that someone left while I was grocery shopping last year and ever since another student hit my car in the school parking lot, the trunk latch hasn't worked and I've had to tie it down with a bungee cord. *The interior of my car is no better than the exterior.* The upholstery and carpet are stained from years of carrying around two kids and a dog and the headliner is coming loose in several places. Who can blame my kids for not wanting their friends to ride in such a car?

My car is about ready for the junk pile. Even though I hate the thought of spending the money, I guess it's about time to start looking for a later model used car. *Even if I have* to work more hours to make the payments, it'll be worth it to have a car *that won't leave me stranded,* that won't cost and arm and a leg in repairs, and that my kids won't be embarrassed to be seen in.

WRITING PRACTICE 4   If possible, get feedback on your essay from peers or your instructor. If you cannot get feedback from someone else, analyze the strengths and weaknesses of your essay by using the Essay Revision Checklist on page 82.

Editing

Once you are satisfied with the content and form of your writing, edit your essay for mechanical errors. Editing is one of the most important skills in writing. All too often, writers receive low grades on their work because they have neglected to edit carefully. No one intends to turn an essay in with errors, but finding errors takes time and attention to detail.

Using an editing checklist like the one below can help you catch and correct errors in your English because it can help you focus on one type of error at a time. When you edit, you should read your essay five or six times, focusing on one type of error each time—fragments, verb errors, comma errors, spelling errors, and so on—paying particular attention to errors you have had trouble with in the past.

One reason it is so hard to spot errors is that we tend to read what we *intended* to write down rather than what is actually on the page. A technique that you might want to try is reading your essay backward, starting at the bottom and moving to the top. Reading backward forces you to focus on the words rather than on the content

Another technique that may be helpful is called tracking. Tracking means using a pencil to point to each word as you read it. Tracking can help slow your reading down and help you focus on one word at a time.

All of these techniques are intended to help you find errors so that you can correct them before you turn in your essay.

As you learn about the following skills, add them to your editing checklist.

Editing Checklist ✓

1. Check for run-ons and fragments. Is there one complete sentence between every two periods? (Identify the subject and the verb, and make sure the word group expresses a complete thought.)

2. Check every verb. Do subjects and verbs agree? Is proper verb tense used? Be sure to check the problem phrases such as *there is/there are* and pay attention to singular subjects such as *everyone.*

3. Use the dictionary or computer spell check to catch capitalization errors and misspellings. Remember, though, that the spell check will not catch errors with problem words such as *there/their.*

4. Remember your personal list of errors. Check your writing for any of these errors.

5. Check for apostrophes in contractions and possessives.

6. Check commas.

7. Check pronouns. Do they agree with their antecedents? Is the reference clear?

8. Look for any missing words or letters by reading the writing slowly from the last sentence to the first.

9. Check for parallelism in pairs, series, and comparisons.

10. Check for dangling and misplaced modifiers.

11. Check semicolon and colon use.

PEER EXAMPLE

Beth Edits One Body Paragraph

Worst of all, my kids are embarrassed to be seen in our car because it looks so terrible. The once-shiny paint is now dull and bleached from road salt, and there are patches of rust around the wheel wells and fenders. There is a dent in the passenger door that someone left while I was grocery shopping last year, and ever since another student hit my car in the school parking lot, the trunk latch hasn't worked, and I've had to tie it down with a bungee cord. The interior of my car is no better than the exterior. The upholstery and carpet are stained from years of carrying around two kids and a dog, and the headliner is coming loose in several places. Who can blame my kids for not wanting their friends to ride in such a car?

WRITING PRACTICE 5   Use the Editing Checklist to proofread your essay for errors.

Essay Writing Process Prompts

Here are the complete essay writing process prompts. You may wish to refer to them whenever you write an essay.

1. **Understanding the assignment**

   Assignment: _____

   Length: _____

   Due date: _____

   If necessary, use a narrowing tree or brainstorming to narrow your topic to a subject that interests you and that you can develop in the length of paper you have been assigned. You may find it helpful to use scratch paper.

   Narrowed topic: _____

2. **Determining the writing context**

   Decide on your purpose, audience, and tone. Then write a tentative thesis.

   Purpose: _____

   Audience: _____

   Tone: _____

   Tentative thesis: _____

3. Generating ideas

Generate ideas by brainstorming, freewriting, listing, clustering or dividing. You may find it helpful to use scratch paper. Come up with as many ideas as possible. Keep your purpose and audience in mind as you generate ideas to support your topic sentence.

4. Organizing ideas

- Examine the ideas you have generated and revise your tentative thesis to fit the ideas generated.

- Select the main ideas you will use to support your thesis. Remember that you will develop one main idea in each body paragraph of the essay.

- Generate additional ideas if you don't have enough main ideas to support your thesis.

- Using the Essay Outline Template below, write a tentative topic sentence for each body paragraph (next to each Roman numeral).

- Generate ideas to develop each body paragraph.

- Decide which supports to use and the order in which to present them. Add them to your outline.

- Revise your thesis statement to fit the ideas you will develop in the essay.

- Generate ideas for the introduction and conclusion after you have written a draft of the body paragraphs.

Essay Outline Template
(*Note:* Use as many main topics, support topics, and specific supports as necessary.)

   I. Introduction

      Thesis: _____

  II. Main topic _____

     A. Support topic _____

     B. Support topic _____

     C. Support topic _____

III. Main topic _____

    A. Support topic _____

    B. Support topic _____

    C. Support topic _____

IV. Main topic _____

    A. Support topic _____

    B. Support topic _____

    C. Support topic _____

V. Conclusion _____

5. **Drafting**

Body

Write a draft for each of your body paragraphs, incorporating the information from your outline into your sentences. Focus on communicating your main ideas as clearly as possible.

Introduction

Use a technique such as brainstorming, freewriting, listing, clustering, or dividing to generate ideas for your introduction. How can you get your reader's attention? Can you think of a story or anecdote to dramatize the point of your essay? What background information does the reader need to understand your thesis?

Conclusion

Generate ideas for your conclusion. Can you refer back to something in your introduction to conclude your paper? Can you emphasize or restate the main points of your essay?

6. **If possible, get feedback on your essay from peers or your instructor.** If you cannot get feedback from someone else, analyze the strengths and weaknesses of your essay using the Essay Revision Checklist on page 82.

Getting the Essay Back

Contrary to popular belief, the process isn't over when you get your graded paper back from your instructor. Part of the process of improving your writing is learning from your mistakes. The last thing most students want to do when they get back a paper is pay attention to the errors that have been marked, but figuring out what you did wrong is the key to improving your performance. Just as in sports, you need to listen to your coach if you hope to play your best. Think of your instructor's marks and comments as a way of helping you improve.

First, you need to make sure you understand the errors your instructor has marked. If you don't understand the marks, ask your instructor to explain them. Next, you need to know how to correct the errors. One way to do this is to look up each one in Part VI, "Writing Elements and Skills." Detailed instruction and practices are available for the common grammar and punctuation errors.

Next, record the errors your instructor has marked in your essay on a **personal error list**. This will help you keep track of the types of errors you have made so that you can avoid repeating them. Although it may take several minutes to record errors on your personal error list, learning to correct past errors is the best way to avoid making those same errors again. A template for your personal error list is available in the appendix at the end of this book. Your completed personal error list also serves as a great way to review before a test or before an in-class writing. Simply take your error list out and review it for a few minutes before you begin writing. That way your past errors are fresh in your mind and you are less likely to repeat them.

EXAMPLE

Sample
Error List

Error	Explanation/Rule	Correction
1. recieved	spelling	received
2. use to go	spelling	used to go
3. alot	spelling	a lot
4. Always being late for class.	I am always late for class.	fragment

Part III

The Structure of the Paragraph

Chapter 6
The Paragraph

A paragraph is a unit of thought made up of a set of related sentences. All the sentences of the paragraph work together to develop a single idea. A paragraph can stand alone as an independent discussion of one idea, or paragraphs can be put together into a larger unit such as an essay.

While Chapter 4 explains the step-by-step process that writers use to develop a topic, this chapter shows you the parts of the paragraph and how they work together. You will explore many paragraphs written by the four student peers (Beth, Tony, Alicia, and Dan) on topics similar to ones you may be asked to write about. The practices and exercises in this chapter will make you familiar with the parts of the paragraph and the requirements for each part. Learning to write paragraphs will prepare you for writing essays and compositions by teaching you how to organize ideas and present them clearly and logically.

The Paragraph's Structure

The paragraph contains three parts. The **topic sentence** states the main idea of the paragraph. Sentences in the body of the paragraph **support** the main idea with specific details. The **conclusion** summarizes the ideas in the paragraph. All the parts of the paragraph work together.

> Here is a paragraph I wrote in my writing class. I've labeled the different parts to give you an idea of how the paragraph is structured. My friends and I will share a number of our paragraphs in this chapter.

Read All About It

topic sentence —   *main or controlling idea*

The daily newspaper provides <u>a valuable source of information</u>. As everyone knows, a town's daily paper reports the news from around the world. Readers gain knowledge of world affairs by reading about wars starting and stopping, the national economy, and tragedies that befall people every day like auto accidents and home fires. Readers also acquire basic information that is needed to be an informed citizen such as the workings of Congress and the geography of places all around the world. For instance, when the Pope visited Cuba, Americans learned about the history and geography of the island. Just as important to many readers, the newspaper reports on the world of sports and entertainment. Many subscribers eagerly await the morning paper to find out the latest box scores of favorite teams or the television and movie listings for the day. Also, the newspaper predicts the weather, and the advertising helps readers save money by publishing information on the latest sales. Most important, the newspaper connects us to our community by publishing important announcements like births, deaths, weddings, and the events occurring in town like fairs and government meetings. Reading the newspaper helps us develop our intelligence as citizens by providing us with important information about our world.

Support

Conclusion

The Topic Sentence

The **topic sentence** is the most important part of the paragraph because it creates the focus for the rest of the sentences. It states the **main** or **controlling idea** that the rest of the paragraph will develop or support.

EXAMPLES

The daily newspaper provides <u>a valuable source of information</u>.

Trout Pond holds <u>special meaning to my family</u>.

I'm <u>lucky to have my roommate</u>, Bud.

The interior of the new Supra minivan is <u>designed for the driver's safety and comfort</u>.

Underline the words that express the main idea of each topic sentence.

Exercise 1

1. Credit cards can get consumers into trouble.

2. Computers are becoming an important part of the modern home.

3. Raising a child alone is a challenge.

4. My next-door neighbor is one of the kindest people I've ever known.

5. There should not be a required attendance policy in college.

Statement of Opinion

The topic sentence should express a main idea that can be developed with stated reasons. This statement is usually an **opinion, feeling, attitude, belief,** or **point of view** about the topic. It should **not** be **a statement of fact** that needs no development.

EXAMPLES

These facts do not need a paragraph to develop them.	These opinions need a paragraph to be developed or explained.
Fact: The Air and Space Museum is in Washington, DC.	**Opinion:** Visiting the Air and Space Museum in Washington, DC, was the best part of our trip.
Fact: The Marshalls are my neighbors	**Opinion:** I really enjoy having the Marshalls as my neighbors.
Fact: More Americans are obese than ever before.	**Opinion:** The health risks of obesity should not be ignored by overweight Americans.

Identify these statements as fact (F) or opinion (O).

Exercise 2

____ 1. There are more students enrolled in college this year than any year in the past decade.

____ 2. Woodstoves provide an economical alternative to gas and electric home heating.

____ 3. The campus police are here to serve the college community.

____ 4. My grandparents came to the United States from Lebanon.

____ 5. The plane we took to New York was a turboprop.

Focus

Because the topic sentence determines what the rest of the paragraph will develop, it's important that the topic sentence create an **adequate focus** for the paragraph. The topic sentence should be explained or developed in five to ten sentences. If the main idea is too broad, it cannot be adequately developed in one paragraph; if it is too narrow, an entire paragraph is not needed to develop it.

EXAMPLES

Too broad: The causes of the Civil War are complex.	The focus of this topic sentence is too broad because it will take more than three to ten sentences to support it. It deserves an entire book. The writer should narrow the focus to one element of the Civil War.
Adequate focus: The Battle of Bull Run had a number of strange coincidences.	The writer has narrowed the focus of the Civil War to one battle. This topic sentence can be supported with three to four examples of strange coincidences.
Too narrow: My daughter has a beautiful smile.	The focus of this topic sentence is too narrow because the writer will have trouble finding three to four examples to support this sentence. This statement would work well as a support in a paragraph more broadly focused on the daughter's overall beauty.
Adequate focus: My daughter is very attractive.	This topic sentence can be developed with three to four reasons.

Exercise 3

Given an assignment to write one paragraph, tell whether the focus of each topic sentence below is either adequate (A), too broad (B), or too narrow (N).

____ 1. The car I own has been very expensive to maintain this year.

____ 2. Everyone needs an education.

____ 3. Steroids do more harm than good.

____ 4. Goats will eat almost anything.

____ 5. John Irving is one of my favorite authors.

Placement

The **placement** of the topic sentence should aid the reader in understanding the ideas that are developed. The topic sentence is usually the first sentence of the paragraph, but it can be placed anywhere in the paragraph. In order to create a different process of understanding for the reader, sometimes writers place the topic sentence in the second or third sentence or at the end of the paragraph.

PEER EXAMPLE

Topic sentences at end of paragraph

> " I placed the topic sentence at the end of the paragraph because I wanted the reader to come on this main point at the end of the description of the road, just as I find my girlfriend after experiencing the long and winding road. "

A Difficult Destination

My girlfriend, Sally Jenkins, lives at the end of a long and winding and narrow dirt road that takes me forever to travel. There are so many potholes and tree roots that I have to creep along at under ten miles per hour so I don't break an axle. It is even worse after a hard rain when the puddles hide the potholes and force me to inch along the shoulder of the dirt road, or else my truck and I are in danger of drowning. When the weather is dry, I have to be careful that my truck's tires don't lose traction in the loose sand and get stuck. The worst time is at night when I'm in danger of getting lost because I have trouble picking out the landmarks that tell me where I am, and there is no street sign for the dirt lane that feeds into her driveway. **Picking up my girlfriend for a date is a real challenge!**

PEER EXAMPLE

Topic sentences in middle of paragraph

> " I decided to give some background with my first two sentences, so my topic sentence is the third sentence of the paragraph. "

My Sanctuary

As a child growing up with six brothers and sisters, I never had much time or space to myself, so I promised myself that when I grew up I would have a space I could call my own. Today I'm lucky enough to have that dream come true. **The workshop at the back of our 1890s Victorian house is the place I enjoy spending time by myself.** I relax in my workshop by building model planes that I fly in competitions. I feel comfortable here because this space is the one organized place in my life. I have my tools hanging on the wall so I can find anything I need quickly. Moreover, the room contains the equipment I need for my hobby such as a paddle fan to help clear the air of the fumes from the glue I use and a sink to wash up in when I make a mess. As I work, I can listen to a my favorite music, a Yankees' game, or an Olde Time Radio show without bothering anyone and without being told to turn it down. I also enjoy being able to light up an occasional cigar without causing a major fight with the woman of the house. This tiny work area gives me a place to relax and be myself.

Exercise 4

Identify the topic sentence that would best express the main idea of the paragraph.

Because seat belt use is required by law, drivers can be ticketed for failing to use restraining devices. Those who use seat belts regularly not only avoid being ticketed for breaking the seat belt law but may avoid other tickets as well because an officer who stops a driver for a traffic infraction such as speeding is more likely to be lenient if he sees that the driver is wearing a seat belt. Not only are those who consistently wear seat belts less likely to be ticketed, but also they are less likely to be injured if an accident should occur. Seat belts prevent passengers from hitting the dashboard or flying through the windshield when a collision occurs; therefore, they prevent serious injury and they save lives. The mandatory seat belt law has dramatically decreased the number of automobile fatalities in the United Sates each year. With ever-increasing numbers of cars on the road and with speed limits once again rising, motorists have more reason than ever to buckle up before they leave their driveways.

A. Seat belts are required by law to be used.

B. Seat belts prevent injuries in accidents.

C. Motorists have more reason than ever to buckle up before they leave home.

D. Seat belt laws have made the roads safer for motorists.

Generating a Topic Sentence

In college writing classes, you will generate a topic sentence from the topic you are given by your instructor. The writing topic may be a word or phrase (such as "smoking," "a good friend," or "college pressures"), or the topic may be a discussion question or prompt (such as "Explain why you like or dislike your job"). Often, you can use the words in the writing topic to help generate a topic sentence that expresses your opinion or point of view about the topic.

You should determine your purpose and your audience before generating a topic sentence. Sometimes the purpose is stated or implied in the discussion prompt with words like *convince* or *explain*. The audience can be the general reader, meaning someone like you, or it could be stated in the discussion prompt: "Convince your parents to buy you a new car." For a detailed discussion of audience, purpose, and tone, see Chapter 3.

EXAMPLES

Topic: a good friend
Topic sentence: Jose Morales is a good friend to me.

Topic: college pressures
Topic sentence: A freshman feels a lot of pressures when starting college.

Topic: Explain to a new employee why you like or dislike your job.
Topic sentence: I enjoy my job as a cashier at Handy's very much.

Generate a topic sentence for each topic.

WRITING PRACTICE 1

1. a sport you enjoy or don't enjoy watching or playing

   _____

   _____

   _____

2. Choose a course you are taking and explain why you like or dislike it.

   _____

   _____

   _____

3. Whom do you admire most and why?

   _____

   _____

   _____

Support

The body of the paragraph provides **support** for the main idea expressed in the topic sentence. **Supporting details** develop the main idea or controlling idea in the topic sentence by **proving, illustrating, explaining,** or **defining** the main idea. The number of supporting details can vary. Most paragraphs contain a minimum of three.

Beth

"" Here is a paragraph I wrote about the minivan my parents helped me buy last summer. In order to prove the main idea—that my new van is designed for the driver's safety and comfort—I got into my van and examined all the different features. Of course, I included information about the instrument panel, but I also looked for other features, such as the mirrors, that would help me prove my main idea. ""

A Luxury Ride

topic sentence ———

controlling or main idea

The interior of the new Supra minivan is designed for the driver's safety and comfort. When a motorist enters the vehicle, she is offered choices for adjusting the seat's height, distance from the steering wheel, and lower back support, which ensures that every driver is properly positioned to operate the vehicle without straining, stretching, or hunching down. In front of the driver, there is a beautifully displayed instrument panel with a digital display that is lit in bright colors for easy reading. Moreover, the console next to the driver anticipates her needs with its cup holders and organizer tray for tapes or CDs. When the van is moving, a computerized voice warns of unlocked doors or seat belts that are not fastened, which puts a driver at ease when carrying a vanload of kids. The driver can even control the mirror on the passenger door to get a better look at the lanes of traffic, and the mirror on the back gate lets the driver feel confident when backing into a parking space. The Supra's interior makes driving a pleasure.

Support

1. Seats

2. instrument panel

3. console

4. computerized voice

5. mirror

Specific Detail

In order to develop, explain, or prove the topic sentence, good writers give lots of specific information in their supports and make sure that the information directly relates to the main idea in the topic sentence.

Supports develop the topic sentence by giving **examples, facts, statistics,** or **concrete information**.

Relation to Topic Sentence

The specific details should **relate directly** to the main idea. Supporting sentences often explain how the detail proves the topic sentence. However, an actual statement explaining **how the support relates to the topic sentence** is not always necessary in the paragraph, but by reasoning out the relationship, the writer can make the logic clear to the reader.

> In my paragraph, I wanted to give lots of the details about Trout Pond, and I also was careful to explain how each detail develops the main idea in the topic sentence.

Tony

Save the Pond

specific detail

specific detail

Trout Pond holds special meaning to my family. First, Trout Pond was dug by hand over a century ago by my ancestors as a place to wash clothes, but as the years have passed, it has come to mean much more than a wash place. This twenty-by-seventy-foot oval body of water a quarter mile from the family farm has always served as a quiet retreat for members of my family. Whenever relatives need to think or pray or maybe just cry a little, they just sneak away to the oak-shaded banks of the little pond. In addition, this still body of water is an oasis for wildlife that attracts birds, otter, and deer. It also holds lots of rich memories for my entire family; for example, my father proposed to my mother under the live oak that stretches over the northern rim of the pond, and he was sitting under that same tree when he heard a cry to come quickly because my pregnant mother's water had broken and I was on my way. Trout Pond has also helped my family survive by providing fish and game for our dinner when times were tough. The history of Trout Pond and the history of my family are intertwined, and I hope my children and their children can continue to enjoy it in the future.

relation to topic sentence

relation to topic sentence

specifics

Example

Unity

If sentences don't directly relate to the topic sentence, then the reader can get distracted and confused. In order for the paragraph to achieve **unity**, every sentence in the body of the paragraph should contribute to supporting the topic sentence.

Nonsupport: Topic Sentence: I'm lucky to have my roommate, Bud. *I haven't had a roommate in a long time.* I enjoy Bud because he has the same priorities I do….

The sentence in italics does not support the topic sentence. It simply adds extra information that does not contribute to the controlling idea of "lucky to have my roommate."

Good support: *Although I haven't had a roommate in a long time, I enjoy Bud because he has the same priorities I do.*

Sometimes extra information can be combined with a support so as not to interrupt the unity of ideas.

Exercise 5

Cross out the sentence that does not support the topic sentence because it does not prove or explain why the topic sentence is true.

1. Topic sentence: A child should have a pet.

   Support:

   A. Owning a pet teaches a child to accept responsibilities.

   B. Having a pet helps a child learn to respect all animals and their rights.

   C. Most pets take very little time to care for.

   D. Pets are cute and cuddly.

2. Topic sentence: Trees are a valuable resource.

   Support:

   A. The roots of trees help to prevent soil erosion.

   B. Trees provide oxygen for all animals to breathe.

   C. There are many different sizes and shapes of trees and their leaves.

   D. Many trees provide fruits and nuts for people and animals to eat.

3. Topic sentence: Being sick can be expensive.

   Support:

   A. The cost of pills can reach five dollars apiece.

   B. If an employee misses work, he can lose pay.

   C. A visit to the doctor may cost as much as $150.

   D. I don't like to spend money unnecessarily.

4. Topic sentence: In this country, many people have trouble eating a balanced diet.

   Support:

   A. Many people skip meals to lose weight.

   B. If you don't eat a balanced diet, you should take extra vitamins and minerals.

   C. Many people are used to having a burger and fries for their main meal.

   D. Canned foods do not have all their natural nutrition, and many people eat canned vegetables instead of fresh ones.

5. Topic sentence: Living in the northern United States during the winter must be very difficult.

Support:

    A. The temperature in some northern areas goes down below freezing.

    B. When the streets are covered with snow, traffic moves very slowly, and driving may be dangerous.

    C. It costs much more to heat a house in the north than in the south because it is so much colder in the north.

    D. Harsh snow and ice storms can wipe out electricity for days.

Building Strong Support Using a Map or an Outline

Good writers build strong support by brainstorming ideas and then organizing these ideas on paper before they begin writing their paragraph. They plan their supports using a map or an outline. They brainstorm ideas for their supports, add details to their ideas, and then figure out the reason that this information supports the topic sentence. Once they have this information organized, they can write strong supports.

Map

A basic paragraph **map** consists of a topic sentence, a list of supports in the order they will be presented, and a list of the specific details that will be used to develop each area of support. A more detailed map may contain an indication of the reasoning behind each support or a statement explaining how or why the support relates to the topic sentence.

Topic sentence:_____

Area of Support	Specific Details	Topic Sentence
1.		
2.		
3.		
4.		
5.		

Tony

Topic sentence: Trout Pond holds special meaning to my family.

Area of Support	Specific Details	Relation to Topic Sentence
1. created by ancestors	dug by hand	for washing clothes
2. place to get away	to think, pray, cry	a retreat
3. attracts wildlife	birds, otter, deer	oasis for animals as area gets built up
4. family history	dad's proposal & my delivery	rich memories
5. provides food	fish & game	supported us when times were rough

Outline

Another way to organize the same information is with an **outline**. As explained in Chapters 4 and 5, an outline is a formal structure that helps you organize support topics and subtopics. The outline will help you incorporate both specific details and a relation to the topic sentence if one is appropriate.

Outline Form

Topic sentence:_____

_____

   I. Support #1
     A. Specific details
     B. Relation to topic sentence
  II. Support #2
     A. Specific details
     B. Relation to topic sentence
 III. Support #3
     A. Specific details
     B. Relation to topic sentence
 IV. Support #4
     A. Specific details
     B. Relation to topic sentence
  V. Support #5
     A. Specific details
     B. Relation to topic sentence

Tony's Phrase outline

Topic sentence: Trout Pond holds special meaning to my family.

   I. Created by ancestors
     A. dug by hand
     B. for washing clothes
  II. Place to get away
     A. to think, pray, cry
     B. a retreat
 III. Attracts wildlife
     A. birds, otter, deer
     B. oasis for animals as area gets built up
 IV. Family history
     A. dad's proposal & my delivery
     B. rich memories
  V. Provides food
     A. fish & game
     B. supported us when times were tough

Generate ideas for supporting the topic sentence using the outline below. **WRITING PRACTICE 2**

Topic sentence: This writing course I am taking can be challenging.

   I. Support idea #1: **tests**

     A. Specific details: _____

     B. Relation to the topic sentence:_____

   II. Support idea #2: **completing assignments**

     A. Specific details: _____

     B. Relation to the topic sentence:_____

  III. Support idea #3: **making deadlines**

     A. Specific details: _____

     B. Relation to the topic sentence:_____

Coherence

Once you have made a map or outline of your supports for your topic sentence, you are ready to put them into a logical order and begin writing sentences. Effective supports are organized logically in order for the paragraph to achieve **coherence.**

Two tools that help make paragraphs coherent are **transitions** and **repeated key words**. Using transitional words and phrases can help you clarify the relationship between ideas. Similarly, repeating key words or concepts introduced in earlier supports can help you show the relationship between ideas and thus tie the paragraph together. However, be careful not to overdo the repetition; vary the descriptive phrases in which the key words appear so that you maintain coherence without making your writing boring.

PEER EXAMPLE

Transitory and repeated keywords

Tony

❝ When I first wrote my paragraph about Trout Pond, I didn't like the way I was repeating *Trout Pond* over and over again in each support. My instructor pointed out that the repeated references to the pond helped create coherence in the paragraph, but she encouraged me to use different descriptive phrases to keep the repeated references to the pond from becoming dull.

Please take a look again at my paragraph to see how I used repeated key words with different descriptive phrases (in boldface type) for the pond. I also use a number of transitions (in italics) to achieve coherence. ❞

Save the Pond

Trout Pond holds special meaning to my family. *First,* **Trout Pond** was dug by hand over a century ago by my ancestors as a **place** to **wash** clothes, but as the years have passed, it has come to mean much more than a **wash place**. **This twenty-by-seventy-foot oval body of water** a quarter mile from the family farm has always served as a quiet retreat for members of my family. Whenever relatives need to think or pray or maybe just cry a little, they just sneak away to the oak-shaded banks of **the little pond**. *In addition,* **this still body of water** is an oasis for wildlife that attracts birds, otter, and deer. It *also* holds lots of rich memories for my entire family; **for example**, my father proposed to my mother under the **live oak** that stretches over the northern rim of **the pond**, and he was sitting under that **same tree** when he heard a cry to come quickly because my pregnant mother's water had burst and I was on my way. Trout Pond has also helped my family survive by providing fish and game for our dinner when times were tough. The history of Trout Pond and the history of my family are intertwined, and I hope my children and their children can continue to enjoy it in the future.

Organization of Supports

There are many logical ways to organize supporting statements. The most common are

- Time relation
- Space relation
- Order of importance

Supports organized by time are ordered from **past to present** or **present to past.**

Tony

PEER EXAMPLE

Time relation

    My supports are organized by time, from past to present. I wanted to explain how General Colin Powell is an excellent role model by using the facts of his life from his beginnings until he left the armed services. The first support explains how and where General Powell grew up, and then the rest of the supports tell of his career from college to retirement and beyond. The words related to time are in boldface type.

The General

Colin Powell is an excellent role model for African American men. Although General Powell rose to the highest rank in the military as the head of the Joint Chiefs of Staff of the Armed Forces, he had to overcome his modest **beginnings** as the son of poor Jamaican immigrants who lived in a lower-middle-class neighborhood in Brooklyn. Instead of dropping out of school as many of his peers did, he worked hard and went to college, where he discovered ROTC. **In the Army**, his hard work paid off as he **rose steadily** through the ranks. His success as commander-in-chief shows black men that they can be successful and effective as leaders in America. Not only has General Powell been successful in his career, but he has been a good family man and a good human being as well. He has been married to the same woman for **decades**, and they have two children. His respect for his wife was demonstrated when he followed her advice and didn't run for vice president **in 1996. Now** that General Powell is retired from the military, he has turned his attention to the well-being of young people by becoming a spokesman for literacy campaigns and anti-drug campaigns. He also lectures around the country encouraging young people to work hard, stay in school, and get ahead. Many people believe that he could be elected president of the United States of America, which demonstrates that there are paths of opportunity open to black men who possess the drive and determination to succeed in America in other endeavors besides sports and entertainment.

Supports can be organized by words that indicate **space relations**.

Beth

> I tried to draw the readers a picture of my minivan by organizing my paragraph's support spatially, from entering the van to the driver's controls. The words that indicate space relations are in boldface type.

A Luxury Ride

The interior of the new Supra minivan is designed for the driver's safety and comfort. When a motorist **enters** the vehicle, she is offered choices for adjusting the seat's height, distance from the steering wheel, and lower back support, which ensures that every driver is properly positioned to operate the vehicle without straining, stretching, or hunching down. **In front of** the driver, there is a beautifully displayed instrument panel with a digital display that is lit in bright colors for easy reading. Moreover, the console **next to** the driver anticipates her needs with its cup holders and organizer tray for tapes or CDs. When the van is moving, a computerized voice warns of unlocked doors or seat belts that are not fastened, which puts a driver at ease when carrying a vanload of kids. The driver can even control the mirror **on** the passenger door to get a better look at the lanes of traffic, and the mirror **on** the back gate lets the driver feel confident when backing into a parking space. The Supra's interior makes driving a pleasure.

Supports can be organized by **order of importance**.

PEER
EXAMPLE

Order of
importance

> Since building model planes is the most enjoyable time I spend in my workshop, I used it as my first support in the paragraph I wrote about my favorite place. Smoking a cigar is the least important support and therefore comes last.

My Sanctuary

As a child growing up with six brothers and sisters, I never had much time or space to myself, so I promised myself that when I grew up I would have a space I could call my own. Today I'm lucky enough to have that dream come true. The workshop at the back of our 1890s Victorian house is the place I enjoy spending time by myself. **I relax in my workshop by building model planes that I fly in competitions.** I feel comfortable here because this space is the one organized place in my life. I have my tools hanging on the wall so I can find anything I need quickly. Moreover, the room contains the equipment I need for my hobby such as a paddle fan to help clear the air of the fumes from the glue I use and a sink to wash up in when I make a mess. As I work, I can listen to a my favorite music, a Yankees game, or an Olde Time Radio show without bothering anyone and without being told to turn it down. **I also enjoy being able to light up an occasional cigar without causing a major fight with the woman of the house.** This tiny work area gives me a place to relax and be myself.

Often the **strongest supports come first and last**, with less important supports in between.

PEER
EXAMPLE

Order of
importance

> In this paragraph, I discuss the most important functions of the newspaper in my first and last supports.

Read All About It

The daily newspaper provides a valuable source of information. As everyone knows, a town's daily paper reports the **news from around the world**. Readers gain knowledge of world affairs by reading about wars starting and stopping, the national economy, and tragedies that befall people every day like auto accidents and home fires. Readers also acquire basic information that is needed to be an informed citizen such as the workings of Congress and the geography of places all around the world. For instance, when the pope visited Cuba, Americans learned about the history and geography of the island. Just as important to many readers, the newspaper reports on the world of sports and entertainment. Many subscribers eagerly await the morning paper to find out the latest box scores of favorite teams or the television and movie listings for the day. Also, the newspaper predicts the weather, and the advertising helps readers save money by publishing information on the latest sales. **Most important, the newspaper connects us to our community** by publishing important announcements about births, deaths, weddings, and the events occurring in town like fairs and government meetings. Reading the newspaper helps us develop our intelligence as citizens by providing us with important information about our world.

Circle the letter in each support area of the strongest support for the topic sentence.

Exercise 6

Topic sentence: Raymundo's, a steak house on the town square, is a great place to take a family out to dinner.

1. **SUPPORT AREA #1: Food**

   A. This restaurant serves a marvelous array of fresh hot rolls, juicy roast beef, crispy chicken, and a monster salad bar filled with luscious fruits and vegetables.

   B. While waiting for the food to be served, the aroma of the piping-hot food would cause a person's mouth to water.

   C. With entrées including everything from New York strip steaks to hamburgers, and a "mega bar" that houses a huge selection of salad items, chicken wings, and numerous pasta dishes, Raymundo's is able to satisfy any family member's appetite, no matter how extreme.

2. **SUPPORT AREA #2: Service**

   A. The waiters at Raymundo's are very polite and are also willing to get a customer anything he may need to make his meal more enjoyable.

   B. The fast and friendly service enables parents to feed their children quickly, and this allows the parents to eat their meal without having to fuss with hungry kids.

   C. Most of the time, Raymundo's has lots of servers on duty who provide special services for all family members.

3. SUPPORT AREA #3: Atmosphere

A. The atmosphere is lightly scented with hickory smoke and oven-fresh baked breads.

B. The wonderful nice atmosphere makes my family feel right at home.

C. The atmosphere at Raymundo's is family-oriented, so parents don't have to worry if the kids start to cry because Raymundo's has its own clown to cheer them up.

4. SUPPORT AREA #4: Cleanliness

A. Even with hundreds of little mess makers passing through Raymundo's doors each day, the busboys do an incredible job of keeping the dining area spotless, and this makes each family feel like they are the first people to have eaten in the restaurant.

B. Raymundo's tables are always wiped to a shine, and the china and utensils are immaculate.

C. Raymundo's keeps such a clean and well-organized restaurant that it makes customers feel comfortable about eating food there.

5. SUPPORT AREA #5: Prices

A. The sale prices on meals for a family are so cheap that they save any size family a lot of money.

B. The price range at Raymundo's may be a little higher than at fast-food places, but the quantity and quality of food more than make up for the slightly higher price.

C. Since the average meal costs a mere $6.95, a family of four can eat dinner out and not break its budget.

The Conclusion

The conclusion is the last sentence of the paragraph. It either sums up the paragraph by reminding the reader of the main idea or interprets the significance of the support. It should not start a new argument.

EXAMPLE

Look again at Dan's paragraph on newspapers on page 110.

Inappropriate conclusion: Since the newspaper is so valuable, I believe that everyone should be required to subscribe.

Appropriate conclusion: Reading the newspaper helps us develop our intelligence as citizens by providing us with important information about our world.

The Title

Most writers choose to make a title for their paragraphs when the paragraph stands alone as an independent piece of writing. The title gives the reader a clue as to the topic of the paragraph and the main idea. It is a sentence fragment, or sometimes a question, and is written above the paragraph in the middle of the page. The title is capitalized according to standard rules (see Chapter 22). Remember that the title that accompanies your own writing should not be underlined, italicized, or placed within quotation marks.

EXAMPLES

Correct title form:

Read All About It

A Luxury Ride

Save the Pond

Incorrect title form:

Read all about it

"A Luxury Ride"

<u>Save the Pond</u>

Writing Topics

Write a paragraph for one of the following topics. To view writing process prompts for writing the paragraph, turn to Chapter 4. Begin by generating a topic sentence; then map or outline supports. Once you have all your ideas on paper, write the paragraph and make sure it has five to ten sentences.

1. Explain how an important technological innovation like the computer, the microwave oven, the telephone answering machine, the cell phone, or e-mail has changed the way we live.

2. Write about the benefits of a certain sport or recreational activity.

3. Argue that a product you can buy should be banned.

4. Discuss the best ways to prepare for a test.

5. Choose a well-known person and prove that this person is either a good or a bad role model.

6. If you could choose one experience in your life to relive, what would it be? Why do you choose it?

7. Where do you like to relax? Explain the attraction a particular place has for you as a place for relaxation.

8. Argue how one of your major roles in life (spouse, student, parent, employee) is difficult.

Part IV

The Structure of the Essay

Chapter 7
The Essay

Most of the writing you do in college will be in the format of an essay. The word *essay* comes from a French word meaning "to attempt or try." The essay is an attempt at developing a main idea in a number of paragraphs. An essay can be four or five paragraphs long, or it can be as long as an entire book. Although there is nothing special about the five-paragraph essay, it is commonly used in college because it can be written in a class period.

Most beginning college writers dread the idea of having to write an essay. They fear that they won't have enough to say to fill up four or more paragraphs, and they worry that they won't know how to organize their writing. As you go through the lessons, you will notice a number of differences between the student essays and the professional essays used as examples. The classic five-paragraph essay is a good learning tool, but in order to interest their audience and make their point, professional writers usually use shorter paragraphs and a less formal organization that lacks overt thesis statements and topic sentences. Writers and editors deliberately keep the paragraphs in newspaper and magazine articles short because the column format makes short paragraphs easier to read. Academic writing, however, in which students practice supporting and developing their ideas, requires longer, more structured paragraphs.

This chapter will show you how the essay follows the same format as the paragraph. You will learn about the parts of the essay and investigate lots of examples written by student peers and professional writers. These examples will help you use the essay form in your writing.

Academic Essays	Professional Essays
Formal structure	Informal structure
Thesis overt	Thesis sometimes implied
Topic sentences overt	Topic sentences sometimes implied
Paragraphs well developed	Short paragraphs used to retain attention

From Paragraph to Essay

The overall design or **form of the essay** is similar to that of the paragraph. Both the essay and the paragraph develop a main idea with support and end the writing with a conclusion. However, the essay uses paragraphs to support the main idea and conclude the writing whereas the paragraph uses sentences. Moreover, the essay presents the main idea or thesis statement at the end of the first paragraph, which is called the introduction. The support for the main idea comes in paragraphs in the body of the essay. Finally, the essay is summed up in the last paragraph, called the conclusion.

Paragraph	Structure	Essay
Topic sentence (one sentence)	⟵ MAIN IDEA ⟶	Thesis (one to two sentences at the end of the introduction)
Support sentences	⟵ BODY ⟶	Support paragraphs
Conclusion sentence	⟵ CONCLUSION ⟶	Conclusion paragraph

PEER EXAMPLE

Dan

" I wrote an essay on the newspaper by expanding ideas in my paragraph about the importance of the newspaper. I used the same main idea in my essay that I used in my paragraph, and I chose as body paragraphs the three areas from my paragraph that seem the most important kinds of information that the newspaper provides. I was then able to give much more specific detail about these kinds of information than I was in the one paragraph I wrote about the newspaper. Read my paragraph, and then see how I expanded it into the essay that follows. "

Read All About It

The daily newspaper provides a valuable source of information. As everyone knows, a town's daily paper reports the **news** from around the world. Readers gain knowledge of world affairs by reading about wars starting and stopping, the national economy, and tragedies that befall people every day like auto accidents and home fires. Readers also acquire **background information** that is needed to be an informed citizen such as the workings of Congress and the geography of places all around the world. For instance, when the pope visited Cuba, Americans learned about the history and geography of the island. Most important, the newspaper **connects us to our community** by publishing important announcements about births, deaths, weddings, the events occurring in town like fairs and government meetings. Reading the newspaper helps us develop our intelligence as citizens by providing us with important information about our world.

Topic Sentence
(Main Idea)

Support ideas:
News
Background info
Connection to community

Conclusion

Our Daily Tutor

Around six o'clock in the morning, a loud thump can be heard at many front doors. For millions of Americans, it is one of the most cherished sounds of the day, for it heralds the arrival of the daily newspaper. Some of us enjoy the ritual of reading the paper as we sip our coffee while others take the paper to work and read it along the way. A few even have the patience to wait until they come home from work at the end of the day. Of course, not every American reads the paper every day, but most of us do spend the twenty-five cents to one dollar when some important event occurs. In fact, newspaper readership has been falling steadily for many years. Many people avoid the news because they find it depressing. However, what all Americans should realize is that citizens of a democracy need to be informed in order to make intelligent choices at the ballot box and to participate in the public debates that help shape our country's course. **The daily newspaper provides a valuable source of information.** Not only does it report the news, but it provides valuable background information that helps us understand how our world works, and it connects us to our community and culture.

Introduction

Thesis
(Main Idea)

Reading the daily news makes us better citizens by informing us about what is happening in the world around us. First, the international news alerts us to developments around the world that may have profound consequences. For example, when another country tests a nuclear weapon or a region erupts in violence, the news may not be pleasant, but our understanding is crucial because such events affect all of us and perhaps even the future of the planet. In addition, our awareness of current events can get us involved in causes such as stopping the spread of nuclear weapons or righting the wrongs that create regional hatreds. Second, the national news keeps us in touch with events closer to home. We learn of political developments in Washington that may change the

Support Paragraph #1:
The News

way we live, and we make judgments about our leaders' actions that will influence the way we vote in the next election. Last but not least, the state and local news keeps us in touch with our regional politicians and with issues like economic development that affect our area. All this information goes into our personal data bank and informs our voice in the great chorus of American democracy.

Support Paragraph #2: Background Information

Almost as important as the news is the background information the newspaper supplies in order to give the news an understandable context. We are shown detailed maps of regions that are experiencing a conflict or natural disaster, and we are given the historical background to news events like the Balkan war in the 1990s. When El Niño emerged recently, newspapers ran detailed accounts of the weather system's causes, effects, and possible future. In addition, the workings of government institutions like Congress and the Supreme Court are regularly explained. New scientific developments like vaccines for AIDS and the cloning of sheep are also explained in language all of us can understand. The newspaper gives us not only the information but also the understanding we need to make sense of developments in our world.

Support Paragraph #3: Connection to Community

Most important, the newspaper offers us a vivid connection to our community. By reading the paper, we learn of important civic meetings that offer us the opportunity to get involved on the local level to help improve our neighborhoods. Moreover, our local newspaper helps give our town an identity and connects us to our neighbors. We keep abreast of the activities of local clubs and teams, and we learn of births, marriages, and deaths in our town. We read letters to the editor that tell us what our neighbors think of issues big and small, and we also participate in the pride of ownership when we read of local residents who win awards or gain recognition for outstanding accomplishments. After reading the paper over breakfast, we walk out the door feeling more engaged in our community.

Conclusion

Our world is becoming more complex each day, and it is often a struggle to make sense of such rapidly changing times. Luckily, we have an ally in the newspaper that is delivered to us every morning. The daily newspaper deserves our time and attention, for it brings us the information we need to better understand our world and to be engaged citizens. Armed with knowledge of current affairs, the background information to make sense of the affairs, and appreciation for our community, we are better equipped to participate as responsible citizens in a democratic nation.

The Introduction

Because it establishes the reader's attitude toward both the topic and the writer, the **introduction** is the most important part of the essay. An interesting introduction will make the reader want to read the rest of the essay.

The introduction to an essay should

- Get the reader **interested in the topic** (attention-getter).

- Provide **background information** about the topic (factual material).

- State **the thesis** of the essay (main idea).

In the following example, professional writer Michael Ryan creates interest by listing surprising facts about famous people. Who would have suspected that Albert Einstein, one of the greatest theoretical scientists of all time, was considered slow by his teachers? This sort of surprising information raises readers' curiosity about what accounts for greatness and makes them want to read on. (The complete essay is on page 533.) Remember that professional writers often prefer a number of short paragraphs to grab the reader's attention. In an academic essay, the attention-getter is usually located at the beginning of the introductory paragraph.

PROFESSIONAL EXAMPLE

From "Who Is Great?"

Michael Ryan

As a young boy, Albert Einstein did so poorly in school that teachers thought he was slow. The young Napoleon Bonaparte was just one of hundreds of artillery lieutenants in the French Army, and the teenage George Washington, with little formal education, was being trained not as a soldier but as a land surveyor.

Despite their unspectacular beginnings, each would go on to carve a place for himself in history. What was it that enabled them to become great? Were they born with something special? Or did their greatness have more to do with timing, devotion and, perhaps, an uncompromising personality?

For decades scientists have been asking such questions. And, in the past few years, they have found evidence to help explain why some people rise above, while others—similarly talented, perhaps—are left behind. Their findings could have implications for us all.

The Attention-Getter and Background Information

Most essays don't begin immediately with the thesis. Instead, they start gradually by getting the reader ready for the thesis. Background information, like background music in a movie, gets the reader in the mood to read the essay. The introduction almost always begins with an **attention-getter** and **background information** about the topic to prepare for the thesis that will come afterward. Essays can begin with a specific fact in order to develop a general idea, or they can start with a generality and develop particular examples.

Attention-getters and background information can take many forms, some of which are listed below. You can use any of these strategies alone or in combination. Remember that the purpose of the introduction is to prepare the reader to read, understand, and agree with the thesis, so it's important to provide whatever information is necessary to get the reader on the same wavelength as the writer. Imagine you were going to read your essay—what would get you interested?

- **A story or anecdote:** A good story is like a picture, and as the old saying goes, a picture is worth a thousand words. A story that illustrates the point you plan to make in the essay will get the reader interested and predisposed in favor of your slant on the topic.

Peer example:

"Flintstone and Kramden," by Dan Tribble, p. 200

Professional examples:

"Why Happy Families Are Different," by John Obedzinsky, p. 503

"Not in Our Town," by Edwin Dobb, p. 465

"What's Your Emotional IQ?" by Daniel Goleman, p. 480

- **History, facts, or information about the topic**

Sometimes a topic is so complex that a review of what has happened legally, socially, medically, or politically with the topic must be reported before the reader can appreciate the significance of the thesis your essay will develop. Facts can also help define the significance and the implications of your topic.

Peer example:

"Deadbeat Dads," by Tony Anderson, p. 216

Professional example:

"Who Is Great?" by Michael Ryan, p. 533

- **An appropriate quotation:** Sometimes a quote from a historical figure or an authority in the field can get the reader's attention.

Peer example:

"How to End a Relationship," by Alicia Martinez, p. 182

- **A problem the reader should know about concerning the topic:** Sometimes the reader needs to be alerted to a problem or to the scope of the problem in order to understand your thesis.

  Professional example:

  "A Brother's Murder," by Brent Staples, p. 539

- **A question that limits your topic:** The answer to the question is your thesis.

  Professional example:

  "Who Are Our Heroes?" by Ponchitta Pierce, p. 504

- **A statement that popular ideas about your topic are wrong**

  State popular ideas about your topic and show how you intend to disprove them.

  Peer example:

  "Put Away the Paddle," by Tony Anderson, p. 258

- **A reference to something else:** Establish common ground with the reader by referring to something well known that is related to the topic. The reference may be to a historical event, a current event, or a literary work, for example.

- **A strong opinion:** Sometimes you can get the reader's attention by shocking him or her through a strong statement of opinion.

Appeal to Audience

Effective background information addresses the audience of the essay. Because background information is directed at the reader, it is important to consider your audience. What will get your particular readers interested? For example, the kind of information that would get a parent interested in an essay about dating would be different from the kind that would get teenagers interested. Even among teenagers, boys and girls would each be interested in different background information.

In the following example, professional writer Grace Bennett appeals to her audience, which is clearly parents of young children, by telling a story that any parent can identify with. This technique gets readers involved and makes them want to find out why telling white lies to children is not a good idea. (The complete essay is on page 460.)

Grace Bennett   **From "Why White Lies Hurt"**

"Where's my doll? We lost Baby!" cried five-year-old Ariel Rosen of Millwood, New York. Ariel, her mom Shari, my daughter Anna, and I were standing in line at a bagel place. Shari had apparently left Ariel's doll at our local community center, where the girls had just finished a late morning class. Now all hell threatened to break loose.

Then, as I watched, Shari pulled a cellular phone from her purse, pretended to dial the center, and embarked on a make-believe conversation with the "lady at the desk."

"You see my daughter's doll on the table? Oh, good. We'll come pick it up in a little while. Thank you. Bye!… You see, Ariel, they'll hold Baby for us until later." Ariel smiled broadly. Her whole body seemed to relax. Satisfied with her mom's fib, she was content enough now to sit down to lunch.

"That sure did the trick!" I commented.

"I'm the queen of white lies." Shari smiled, but she looked slightly embarrassed. "Anyway, I know exactly where we left the doll. I'm not worried about finding it later."

"Oh, you don't have to explain," I told her. "I've used white lies with Anna."

In fact, most parents can empathize with another mother's or father's decision to tell a "little white lie" to avoid an unpleasant scene with their preschooler, particularly in public. "It's important to pick your battles," more than one parent told me. And telling an occasional untruth seems like a small price to pay for family harmony.

Length and Placement

How much background information to provide depends on the length of the essay and the strategy the writer uses to get the reader prepared for the thesis. In general, an essay of five paragraphs should include three to six sentences of background *before* the thesis. All the background information must come before the thesis is presented to point the reader toward the main idea that the essay will develop.

Dan

" In my essay about the newspaper, I was nervous about making the background too long because my essay is only five paragraphs. I wanted to begin with an attention-getter and decided to start with a little scene of the paper arriving and people reading it at different times of the day. Then I explained why this topic should be important to the reader. I gave all the background information before I gave my thesis. "

Thesis

The **thesis** of the essay presents the main idea that the essay will develop. The thesis creates a focus for the essay and should not be too broad nor too narrow for your assignment. A thesis that is too broad is a statement that is too large to be adequately developed in the length essay you have been assigned. A thesis that is too narrow is a statement that is not large enough to be developed into an essay. A well-focused thesis presents a main idea that can be adequately developed in the number of paragraphs or pages you have been assigned to write.

EXAMPLES

Too broad: People are unhealthy for many reasons.

Adequate focus: The diet of many American teenagers is unhealthy.

If you've been assigned to write a short essay, you wouldn't even be able to list all the reasons people are unhealthy. You'd be much better off focusing on a specific group of people and/or a specific reason or set of reasons why they are unhealthy.

Too narrow: American teenagers consume too much salt.

Adequate focus: The diet of many American teenagers is unhealthy.

While you might be able to develop a good paragraph about the diet of American teenagers being loaded with salt, unless you are taking a nutrition class that requires in-depth reporting, it's unlikely you'd have enough information to develop an entire essay around this topic.

Blueprinted Thesis

A **blueprinted thesis** lists the major points the essay will develop. The points should be listed in the order that they will appear in the body paragraphs. The list may appear in the thesis statement or in a separate sentence after the thesis statement. The major points in the series must be **parallel**. In other words, areas listed in the thesis should be expressed in the same grammatical form (see Chapter 38).

Because some instructors prefer a blueprinted thesis and some do not, you should check with your instructor to find out whether a list of main points should be included.

Dan

> " In the introduction to my essay on Raintree, I state my thesis and list the main points I use to develop the thesis in one sentence. In the body, I develop the points in the same order as I list them. All three points are nouns, and the pronoun *its* is repeated in all three elements to emphasize their symmetry. "

Raintree is a great place to take the entire family out to dinner because of **its convenience, its menu,** and **its atmosphere.**

PITFALLS

There are some common errors you should watch out for when writing an introduction:

- Avoid a boring or uninteresting introduction.
- Avoid placing the thesis before the background information.
- Avoid making your thesis too broad or too narrow.
- Avoid faulty parallelism in a blueprinted thesis.
- Avoid discussing main points in any order other than the order they are listed in a blueprinted thesis.

Body Paragraphs

Each paragraph in the **body** of the essay develops **one main point** (topic sentence) that **supports the thesis** of the essay. The topic sentence should present an idea that can be developed in one paragraph, and the topic sentence should support the thesis of the essay.

The body paragraphs in an essay follow the traditional paragraph pattern of topic sentence, support, and conclusion. Of course, not every paragraph begins with the topic sentence, especially in professional writing; but for most academic writing, it's a good idea to place the topic sentence first in order to make sure that there is no room for confusion as to the main idea of the paragraph.

Each body paragraph should directly support the thesis statement. In other words, each body paragraph is a separate support or reason why the thesis of the essay is true. A body paragraph usually has a minimum of three supporting details that develop the topic sentence. These supports are often developed with examples.

Most writers organize the ideas for their essay using an **outline**. As explained in Chapters 4 and 5, an outline is a formal structure that helps you organize support topics and subtopics. Outline form is broken down into main headings, support headings, and details. Use as many main headings, support headings, and details as you need to develop your topic. Main headings are indicated with Roman numerals (I, II, III, IV, V). Support headings are indicated with capital letters (A, B, C). Details are indicated with numbers (1, 2, 3). Each heading that is broken down should have at least two subheadings. If you have an A, you need a B; if you have a 1, you need a 2.

PEER EXAMPLE

> ❝ I wanted to explain in this essay how my new minivan meets my needs as a parent. I decided to cover three main points: the van's exterior, the van's interior, and the van's performance. Each body paragraph covers one main point. I begin each body paragraph with a topic sentence that supports the essay's thesis, and I supply at least three supporting details to develop or explain the topic sentence in each body paragraph. Notice that I ended each of my body paragraphs with a conclusion. I've included my outline to the essay to show how I planned my ideas before writing. ❞

A Luxury Ride

My son had a big grin on his face as I got ready to drive him to Cub Scouts yesterday. When I asked him what I did to deserve that smile, he pointed gleefully at our new vehicle. We had traded in Miss Debbi, an ancient sedan that I had inherited from an aunt back in the late 80s, for a sleek teal-green minivan. Even though I was grateful to our old car for getting me through those early years as a mother, as my babies became youngsters, Miss Debbi got creakier and rustier and uglier, and my son and daughter were plainly embarrassed to be seen in her. What took Miss Debbi to her grave, though, were the credit card bonus points that my father contributed toward a new vehicle. Dear old dad was the hit of our family when he suggested that we look for something larger and safer than my old clunker. As I gathered up my son and his gear to take him to Scouts, **I realized how perfectly this new minivan meets my needs as a parent.**

First, the exterior of the van offers me style, safety, and convenience. Compared to my old clunker, the minivan is the height of **style** with its teal-green exterior and aerodynamic design. Surprisingly, the van is not much longer than my old sedan, and with the cab forward design, it has the appearance of a bullet train. The steel frame and advanced bumpers offer **safety** in the event of a crash, and the latest development in impact resistant skin panels means my van won't get dented every time someone's shopping cart bounces against it in a parking lot. In addition, the van isn't much higher than my old sedan, which makes it **convenient** for

I. Introduction
    A. Background Info

    B. Thesis

II. The exterior of my van offers me style, safety, and convenience.
    A. Style
    B. Safety
    C. Convenience

me to stash lawn chairs, cooler, and tent on the roof racks when we go camping. I also like the side door that slides wide open to load kids and dogs. For groceries, the hatchback allows me to stuff bags and cartons in the rear compartment without upsetting the kids camped in the middle seats. Finally, the keyless entry is a fabulous feature for a single woman with her arms full of packages and children.

Not only does the exterior of the new minivan perfectly suit my needs as a parent, but the interior is designed for the driver's safety and comfort. When a motorist enters the vehicle, she is offered choices for adjusting the **seat's** height, distance from the steering wheel, and lower back support, which ensures that every driver is properly positioned to operate the vehicle without straining, stretching, or hunching down. In front of the driver of a minivan, there is a beautifully displayed **instrument panel** with a digital display that is lit in bright colors for easy reading. Moreover, the **console** next to the driver anticipates her needs with its cup holders and organizer tray for tapes or CDs. When the van is moving, a computerized voice warns of unlocked **doors** or unfastened seat belts, which puts a driver at ease when carrying a vanload of kids. The driver can even control the **mirror** on the passenger door to get a better look at the lanes of traffic, and the mirror on the back gate lets the driver feel confident when backing into a parking space.

Finally, the van's performance features make it a pleasure to drive. The engine provides the power of **six cylinders**, which gives me the acceleration to enter freeway traffic effortlessly. I also enjoy the **cruise control** out on the highway for my long drives from home to school. Last week, I discovered the benefits of the **antilock brakes** when I had to avoid a fender bender ahead. My old car's brakes would have locked up, and I would have skidded into that huge truck in my path. Instead, the van's brakes didn't grab, so I kept control and was able to maneuver around the crackup. Probably the feature of my new van that I appreciate most often is the **fuel economy** because I'm not spending any more on fuel than I was on my old heap. The power and economy of my new minivan are an exceptional combination.

My son just informed me that he volunteered me to drive half his scout troop to its jamboree in our new van, which he has nicknamed Miss Betty, and he gave me a big hug. Outside sits the best gift I've ever received and one of the most important tools for a parent like me. My sleek new minivan is stylish and convenient outside, safe and comfortable inside, and powerful and economical on the road. Miss Betty is the best vehicle I could ever drive as a parent.

III. The interior of new minivans are designed for the driver's safety and comfort.

   A. Seats

   B. Instrument panel

   C. Console

   D. Doors

   E. Mirrors

IV. The van's performance features make it a pleasure to drive.

   A. Six cylinders

   B. Cruise control

   C. Antilock brakes

   D. Fuel economy

V. Conclusion

The Conclusions in the Body Paragraphs

Body paragraphs may end with a strong supporting detail or may end with a conclusion that sums up the ideas presented in the paragraph. The necessity for a conclusion, or summary statement, depends on the length and complexity of the paragraph. If a paragraph is short or the main idea of the paragraph is simple, a conclusion may not be needed.

Transitions

Effective body paragraphs use transitions *within* paragraphs to create coherence.

PEER
EXAMPLE

Transition
within
paragraphs

> " Because I had three primary supports in this paragraph, I signaled the move to each major support with the transitions *first, second,* and *last but not least.* Within the first support area, I showed the relationship between the sentences with *for example* and *in addition.* "

Reading the daily news makes us better citizens by informing us about what is happening in the world around us. **First,** the international news alerts us to developments around the world that may have profound consequences. **For example,** when another country tests a nuclear weapon or a region erupts in violence, the news may not be pleasant, but our understanding is crucial because such events affect all of us and perhaps even the future of the planet. **In addition,** our awareness of current events can get us involved in causes such as stopping the spread of nuclear weapons or righting the wrongs that create regional hatreds. **Second,** the national news keeps us in touch with events closer to home. We learn of political developments in Washington that may change the way we live, and we make judgments about our leaders' actions that will influence the way we vote in the next election. **Last but not least,** the state and local news keeps us in touch with our regional politicians and with issues like economic development that affect our area. All this information goes into our personal data bank and informs our voice in the great chorus of American democracy.

Effective body paragraphs also provide transitions *between* paragraphs of support.

PEER
EXAMPLE

Transition
between
paragraphs

> " I used transitions at the beginning of each of my body paragraphs to help lead the reader through my essay. In the second paragraph, I announced my first support with the word *first.* In my third paragraph I referred back to the first point I'd made and then introduced my second point, and in my fourth paragraph I announced my final support. "

Thesis: As I gathered up my son and his gear to take him to Scouts, I realized how perfectly this new minivan meets my needs as a parent.

Topic sentence #1: First, the exterior of the van offers me style, safety, and convenience.

Topic sentence #2: Not only does the exterior of the new minivan perfectly suit my needs as a parent, but the interior is designed for the driver's safety and comfort.

Topic sentence #3: Finally, the van's performance features make it a pleasure to drive.

Number

The number of body paragraphs in an essay will depend on the number of points needed to develop the thesis. The length of your essay may be determined by your assignment, or it may be left up to you. Even though we show you lots of five-paragraph essays as models, the number of paragraphs in your essays may vary depending on what you have to say and how many points you wish to present.

Order

The body paragraphs should be presented in a logical order. You can choose to organize your body paragraphs in a number of ways; the important consideration is to make the order clear and logical to the reader. If the areas the essay will develop are spelled out in a blueprinted thesis, the body paragraphs should be developed in the same order that they are listed in the thesis.

The body paragraphs could be presented

- In chronological order.
- In order of importance.
- According to some other structuring principle.
- With a combination of the above plans.

PEER EXAMPLE

 Chronological Order

❝ In my essay about what happened on the night of my prom, I decided to organize the body paragraphs chronologically according to what happened first, second, and third that night. ❞

Thesis: Unfortunately, my senior prom was a disaster.

Topic sentence #1: I thought I had everything arranged well **in advance** of the night of the prom.

Topic sentence #2: My date was forgiving enough until we arrived fifteen minutes **late at the four-star French restaurant** where I had made reservations months in advance.

Topic sentence #3: By the time we **arrived at the prom**, my date was barely speaking to me.

Dan

" In my essay about reading the newspaper, all my points are important, so I chose to base the order of importance on most obvious to least obvious. I started with the most obvious benefit of the newspaper, which most people would agree is the news. Less obvious, but just as important, is the background information the newspaper provides. Least obvious, but most important to me, is the connection to the community the newspaper provides. "

Thesis: The daily newspaper provides a valuable source of information. Not only does it report the news, but it provides valuable background information that helps us understand how our world works, and it connects us to our community and culture.

Topic sentence #1. Reading the daily news makes us better citizens by informing us about international, national, and local news

Topic sentence #2. Almost as important as the news is the **background information** the newspaper supplies in order to give the news an understandable context

Topic sentence #3. Most important, the newspaper offers us a **vivid connection to our community**.

Beth

" I suppose my essay was organized spatially. I started with the exterior of the van, then discussed the interior, and ended up with performance. "

Thesis: As I gathered up my son and his gear to take him to Scouts, I realized how perfectly this new minivan meets my needs as a parent.

Topic sentence #1: First, the **exterior** of the van offers me style, safety, and convenience

Topic sentence #2: Not only does the exterior of the new minivan perfectly suit my needs as a parent, but **the interior** is designed for the driver's safety and comfort.

Topic sentence #3: Finally, the **van's performance** features make it a pleasure to drive.

PEER EXAMPLE

Tony

Combined Structuring Principles

"In my essay on General Colin Powell, I chose to discuss Powell's military career first because that's what he is best known for. His concern and affection for his family became known when, at his wife's urgings, he declined to run for vice president. His career as a statesman is his most recent and perhaps his most important success. So my essay is a combination of chronological order and order of importance."

Thesis: This distinguished man is an excellent role model for African American men.

Topic sentence #1: Colin Powell's **military career** shows African American males that they can succeed in a traditionally white institution like the armed services.

Topic sentence #2: Colin Powell serves as an example of the power a **strong family** has to anchor us in enduring values.

Topic sentence #3: After retiring from the military, General Powell has taken his place as **a senior statesman**, a new role for an African American male.

PITFALLS

There are some common errors you should watch out for when writing body paragraphs:

- Avoid topic sentences that don't support the thesis.

- Avoid topic sentences that are too broad or too narrow to be developed in a paragraph.

- Avoid poorly developed body paragraphs.

- Avoid body paragraphs that do not use transitions within and between paragraphs.

- Avoid body paragraphs that are not presented in logical order.

The Conclusion

The **conclusion** to the essay is the **final paragraph**. If the essay is very long, the conclusion might be more than one paragraph, but essays of five to ten paragraphs generally have only one paragraph of conclusion.

The two most common techniques for concluding an essay are to

- **Refer back** to the story, problem, question, or quote that began the introduction.

- **Emphasize** the important points.

- Remind the reader of the thesis of the essay and how its major details are developed.

PEER
EXAMPLE

> I decided to end my essay by referring back to the story I used in the introduction about taking my son to Boy Scouts. The fact that my son is volunteering me to drive and that he has named our new van says how he feels about this new member of our family.

Luxury Ride

My son just informed me that he volunteered me to drive half his scout troop to its jamboree in our new van, which he has nicknamed Miss Betty, and he gave me a big hug. Outside sits the best gift I've ever received and one of the most important tools for a parent like me. My sleek new minivan is stylish and convenient outside, safe and comfortable inside, and powerful and economical on the road. Miss Betty is the best vehicle I could ever drive as a parent.

PEER
EXAMPLE

> In my essay on the newspaper, I wanted to emphasize the points I make in the body and show once again how important the information we get through the newspaper is if we are to participate responsibly in the decisions we have to make as voters.

Daily Tutor

Our world is becoming more complex each day, and it is often a struggle to make sense of such rapidly changing times. Luckily, we have an ally in the newspaper that is delivered to us every morning. The daily newspaper deserves our time and attention, for it brings us the information we need to better understand our world and to be engaged citizens. Armed with knowledge of current affairs, the background information to make sense of the affairs, and appreciation for our community, we are better equipped to participate as responsible citizens in a democratic nation.

Length

The conclusion is generally not as long as the introduction. The length of the conclusion depends on the length and complexity of the essay. An essay of five or six paragraphs should present a conclusion of three to ten sentences.

PITFALLS

There are some common errors you should watch out for when writing conclusions:

- Avoid beginning the conclusion with *in conclusion, finally,* or *to summarize* because it is obvious to the reader that you are going to conclude your essay in the last paragraph.

- Avoid sounding mechanical in summarizing the essay, and do not repeat the thesis statement or list the major details word for word from the introduction.

- Avoid beginning a new argument in the conclusion.

The Title

Like the title of a paragraph (see Chapter 6), the title of an essay gives the reader a clue as to the topic of the paragraph and the main idea. It is a sentence fragment, or sometimes a question, and is written above the essay in the middle of the page. The title is capitalized according to standard rules (see Chapter 22). Remember that the title that accompanies your own writing should not be underlined, italicized, or placed within quotation marks. Your title should not be the same as the subject or topic you have been assigned, but should be a unique name for your specific essay.

Incorrect: A Source of Information You Enjoy Reading

Correct: Getting the Most from Internet Newsgroups

Our Daily Tutor	**DAN:** My focus in this essay is on how the news-paper teaches us, so as I wrote the first draft in the writing lab and heard someone call for a tutor, I knew I had my title.	Titles
Luxury Ride	**BETH:** Luxury was a word I wanted in my title. I also played around with van in the title but decided in the end to use Luxury Ride.	

Review Exercise 1

Circle the best answer.

1. What is the main idea of an essay called?

    A. introduction

    B. topic sentence

    C. thesis

2. Where is background information in an essay placed?

    A. after the thesis

    B. at the beginning of the introduction before the thesis

    C. anywhere in the introduction

3. What is the main purpose of background information?

    A. to introduce the reader to the subject of the essay

    B. to present the thesis

    C. to give background about the writer

4. What should paragraphs in the body of the essay include?

    A. at least five supporting details

    B. a topic sentence

    C. background about the paragraphs

5. How does the topic sentence in a body paragraph relate to the thesis statement?

    A. It supports the thesis statement of the essay.

    B. It states a fact about the subject of the essay.

    C. It concludes the introduction.

continues

continued

6. The number of sentences within body paragraphs should be consistent throughout the essay.

   True   False

7. The number of body paragraphs in an essay may vary.

   True   False

8. The concluding paragraph should remind the reader of the thesis and the main points in the body of the essay.

   True   False

9. The title of your essay should be underlined.

   True   False

10. It is acceptable to capitalize every word in a title.

    True   False

Review Exercise 2

Identify each paragraph below as an introduction, a body paragraph, or a conclusion.

1. _____ One of the best things about Raintree is its convenience. We live five minutes away, so it's easy to jump in the car at the last minute and be there in no time. I for one certainly appreciate not having to drive across town and fight traffic after a hard day at the office. The restaurant also offers plenty of parking. I've never had to circle the lot looking for a parking space as I have in other restaurants. Best of all, the service is fast and friendly. We're generally seated immediately, and the waitress takes our orders quickly. She brings our drinks and bread before the kids have a chance to get antsy. She also checks in periodically throughout our meal to see if we need anything and to refill our drinks. All of these qualities make eating at Raintree a hassle-free dining experience.

2. _____ We're lucky our whole family can agree on a restaurant we all like. I don't dare think about what their favorite restaurant may be when they're in their teens—The Hard Rock Café or some diner with waitresses on roller skates. For now, I'm grateful we can all agree on Raintree, where we can enjoy a good meal, friendly service, and comfortable surroundings at a price I can afford. Raintree makes it easy to enjoy each other's company.

3. _____ Going out to eat with kids can be an enjoyable or not so enjoyable experience depending on the kids and depending on the restaurant. When my two kids were little, the restaurants they liked were not exactly high on my wife Diane's and my list. For years, the only place they wanted to go was McBurger. My wife and I suffered through many Big Burger meals just to make the kids happy. Luckily, our kids have grown up, and their tastes have changed. Now when I ask where they want to go for dinner, they vote for Raintree, and Diane and I smile because we are as happy with their choice as they are. Raintree is a great place to take the entire family out to dinner because of its convenience, its menu, and its atmosphere.

4. _____ The atmosphere in Raintree is one the whole family can enjoy. The lighting is low and peaceful, and the music is low enough to provide background without being obnoxious. The restaurant has mostly booths, which provide intimate seating, unlike the barn-style dining rooms of some restaurants. The restaurant is decorated with sports and entertainment paraphernalia such as team pennants and movie posters, which gives it a casual but adult atmosphere. They also have TV monitors hung from the ceiling, so if anyone gets bored, they can watch a game. My kids think it's cool because they might run into one of their friends, and from our point of view, there is plenty to keep the kids amused during dinner. Anything that keeps them happy keeps Diane and me happy too.

5. _____ Not only is Raintree convenient, but it also has great food. The menu offers a variety of dishes to please the entire family. There are steaks, ribs, and fajitas for me; burgers, grilled cheese sandwiches, and fries for the kids; and all kinds of salads for Diane. The quality of the food is also excellent, and the portions are large. No one has ever complained about leaving Raintree hungry. Best of all, the bill won't break the bank. Kids' meals are under three dollars, the sandwich platters and salads are around five dollars, and full dinners are around eight dollars. Diane appreciates the fact that the kids get a nutritious meal that they like, and I appreciate not having to spend and arm and a leg on it.

Review Exercise 3

Determine the correct order for the thesis, topic sentences, and conclusion by correctly placing the number of each sentence into the outline below.

1. Not only is Raintree convenient, but it also has great food.

2. The atmosphere in Raintree is one the whole family can enjoy.

3. Raintree is a great place to take the entire family out to dinner because of its convenience, its menu, and its atmosphere.

4. We're lucky our whole family can agree on a restaurant we all like.

5. One of the best things about Raintree is its convenience.

    I. Thesis:_____

    II. Topic sentence #1:_____

    III. Topic sentence #2:_____

    IV. Topic sentence #3:_____

    V. Conclusion:_____

Review Exercise 4

Determine the correct order for the thesis and topic sentences of the body paragraphs by placing 1 next to the thesis and 2, 3, and 4 next to the topic sentences in the most logical order.

1. A Good Health Club

    _____ In addition to a modern, well-maintained facility, a good club will boast the latest in exercise equipment and classes.

    _____ A good health club can be recognized by examining its component parts: facilities, programs, and staff.

    _____ One of the most obvious qualities of a good health club is its facilities.

    _____ What makes a good club outstanding, however, is its staff and amenities.

2. Corporal Punishment

    _____ Corporal punishment aggravates antisocial behavior.

    _____ Finally, corporal punishment instills fear rather than respect.

_____ Corporal punishment is counterproductive because it aggravates antisocial behavior in the student, breaks down communication between teacher and student, and instills fear rather than respect.

_____ In addition to aggravating antisocial behavior, corporal punishment blocks the opportunity for communication between teacher and student.

3. How to Break Off a Relationship

_____ First, I try not to break up with a boyfriend unless I'm sure the relationship can't be saved.

_____ I try to follow the guidelines I learned as a child in Sunday school: I try to treat others the way I would want to be treated myself.

_____ Once it's clear that a breakup is inevitable, I try to tell my soon-to-be ex-boyfriend as quickly and kindly as I can.

_____ Even though following this process may take longer than the cruel-and-quick method, the results are worth it.

4. An Admirable Man

_____ Not only was my dad honest, but he was also the hardest-working man I've ever known.

_____ My father showed me the meaning of honesty.

_____ By setting a good example for me, my father showed me the meaning of honesty, hard work, and generosity.

_____ My father was also an enormously generous man.

5. Repetition in *Teletubbies*

_____ First, the characters themselves, Tinky Winky, Dipsy, La La, and Po, are four variations on a theme.

_____ Not only are the *Teletubbies* repetitions of one another, but sequences of actions are repeated within each show.

_____ The show is *Teletubbies*, a British show aimed specifically at toddlers, and the repetition I noticed is no accident. *Teletubbies* uses repetition in a number of ways to appeal to toddlers and help them learn.

_____ Similarly, the repetition of sequences from previous shows provides predictability, familiarity, and pleasure.

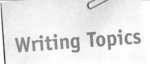

Writing Topics

Write an essay for one of the following topics. To view writing process prompts for writing the essay, turn back to Chapter 5.

- Choose a sport you enjoy and explain how it teaches important values. Or tell which sport you think best reflects the American character.

- Explain why you like or dislike your car. Or choose a brand and type of car that you would like to own and explain why.

- Choose a favorite natural wonder like a lake, park, or river and prove that it should be preserved.

- Discuss whether or not the United States should be involved in peacekeeping missions around the world. Or discuss the pros or cons of one such mission, like our presence in the Persian Gulf.

- Prove the importance of a trend in clothing, music, lifestyle, politics, entertainment, or technology.

- Explain the causes, effects, or solutions to daily stress.

- Discuss the best ways to prepare for a test.

- Choose a celebrity and prove that this person is a good or a bad role model.

- Argue that a product you can buy should be banned.

- Who is a famous person, living or dead, that you'd like to meet?

Part V

Rhetorical Patterns

Introduction

Rhetoric simply means the art of speaking or writing effectively. Rhetorical patterns are ways of organizing information, and they can be used to structure paragraphs, essays, and exams. Becoming familiar with the various rhetorical patterns can help you become a better writer or speaker because you will learn various strategies for organizing and presenting information. Any of these patterns can be used alone or in combination, and they can be used to inform or to persuade. Studying the rhetorical patterns can give you invaluable strategies for presenting ideas, but you need to be aware that the organization of your ideas is only one part of the rhetorical context. Becoming an effective writer or speaker also has to do with analyzing your purpose, audience, and tone, all of which are discussed in detail in Chapter 3, First Steps in the Writing Process.

Many of the patterns analyzed in this chapter will be familiar to you from your reading and from your experience of life. Describing, giving examples, comparing, and sorting are skills we use daily to help us process information and understand the world. Although you are familiar with these skills, you may never have analyzed these patterns in detail or studied how to use them to improve your writing. Our approach is to show you what each pattern looks like in student writing and then to break each pattern down into its component parts to model how you might employ those structures in your writing. In addition to the traditional rhetorical patterns of description, narration, example, process analysis, comparison/contrast, cause/effect, definition, and classification, we also cover summary, analysis, and argument because they are frequently required in college level writing.

For each of the eleven patterns, we begin with a brief **definition** of the pattern, followed by an **example** paragraph and/or essay written by one of the four student peers (Alicia, Dan, Beth, and Tony). Next, we examine the structure of each pattern by providing sample **outlines** for a paragraph and essay, sample **thesis statements**, and common **transitions** used for each pattern. We provide advice to keep in mind as you develop your paper under **Tips** and warn against problems to avoid with each pattern under **Pitfalls**.

All of these resources are intended to give you an overview of the pattern before you start writing. Once your instructor has given you a topic or you have chosen one of our **topics for writing**, you can use the **writing process prompts** for each pattern to guide you through the writing process. As you write, you can consult the lesson to see examples, outlines, tips, transitional devices, or pitfalls.

Chapter 8
Description

In a description, the writer paints a word picture of a person, place, or object by appealing to one or more of the five senses (smell, taste, hearing, touch, and sight). Description is useful in many kinds of writing because it helps the reader see the people, places, or objects being described. Good description depends on the effective use of specific detail. Writing "There was a flower in a vase" doesn't help the reader see the flower as clearly as writing "There was a long-stemmed red rose in a slender crystal vase." The more specific you can be, the more you will help the reader see the scene you have in mind. Use concrete and specific nouns and verbs, descriptive adjectives and adverbs, and vivid images. (For additional help in choosing effective language, consult Chapter 23.)

Examples of Description
Description of a Person

PEER
EXAMPLE

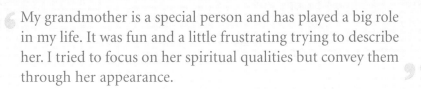

> My grandmother is a special person and has played a big role in my life. It was fun and a little frustrating trying to describe her. I tried to focus on her spiritual qualities but convey them through her appearance.

Grandma Anderson

My grandmother is a special lady. She stands barely five feet tall and weighs under a hundred pounds, but her will is as strong and fierce as a lion's. As long as I've known her, her gray hair has been pulled into a tight braid at the back of her head, and she has worn the same simple cotton dresses she has worn all her life. Only on Sunday, when she goes to church, does she put on the lace-trimmed black dress that is shiny with starch and ironing. Her face is small and lined with her years, but her eyes are as bright and attentive as a hawk's. She misses nothing in the world or in you. When I was young, I believed she could read my mind because she would take one look at me and know what I was feeling. I still sometimes believe she can read my mind today. Although her frame is bent slightly with her more than eighty years, her smile is as warm and free as a teenager's. Because I love and respect my grandmother, nothing gives me greater pleasure than to sit down at her dinner table and see her face light up when I ask for a second helping of her famous peach cobbler.

Description of a Place

PEER
EXAMPLE

Dan

> One of my favorite places to spend time is Clearwater Lake. I seem to relax and leave my troubles behind whenever I'm there. One of the problems I had in describing the lake was settling on a time of year to describe it. I go there all year long, so I know what it looks like in the spring, summer, fall, and winter. I finally decided that the lake is at its most spectacular in the fall.

Clearwater Lake

Fishing on Clearwater Lake puts me in touch with nature. Clearwater Lake is a small lake nestled in the Adirondack Mountains. The glassy lake is ringed with aspen, larch, birch, and fir trees, and in the fall, the mountainsides are on fire with brilliant oranges, reds, and yellows. I arrive at the lake early, with mist still clinging to the surface of the water like smoke. I slide my canoe silently into the clear, cold water, step in, and push off the sandy bank. Each stroke of the paddle pulls me farther out into the lake, the wind crisp and cold against my cheeks. The world seems to go silent around me; only the sound of my paddle moving through the water breaks the silence. Once on the lake, I am cut off from the world of work and school and family, and I'm free to meditate on the beauty and tranquillity of the spot.

Description of an Object

PEER
EXAMPLE

Beth

> My grandmother's rocking chair sits in my living room today, and even though she's dead, her rocking chair reminds me of her and brings her back to life for me. Sometimes special

objects can represent the person we associate with them, and the rocker comforts me today just as my grandmother comforted me when I was a child. "

Memaw's Rocker

My grandmother's rocking chair sits empty in the corner of the living room. The simple unpainted cane rocker would be of little interest to an antique dealer, but I wouldn't part with it for the world. The seat is cupped slightly from years of use: afternoons and evenings when she sat shelling peas, darning socks, or knitting sweaters. The arms are sanded smooth from the constant motion of her thin arms. The chair is silent now, but if I close my eyes, I can still hear the squeak of the rockers against the pine floor and hear the click of her knitting needles. They were sounds that always comforted me and made me feel as if everything were right with the world. Even today, I can't look at the rocker without seeing Memaw smiling at me over the rim of her glasses and hearing her say she loves me.

How Is a Description Organized?

Descriptions can be organized spatially (left to right, top to bottom, etc.); chronologically (in time order); or in order of importance (the thing that strikes you first or that is dominant about what you are describing). The subject and purpose of your description will guide your choice and organization of details.

PARAGRAPH OUTLINE	PEER EXAMPLE
Topic sentence: Subject of description	Topic sentence:
I. Major topic #1	My grandmother is a special lady.
A. Supporting detail	I. Appearance
B. Supporting detail	A. Five feet tall
II. Major topic #2	B. Under 100 lbs.
A.Supporting detail	C. Strong will
B.Supporting detail	D. Frame bent with years
III. Major topic #3	E. Smile like teenager's
A.Supporting detail	F. Gray hair in braid
B.Supporting detail	II. Clothing
	A. Simple cotton dresses
	B. Lace-trimmed black dress for church
	III. Face
	A. Small, wrinkled
	B. Eyes bright as hawk's

Tony

Tony

ESSAY OUTLINE	PEER EXAMPLE

I. Introduction
   Thesis: Subject of description
II. Major topic or description #1
   A. Support topic
      1. Specific support
      2. Specific support
   B. Support topic
   C. Support topic
III. Major topic or description #2
   A. Support topic
      1. Specific support
      2. Specific support
   B. Support topic
   C. Support topic
IV. Major topic or description #3
   A. Support topic
      1. Specific support
      2. Specific support
   B. Support topic
   C. Support topic
V. Conclusion
	I. Introduction
	   Thesis: My grandmother Marie is one of my favorite people.
	II. Appearance
	   A. Build
	      1. Height, weight
	      2. Frame
	      3. Hair
	   B. Expression
	      1. Smile
	      2. Sparkling eyes
	   C. Features
	      1. Hands
	      2. Eyebrows
	III. Values
	   A. Love
	      1. Family
	      2. Animals
	      3. People in need
	   B. Hard work
	      1. House
	      2. Yard
	      3. Charity
	IV. What she teaches me
	   A. Cooking
	   B. Appreciation of nature
	   C. Stories
	V. Conclusion

Sample Thesis Statements for Description

The thesis or topic sentence generally presents the subject of the description and/or establishes the tone or mood of the description. It controls the details you will include.

EXAMPLES

Pop stole the show at the family reunion.	The subject of the description is Pop, and the attitude seems to be positive.
My room reflects my personality.	The subject of the description is both the writer's room and the writer because the room reflects the writer's personality.

Big Shoals is a place I go to escape the stress of everyday life.	The subject of the description is Big Shoals and the attitude is that it is relaxing.
My science teacher, Mr. Mathews, is a distinguished-looking man.	The writer announces the subject of the description, his science teacher, and his or her attitude toward him.
My 1974 Dodge station wagon is a beauty.	The writer announces the subject of the description and his or her attitude toward it.

Transitional Devices for Description

Because there are no transitions that relate specifically to description, you would use the transitions that best show the relationship between the ideas you are expressing.

Tips on Planning a Description

1. Have a purpose in mind for the description. Are you trying to give an objective description, or are you trying to convey attitude, opinion, or mood about your subject?

2. Because descriptions of people, places, and objects are different, you will have different considerations for each.

   a. If you are describing a person, try to help the reader see the person and his or her character by describing appearance, dress, mannerisms, dress, actions, and/or speech. Descriptive details can be used to suggest personality or character.

   b. If you are describing a place, scene, or activity, you will need to select a physical perspective or viewpoint on the subject and stick to it. For example, if you were describing a room from the perspective of someone standing on a ladder looking in a window, you would notice certain things and not others. Your perspective might also include the time of day and season of the year of your description. You would notice different things in the fall and spring, in the morning and at night. You should remain consistent with the perspective you select.

   c. If you are describing an object, try to help the reader see the object and its meaning to you. Descriptions of objects rely on the five senses (sight, sound, touch, taste, and smell) to evoke the physical appearance and emotional associations of the object.

3. Decide on an emotional perspective or attitude toward your subject and keep it in mind as you select details. Do you like or dislike this subject? What is the dominant impression or mood you wish to evoke? This mood or feeling will be a unifying element in your description. By keeping it in mind, you can reject all details that do not fit. Try not to confuse the reader by giving some positive and some negative details.

4. Make a list of things seen, heard, smelled, tasted and felt, choosing those things that fit your physical and/or emotional perspective.

PITFALLS

1. *Avoid disorganized descriptions.* If your description is haphazard or jumps around, you will confuse the reader.

   Example:

   Topic sentence: I want to live in this house forever.
       I. The Garden
         A. Adds beauty to the home
         B. Is rewarding to work in
       II. The Kitchen
         A. Is the family's center of activity
         B. Has been remodeled with all new appliances
      III. Winter Sled Hill
         A. Allows backyard hill sledding
         B. Entices children to challenge each other

   If you describe something on the outside of a house, then something on the inside, and then something on the outside again, the reader will have trouble picturing your subject.

2. *Avoid inconsistent descriptions.* A description that is not consistent in physical perspective or emotional perspective will confuse the reader.

   Example: A vacation place description; fall and spring details mixed in the outline

   Suppose you are writing about a place. You will confuse your reader if you inadvertently combine descriptions from two different seasons of the year.

Example: A description of your boss; good and bad behaviors mixed

    I. Personality
        A. Is friendly
        B. Sometimes yells at us
    II. Scheduling
        A. Won't give me time off
        B. Plays favorites
   III. Supervision
        A. Gives clear feedback
        B. Shows us how to improve

If you switch back and forth between positive and negative details about a person, this inconsistency will cause the reader to be uncertain of what to think about your subject.

3. *Avoid generalizations and abstractions.* General statements and abstractions don't create an image in the reader's mind and therefore don't help the reader see the subject of your description.

Example: My cousin could best be described as average.

    I. Appearance
        A. Average height, build
        B. Nondescript features
    II. Personality
        A. Quiet
        B. Boring

Abstract words such as beautiful, lovely, and wonderful mean different things to different people, so they won't help your reader visualize what you have in mind. You should also avoid describing something as average or boring because such words don't help the reader see your subject and may stop the reader from reading further.

1. Write a description of an object without using the name of the object. Try describing the object with your eyes closed. This forces you to focus on senses other than sight.

2. Write a physical description of someone you know or have seen on TV or in a photograph. Use concrete language and specific detail to create a word picture of the person.

3. Write a description of the same person you described in topic 2, but also include all the nonphysical characteristics that make the person who he or she is. Consider mannerisms, speech quirks, attitudes, values, and behavior, anything that helps make the person come to life for the reader.

4. Describe one of your favorite relatives. What makes him or her so special? Make sure you include mannerisms, patterns of speech, and anything that reveals his or her personality.

5. Choose a place that is important to you and decide on an adjective that describes the emotion or feeling of the place (peaceful, frightening, etc.). Don't use this descriptive word in the description, but select details that elicit that mood or feeling in the reader. When the reader finishes your description, he or she should be able to name the emotion you had in mind when you wrote it.

6. Select a place that you like or are familiar with and write two descriptions of the same place at different times of the day or in different seasons. Try to pick times that show a contrast in the mood or quality of the place. For example, you might write one paragraph describing the football stadium during a game and another paragraph describing the stadium after the game.

7. Describe an outdoor place that is or was special to you (park, river, beach, tree house, or playground).

8. Describe the house you remember best as a child (or perhaps your childhood room) and the feelings you associate with it.

9. Describe the place you most loved to spend time as a child.

10. Describe your favorite place to vacation or relax.

Writing Process Prompts for Description

Describing a Person

1. Select a dominant mood or impression you wish to convey. Write a tentative main idea statement.

_____

_____

2. Describe the person's appearance.

Consider

Face (eyes, eyebrows, jaw, mouth, chin, expression): _____

_____

Hair (color, length, texture, style): _____

_____

Height: _____

Weight: _____

Posture:_____

Clothing:_____

_____

_____

3. What physical features suggest your subject's personality?

_____

_____

_____

4. Consider describing your subject's behavior.

   Mannerisms (e.g., gestures):

   _____

   Speech (e.g., expressions): _____

   _____

   Attitude: _____

   _____

   Values:_____

   _____

   Actions:_____

5. What behaviors suggest your subject's personality?

   _____

   _____

   _____

6. Brainstorm specific details for each main point you wish to include.

_____

_____

_____

_____

_____

_____

_____

_____

_____

_____

_____

7. If you are working on a paragraph, use the following paragraph outline to help you organize your ideas. Add as many supports and specifics as you need for your topic.

Topic sentence: _____

I. Major topic #1 _____

   A. Supporting detail_____

   B. Supporting detail_____

II. Major topic #2 _____

   A. Supporting detail_____

   B. Supporting detail_____

III. Major topic #3 _____

   A. Supporting detail_____

   B. Supporting detail_____

(Skip to prompt 9.)

8. If you are working on an essay, outline your body paragraphs based on the ideas you have generated. Use the essay outline to help you organize your ideas. Add as many supports and specifics as you need for your topic.

    I. Introduction

    Thesis: _____

    II. Major topic _____

        A. Support topic_____

        B. Support topic_____

        C. Support topic _____

    III. Major topic _____

        A. Support topic _____

        B. Support topic _____

        C. Support topic _____

    IV. Major topic _____

        A. Support topic _____

        B. Support topic _____

        C. Support topic _____

    III. Conclusion_____

- Use techniques such as brainstorming, freewriting, listing, clustering, or dividing to generate ideas for your introduction. How can you get your reader's attention?

- Generate ideas for your conclusion. Can you refer back to something in your introduction to conclude your paper? Can you restate the main points of your essay?

9. Working from your outline, write a draft of your paragraph or essay.

10. When the draft is completed, request feedback from your instructor and from peers.

11. Revise your writing using the feedback you received or using the Revision Checklist on page 62 (for a paragraph) or page 82 (for an essay).

12. Edit your writing using the Editing Checklist on page 65 (for a paragraph) or page 87 (for an essay).

Describing a Place

1. Select a viewpoint or perspective on the scene. (Where are you standing as you view the scene?) The perspective can help you determine the order and arrangement of your descriptive details.

2. Select a time of day.

3. Select a season of the year.

4. Select a mood, feeling, or emotion.

5. Make a list of things seen, selecting those that fit the perspective, time, season, and mood selected above. Write down what you would probably see first, second, third, and so on.

6. Make a list of things heard.

7. Make a list of things smelled.

8. Make a list of things felt physically.

9. Generate a tentative topic sentence or thesis statement.

10. Brainstorm specific details for each main point you wish to include.

11. If you are working on a paragraph, use the following paragraph outline to help you organize your ideas. Add as many supports and specifics as you need for your topic.

Topic sentence: Subject of description

    I. Major topic #1 _____

      A. Supporting detail_____

      B. Supporting detail_____

   III. Major topic #2 _____

      A. Supporting detail_____

      B. Supporting detail _____

   III. Major topic #3 _____

      A. Supporting detail_____

      B. Supporting detail _____

(Skip to prompt 13.)

12. If you are working on an essay, outline your body paragraphs based on the ideas you have generated. Use the essay outline to help you organize your ideas. Add as many supports and specifics as you need for your topic.

    I. Introduction _____

       Thesis: _____

    II. Major topic _____

      A. Support topic _____

      B. Support topic _____

      C. Support topic _____

   III. Major topic _____

      A. Support topic _____

      B. Support topic _____

      C. Support topic _____

   IV. Major topic _____

      A. Support topic _____

      B. Support topic _____

      C. Support topic _____

    V. Conclusion_____

- Use techniques such as brainstorming, freewriting, listing, clustering, or dividing to generate ideas for your introduction. How can you get your reader's attention?

- Generate ideas for your conclusion. Can you refer back to something in your introduction to conclude your paper? Can you restate the main points of your essay?

13. Working from your outline, write a draft of your paragraph or essay.

14. When the draft is completed, request feedback from your instructor and from peers.

15. Revise your essay using the Revision Checklist on page 62 (for a paragraph) or page 82 (for an essay).

16. Edit your essay using the Editing Checklist on page 65 (for a paragraph) or page 87 (for an essay).

Describing an Object

1. Describe the physical properties of the object:

   What does the object look like? Consider shape, color, size, and appearance.

   _____

   _____

   What does it feel like? Consider weight, texture, and consistency.

   _____

   _____

   What does it sound like? _____

   _____

   What does it smell like? _____

   _____

   What does it taste like? _____

   _____

2. Describe the emotional properties of the object.

   What do you associate with the object?_____

   _____

   _____

   What does it remind you of or make you think of? _____

   _____

   _____

   What does it make you feel? _____

   _____

   _____

3. Write a tentative main idea or thesis statement and brainstorm specific details for each main point you wish to include.

_____

_____

_____

_____

4. If you are working on a paragraph, use the following paragraph outline to help you organize your ideas. Add as many supports and specifics as you need for your topic.

Topic sentence: Subject of description

    I. Major topic #1 _____

      A. Supporting detail_____

      B. Supporting detail_____

    II. Major topic #2 _____

      A. Supporting detail_____

      B. Supporting detail_____

    III. Major topic #3 _____

      A. Supporting detail_____

      B. Supporting detail_____

(Skip to prompt 6.)

5. If you are writing an essay, examine the list of ideas generated to determine whether you can break your ideas into logical divisions around which to structure your paragraphs. Outline your body paragraphs based on the ideas you have generated. Use the following essay outline to help you organize your ideas. Add as many supports and specifics as you need for your topic.

    I. Introduction

      Thesis: Subject of description

    II Major topic _____

      A.Support topic _____

      B.Support topic _____

      C.Support topic _____

III. Major topic _____

    A.Support topic _____

    B.Support topic _____

    C.Support topic _____

IV. Major topic _____

    A.Support topic _____

    B.Support topic _____

    C.Support topic _____

 V. Conclusion_____

- Use techniques such as brainstorming, freewriting, listing, clustering, or dividing to generate ideas for your introduction. How can you get your reader's attention?

- Generate ideas for your conclusion. Can you refer back to something in your introduction to conclude your paper? Can you restate the main points of your essay?

6. Working from your outline, write a draft of your paragraph or essay.

7. When the draft is completed, request feedback from your instructor and from peers.

8. Revise your essay using the Revision Checklist on page 62 (for a paragraph) or page 82 (for an essay).

9. Edit your essay using the Editing Checklist on page 65 (for a paragraph) or page 87 (for an essay).

Chapter 9
Narration

In narration, the writer tells a story about a series of events. That may sound easy, but storytelling isn't as easy as it sounds. First, the writer has to tell the story clearly enough for the reader to follow what happened when. Second, the writer has to tell the story dramatically enough to keep the reader's attention and interest. One way to keep a reader's attention is by describing the people and places in the story vividly.

Generally, narratives are told chronologically, and they answer the six basic journalistic questions: Who? What? When? Where? Why? and How? Narration often uses the first person (I, we) because the writer is recounting personal experience.

Examples of Narration

PEER EXAMPLE

Paragraph

Tony

> The memory of my prom night is still fresh in my mind, so it was easy to write about. It was one of those nights when everything that could go wrong did.

Disaster Prom

My senior prom was a disaster. I had arranged to borrow my brother's new Camaro, but he didn't get home until right before I was supposed to leave, and in my rush, I neglected to check the gas gauge. As a result, I ran out of gas and had to hitchhike in my tux to the nearest filling station. I arrived at my date's house sweaty and was met by her scowling father, who clearly disapproved of anyone who would keep his precious daughter waiting on such an important night. My date was forgiving enough until we arrived fifteen minutes late at the four-star French restaurant where I had made reservations months in advance. We were informed by a surly maître d' that we had lost our reservations and would have a one-hour wait if we wanted to stay. Instead, we opted for a local restaurant that offered a fancy seafood buffet, but we felt ridiculous in our formal clothes when everyone else was dressed casually. My date's dress was so tight that she could barely eat a bite of food, and I was so miserable that I ate too much and ended up feeling queasy. By the time we arrived at the prom, my date was barely speaking to me. The prom was held in the gym, which had been only superficially decorated by potted plants and a canopy of balloons, and the band played mostly punk rock, which was impossible to dance to. Then, someone bumped my elbow, and I sloshed my drink all over the front of my date's blue satin dress, which sent her running to the bathroom in tears. I suppose that was the last straw because by the time I dropped her off, she was so furious that she refused to kiss me goodnight, and she never went out with me again. All in all, my senior prom was an experience I would just as soon have skipped.

PEER EXAMPLE

Tony

Essay

> 66 In writing an essay on my prom night, I divided the night into major chunks of time and tried to include as many details as I could about what happened and how I was feeling. 99

Disaster Prom

For some people, the senior prom is the culmination of four years of high school and is more important and certainly more memorable than graduation. They proudly display their prom pictures on their mantels, and they remember prom night as one of the best in their lives. It didn't quite work that way for me. I changed schools my senior year because my parents moved from one area of Atlanta to another. As a result, my date for the prom was a girl I had met in my English class but barely knew. I still have the picture of the two of us that night, but I don't have the heart to display it because even though I look good in my tux and she looks beautiful in her blue satin dress and orchid corsage, I can't look at the picture without remembering that just after the flash went off, she turned away in anger. Unfortunately, my senior prom was a disaster.

I thought I had everything arranged well in advance of the night of the prom. I had persuaded my brother to lend me his shiny new red Camaro in exchange for mowing his lawn for two months. At the time, it seemed like the trade was well worth it because I could just imagine the look in my date's eyes when I picked her up in my brother's cool car. Unfortunately, my brother didn't show up until right before I was supposed to leave, and in my rush I neglected to check the gas gauge. As a result, I ran out of gas and had to hitchhike in my tux to the nearest filling station. I arrived at my date's house twenty minutes late and sweaty. When her father opened the door, it was clear from the scowl on his face that he was not pleased with anyone who would keep his precious daughter waiting on such an important night.

My date was forgiving enough until we arrived fifteen minutes late at the four-star French restaurant where I had made reservations months in advance. We were informed by a surly maître d' that we had lost our reservations and would have a one-hour wait if we wanted to stay. Instead, we opted for a local restaurant that offered a fancy seafood buffet, but we felt ridiculous in our formal clothes when everyone else was dressed casually. It was already clear that the evening was not going well, and my date didn't have much to say. Her dress was so tight that she could barely eat a bite of food, and I was so miserable that I ate too much. The tension and the greasy fried food combined to make me feel slightly queasy.

By the time we arrived at the prom, my date was barely speaking to me. The prom was held in the gym, which still looked very much like a gym in spite of the potted plants and canopy of balloons. To make matters worse, the band the prom committee had hired played mostly punk rock music, which was impossible to dance to. Everyone just milled around awkwardly and didn't know what to do. The music was too loud to hear yourself talk, and the strobe lights at once blinded me and made me feel dizzy. Not an hour after we arrived, someone bumped my elbow, and I sloshed my drink all over the front of my date's blue satin dress, which sent her running to the bathroom in tears. I suppose for her that was the last straw.

By the time I dropped her off, she was so furious that she refused to say goodnight, let alone kiss me goodnight. Needless to say, she never went out with me again. I spent two hot summer months mowing my brother's lawn to pay for borrowing his car, and when my prom picture arrived in the mail, I put it in a drawer without looking at it. All in all, my senior prom was an experience I would just as soon forget.

How Is Narration Organized?

Narratives are generally told in chronological order, so the story you are telling will dictate the organization of your paragraph or essay. Try to structure your essay around logical divisions in the events you are recounting.

Tony

PARAGRAPH OUTLINE	PEER EXAMPLE

Topic sentence: Subject of story
   I. Event or major division #1
     A. Supporting detail
     B. Supporting detail
  II. Event or major division #2
     A. Supporting detail
     B. Supporting detail
 III. Event or major division #3
     A. Supporting detail
     B. Supporting detail
	Topic sentence: My senior prom was a disaster
	   I. Brother's car
	     A. Brother brought car late
	     B. Ran out of gas
	  II. Late picking her up
	     A. Sweaty
	     B. Father angry
	 III. Restaurant
	     A. Lost reservations
	     B. One-hour wait
	     C. Ate at local seafood restaurant
	 IV. Prom
	     A. Gym superficially decorated
	     B. Everyone awkward
	     C. Couldn't dance to band
	     D. Spilled punch on date's dress
	  V. Date in tears
	     A. Wouldn't speak to me
	     B. Never went out with me again

ESSAY OUTLINE	PEER EXAMPLE

I. Introduction
   Thesis: Event to be
   narrated
II. Event or division #1
   A. Support topic
      1. Specific support
      2. Specific support
   B. Support topic
   C. Support topic
III. Event or division #2
   A. Support topic
   B. Support topic
      1. Specific support
      2. Specific support
   C. Support topic
IV. Event or division #3
   A. Support topic
   B. Support topic
   C. Support topic
      1. Specific support
      2. Specific support
V. Conclusion
	I. Thesis: My senior prom
	   was a disaster.
	II. Before dinner
	   A. Everything arranged
	      1. Borrow brother's
	         car
	      2. Mow lawn in
	         exchange
	   B. Car ran out of gas
	   C. Late picking her up
	   D. Father angry
	III. Dinner
	   A. Lost reservations
	      1. Surly maître d'
	      2. One-hour wait
	   B. Ate at local seafood
	      restaurant
	      1. Felt ridiculous
	      2. She wouldn't talk
	      3. She couldn't eat
	         and I ate too much
	IV. Prom
	   A. Gym superficially
	      decorated
	   B. Everyone awkward
	   C. Couldn't dance to band
	   D. Strobe lights blinding
	   E. Spilled punch on date's
	      dress
	V. Conclusion
	   A. Date angry
	   B. Never went out with
	      me again
	   C. Two months mowing
	      brother's lawn
	   D. An experience I would
	      just as soon forget

Sample Thesis Statements for Narration

The thesis or topic sentence presents the subject of the narration and its significance.

EXAMPLES

My car accident was the most terrifying experience of my life.	This thesis tells us that the subject is the writer's car accident and reveals the writer's attitude toward the events.
Our family's Christmas vacation turned into a disaster.	This thesis also announces the subject, Christmas vacation, and indicates an opinion about it, that it was a disaster.
My trip out west with my girlfriend ended our relationship.	The subject is the writer's trip out west, and its significance is that it ended his relationship with his girlfriend.

Sometimes the topic sentence of a narrative paragraph begins telling the story.

EXAMPLES

On the morning of my graduation from high school, I woke feeling sick.	This thesis tells us that the subject is the writer's high school graduation and reveals that it did not go as planned.
We began our Christmas vacation as we always did, by leaving for Grandma's house before dawn.	The writer begins telling the story of her Christmas vacation by starting when her family left the house. Notice that she lets the reader know what the story will be about and gives us a clue that things will not go as normally in the story she is about to tell.

Transitions

Transition words used in narration are generally time markers:

afterward	in the end
at last	meanwhile
at the same time	next
at this point	soon after
by this time	subsequently
eventually	then
finally	to begin with
first, second, third, etc.	

Tips on Planning a Narration

1. Decide on the story you want to tell, and think about what the story means to you. Did you learn something through the experience? What would you like the reader to learn by reading your story? What feeling or attitude would you like the reader to have about the story you are telling?

2. Think through (or outline) what happened first, second, third, and so on. Try not to leave out anything the reader will need to understand the story. For example, if you were telling the story of your car accident, you wouldn't want to neglect to mention who was driving or what caused the accident.

3. Try to divide the action into major blocks. You may find, however, that you have to write out the entire story to see where the logical breaks in the action are. For example, you might want to divide a narrative about a car accident into what happened before the accident, what happened during the accident, and what happened after.

4. Focus on the people involved in your narrative, and try to describe them accurately and colorfully.

5. Focus on the feelings you experienced at different times in your story. Try to make these feelings clear to the reader.

PITFALLS

1. *Avoid stringing together a series of events without dramatizing any of them or showing their significance.* No one wants to read a mere series of "this happened and then this happened and then we did this."

2. *Avoid a list.* Make sure the events are logically connected with appropriate transitions to help the reader follow the sequence of events.

Writing Topics

1. Retell a story your family tells about you or some other member of the family. What does the story or the way it is told reveal about your family's attitude toward the event or person? Does the story say something about what your family values?

2. Describe a school activity that made you feel awkward or confident. Write a topic sentence that describes how you felt.

3. Describe an activity you did after school with friends.

4. Describe a junior high or high school dance or social event.

5. Describe a family gathering or holiday celebration.

6. Tell the story of how you met your girl/boyfriend or spouse.

7. Tell the story of a dramatic moment in your life (the happiest, scariest, most embarrassing, etc.).

8. Did you ever get in trouble as a kid or as an adult? Tell the story of what happened and what you learned as a result.

9. Tell the story of how you made significant decision in your life (going to school, getting married, quitting a job, applying for a scholarship, etc.). Try to dramatize who you were at the time, what factors influenced your decision, and how the decision has affected you.

10. Recount a frustrating experience (buying a car, registering for classes, going to court, etc.).

1. Select the subject for your narration.

   _____

2. Determine your purpose, audience, and tone.

   Purpose: _____

   Audience: _____

   Tone: _____

3. Write a tentative thesis or main idea statement.

   _____

   _____

4. List what happened in chronological order.

   1._____

   2._____

   3._____

   4._____

   5._____

   (Add more as needed.)

5. Examine the list to make sure you haven't left out anything the reader needs to know in order to understand or follow your story.

6. For a paragraph, use the following outline to help organize your ideas. Add as many supports and specifics as needed for your topic. (Then skip to prompt 8.)

   Topic sentence:_____

   I. Event or major division #1 _____

   A. Supporting detail_____

   B. Supporting detail_____

   II. Event or major division #2 _____

   A. Supporting detail _____

   B. Supporting detail _____

   III. Event or major division #3 _____

   A. Supporting detail _____

   B. Supporting detail _____

Writing Process Prompts for Narration

7. If you are writing an essay, examine the list you generated to determine whether you can break the events into major stages or chunks around which to structure your body paragraphs. Use the following outline to help organize your ideas. Add as many supports and specifics as needed for your topic.

   I. Introduction

     Thesis: _____

   II. Event or division #1 _____

     A. Support topic_____

     B. Support topic_____

     C. Support topic _____

   III. Event or division #2 _____

     A. Support topic_____

     B. Support topic_____ _____

     C. Support topic _____

   IV. Event or division #3 _____

     A. Support topic_____

     B. Support topic_____

     C. Support topic _____

   V. Conclusion

- Generate ideas for your introduction. How can you get your reader's attention?

- Generate ideas for your conclusion. Can you refer back to something in your introduction to conclude your paper? Can you restate the main points of your essay?

8. Working from your outline, write a draft of your narration.

9. Get feedback on your writing to find out if your story is clear and vivid to your reader. Is it entertaining?

10. Revise your writing using the feedback you received or using the Revision Checklist on page 62 (for a paragraph) or page 82 (for an essay).

11. Edit your writing using the Editing Checklist on page 65 (for a paragraph) or page 87 (for an essay).

Chapter 10
Illustration or Example

The writer uses examples or illustration to develop a general idea or prove a general statement. Examples are specific and concrete, not general or abstract. They explain, clarify, or demonstrate a general idea. An illustration is an extended, developed example.

Examples help readers understand the writer's ideas by making abstract ideas concrete and easier to understand. Just as a picture or illustration helps the reader see and understand the writer's ideas, examples or illustrations help the reader understand a general idea. Examples are also more memorable than abstractions. Most students remember the examples an instructor used in class long after they've forgotten the point the instructor was trying to make. Examples keep the reader's attention and make writing vivid and memorable.

Examples of Illustration or Example

PEER EXAMPLE

> “ Having to come up with concrete examples of my father's honesty helped me appreciate this remarkable man. ”

Paragraph

Dan

An Honest Man

My father showed me the meaning of honesty. I never heard him tell a lie, even the kind of white lie we tend to use to save ourselves time or money or hassle. Once when a cashier gave him change for a twenty rather than the ten he had given her, he handed back the extra ten dollars and told her she'd made a mistake. Needless to say, she was astounded by his unexpected honesty. Another time when he accidentally backed into a car in a parking lot and put a small scratch on its fender, he left a note on the windshield with his name and phone number. Most important, he always took responsibility for his actions, and if something went wrong, he was the first to admit his mistake. When the crops failed or an animal died, if it was his fault, he admitted it. He always said it takes a man to admit his mistakes rather than run away from them. By watching my father, I learned what it means to be honest.

PEER EXAMPLE

Essay

Dan

An Admirable Man

My dad didn't have a college degree, but he was an intelligent man. He could fix most things, from cars to toasters to radios, and he had a knack for nurturing growing things such as crops and animals and children. My father was well liked and well respected in our community, and nobody deserved his reputation more than he did. Most of the things I learned of value in my childhood came from watching my father and learning from him. By setting a good example for me, my father showed me the meaning of honesty, hard work, and generosity.

My father showed me the meaning of honesty. I never heard him tell a lie, even the kid of white lie we tend to use to save ourselves time or money or hassle. Once when a cashier gave him change for a twenty rather than the ten he had given her, he handed back the extra ten dollars and told her she'd made a mistake. Needless to say, she was astounded by his unexpected honesty. Another time when he accidentally backed into a car in a parking lot and left a small scratch on its fender, he left a note on the windshield with his name and phone number. He always took responsibility for his actions, and if something went wrong, he was the first to admit his mistake. When the crops failed or an animal died, if it was his fault, he admitted it. He always said it takes a man to admit his mistakes rather than run away from them. By watching my father, I learned what it means to be honest.

Not only was my dad honest, but he was also the hardest-working man I've ever known. His day began before daylight when he got up to feed and water the animals and take care of household chores. In winter, he had to get up a half an hour earlier to bring in wood for the stoves and shovel the snow out of the driveway. After helping Mom get the kids off to school, he headed out the driveway in his pickup truck to drive thirty miles to his job working for the physical plant of a large corporation. Rain or snow, he never missed a day of work. At work he did everything from installing desks to fixing electrical problems. His job kept him on his feet most of the day, and when he came home at five, he was tired, but he was never too tired to help with dinner or to complete whatever jobs needed doing around the house.

My father was also an enormously generous man. He helped out whenever anyone in our community needed a roof repaired, a fence mended, or a crop brought in. He also volunteered his time to coach our Little League baseball team and to serve as a volunteer firefighter. He was generous not only with others, but also with his kids. He was never too busy to help out with a school project, toss a baseball with us in the front yard, or just sit on the porch swing and talk. I don't know how he found the time to do everything he did, but he believed it was his responsibility to help others.

There aren't many men like my dad, and the older I get, the more I appreciate and admire him. The old saying "Actions speak louder than words" is certainly true of my father. He didn't preach about how to be a good person, but he was one. I learned good values from watching him and from the example he set. I only hope I can set as good an example for my children.

How Is an Example Organized?

Example or illustration paragraphs and essays begin with a general or abstract idea, which is then supported by individual examples or an extended illustration and details.

PARAGRAPH OUTLINE	PEER EXAMPLE

Topic sentence: General or abstract idea
   I. Example #1
     A. Supporting detail
     B. Supporting detail
  II. Example #2
     A. Supporting detail
     B. Supporting detail
 III. Example #3
     A. Supporting detail
     B. Supporting detail

Topic sentence: My father showed me the meaning of honesty.
   I. Never told a lie
  II. Returned extra change
 III. Left note on car he backed into
 IV. Admitted mistakes
     A. Crops failed
     B. Animal died

Dan

ESSAY OUTLINE	PEER EXAMPLE

I. Introduction
Thesis: General idea(s) to be illustrated through example
II. General idea or example #1
  A. Support topic
   1. Specific support
   2. Specific support
  B. Support topic
  C. Support topic
III. General idea or example #2
  A. Support topic
  B. Support topic
  C. Support topic
   1. Specific support
   2. Specific support
IV. General idea or example #3
  A. Support topic
  B. Support topic
   1. Specific support
   2. Specific support
  C. Support topic
V. Conclusion
	I. Introduction
	Thesis: By setting a good example for me, my father showed me the meaning of honesty, hard work, and generosity.
	II. Honesty
	  A. Never told a lie
	  B. Returned extra change
	  C. Left note on car he hit
	  D. Admitted mistakes
	   1. Crops failed
	   2. Animal died
	III. Hard work
	  A. Around house
	   1. Feed animals
	   2. Household chores
	   3. Bring in wood
	   4. Shovel snow
	   5. Help with kids
	  B. Job in physical plant of corporation
	   1. Drove 30 miles rain or snow
	   2. On feet all day
	    a. Moving furniture
	    b. Electrical repairs
	   3. Came home tired
	IV. Generosity
	  A. Helped neighbors
	   1. Repair roofs
	   2. Mend fences
	   3. Bring in crops
	  B. Coached Little League
	  C. Volunteer firefighter
	  D. Never too busy for kids
	   1. Help with schoolwork
	   2. Toss a baseball
	   3. Sit and talk
	V. Conclusion

Sample Thesis Statements for Example or Illustration

The thesis or topic sentence is the general statement that the example or illustration is intended to support or illustrate.

EXAMPLES

My mother was always generous with her children.	The writer will give examples that illustrate the generosity of his or her mother.
Experience is the best teacher.	The writer will support the belief that experience is the best teacher by giving examples or by giving one long illustration.
Beauty is only skin deep.	The writer will show the truth of the abstract statement that beauty is only skin deep by giving examples or illustrations.
I've learned from my mistakes.	The writer will illustrate the statement that he has learned from his mistakes by giving examples.

Transitions

In example or illustration, many transitions may be appropriate depending on the content.

Example or illustration

as a matter of fact	in fact
certainly	in other words
for example	likewise
for instance	specifically
indeed	to illustrate

Transitions that show order or sequence are often useful, as are transitions that show addition.

Order or Sequence

first	last
second	most important
next	

Addition

also	in addition
besides	likewise
for instance	moreover
furthermore	similarly

Tips on Planning an Example or Illustration

1. Decide on the general statement or idea you would like to support or illustrate.

2. Formulate a tentative thesis or main idea statement.

3. Decide which form will work best for your topic, exemplification (several short examples) or illustration (one or more long examples).

4. If you chose exemplification, generate a list of specific examples that support or prove your thesis.

   Example: Using examples to support the statement "My uncle was a good role model," you would develop a list that might include the time he helped your father financially, the time he lost his job and started his own business, and the time he broke his favorite fly rod and didn't lose his temper. If you are writing an essay, you will need to generate a more extensive list and look for areas of similarity around which to structure paragraphs.

5. If you chose illustration, generate one or more concrete examples that support or prove your thesis and develop them in as much detail as possible.

   Example: Using illustration to support the statement "Jackson Hole offers many recreational opportunities," you might recount a day you spent skiing, horseback riding, shopping, and eating in Jackson Hole. If you are writing an essay, you will need to divide your illustration into major blocks around which to structure paragraphs.

1. *Avoid giving disconnected examples.* Make sure each example is tied directly to your topic sentence or thesis. Examples are of little value if the reader doesn't see the connection between the example and the idea it is intended to illustrate.

2. *Avoid trying to prove a controversial opinion with one example.* Even if it is well developed and interesting, one example is unlikely to convince your reader to share your opinion.

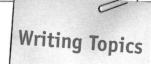

Writing Topics

Use examples or illustration to support one of the following statements:

1. No one is perfect.

2. Where there's a will there's a way.

3. Family gatherings can be trying.

4. _____ fashions show _____. (Example: Retro fashions illustrate the wearer's nostalgia for the past.)

5. Commercial children's television has _____ (great children's programs, an excessive amount of violence, too many advertisements, etc.).

6. _____ is an excellent role model.

7. Gardens can be _____ (rewarding, a nightmare, lots of work, etc.).

8. Kids' stories about schools reveal how common disruptive behavior has become.

9. Adversity can strengthen character.

10. The Internet can save consumers money when it comes to buying a _____ (car, computer, camera, plane ticket, etc.).

1. Determine the idea you wish to illustrate or explain.

2. Determine your purpose, audience, and tone.

Purpose: _____

Audience: _____

Tone: _____

Writing Process Prompts for Illustration or Example

3. Write a tentative main idea or thesis statement.

_____

_____

4. Keeping the length of your assignment in mind, decide whether exemplification (several short examples) or illustration (one or more long examples) will work best for your topic.

   A. To use examples, generate a list of specific examples that support or prove your thesis.

      1._____

      2._____

      3._____

      4._____

      5._____

      (Add more as needed.)

   B. To use illustration, generate one or more concrete examples that support or prove your thesis and develop them in as much detail as possible.

      1._____

      (Add more as needed.)

5. For a paragraph, use the following outline to help you organize your ideas. Add as many supports and specifics as you need for your topic. (Then skip to prompt 7.)

Topic sentence: General or abstract idea
    I. Example #1
      A. Supporting detail
      B. Supporting detail
    II. Example #2
      A. Supporting detail
      B. Supporting detail
   III. Example #3
      A. Supporting detail
      B. Supporting detail

6. If you are writing an essay, examine the list you generated to determine whether you can break the ideas or examples into logical divisions around which to structure your paragraphs. Use the following essay outline to help you organize your ideas.

    I. Introduction

       Thesis: _____

   II. Example #1 _____

       A. Support topic_____

       B. Support topic_____

       C. Support topic _____

  III. Example #2 _____

       A. Support topic_____

       B. Support topic_____

       C. Support topic _____

  IV. Example #3 _____

       A. Support topic_____

       B. Support topic_____

       C. Support topic _____

   V. Conclusion

- Generate ideas for your introduction. How can you get your reader's attention?

- Generate ideas for your conclusion. Can you refer back to something in your introduction to conclude your paper? Can you restate the main points of your essay?

7. Working from your outline, write a draft of your example or illustration.

8. Get feedback on your writing.

9. Revise your writing using the feedback you received or using the Revision Checklist on page 62 (for paragraphs) or page 82 (for essays).

10. Edit your writing using the Editing Checklist on page 65 (for paragraphs) or page 87 (for essays).

Chapter 11
Process Analysis

In process analysis, the writer describes how to do something or how something happens by describing the steps or stages in the process. The writer breaks down the process into steps and describes the steps in detail in order to inform or persuade the reader about that process. Process analysis may be used to describe a simple process such as how to bake a cake or change the oil in a car, or it may be used to describe a complex process such as how a scientist conducts an experiment or how Congress passes a law.

Examples of Process Analysis

PEER EXAMPLE

Paragraph

Alicia

" In both my paragraph and essay, I analyzed the process I follow when breaking up with a boyfriend, and I also tried to persuade my audience that there is no point in hurting someone unnecessarily. "

How to End a Relationship

When it comes to breaking off a relationship, I try to follow the golden rule I learned as a child in Sunday school: I try to treat others the way I would want to be treated myself. First, I try not to break up with a boyfriend until I'm sure the relationship can't be saved. I tell my boyfriend if one of his behaviors is bothering me, and I try to work out conflicts before they get out of hand. Even if he chooses not to change his behavior, at least I have given him a chance. If nothing else, giving a boyfriend a chance to change makes me feel less guilty about breaking up. Once it's clear that a breakup is inevitable, I try to tell him as quickly and kindly as I can. There is no point in hurting someone unnecessarily, so I try to be firm but kind. I let him know that he's a great person and I still care for him, but I'm no longer in love with him and I'm not interested in continuing the relationship. Even though following this process may take longer than the cruel-and-quick method, the results are worth it. I feel good about myself, and I've managed to remain friends with many of my ex-boyfriends.

PEER EXAMPLE

Essay

How to End a Relationship

According to Paul Simon, "There must be fifty ways to leave your lover." Unless a woman intends to marry the first man she goes out with, breaking up with a boyfriend is inevitable. Methods of breaking off a relationship are as different as the people who practice them and can range from cruel to kind. One of my girlfriends swears by her quick-and-dirty method. She starts going out with her boyfriend's best friend if she wants to break up. She swears it works every time. Even though her technique may be fast and sure, I prefer a slower, kinder method. I try to follow the guidelines I learned as a child in Sunday school: I try to treat others the way I would want to be treated myself.

First, I try not to break up with a boyfriend unless I'm sure the relationship can't be saved. I try to work out conflicts and problems before they get out of hand. I let my boyfriend know if one of his behaviors such as smoking bothers me, and I tell him if I am feeling ignored when he watches football for three hours on Saturday night. Even if he chooses not to change his behavior, at least I have given him a chance. It's a technique I learned at work from a supervisor who said she never fired anyone without giving her a chance to improve her shortcomings. If nothing else, giving a boyfriend a chance to change makes me feel less guilty about breaking up.

Once it's clear that a breakup is inevitable, I try to tell my soon-to-be ex-boyfriend as quickly and kindly as I can. My mother always told me, "What goes around, comes around," and I've tried to take her advice into consideration in the way I tell a boyfriend that I'm not interested in continuing the relationship. There is no point in hurting someone unnecessarily, so I try to be firm but kind. I avoid saying things like "I'm breaking up with you because you're a jerk or a slob." Instead I try to let him know that he's a great person, but that I'm no longer in love with him and I'm not interested in continuing the relationship.

Even though following this process may take longer than the cruel-and-quick method, the results are worth it. First of all, I feel good about myself and feel like I've lived up to my own standards by not hurting anyone unnecessarily. Second, by being kind, I can often remain friends with my ex-boyfriends. It's always better to keep a friend than to make an enemy. My ex-boyfriends have helped me fix a flat tire and repair the gutters on my mother's house. Especially in a small town like this one, it's wise not to have everyone you ever dated saying mean things about you behind your back.

How Is Process Analysis Organized?

The process you are analyzing will dictate the structure of your paragraph or essay. Break the process down into its component parts (or steps) and structure your writing around logical divisions in the process you are analyzing.

PARAGRAPH OUTLINE	PEER EXAMPLE

Alicia

PARAGRAPH OUTLINE	PEER EXAMPLE

Topic sentence: Process to be analyzed
   I. Step #1
      A. Supporting detail
      B. Supporting detail
  II. Step #2
      A. Supporting detail
      B. Supporting detail
 III. Step #3
      A. Supporting detail
      B. Supporting detail
	Topic sentence: When it comes to breaking off a relationship, I try to follow the guidelines I learned as a child in Sunday school: I try to treat others the way I would want to be treated myself.
	   I. Don't break up unless necessary
	      A. Tell him if behavior bothers me
	      B. Try to work out problems
	  II. Be firm but kind
	      A. Don't hurt him unnecessarily
	      B. Tell him I still care for him

Alicia

ESSAY OUTLINE	PEER EXAMPLE

I. Introduction
Thesis: Process to be analyzed
II. Step #1
   A. Support topic
     1. Specific support
     2. Specific support
   B. Support topic
   C. Support topic
III. Step #2
   A. Support topic
   B. Support topic
     1. Specific support
     2. Specific support
   C. Support topic
IV. Step #3
   A. Support topic
   B. Support topic
   C. Support topic
     1. Specific support
     2. Specific support
V. Conclusion
	I. Thesis: When it comes to breaking off a relationship, I try to follow the guide-lines I learned as a child in Sunday school: I try to treat others the way I would want to be treated myself.
	II. Don't break up unless necessary
	   A. Tell him if behavior bothers me
	   B. Try to work out problems
	   C. Give him a chance to change
	   D. Feel less guilty
	III. Be firm but kind
	   A. "What goes around, comes around."
	   B. Don't hurt him unnecessarily
	   C. Tell him I still care for him
	IV. Conclusion—results
	   A. Feel good about myself
	   B. Stay friends with ex-boyfriends
	     1. Help when I need it
	     2. No gossip

Sample Thesis Statements

The thesis or topic sentence names the process that will be described or analyzed. Often the thesis contains an attitude or opinion about the process.

EXAMPLES

Changing a tire is easy if you follow the right steps.	This thesis lets us know that the process to be analyzed is changing a tire, and it gives us an opinion that it is easy if you follow the right steps.
You don't have to be Italian to make pasta carbonara.	This thesis also announces the process and indicates an opinion.
Anyone can fail a class if she tries hard enough.	The subject is failing a class, and the opinion is that you have to make an effort to do it. It's a good bet the tone of this paper is going to be sarcastic.
Bathing a dog doesn't have to be a miserable experience for either party.	The topic is bathing a dog, and the opinion is that it doesn't have to be unpleasant.

Transitions

Transitions for process analysis are generally **time and sequence** markers:

afterward	eventually	next
at last	finally	soon after
at the same time	first, second, third, etc.	subsequently
at this point	in the end	then
by this time	meanwhile	to begin with

Tips for Planning a Process Analysis

1. First, divide the process into logical major parts. For example, if you are describing how to buy a car, you might want to divide the process into the actions you take before you go to a dealership (consult *Consumer Reports*, talk to friends, prepare a list of questions, etc.), actions you take when you are looking at the car, and actions you take when you are negotiating.

2. Next, list the individual steps or stages in the process, making sure not to leave out any steps, including any preparation that might be necessary. For example, if you were describing how to change a tire, you would want to include directions on how to jack the car properly before changing the tire.

3. Describe each step in detail. Try not to leave anything out. Remember that your readers may not be familiar with the process you are describing, so your directions will have to be explicit and complete. For example, if you are writing to a general audience about how to change a tire and include the direction "Remove the lug nuts," you shouldn't assume the reader knows what lug nuts are or how to remove them; you will have to explain these details.

4. Anticipate any problems that might arise at each step in the process, and tell the reader how to avoid or remedy the problem. For example, if you are describing how to change a tire, you would want to explain what to do if any of the lug nuts stick.

PITFALLS

Avoid incomplete directions. For example, if you forget to tell your reader to add baking powder to the cake batter, more than likely the cake will not rise. If you forget to tell your reader to engage the parking brake before he or she jacks the car, your reader could be seriously injured.

Writing Topics

1. Describe your writing process.

2. Describe the process of passing a difficult class.

3. Describe how you chose your doctor, vet, dentist, or some other service provider.

4. Describe how to buy (or sell) a stereo, car, hair dryer, or some other product.

5. Describe how to impress a date.

6. Describe how you decided to get married, get divorced, or make any other major life choice.

7. Describe how to plant a garden.

8. Describe how to build a tree house, lamp, model airplane, stereo speaker, or some other object.

9. Describe how to change a tire, pitch a tent, frost your hair, or complete some other process.

10. Describe how to make your favorite recipe.

Writing Process Prompts for Process Analysis

1. Select the subject for your process analysis.

2. Determine your purpose, audience, and tone.

   Purpose: _____

   Audience: _____

   Tone: _____

3. Write a tentative thesis statement.

   _____

   _____

4. List all the steps in your process in chronological order.

   1._____

   2._____

   3._____

   4._____

   5._____

   (Add more as needed.)

5. Examine the list to make sure you have not left any step out.

6. For a paragraph, use the following outline to help you outline your ideas. Add as many supports and specifics as you need for your topic. (Then skip to prompt 8.)

   Topic sentence: Process to be analyzed
       I. Step #1
          A. Supporting detail
          B. Supporting detail
      II. Step #2
          A. Supporting detail
          B. Supporting detail
     III. Step #3
          A. Supporting detail
          B. Supporting detail

7. If you are writing an essay, examine the list you generated to determine whether you can break the process into major stages around which to structure your paragraphs. Outline your body paragraphs using the following essay outline. Add as many supports and specifics as you need for your topic.

    I. Introduction

       Thesis: Process to be analyzed _____

    II. Major step or division #1_____

      A. Support topic_____

      B. Support topic_____

      C. Support topic _____

    III. Major step or division #2_____

      A. Support topic_____

      B. Support topic_____

      C. Support topic _____

    IV. Major step or division #3_____

      A. Support topic_____

      B. Support topic_____

      C. Support topic _____

    V. Conclusion

- Use a technique such as brainstorming, freewriting, listing, clustering, or dividing to generate ideas for your introduction. How can you get your reader's attention?

- Generate ideas for your conclusion. Can you refer back to something in your introduction to conclude your paper? Can you restate the main points of your essay?

8. Working from your outline, write a draft of your process analysis.

9. Get feedback on your writing.

10. Revise your writing using the feedback you received or using the Revision Checklist on page 62 (for a paragraph) or page 82 (for an essay).

11. Edit your writing using the Editing Checklist on page 65 (for a paragraph) or page 87 (for an essay).

Chapter 12
Cause and Effect

Causes and effects focus on why things happen and what their results or consequences are. Causes are the reasons why something happened; they answer the question "Why did the event happen?" The causes of a car accident might be bad weather conditions, inattention on the driver's part, or faulty brakes. Causes occur before the event and make the event happen.

Effects are the direct results or consequences of an event; they respond to the question "What happened because of the event?" The effects of a car accident might be injury, litigation, or increased insurance premiums. Effects come after the event and are the direct results of the event.

The study of causes and effects is central to many disciplines. For example, historians analyze causes and effects of historical events. What were the causes of the Civil War? What were the results of the Treaty of Versailles? Scientists attempt to unravel causes and effects as well. What causes cancer cells to multiply in the body? What effect do they have on healthy cells? What effect does shade have on plant growth? What are the effects of overfishing, pollution, or dams on the salmon population?

Examples of Cause and Effect

PEER EXAMPLE

Cause Paragraph

66 Writing about the reasons I decided to return to school helped me remember how much I want a degree and helped me stay motivated. 99

Going Nowhere

My decision to return to school was motivated by my desire to better myself. After working for minimum wage for two years, I realized that without a degree, I couldn't earn enough money to support myself, let alone support a family. My salary barely covered my living expenses, and I had nothing left over for emergencies, extras, or savings. Without a degree, I had no hope of getting a promotion or a raise. My job and my life were going nowhere, and I was beginning to feel like a loser. I needed to make a change; I needed to do something to turn my life around and have a brighter future. When I found out I could take classes part-time and still keep my job, I decided that going back to school was the perfect solution. It would allow me to work toward a degree while supporting myself.

PEER EXAMPLE

Effect Paragraph

Beth

 Returning to school has changed my life, and writing this paragraph helped me analyze the effects, both good and bad.

Poor but Proud

My decision to return to school has had a big impact on my life. First, because of the added expense of books and tuition, I have even less spending money than I did before I came back to school. This has meant that I've had to postpone making big purchases such as replacing the dishwasher when it broke, and I've had to cut back on small expenses such as going out to eat and going to the movies. Not only do I have less money than before I went back to school, but I also have less time. Rather than watching TV after dinner, I now study. Gone are the days when I could spend hours hanging out with my friends. These days most of my free time is spent studying and completing reading and writing assignments for my classes. By far the most important effect on my life, however, has been the change in the way I see myself. Through my experiences in school, I have gained a new respect for myself. I have learned I can set my mind to something and do it, and this new confidence in myself far outweighs the temporary inconveniences of not having as much time or money as I once did.

How Is Cause and Effect Organized?

Cause/effect paragraphs and essays generally focus on the causes or the effects of an event, problem, or phenomenon. Some longer essays examine both causes and effects.

PARAGRAPH OUTLINE	PEER EXAMPLE

Topic sentence: Causes or effects of an event or phenomenon
   I. Cause or effect #1
     A. Supporting detail
     B. Supporting detail
   II. Cause or effect #2
     A. Supporting detail
     B. Supporting detail
   III. Cause or effect #3
     A. Supporting detail
     B. Supporting detail
	Topic sentence: My decision to return to school has had a big impact on my life.
	   I. Less money
	     A. No big purchases
	     B. No eating out, movies
	   II. Less time
	     A. No TV after dinner
	     B. No hanging out with friends
	     C. Free time is study time
	   III. New attitude
	     A. Respect
	     B. Confidence

Beth

ESSAY OUTLINE	PEER EXAMPLE

I. Introduction
     Thesis: Causes or effects of an event or phenomenon
   II. Cause or effect #1
     A. Support topic
     B. Support topic
     C. Support topic
   III. Cause or effect #2
     A. Support topic
     B. Support topic
     C. Support topic
   IV. Cause or effect #3
     A. Support topic
     B. Support topic
     C. Support topic
   V. Conclusion
	I. Introduction
	     Thesis: The effects of my promotion were an increase in my salary, my respect, and my responsibilities.
	   II. Increase in salary
	     A. New car
	     B. Save for vacation
	     C. Take family out to eat
	   III. Increase in respect
	     A. At work
	        1. Boss asks me for ideas
	        2. Colleagues
	     B. Family
	     C. Self-respect
	   IV. Increase in responsibilities
	     A. New accounts
	        1. Dealing with clients
	        2. Producing reports
	     B. Supervision
	     C. Managing time
	   V. Conclusion

Dan

Sample Thesis Statements for Cause and Effect

The topic sentence or thesis should present the event or phenomenon that will be analyzed and announce whether causes, effects, or both will be examined.

 **EXAMPLE**

Salmon populations have dwindled due to overfishing, pollution, and the presence of dams on spawning runs.	This thesis examines the causes of the decline in the salmon population. Since it announces the three causes the essay will examine, we call it a blueprinted thesis.
World War II devastated the economy of Germany.	This thesis announces a focus on the effects of World War II on the German economy.
Acid rain is an environmental catastrophe with complex causes and devastating effects.	This essay will examine both the causes and effects of acid rain in an attempt to persuade the reader to do something about the problem.

Transitions

There are no transitions specific to cause. Use those transitions that show you are **adding** causes to the ones already discussed or those that show **sequence**.

Addition

also	in addition
as a matter of fact	in fact
besides	likewise
for instance	moreover
furthermore	similarly

Sequence

afterward	eventually	next
at last	finally	soon after
at the same time	first, second, third, etc.	subsequently
at this point	in the end	then
by this time	meanwhile	to begin with

There are three transitions especially useful in effect:

as a result

consequently

therefore

Tips on Planning Cause or Effect

1. Keep the purpose and length of your paper in mind as you decide whether to focus on causes, effects, or both. It would be difficult to do justice to the causes and effects of World War I in a short essay.

2. List all the causes and/or effects you can think of for your event or phenomenon.

3. Examine each cause or effect to determine if it is a direct cause or effect of your event. If you can discuss the cause or effect without having to discuss any other causes or effects, then more than likely it is a direct cause. For example, the direct causes of your car accident might be the slick road, the bad condition of your brakes, and your slow reaction to the car stopping in front of you. Indirect causes might be the lack of funds that led to your not getting your brakes fixed and the fact that you stayed up all night writing a paper. You may wish to discus secondary or indirect causes in your essay, but do not present them as direct or primary causes.

4. If there are numerous causes and/or effects to discuss, group them into related categories (political, economic, social, physical, emotional, etc.).

5. Clearly establish or demonstrate the cause or effect relationship present. Make sure the reader can understand how A caused B or how C was the result of B.

1. *Avoid mistaking coincidence (two unrelated things happening together) for cause or effect.* Just because something happened before an event doesn't mean it caused the event to happen. Similarly, just because something happened after an event does not mean it is a result or consequence of the event.

PITFALLS

2. *Avoid oversimplification.* Many problems have complex causes and complex effects. It would be an oversimplification to say that any one change would solve all the problems we face in our country. Politicians often want to convince the public that they have the solutions to all the problems of society while their opponents are the cause of all the problems.

3. *Don't confuse affect and effect.*

   Affect is a verb meaning "to influence."

   Example:

   > The movie seriously *affected* my mood.

   > The prescription drug did not *affect* his driving.

   Effect is usually used as a noun meaning "result."

   Example:

   > The *effects* of the flood devastated the community.

   > The drug seemed to have no *effect.*

   When used as a verb, *effect* means "to make or to cause to happen."

   Example:

   > He *effected* changes in his routine.

   > I will *effect* the changes as soon as possible.

Writing Topics

1. Discuss the causes or effects of stress on students.

2. Discuss the causes or effects of a problem your child is having or has had at school or at home.

3. Describe the effects of staying up too late, drinking too much coffee, overeating, or doing some other activity to excess.

4. Discuss the effects of growing up with liberal, authoritarian, or conservative parents.

5. Discuss the causes or effects of starting college or dropping out of college.

6. Discuss the causes or effects of going on a diet.

7. Describe what caused you to lie to someone you love or the effects of the lie.

8. Discuss the effects of winning the lottery or inheriting a great deal of money.

9. Discuss the causes or effects of quitting a job.

10. Discuss the causes or effects of a disagreement you had with your spouse, child, or close friend.

Writing Process Prompts for Cause and Effect

1. Select the subject for your cause or effect essay, keeping the length of the essay in mind.

2. Will you examine causes, effects, or both?

3. Determine the purpose, audience, and tone of your essay.

   Purpose: _____

   Audience: _____

   Tone: _____

4. Write a tentative topic sentence or thesis statement.

   _____

   _____

5. List all the causes or effects of your event, problem, or phenomenon.

   1. _____

   2. _____

   3. _____

   4. _____

   5. _____

   (Add more as needed.)

   Examine each item on your list to determine that it is an independent cause or effect.

6. Generate support for each of your causes or effects. How can you show your audience how each item you listed in prompt 5 is a cause or effect of your event, problem, or phenomenon?

7. For a paragraph, outline your paragraph using the following paragraph outline, changing it to fit your topic. (Then skip to prompt 9.)

Topic sentence:_____

    I. Cause or effect #1 _____

       A. Support topic_____

       B. Support topic_____

       C. Support topic _____

    II. Cause or effect #2 _____

       A. Support topic_____

       B. Support topic_____

       C. Support topic _____

   III. Cause or effect #3 _____

       A. Support topic_____

       B. Support topic_____

       C. Support topic _____

8. For an essay, outline your body paragraphs, developing one for each major cause or effect. Add as many supports and specifics as you need for your topic. Use the following essay outline, changing it as needed to fit your topic

    I. Introduction _____

       Thesis: _____

    II. Cause or effect #1 _____

       A. Support topic_____

       B. Support topic_____

       C. Support topic _____

   III. Cause or effect #2 _____

       A. Support topic_____

       B. Support topic_____

       C. Support topic _____

   IV. Cause or effect #3 _____

       A. Support topic_____

       B. Support topic_____

       C. Support topic _____

    V. Conclusion_____

- Use a technique such as brainstorming, freewriting, listing, clustering, or dividing to generate ideas for your introduction. How can you get your reader's attention?

- Generate ideas for your conclusion. Can you refer back to something in your introduction to conclude your paper? Can you restate the main points of your essay?

9. Working from your outline, write a draft of your cause or effect paragraph or essay.

10. Get feedback on your writing.

11. Revise your writing using the feedback you received or using the Revision Checklist on page 62 (for a paragraph) or page 82 (for an essay).

12. Edit your paragraph or essay using the Editing Checklist on page 65 (for a paragraph) or page 87 (for an essay).

Chapter 13
Comparison and Contrast

In comparison and contrast, the writer places two subjects side by side and examines their similarities and/or differences in order to clarify the qualities of each (inform) or to make a point (persuade). Comparison and contrast can be used independently (just similarities or differences) or in combination (both similarities and differences). Comparison and contrast are frequently called for in essay exams because they allow you to show your knowledge of two subjects while analyzing the relationship between them.

Examples of Comparison/Contrast:

PEER
EXAMPLE

Comparison
Paragraph

> ❝ I wrote this paragraph to point out the interesting similarities I saw in two TV sitcom characters I used to watch in reruns as a kid. It fascinated me to realize how similar these two characters were in spite of the different settings of the shows. ❞

Flintstone and Kramden: Two Peas in a Pod

Fred Flintstone of *The Flintstones* and Ralph Kramden of *The Honeymooners* are remarkably similar. The first of the similarities is their appearance. Both have black hair and five o'clock shadows; in addition, both have large paunches and wear loud, baggy clothes. Their personalities are also similar. Both have large appetites, boisterous personalities, and a tendency to act before they think. Moreover, they both have best friends who play second fiddle to them: Barney Rubble for Fred and Ed Norton for Ralph. Additionally, both Fred's and Ralph's favorite activity on a Friday night is to go out bowling with the guys. Finally, when Fred and Ralph put down their bowling balls, they earn their living by working remarkably similar jobs. Fred drives a truck in a gravel pit, and Ralph drives a city bus. In spite of the differences in the two shows' settings, the main characters share a number of similarities.

Contrast
Paragraph

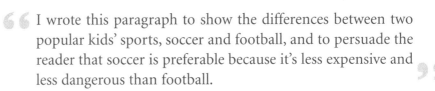

" I wrote this paragraph to show the differences between two popular kids' sports, soccer and football, and to persuade the reader that soccer is preferable because it's less expensive and less dangerous than football. "

All Sports Are Not Created Equal

Although football and soccer are both popular sports for kids, football is more expensive and more dangerous than soccer. Because of the specialized equipment necessary for football, parents must pay well over one hundred dollars for a two-month season of peewee football. In addition to this fee, the shoes and protective gear each child must purchase can easily cost upwards of fifty dollars. On the other hand, a season of youth soccer, which runs for two months in the fall and two months in the spring, costs only seventy-five dollars. Soccer shoes, which generally cost between fifteen and twenty-five dollars, are recommended but not required. Not only is football more expensive than soccer, but it is also more violent and therefore more dangerous. Children tackle and block one another, and these maneuvers result in frequent bruises, strains, and pulls. More serious injuries such as fractures, broken bones, and concussions are not unusual. Soccer, on the other hand, is not a contact sport and is therefore less likely to result in injury. Children can fall and bump into one another, but these accidental contacts rarely result in anything more serious than grass stains or loss of breath. Given the differences in these two sports, there is no question that I would prefer my son to play soccer rather than football.

Comparison/
Contrast
Essay

" I wrote this essay to point out the interesting similarities I saw in two TV sitcom characters I used to watch as a kid. It fascinated me to realize how similar these two characters are in spite of the different settings of the shows. "

Flintstone and Kramden: Two Peas in a Pod

When I look back at my childhood, one of my fondest memories is racing home from school to settle down for an afternoon of watching television. My mother would fix me a snack, and I would flip through the channels until I located my favorite programs. I would start the afternoon with cartoons and end the evening with situation comedies. Two of my favorite programs were reruns of *The Flintstones* and *The Honeymooners*. *The Flintstones* was a cartoon set in the Stone Age while *The Honeymooners* was a situation comedy performed by live actors and set in the 1950s. Although *The Flintstones* was intended to appeal to kids and *The Honeymooners* was intended to appeal to adults, I enjoyed them both. Despite the two shows' obvious differences in form and setting, the main characters of the shows share a number of similarities. Fred Flintstone of *The Flintstones* and Ralph Kramden of *The Honeymooners* are similar in appearance, habits, and occupations.

The most striking similarity between Fred Flintstone and Ralph Kramden is their appearance. Both are large men with potbellies who wear colorful, baggy clothes. Both have dark hair, and because they both hate shaving, they have heavy five o'clock shadows. Not only do they look alike, but also they act alike as well. Fred and Ralph have boisterous personalities, and they both tend to act before they think. As a result, both men are forever getting in trouble because of their big mouths.

As well as having similar appearances, Fred and Ralph engage in similar social activities. Both men's favorite pastime is to go bowling on Friday nights with the guys. They both belong to bowling teams, and both take their bowling seriously. Their favorite bowling partners are their best friends, Barney Rubble and Ed Norton. Interestingly, Barney and Ed have similar personalities and both play second fiddle to their larger, more adventuresome friends.

Finally, when Fred Flintstone and Ralph Kramden put down their bowling balls, they earn their living by working similar jobs. Fred drives a truck in a gravel pit where he is responsible for moving boulders from one side of the pit to another. Similarly, Ralph drives a city bus; the only difference is that he moves people instead of boulders. Both men work 8:00 to 5:00 jobs that require little education and for which they are paid relatively low wages. As a result, they both live middle class life styles.

As a kid I enjoyed *The Flintstones* and *The Honeymooners*. It wasn't until I was an adult that I noticed the similarities in the shows' main characters. The similarities are so strong that it's almost as if they are the same story recast in different formats and settings. Both shows reflect a conventional 50s ideal of the American family and a certain type of conventional male role. Despite the differences in their settings, Fred and Ralph were cut from the same cloth.

How Is Comparison/Contrast Organized?

Paragraphs and essays that compare and/or contrast two subjects use either a subject-by-subject or a point-by-point structure. In a **subject-by-subject** structure, the writer describes one subject first and then moves on to the second subject. In such a structure, the writer would discuss everything about subject A before moving on to discuss subject B. This structure results in larger blocks devoted to each subject.

In a **point-by-point** structure, the writer organizes his or her writing around points of similarity or difference between the two subjects, so each subject is discussed in relation to a point of similarity or difference. This structure results in both subject A and B being discussed within a paragraph.

Dan

SUBJECT-BY-SUBJECT PATTERN	PEER EXAMPLE

Topic sentence: Similarities and/or differences in Subjet A and Subject B.
 	
   I. Subject A
      A. Point #1
      B. Point #2
      C. Point #3
      D. Point #4
      E. Point #5
 	
  II. Subject B
      A. Point #1
      B. Point #2
      C. Point #3
      D. Point #4
      E. Point #5
	Topic sentence: Fred Flintstone and Ralph Kramden are remarkably similar.
	
	   I. Fred Flintstone
	      A. Appearance
	      B. Personality
	      C. Friend
	      D. Sport
	      E. Job
	
	  II. Ralph Kramden
	      A. Appearance
	      B. Personality
	      C. Friend
	      D. Sport
	      E. Job

POINT-BY-POINT PATTERN

PEER EXAMPLE

Topic sentence: Similarities and/or differences in Subject A and Subject B.
- I. Main point #1
- A. Subject A
- B. Subject B
- II. Main point #2
- A. Subject A
- B. Subject B
- III. Main point #3
- A. Subject A
- B. Subject B
- IV. Main point #4
- A. Subject A
- B. Subject B
- V. Main point #5
- A. Subject A
- B. Subject B

Topic sentence: Fred Flintstone and Ralph Kramden are remarkably similar.
- I. Appearance
- A. Fred
- B. Ralph
- II. Personality
- A. Fred
- B. Ralph
- III. Friends
- A. Fred (Barney Rubble)
- B. Ralph (Ed Norton)
- IV. Activities
- A. Fred
- B. Ralph
- V. Jobs
- A. Fred
- B. Ralph

SUBJECT-BY-SUBJECT PATTERN

POINT-BY-POINT PATTERN

- I. Introduction
  Thesis:
- II. Subject A
  - A. Point #1
  - B. Point #2
  - C. Point #3
  - D. Point #4
  - E. Point #5
- III. Subject B
  - A. Point #1
  - B. Point #2
  - C. Point #3
  - D. Point #4
  - E. Point #5
- IV. Conclusion

- I. Introduction
  Thesis:
- II. Main idea #1
  - A. Support topic
  - B. Support topic
  - C. Support topic
- III. Main idea #2
  - A. Support topic
  - B. Support topic
  - C. Support topic
- IV. Main idea #3
  - A. Support topic
  - B. Support topic
  - C. Support topic
- V. Conclusion

Dan

Point-by-Point Essay Outline

I. Introduction
   Thesis: Fred Flintstone of *The Flintstones* and Ralph Kramden of *The Honeymooners* are similar in appearance, habits, and occupations.
II. The most striking similarity between Fred Flintstone and Ralph Kramden is their appearance.
   A. Appearance
      1. Large
      2. Pot bellies
      3. Colorful clothes
      4. Dark hair
      5. Five o'clock shadow
   B. Personality
      1. Boisterous
      2. Act before they think
      3. Big mouths
III. As well as having similar appearances, Fred and Ralph engage in similar social activities.
   A. Bowling with guys
   B. Bowling teams
   C. Bowling partners
      1. Barney Rubble
      2. Ed Norton
   D. Similarity of friends
IV. Finally, when Fred Flintstone and Ralph Kramden put down their bowling balls, they earn their living by working similar jobs.
   A. Fred drives truck
   B. Ralph drives bus
   C. Hours
   D. Pay
V. Conclusion

Sample Thesis Statements

   The topic sentence of a paragraph or the thesis of an essay should name the subjects (A and B) and announce the focus on contrast and/or comparison.

   In a blueprinted thesis, the writer spells out the main points the essay will cover. In a general thesis, the writer states a general opinion but leaves the enumeration of points to the body of the essay.

Comparison
Thesis

Fred Flintstone of *The Flintstones* and Ralph Kramden of *The Honeymooners* are remarkably similar.

The topic sentence names the subjects of the comparison, Fred and Ralph, and announces the focus on similarities.

When we moved from Chapel Hill to Richmond, I discovered my new and old neighborhoods were not as different as I had expected.

This topic sentence names the subjects, Chapel Hill and Richmond, and announces comparison as the focus.

My neighborhoods in Chapel Hill and Richmond had similar kinds of kids and similar activities. (blueprinted thesis)

Notice how this topic sentence names the subjects Chapel Hill and Richmond and spells out the areas of similarity.

Contrast
Thesis

Although football and soccer are both popular sports for kids, football is more expensive and more dangerous than soccer.

The topic sentence names the subjects, football and soccer, and spells out the areas of difference.

My junior and senior years in high school were as different as night and day.

This topic sentence names the subjects, my junior and senior years, and announces contrast as the focus.

My junior and senior years in high school differed in the amount of work expected of me and the amount of freedom I had. (blueprinted thesis)

Notice that this main idea statement names the two subjects to be compared, my junior and senior years, and spells out the differences that the writer will develop.

EXAMPLE

Comparison/ Contrast Thesis	Despite the two shows' obvious differences in form and setting, the main characters of the shows share a number of similarities. Fred Flintstone of *The Flintstones* and Ralph Kramden of *The Honeymooners* are similar in appearance, habits, and occupations.	The thesis names the subjects of the comparison, Fred and Ralph, and lists their similarities.
	Although ultralight and single-engine planes are visually similar, they differ in construction, flight requirements, and cost.	The thesis announces the subjects of the essay, ultralight and single-engine planes, and spells out their differences.
	Although Shakespearc's *Hamlet* and Steve Martin's *L.A. Story* are from different periods and are different genres, they are similar in plot, theme, and characterization. (blueprinted thesis)	This essay will emphasize similarities.

Transitional Devices for Comparison/Contrast

Transitions used in comparison generally show similarity or addition, and transitions used in contrast generally show difference or dissimilarity, but many transitions can be appropriate in comparison or contrast depending on the content.

Common transitional devices used for comparison:

also	in addition
as a matter of fact	in fact
besides	likewise
for instance	moreover
furthermore	similarly

Common transitional devices used for contrast:

conversely	nonetheless
however	otherwise
instead	on the contrary
nevertheless	on the other hand

Tips for Planning Comparison/Contrast

1. Select the subjects for your comparison/contrast with a purpose and audience in mind. There should be a reason for bringing the two topics together. Are you trying to help the reader understand the subjects or persuade the reader that one subject is preferable to the other? There wouldn't be any good reason to compare/contrast knives and forks, for example, because such a comparison would serve no useful purpose for the reader. There should also be a basis for your comparison. For example, it wouldn't make sense to compare apples and Star Trek because they aren't in the same category and therefore the comparison wouldn't make sense. Try to compare/contrast two things that share a basis for comparison (two teachers, two cars, two players, two air conditioners, etc.).

2. List similarities and differences in your subjects, making sure you discuss the same topics for subject A and subject B.

   Example:

Health Club A	Health Club B
1. Location	1. Location
2. Price	2. Price
3. Classes	3. Classes
4. Machines	4. Machines

3. Decide if your subjects share more similarities or differences. You will want to emphasize either similarities or differences so that you leave a clear impression with your reader.

PITFALLS

1. *Avoid obvious comparisons.* It's not very interesting to hear what we already know, so try examining similarities or differences that aren't obvious to the reader.

Example

Topic: Similarities in two fast-food restaurants

similar prices similar menus similar service	It wouldn't be very interesting to write about what is similar in two fast-food restaurants because your reader already knows that. Think about how you would respond if someone tried to explain how two fast-food restaurants are similar. More than likely, you'd say, "Come on, that's obvious." It would be much more interesting to examine differences in subjects we think of as similar.

Topic: Differences between a fast-food restaurant and a four-star French restaurant.

different food different service different prices	If you choose a write about the differences between a fast-food restaurant and a four-star French restaurant, the topic is also poor because it's not going to be news to anyone that these two types of restaurants are different. You'd be much better off focusing on the differences of two subjects that seem similar.

2. *Avoid incomplete comparisons.* A comparison that does not discuss the same elements for both subjects (A and B) would confuse the reader.

Example:

Assignment: Compare/contrast two cars

Car A	Car B	This comparison does not discuss the same
1. price	1. features	elements for both cars. To make it complete, you
2. performance	2. appearance	would have to add a discussion of the price of car
3. reliability	3. reliability	B, the featuresof car A, the performance of car B,
		and the appearance of car A.

3. *Avoid confusing comparisons.* A comparison that evenly balances the similarities and differences in two subjects can confuse the reader. The writer should emphasize either the similarities or the differences.

Example:

Assignment: Compare/contrast two CD players	**Suppose your assignment is to compare and contrast two models of CD players.**
I. Similarities	"Which is it?" the reader may ask.
A. Price	"Are these two CD players similar or
B. Quality	are they different?" When discussing
II. Differences	both similarities and differences, the
A. Sound	writer should emphasize one element
B. Durability	over the other. Essays that focus on
	contrasts may acknowledge similarities in the introduction and vice versa.

Writing Topics

1. Compare/contrast two guitars, boats, bikes, or other products you know well.

2. Compare/contrast two TV shows, magazines, or movies.

3. Compare/contrast two entertainers, athletes, or leaders.

4. Compare/contrast the portrayal of women, children, the elderly, an ethnic group, or some other category on two TV shows.

5. Compare/contrast the right and wrong way to approach a teacher for help.

6. Compare/contrast attending school full-time and part-time.

7. Compare/contrast two candidates' platforms on the environment, personal freedom, the national debt, or some other issue.

8. Compare/contrast the values endorsed by two children's sports, TV programs, games, or other activities or products.

9. Compare/contrast your spouse, boss, or child on a good day and a bad day.

10. Compare/contrast the advantages and disadvantages of two courses of action.

Writing Process Prompts for Comparison/ Contrast

1. Select the subject for your comparison/contrast. Keep in mind that there should be a reason to bring the two subjects together.

2. Determine the purpose, audience, and tone of your comparison/contrast.

   Purpose: _____

   Audience: _____

   Tone : _____

3. Use a technique such as brainstorming, freewriting, listing, clustering, or dividing to generate a list of similarities and differences for A and B. If you discuss a topic for A, make sure you discuss the same topic for B. Use whichever method is most comfortable or best fits your topic.

   Point-by-Point method

Similarities	Differences
1. _____	1._____
2. _____	2._____
3. _____	3._____
4. _____	4._____

Subject-by-Subject method

Similarities	Differences
Subject A	Subject A
1. _____	1._____
2. _____	2._____
3. _____	3._____
Subject B	Subject B
1. _____	1._____
2. _____	2._____
3. _____	3._____

4. Do A and B share more similarities or differences? Will you discuss only similarities, only differences, or both similarities and differences?

5. Formulate a tentative topic sentence or thesis. Remember to name both A and B and state the focus on either similarities or differences.

6. Choose the outline structure that best suits your topic.

Subject-by-Subject Pattern

Main Idea: Similarities and/or differences in Subject A and Subject B.

   I. Subject A _____

     A. Point #1 _____

     B. Point #2 _____

     C. Point #3 _____

     D. Point #4 _____

     E. Point #5 _____

  II. Subject B _____

     A. Point #1 _____

     B. Point #2 _____

     C. Point #3 _____

     D. Point #4 _____

     E. Point #5 _____

Point-by-Point Pattern

Main Idea: Similarities and/or differences in Subject A and Subject B.

  I. Main point #1 _____

   A. Subject A _____

   B. Subject B _____

  II. Main point #2 _____

   A. Subject A _____

   B. Subject B _____

  III. Main point #3 _____

   A. Subject A _____

   B. Subject B _____

  IV. Main point #4 _____

   A. Subject A _____

   B. Subject B _____

  V. Main point #5 _____

   A. Subject A _____

   B. Subject B _____

7. What main points do you wish to compare/contrast about A and B?

  1. _____

  2. _____

  3. _____

  4. _____

8. Focus on each main point and use a technique such as brainstorming, freewriting, listing, clustering, or dividing to generate specific details for what you want to include about A and B.

  A. _____

  _____

  _____

  _____

B. _____

_____

_____

_____

Repeat for each main point.

9. If you are working on a paragraph, use one of the outline templates in prompt 6 to outline your paragraph based on the ideas you have generated. (Then skip to prompt 11.)

10. If you are working on an essay, use one of the outline templates in prompt 6 to outline your body paragraphs based on the main points you have generated.

   • Use a technique such as brainstorming, freewriting, listing, clustering, or dividing to generate ideas for your introduction. How can you get your reader's attention?

   • Generate ideas for your conclusion. Can you refer back to something in your introduction to conclude your paper? Can you restate the main points of your essay?

11. Working from your outline, write a draft of your paragraph or essay.

12. When the draft is completed, request feedback from your instructor or peers.

13. Revise your writing using the feedback you received or using the Revision Checklist on page 62 (for a paragraph) or page 82 (for an essay).

14. Edit your paragraph or essay using the Editing Checklist on page 65 (for a paragraph) or page 87 (for an essay).

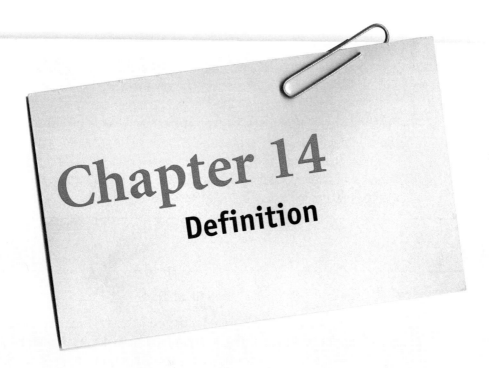

Chapter 14
Definition

In a definition, the writer defines or puts boundaries around a term, concept, or idea in order to clarify its meaning. Definitions answer the question "What is it?" Definitions can be as short as a few words or as long as an essay or an entire book. A simple dictionary definition might be enough to clarify an unfamiliar term, but an extended definition might be needed to define the meaning of liberty or Generation X. The goal of a good definition is to help the reader understand the subject.

An **extended** definition is a long definition that employs a number of techniques to limit, distinguish, or clarify a term or concept. In an extended definition, the writer might use several rhetorical patterns to clarify a subject. For example, a writer might describe, give examples, compare and contrast, analyze (break the subject down into component parts), or examine causes and effects in order to clarify the subject of the definition.

Examples of Definition

PEER EXAMPLE

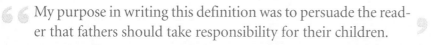

" My purpose in writing this definition was to persuade the reader that fathers should take responsibility for their children. "

Paragraph

Tony

Deadbeat Dads

A deadbeat dad is a biological father who refuses to live up to his financial responsibilities to his child. Any man who fathers a child and fails to support that child financially, whether or not mandated by a court to pay child support, is considered a deadbeat dad. A biological father can be classified as deadbeat regardless of whether he is or ever was married to

Contrast

Effect
Effect

the mother of his child because fatherhood, not marriage, determines responsibility. A deadbeat dad can be distinguished from other deadbeat citizens who default on their legal debts because the deadbeat dad harms those for whom he is morally responsible. The effects of a deadbeat father extend beyond the material realm of financial deprivations, for children of deadbeat dads often suffer from feelings of low self-worth and abandonment. Long after a child has grown up, he may still harbor resentment and hostility toward male authority figures as a result of his deadbeat dad.

**PEER
EXAMPLE**

Essay

Tony

Deadbeat Dads

In 1996, President Bill Clinton signed into law legislation that would make it easier for states to track down fathers who fail to make their child support payments. As a result of this legislation, the paychecks of delinquent fathers can be garnisheed in order to recover child support payments. The problem of deadbeat dads is larger than most people suspect. Nationwide, millions of men have defaulted on their court-mandated child support payments. And this number doesn't include the millions of men who have fathered children whom they have never acknowledged or taken responsibility for. Any man who fathers a child and fails to support that child financially, whether or not he was married to the mother of his child, and whether or not he was mandated by a court to pay child support, should be considered a deadbeat dad. A deadbeat dad is a biological father who refuses to live up to his financial responsibilities to his child.

Contrary to popular belief, most deadbeat dads are gainfully employed and are unwilling rather than unable to make child support payments. They choose not to support their children for a variety of reasons, many of which are understandable but not excusable. Sending part of their paycheck each month to support children they may no longer have contact with reduces the amount of money they have to meet their personal expenses. Additionally, many absent fathers feel it is unfair that they should be burdened by their past, especially if they have taken on the responsibility of a second family. What these delinquent fathers fail to realize is that even if their children are out of sight and out of mind, the needs of the children are no less real.

A deadbeat dad is different from someone who is merely irresponsible or who has defaulted on other types of debt. In these days of easy credit, many people find themselves overextended financially, and as a result, they default on loans and/or credit card payments. However, these people hurt only themselves. They may lose the car or house they were unable to pay for, their credit is affected (making it more difficult for them to borrow again), and they may lose face in their community. On the other hand, the father who fails to make child support payments hurts not himself, but those for whom he is morally responsible. Rather than inconvenience or deprive himself, he deprives those who are unable to support themselves and who are therefore dependent on him. To make matters worse, a father who defaults on his financial responsibility to his children has, up until now, gone largely unpunished. Society has failed to stigmatize deadbeat dads, and courts have failed to enforce even court-mandated child support payments.

The effect of a deadbeat dad on his children is devastating. Most children suffer doubly for having been abandoned emotionally and financially. Not only do they suffer the emotional deprivation of not having a father present, but they may also suffer physical deprivation as well. Many of these children lack adequate shelter, heat, food, and clothing because their mother is unable to earn enough money to cover these expenses. As a result, they grow up with feelings of low self-esteem because they were abandoned. They frequently do poorly in school and get in trouble with the law. Long after these children have grown up, they may still harbor resentment and hostility toward male authority figures as a result of their deadbeat dads.

The problem of deadbeat dads will not disappear any time soon, despite the recent legislation signed by the President. The legislation does nothing to address the hundreds of thousands of biological fathers who never married the mothers of their children and who take no responsibility, either emotionally or financially, for their offspring. Society needs to broaden the definition of what constitutes a deadbeat dad and understand the harmful effects deadbeat dads have on their children if we are to put legislative muscle behind the requirement that fathers help care for their children, at the very least financially.

How Is Definition Organized?

Definition paragraphs and essays use a variety of patterns to limit or define a term or concept. The strategies employed to define the term will determine the structure of the essay.

PARAGRAPH OUTLINE	PEER EXAMPLE

Topic sentence:
  I. Major point #1
    A. Supporting detail
    B. Supporting detail
  II. Major point #2
    A. Supporting detail
    B. Supporting detail
  III. Major point #3
    A. Supporting detail
    B. Supporting detail
	Topic sentence: A deadbeat dad is a biological father who refuses to live up to his financial responsibilities to his child.
	  I. Not determined by court order
	  II. Not determined by marriage
	  III. Contrast with those who default on debts
	  IV. Effect on children
	    A. Low self-esteem
	    B. Resentment and hostility toward authority figures

Tony

Tony

ESSAY OUTLINE	PEER EXAMPLE

I. Introduction
 Thesis: Term to be defined
II. Event or division #1
 A. Support topic
  1. Specific support
  2. Specific support
 B. Support topic
 C. Support topic
III. Event or division #2
 A. Support topic
 B. Support topic
  1. Specific support
  2. Specific support
 C. Support topic
IV. Event or division #3
 A. Support topic
 B. Support topic
 C. Support topic
  1. Specific support
  2. Specific support
V. Conclusion
	Thesis: A deadbeat dad is a bio-logical father who refuses to live up to his financial responsibilities to his child.
	 I. Characteristics
	  A. Employed
	  B. Choose not to make payments
	   1. Reduces their income
	   2. Feel it is unfair burden
	   3. Second families
	   4. Children out of sight, out of mind
	 II. Contrast with other deadbeats
	  A. Other people who default on loans hurt themselves
	   1. Lose car, house
	   2. Bad credit rating
	   3. Lose respect in community
	  B. Deadbeat dads hurt their children
	   1. Those they are responsible for
	   2. Dependent on them
	   3. Not punished by society or law
	 III. Effect on children
	  A. Feel abandoned emotionally and financially
	  B. Physical needs unmet
	   1. Food
	   2. Clothing
	   3. Shelter
	  C. Feelings of abandonment, low self-esteem
	  D. Do poorly in school
	  E. Trouble with the law
	  F. Resentment of authority

Sample Thesis Statements for Definition

The topic sentence or thesis names the subject of the definition and makes it apparent that the term will be defined. Sometimes, a thesis names the class to which the subject belongs and gives particular features that distinguish it from others. In addition, a thesis may reflect the writer's purpose or attitude toward the term.

EXAMPLES

A fanatic is a person who becomes obsessed with his or her beliefs.	This thesis names the term that will be defined, fanatic; it names the class, a type of person; and it gives the person's distinguishing characteristics.
A demolition derby is a contest in which drivers ram old cars into one another until only one is left running.	This thesis places the subject, demolition derby, into a general class, contest, and then gives its distinguishing characteristics.
A good doctor is a doctor who puts patients first.	This thesis also names the term, the class, and the distinguishing characteristics.
My family's definition of acceptable behavior is a hard one to meet.	This thesis names the term or concept to be defined and gives an opinion about it.

Transitions

Because definition can be done in so many ways, there are no transitions specific to this pattern. Use the transitions that are appropriate for the rhetorical patterns you use in defining your subject.

Tips on Planning a Definition

1. Examine the other rhetorical patterns in Part V (description, narration, example/illustration, process analysis, cause/effect, comparison/contrast, classification, summary, analysis/division, and persuasion) and decide which would help clarify the meaning of your subject.

2. Consider examples of what your subject is not. Often it is useful to include a sentence or a paragraph that distinguishes your subject from something with which it might be confused. For example, in a definition of a slang term such as *computer nerd*, you would want to distinguish between a computer nerd and someone who is merely interested in computers.

3. Explore concrete ways to explain abstract terms. For example, if you are defining an abstraction such as friendship, you will need to give lots of concrete examples of what friendship means to you.

4. If you are defining a type of person, consider describing the type's appearance and behavior; providing examples of the type; and differentiating this type from other, similar types.

PITFALLS

1. *Avoid giving only the denotation, or dictionary definition, of the term.* Often the dictionary definition is limited and unclear, and dictionaries don't address connotations, or the emotional associations, of words. For example, defining a cheat simply as "a dishonest person" misses the intensity of the word's negative connotations. The writer could address those connotations of the word by defining a cheat as the worst sort of dishonest person.

2. *Avoid circular definitions.* Don't use the term itself in the definition. For example, you wouldn't want to define a mystery novel as a novel about a mystery. A better definition of a mystery novel would be, "A novel that centers on the suspense of solving an unexplained, unknown, or secret event."

3. *Avoid oversimplification.* If you are defining an abstract term, a single example or explanation will not adequately explain your term because abstract terms tend to have different meanings for different people. For example, a term such as beauty or friendship would require numerous examples and explanations.

Writing Topic

1. Define the role you play in your family (caretaker, peacemaker, rebel, etc.).

2. Define a slang term (gnarly, bad, boss, etc.).

3. Define a type of person (jock, wimp, punk, computer nerd, macho, etc.).

4. Define a good doctor, a good health club, a good tennis racket, or a good running shoe.

5. Define your neighborhood or community.

6. Define what happiness means to you.

7. What is your definition of the perfect mate? What is your spouse's definition of the perfect mate?

8. How would your parents define the perfect child?

9. How would your child define the perfect parent?

10. Define an abstract quality (truth, beauty, integrity, courage, etc.).

---

1. Select the subject for your definition.

2. Determine the purpose, audience, and tone of your paragraph or essay.

   Purpose: _____

   Audience: _____

   Tone: _____

3. Look up the dictionary definition of your term, or write a concise definition that places the term in a class and gives its characteristics.

4. Write a tentative thesis or main idea statement.

   _____

   _____

5. Examine the various rhetorical patterns to see which might help clarify your term.

   Description

   Example/illustration

   Cause/effect

   Comparison/contrast

   Classification

   Analysis/division

6. Select the ideas that best clarify your term from the list you've generated.

Writing Process Prompts for Definition

7. For a paragraph, outline your definition using the following paragraph outline, changing it to fit your topic. Add as many supports and specifics as you need for your topic. (Then skip to prompt 9.)

Topic sentence:_____

    I. Major topic #1 _____

      A. Supporting detail_____

      B. Supporting detail_____

    II. Major topic #2 _____

      A. Supporting detail_____

      B. Supporting detail_____

   III. Major topic #3 _____

      A. Supporting detail_____

      B. Supporting detail_____

8. For an essay, examine the list generated and select three or more areas of definition around which to structure your body paragraphs. Outline your body paragraphs, developing one for each major area of definition. Add as many supports and specifics as you need for your topic. Use the following essay outline, changing it as needed to fit your topic.

    I. Introduction _____

      Thesis: A concise definition of the term _____

      _____

    II. Major topic #1 _____

      A. Support topic_____

      B. Support topic_____

      C. Support topic _____

   III. Major topic #2 _____

      A. Support topic_____

      B. Support topic_____

      C. Support topic _____

   IV. Major topic #3 _____

      A. Support topic_____

      B. Support topic_____

      C. Support topic _____

    V. Conclusion_____

- Use a technique such as brainstorming, freewriting, listing, clustering, or dividing to generate ideas for your introduction. How can you get your reader's attention?

- Generate ideas for your conclusion. Can you refer back to something in your introduction to conclude your paper? Can you restate the main points of your essay?

9. Working from your outline, write a draft of your definition.

10. Get feedback on your writing.

11. Revise your writing using the feedback you received or using the Revision Checklist on page 62 (for a paragraph) or page 82 (for an essay).

12. Edit your essay using the Editing Checklist on page 65 (for a paragraph) or page 87 (for an essay).

Chapter 15
Classification

Classification has to do with sorting things into categories. Children do it when they sort objects by color or shape. Grocery stores do it when they group dairy products or meats or produce together. Music stores do it when they sort CDs by musical genre—rock, jazz, classical. Botanists and biologists use elaborate classification systems when they sort plants and animals into groups based on similar characteristics. Classification is a part of everyday life, and it can be a useful tool in organizing information.

In classifying, the writer sorts subjects into groups or categories. The subject for classification is plural (movies, books, pain medications, etc.). The writer generally classifies or sorts the subject into three or more groups. If the writer sorted the subject into only two categories, the essay might be confused with comparison and contrast.

Examples of Classification

PEER
EXAMPLE

Paragraph

Dan

> ❝ I had a lot of fun trying to come up with categories for the types of campers I have encountered. ❞

Campers

Campers can be classified as weekend partyers, family vacationers, or true outdoorsmen or -women based on their motivations, general preparedness, and attitudes toward nature. Weekend partyers see camping as an opportunity for an extended outdoor party. They arrive at the campsite laden with lawn chairs, games, coolers full of their favorite beverage, and plenty of party snacks. Unfortunately, they often neglect such essential items as appropriate clothing, insect repellent, and food, and they frequently demonstrate ignorance of basic camping techniques such as how to set up a tent. They frequently party late into the night, preventing those around them from getting any sleep, and they leave behind a campsite littered with their trash. The second type of camper, the family vacationer, is motivated by a desire for inexpensive accommodations that also provide educational and entertainment opportunities for the entire family. They bring along trunkloads of tents, chairs, lanterns, and toys, turning their campsites into miniature villages, from which they organize expeditions to nearby natural or manmade attractions. The best parents go out of their way to set a good example for their children by picking up trash and not harming plants or animals. The true outdoorsmen and -women, unlike other campers, are interested in the opportunity to appreciate nature, and they are the least visible and obtrusive type of camper. They are the minimalists of the camping world, arriving with carefully packed essential equipment, and they typically spend their days hiking, fishing, and taking pictures. The clean campsites they leave behind reflect their respect for nature. Campers say a lot about themselves by the way they behave while camping.

PEER EXAMPLE

Essay

Dan

Campers

I've enjoyed camping most of my life. When I was a child, my family camped when we went on vacation because we couldn't afford motels. Through those early experiences, I learned to love being close to nature and roughing it. When I was old enough, I went camping on my own or with friends. Now that I have my own family, I've tried to teach my children to enjoy the great outdoors while respecting and protecting it for their children to enjoy as well. In all my years of camping, I've had plenty of opportunity to observe other campers. Whether I'm camping in a local park or at Yellowstone, I've noticed that campers tend to fall into three categories: weekend partyers, vacationing families, and true outdoorsmen or -women. These types of campers can be differentiated based on their motives for camping, their preparedness, their activities, and their attitudes toward nature.

The least conventional campers are the partyers. The partyers are usually young people who want to socialize away from the watchful eyes of parents and police, and they see camping as an opportunity for an extended outdoor party. They arrive at the campsite laden with lawn chairs, boomboxes, games, coolers full of their favorite beverage, and plenty of party snacks. Unfortunately, they often neglect such essential items as appropriate clothing, insect repellent, tent stakes, cooking utensils and food, and they frequently demonstrate a characteristic ignorance of basic camping techniques such as how to set up a tent. They frequently party late into the night, preventing those around them from getting any sleep, and they leave behind a campsite littered with their trash. They see nature as little more than a backdrop for their parties, and they act as if a professional cleaning crew will clean up behind them. Everyone but the partyers themselves is happy to see these folks pack up their coolers and go home.

The largest and most traditional group of campers is the vacationing families. These families are motivated by their desire for inexpensive accommodations that also provide educational and entertainment opportunities for the entire family. They generally see their campsite as a base from which to organize expeditions to nearby natural or manmade attractions. They bring along trunkloads of tents, chairs, lanterns, and toys, turning their campsites into miniature villages. At their worst, these families arrive in air-conditioned camper vans or trailers, and they bring along TVs, mopeds, and other noisy diversions. These mobile home campers have little awareness, appreciation, or respect for nature, and in order to accommodate them, parks have had to install water and electrical hookups, waste dumping sites, and paved campsites. At their best, camping families go out of their way to teach their children to appreciate and respect nature. They participate in the park's organized nature programs, and parents set a good example for their children by picking up trash and by not harming plants or animals.

The true outdoorsmen and -women are the least obtrusive or visible type of camper. They are motivated by a desire to learn from and appreciate the pristine natural beauty of the areas in which they camp. These campers generally choose wilderness campsites, and they often arrive on foot, carrying carefully packed essential equipment on their backs. Although they are the minimalists of the camping world, they are well prepared for any emergency. They carry lightweight tents, freeze-dried food, compact utensils, insect repellent, first-aid equipment, rain gear, and cold-weather gear. They come so well prepared because they know that the weather can turn quickly and they must be prepared to survive on their own. These campers spend their days hiking wilderness trails, observing and perhaps photographing the flora and fauna of the area. Because they try not to disturb either habitat or animals, they take nothing but pictures and leave nothing but footprints. The clean campsites they leave behind and the spectacular images they carry out with them reflect their reverence for nature.

These three types of campers perceive and make use of nature in different ways. The partyers see nature as a beautiful backdrop for their parties, but they take no responsibility for keeping it beautiful. The family campers wish to be comfortable while being entertained by nature as they might be by a tourist attraction. Last but not least, the true outdoorsmen and -women want to enjoy the pristine beauty of nature on its own terms. If more people shared the attitude of the true outdoorsmen and -women, the natural beauty of our parks and wild areas would stand a better chance of surviving for future generations to enjoy.

How Is Classification Organized?

Classification is a relatively easy pattern to use because it is so structured. Once you've determined your categories and their differentiating characteristics, it's just a matter of plugging in the differentiating characteristics in the same order for each category. If you're careful to keep everything in the same order as you listed it in your thesis, the essay almost writes itself.

Classification paragraphs and essays are structured first by category (classes or types you have divided your subject into) and then by differentiating characteristics (the ways your categories can be distinguished from one another). Categories should be developed in the same order as in the thesis, and the same differentiating characteristics should be discussed in the same order for each category.

I. Introduction
    Topic sentence: Subject of classification
II. Category #1
    A. Characteristic #1
    B. Characteristic #2
    C. Characteristic #3
    D. Characteristic #4
III. Category #2
    A. Characteristic #1
    B. Characteristic #2
    C. Characteristic #3
    D. Characteristic #4
IV. Category #3
    A. Characteristic #1
    B. Characteristic #2
    C. Characteristic #3
    D. Characteristic #4
V. Conclusion

ESSAY OUTLINE   PEER EXAMPLE

I. Thesis:
II. Category #1
   A. Characteristic #1
   B. Characteristic #2
   C. Characteristic #3
   D. Characteristic #4
III. Category #2
   A. Characteristic #1
   B. Characteristic #2
   C. Characteristic #3
   D. Characteristic #4
IV. Category #3
   A. Characteristic #1
   B. Characteristic #2
   C. Characteristic #3
   D. Characteristic #4
V. Conclusion

I. Thesis: Campers can be classified as weekend partyers, family vacationers, or true outdoorsmen or -women based on their motivations, general preparedness, and attitudes toward nature.
II. Partyers
   A. Motivation
   B. General preparedness
   C. Attitude toward nature
III. Family vacationers
   A. Motivation
   B. General preparedness
   C. Attitude toward nature
IV. True outdoorsmen or women
   A. Motivation
   B. General preparedness
   C. Attitude toward nature
V. Conclusion

Sample Thesis Statements for Classification

The topic sentence of a paragraph or the thesis of an essay should name the subject (what is being classified); the method (classify, group, kinds); and the categories (three or more groups). The thesis often includes the differentiating characteristics.

EXAMPLES

Electricians [subject] are classified [method] as foremen, journeymen, and apprentices [categories] based on their education, experience, and salary [differentiating characteristics].

This thesis classifies electricians into three groups (foremen, journeymen, and apprentices) and gives the characteristics that distinguish them (education, experience, and salary).

Tennis enthusiasts should be aware that there are three types [method] of racquets [subject]: wood, graphite, and steel [categories]. These racquets differ in price, flexibility, size, and durability [differentiating characteristics].

This thesis sorts tennis rackets into three groups (wood, graphite, and steel) and gives the differentiating characteristics as price, flexibility, size, and durability.

Nurses [subject] can be classified [method] as registered nurses, licensed practical nurses, or nurse assistants [categories]. These nurses can be differentiated based on their education, salary, and duties [differentiating characteristics].

This thesis gives the three categories of nurses and lists their differentiating characteristics as education, salary, and duties.

Blind dates [subject] fall into three categories [method]: the total loser, the octopus, and the overachiever [categories]. These types can be differentiated based on their appearance and behavior [differentiating characteristics].

This humorous thesis classifies blind dates into three categories based on appearance and behavior.

Transitions

Because there are no transitions that relate specifically to classification, you should use the transitions that best show the relationship between the ideas you are expressing.

Tips on Planning Classification

1. Determine the purpose of your classification. Are you intending to inform your reader about the differences in the categories or persuade him or her that one category is superior to the others?

2. Determine the categories of your classification, making sure that there is no overlap in the categories. Make sure a group won't fit into more than one category.

3. Determine the differentiating characteristics of your categories.

4. Outline your essay, making sure that you discuss the same topics for each class or category and that you discuss them in the same order.

1. *Avoid oversimplification.* Be careful not to stereotype or misrepresent the subjects of your classification.

2. *Avoid overlapping categories.* Make sure your types fit into only one category. For example, you wouldn't want to classify responses to stress as self-destructive, destructive to others, and annoying because annoying responses could be either self-destructive or destructive to others.

3. *Avoid missing categories.* Make sure your categories account for all the types of your subject. For example, it wouldn't be accurate to classify horses as only Appaloosas, quarter horses, or thoroughbreds because there are many other types of horses such as palominos, Clydesdales, etc.

Writing Topics

1. Classify types of a product you know well (guitars, car stereos, dirt bikes, etc.).

2. Classify the types of students or teachers at your school.

3. Classify types of athletes or sports fans in a particular sport.

4. Classify types of rock music, types of country music, types of jazz, or types of some other music genre.

5. Classify types of TV sitcoms, soap operas, talk shows, or some other format.

6. Classify lifestyles among your peers.

7. Classify your peers' attitudes about something (work, money, cheating, drinking, etc.).

8. Classify ways of handling stress, grief, loss, sudden success, or some other emotion or event.

9. Classify types of friends, dates, comedians, parents, athletes, or some other group of people.

10. Describe a classification system used in one of your classes and explain the purpose of the system.

**Writing
Process
Prompts for
Classification**

1. Select the subject for your classification.

2. Determine the purpose, audience, and tone of your classification.

   Purpose: _____

   Audience: _____

   Tone: _____

3. Determine the categories or types of your classification, making sure that the categories fit all the types of your subject and that there is no overlap in categories.

   Category #1_____

   Category #2_____

   Category #3_____   _____

   (Add more as needed.)

4. Determine the differentiating characteristics of your categories.

   Characteristic #1_____

   Characteristic #2_____

   Characteristic #3_____

   Characteristic #4_____

   (Add more as needed.)

5. For a paragraph, replace the general categories and differentiating characteristics in the outline below with the specific ones you generated. (Then skip to prompt 7.)

   Topic sentence: Subject of classification
   - I. Category #1 _____
     - A. Characteristic #1 _____
     - B. Characteristic #2 _____
     - C. Characteristic #3 _____
     - D. Characteristic #4 _____
   - II. Category #2 _____
     - A. Characteristic #1 _____
     - B. Characteristic #2 _____
     - C. Characteristic #3 _____
     - D. Characteristic #4 _____

   III. Category #3 _____

      A. Characteristic #1 _____

      B. Characteristic #2 _____

      C. Characteristic #3 _____

      D. Characteristic #4 _____

6. For an essay, replace the general categories and differentiating characteristics in the outline below with the specific ones you generated.

     I. Thesis: _____

    II. Category #1 _____

      A. Characteristic #1 _____

      B. Characteristic #2 _____

      C. Characteristic #3 _____

      D. Characteristic #4 _____

   III. Category #2 _____

      A. Characteristic #1 _____

      B. Characteristic #2 _____

      C. Characteristic #3 _____

      D. Characteristic #4 _____

   IV. Category #3 _____

      A. Characteristic #1 _____

      B. Characteristic #2 _____

      C. Characteristic #3 _____

      D. Characteristic #4 _____

    V. Conclusion_____

- Use a technique such as brainstorming, freewriting, listing, clustering, or dividing to generate ideas for your introduction. How can you get your reader's attention? Do you need to provide background information to help your reader understand your argument?

- Generate ideas for your conclusion. Can you refer back to something in your introduction to conclude your paper? Can you restate the main points of your essay?

7. Working from your outline, write a draft of your paragraph or essay.

8. Get feedback on your writing.

9. Revise your writing using the feedback you received or using the Revision Checklist on page 62 (for a paragraph) or page 82 (for an essay).

10. Edit your writing using the Editing Checklist on page 65 (for a paragraph) or page 87 (for an essay).

Chapter 16
Summary

When you summarize, you use your own words to briefly report on or explain the ideas from a source such as a book or an essay. You reproduce the contents of a source in a condensed form, focusing on the author's main ideas and reporting them accurately and objectively. You report on the author's ideas but do not evaluate or judge them, so your opinions or ideas shouldn't be included. You must use your own words to express the ideas in the source. If you wish to use the author's words, you must use quotation marks around any words, phrases, and sentences that are the author's.

Examples of Summary

PEER
EXAMPLE

Paragraph

Alicia

> Summarizing an article full of technical information is difficult because you have to understand the article thoroughly in order to condense it.

Bernstein's "Class Society"

In "Is America Becoming More of a Class Society?," Aaron Bernstein argues that the U.S. economy is becoming more stratified based on a worker's educational level. America has traditionally been a land of opportunity in which steady upward mobility was available to everyone. In the period up until the 1980s, all workers, regardless of education or class, made similar economic gains. However, new economic data shows that in the 80s, the American economy began to stratify, with mobility decreasing for workers with low skills and mobility increasing for educated workers. The same patterns of inequality continued into the early 1990s.

235

Today, the salaries of workers with low skills are losing ground to inflation while the salaries of workers with college degrees are increasing. The mobility for low-income groups in the United States is now as low as, if not lower than, that of similar groups in many European countries. Many working families in this country are being forced to rely on food aid to make ends meet. The outlook for the 90s is no different, and the author concludes that the continued division between the classes threatens our democratic identity.

**PEER
EXAMPLE**

Essay

Alicia

Bernstein's "Class Society"

America has traditionally been a land of opportunity in which steady upward mobility was available to everyone. Workers who started at the bottom and worked hard could rise through the ranks to the top of a company. As long as such opportunities were available, Americans have been willing to tolerate wide gaps between rich and poor. However, new economic studies show that mobility is decreasing for the poor while increasing for the affluent and well educated. The American dream of working hard and moving up is no longer a reality for many Americans who find themselves trapped in a series of menial jobs with low pay and no chance for advancement. In "Is America Becoming More of a Class Society?," Aaron Bernstein argues that the U.S. economy is becoming more stratified based on a worker's educational level.

In the period up until the 1980s, the majority of workers, regardless of education or class, made similar economic gains. In the period from 1947 to 1973, the incomes of poor families rose faster than the incomes of rich families, and most economists agree that mobility was significantly greater in the 50s and 60s than it is today. Even as recently as the 70s, however, workers made similar gains regardless of educational level. For example, the ten-year earnings of high school dropouts increased 45 percent, while the earnings of high school graduates increased 42 percent, and the earnings of college graduates increased 53 percent. However, even in the 70s, a growing disparity between the incomes of very poor and the very rich was evident. While the pay of men in the bottom fifth fell behind inflation by 11 percent, the pay of men in the top fifth gained 29 percent. The same trend was evident in the incomes of poor families, which gained only 16 percent, compared to 60 percent for rich families. In spite of this disparity between the top and bottom, the majority of families, 61 percent, were considered middle class.

In the 1980s, the American economy began to stratify, with mobility decreasing for workers with low skills and mobility increasing for educated workers. The earnings of less educated workers dropped behind that of college graduates, with the incomes of high school dropouts gaining only 14 percent, the incomes of high school grads gaining 20 percent, and the incomes of college grads gaining 55 percent. In addition, the disparity between rich and poor that became apparent in the 70s escalated during the 80s. The wages of workers on the bottom lost 34 percent to inflation while the wages of men on the top increased 56 percent over the ten-year period.

The same patterns of inequality continue into the early 1990s. Although most workers lost ground in the early 1990s, the wages of those at the top fell less than those at the bottom, continuing to widen the gap between the rich and poor. For example, wages for men in the top fifth fell by only 1 percent, and that of men with college degrees lost only 0.4 percent, whereas the wages of high school grads fell by 4 percent, and wages of high school dropouts fell by 11 percent. Perhaps most startling, the middle class had shrunk to 50 percent by 1992, and more than one-fourth of the workforce has fallen below the poverty line. This figure doesn't include the 5 to 10 percent of the population that is permanently unemployed. As opportunities for workers at the bottom have decreased, the poor have begun to take on the characteristics of a permanent lower class. The need for emergency food aid has increased dramatically, and American workers at the bottom have less mobility than workers in many European countries.

The outlook for the future is no different, and the author concludes that the continued division between the classes threatens our democratic identity. Our democracy has been based on a stable middle class and on the ideal of economic and social mobility for all. If the gap between rich and poor continues to widen, our democratic identity may suffer.

How Is a Summary Organized?

The organization of a summary is based on the organization of the source. A summary presents the main points of the source in the same order they appear in the source.

Alicia

PARAGRAPH OUTLINE	PEER EXAMPLE
Topic sentence: Thesis of source 　I. Main idea #1 　　A. Supporting detail 　　B. Supporting detail 　II. Main idea #2 　　A. Supporting detail 　　B. Supporting detail 　III. Main idea #3 　　A. Supporting detail 　　B. Supporting detail	Topic sentence: In "Is America Becoming More of a Class Society?" Aaron Bernstein argues that the U.S. economy is becoming more stratified based on a worker's educational level. 　I. America traditionally land of opportunity 　II. Before 1980s all workers made similar gains in income 　III. During 1980s stratification began based on education 　IV. Same patterns of inequality continue into the early 1990s 　V. Continued division between the classes threatens our democratic identity

ESSAY OUTLINE

PEER EXAMPLE

Alicia

ESSAY OUTLINE	PEER EXAMPLE

I. Introduction
   Thesis: Thesis of source
	I. Introduction
	   A. America land of opportunity
	   B. Workers could start at bottom and work up

I. Introduction
   Thesis: Thesis of source
II. Main idea #1
   A. Support topic
      1. Specific support
      2. Specific support
   B. Support topic
   C. Support topic
III. Main idea #2
   A. Support topic
      1. Specific support
      2. Specific support
   B. Support topic
   C. Support topic
IV. Main idea #3
   A. Support topic
      1. Specific support
      2. Specific support
   B. Support topic
   C. Support topic
V. Conclusion

I. Introduction
   A. America land of opportunity
   B. Workers could start at bottom and work up
   C. Americans tolerated disparity as long as opportunity existed
   D. New studies show less mobility for poor
   E. American dream no longer a reality for many working families
Thesis: In "Is America Becoming More of a Class Society?" Aaron Bernstein argues that the U.S. economy is becoming more stratified based on a worker's educational level.
   II. Before 1980s equal gains by all
   A. Before 70s
   B. During 70s, equal gains by all educational levels
      1. High school dropouts gained 45%
      2. High school grads gained 42%
      3. College grads gained 53%
   C. Disparity between gains of rich and poor beginning
      1. Men at bottom -11%
      2. Men at top +29%
      3. Poor families +16%
      4. Rich families +60%
   D. Majority of families in middle class

III. During 1980s, stratification
  A. Mobility decreasing for low-skilled workers, increasing for high
    1. High school drop-outs gained 14%
    2. High school grads gained 20%
    3. College grads gained 55%
  B. Disparity between rich and poor escalated
    1. Wages at bottom -34%
    2. Wages at top +56%
IV. Pattern continues in 1990s
  A. Wages at top fell less than at bottom
    1. High school dropouts -11%
    2. High school grads -1%
    3. College grads -0.4%
  B. Class divisions
    1. Middle class 50%
    2. 25% workers below poverty line
    3. 5%–10% permanently unemployed
  C. Permanent underclass
    1. Need for food aid
    2. Less mobility than in Europe
V. Trend threatens democratic identity
  A. Democracy built on stable middle class
  B. Continued stratification of classes threatens democracy

Sample Thesis Statements for Summary

The thesis restates the main idea or thesis of the source.

In "A Case for Poetry," Marjorie Abrams argues that children should study poetry in grade school.	This thesis announces the thesis of the article that is being summarized.
In the March 1, 1999, *Weekly Gazette*, Mark Cuffy argues that increasing funding for education will provide long-term solutions to the crime problem.	This thesis contains the author, title, and source of the article as well as a restatement of the author's thesis.
In his essay "The Black and White Truth About Basketball," Jeff Greenfield argues that "black" and "white" styles of play are an out-growth of different economic and social conditions.	The writer states the thesis of the essay he will summarize.

Common Transitions for Summary

Transitions that show **addition** and **sequence** are often used in summary.

Addition

also	in addition
as a matter of fact	in fact
besides	likewise
for instance	moreover
furthermore	similarly

Sequence

afterward	eventually	next
at last	finally	soon after
at the same time	first, second, third, etc.	subsequently
at this point	in the end	then
by this time	meanwhile	to begin with

Tips on Planning a Summary

Writing a summary involves two things: thoroughly understanding the content of the source, and reporting it accurately and objectively.

1. Look up unfamiliar vocabulary and make sure you understand the meaning of each word in context. Also make sure you understand any charts, graphs, or illustrations the author uses.

2. Take notes on and/or outline the source. Depending on the length of the original, it may be useful to state the main point of each paragraph in a sentence.

3. Determine the author's thesis and the main points used to support it.

4. Write your summary, reproducing the author's ideas in the order they were presented.

5. Check your summary for accuracy, balance, and coherence.

PITFALLS

1. *Avoid mistaking details for main ideas.* Most examples, quotes, and statistics are support for main ideas. Although they may be interesting and memorable, don't confuse them with main ideas.

Example:

Original: "In the past, companies could hire unskilled people and train them into skilled jobs," says Henry B. Schacht, the former CEO of Cummins Engine Co. who now is chairman of AT&T's $20 billion equipment unit. "My predecessor at Cummins moved from the shop floor and ended up as president." But because Cummins, like many companies, has cut many first-line managerial jobs, "today those stairs don't exist."

Not the main idea: Henry Schacht's predecessor started on the shop floor and eventually became the president

Main idea: Because many companies have cut managerial positions, employees no longer have the ability to rise through the ranks.

2. *Avoid including your opinion.* Remember that a summary condenses but does not evaluate the author's ideas.

Example:

Opinion: Stogan seems way off base in concluding that absenteeism is due to worker burnout.

A summary shouldn't make judgments about the source. It should report objectively on the content.

Summary: Stogan concludes that absenteeism is caused by worker burnout.

This is an improved thesis for a summary essay.

3. *Avoid using the wording of the source.* Remember to use your own words when you summarize. It's a good idea to take notes from the source and use your notes to write the summary.

Example:

Original: "After all, the U.S., unlike more rigid economies in Europe, has always been dynamic enough to provide steady upward mobility for workers."

Unacceptable paraphrase: The U.S. has a dynamic economy that provides steady upward mobility for workers, unlike the more rigid economies in Europe.

This would be an unacceptable paraphrase because it uses the same sentence structure and much of the same phrasing as the original.

Acceptable paraphrase: In the United States, unlike in Europe, workers have always been able to advance.

This is an acceptable summary or paragraph of the original writing.

Writing Topics

1. Summarize an essay from one of your textbooks.

2. Summarize a news story from your local newspaper.

3. Summarize an editorial from your local newspaper.

4. Summarize a TV documentary or special.

5. Summarize a lecture you attended.

6. Summarize a movie or book review.

7. Summarize a chapter from one of your textbooks.

8. Summarize a magazine article.

9. Summarize a book you have read.

10. Summarize the contents of an Internet article or Web site on a particular subject.

Writing Process Prompts for Summary

1. Determine the source you will summarize.

2. Look up any words you are unfamiliar with, making sure you understand their meaning in context. Make sure you understand any graphics.

3. Read the source several times, making sure you thoroughly understand the content.

4. Take notes on and/or outline the source.

5. Identify the author's thesis and state it in your own words.

6. Identify the author's main ideas and state them in your own words.

7. For a paragraph, outline your paragraph using the following paragraph outline, changing it to fit your topic. (Then skip to prompt 9.)

Topic sentence: Thesis of source _____

   I. Main idea #1 _____

     A. Supporting detail_____

     B. Supporting detail_____

  II. Main idea #2 _____

     A. Supporting detail_____

     B. Supporting detail_____

 III. Main idea #3 _____

     A. Supporting detail_____

     B. Supporting detail_____

8. For an essay, outline your body paragraphs, developing one for each major idea. Add as many supports and specifics as you need for your topic. Use the following essay outline, changing it as needed to fit your topic

    I. Introduction _____

      Thesis: Thesis of source _____

   II. Main idea #1 _____

      A. Support topic_____

      B. Support topic_____

      C. Support topic _____

  III. Main idea #2 _____

      A. Support topic_____

      B. Support topic_____

      C. Support topic _____

  IV. Main idea #3 _____

      A. Support topic_____

      B. Support topic_____

      C. Support topic _____

   V. Conclusion_____

- Use a technique such as brainstorming, freewriting, listing, clustering, or dividing to generate ideas for your introduction. How can you get your reader's attention? Do you need to provide background information to help your reader understand your argument?

- Generate ideas for your conclusion. Can you refer back to something in your introduction to conclude your paper? Can you restate the main points of your essay?

9. Working from your outline, write a draft of your summary, reproducing the author's ideas in the order they were presented.

10. Check your summary for accuracy, balance, and coherence.

11. Get feedback on your writing.

12. Revise your writing using the feedback you received or using the Revision Checklist on page 62 (for paragraphs) or page 82 (for essays).

13. Edit your paragraph or essay using the Editing Checklist on page 65 (for paragraphs) or page 87 (for essays).

Chapter 17
Analysis and Division

Both analysis and division can help you divide a large and complicated subject into manageable parts. Just as in a process analysis, where you divide a process into parts, in analysis and division you divide your subject (anything from your neighborhood to the Congress) into its component parts.

In analysis, the writer breaks down a subject into its component parts and examines one or more of the parts in order to clarify the meaning of the whole. For example, a writer might analyze the role of the shortstop in baseball, the role of a character in a short story, or the role of low interest rates in a bull market.

In division, the writer divides a single subject into its component parts, the way a pie is divided into pieces, and examines each of the components in order to clarify the meaning of the whole. For example, a writer might divide the components of a luxury hotel into rooms, service, restaurants, and amenities (pool, sauna, etc.) in order to demonstrate a point about what it takes to be a good luxury hotel or to show that Hotel X is a superb luxury hotel.

The same subject could be divided in multiple ways depending on your interests or purpose. For example, the subject *apartment* might be divided into rooms (kitchen, bedrooms, bathroom, living room, porch) or into aspects an apartment hunter might consider (rent, facilities, size, amenities). Similarly, a book could be divided by physical parts (table of contents, chapters, bibliography, index) or by writing elements (characterization, setting, conflict, and resolution).

Examples of Analysis and Division

PEER EXAMPLE

Analysis

> I chose to analyze how, on the television show *The Magic School Bus*, Ms. Frizzle's appearance and attitude encourage students to be creative.

Ms. Frizzle

Ms. Frizzle's appearance and attitude are central to the message the TV show *The Magic School Bus* teaches about learning. First, Ms. Frizzle's appearance encourages creativity. Her outfits always mirror her lessons; for example, if she intends to have students learn about weather, her dress is covered with thunderclouds, lightning bolts, and rain showers. Next, her attitude is the opposite of that of the traditional elementary school teacher who wants children to be orderly, neat, and quiet. The Frizz, as the students affectionately call her, encourages her students to explore, take risks, be creative, make mistakes, and get dirty. As far as she's concerned, it's all part of the process of learning. In keeping with her attitude, she never lectures to students but instead sets up adventures that allow them to learn firsthand about natural phenomena. Everything about the Frizz, including her clothing and her attitude, encourages students to be creative and learn.

PEER EXAMPLE

Division

> By dividing a good health club into its component parts, I came up with a definition of what a good club should be.

A Good Health Club

A good health club can be recognized by examining its component parts. First and foremost, a good club should offer adequate facilities including large, well-lit exercise and aerobic rooms, dressing rooms, and a pool, sauna, steam room, and whirlpool. Moreover, well-maintained exercise equipment including weight machines, stair machines, bicycles, and rowing machines is a component that should not be overlooked. Next, a good club should offer a full range of classes including high- and low-impact aerobics, step aerobics, and yoga, as well as specialized classes on such topics as diet and nutrition. A well-trained, experienced, and helpful staff is also an essential element in a good club. Finally, a good club will offer such amenities as a nursery for children and a snack bar serving healthy, high-protein refreshments. If a club offers these elements at a price the patron can afford, he or she can't go wrong.

How Are Analysis and Division Organized?

Analysis and division paragraphs and essays are structured around the parts of the subject the writer wishes to examine.

PARAGRAPH OUTLINE	PEER EXAMPLE

Topic sentence: Subject of analysis or division
   I. Element or part #1
     A. Supporting detail
     B. Supporting detail
   II. Element or part #2
     A. Supporting detail
     B. Supporting detail
   III. Element or part #3
     A. Supporting detail
     B. Supporting detail
	Topic sentence: Ms. Frizzle's character and attitude are central to the message *The Magic School Bus* teaches about learning.
	   I. Appearance
	     A. Encourages creativity
	     B. Mirrors lesson
	   II. Attitude
	     A. Opposite of traditional teacher
	     B. Explore, make mistakes, take risks, get dirty
	     C. Importance of learning process
	   III. Teaching
	     A. Sets up adventures
	     B. Students learn actively

Beth

ESSAY OUTLINE	PEER EXAMPLE

I. Introduction
     Thesis: Subject of analysis or division
   II. Element or part #1
     A. Support topic
       1. Specific support
       2. Specific support
     B. Support topic
       1. Specific support
       2. Specific support
     C. Support topic
       1. Specific support
       2. Specific support
       3. Specific support
     D. Support topic
       1. Specific support
       2. Specific support
	Thesis: A good health club can be recognized by examining its component parts.
	   II. Facilities
	     A. Aerobics rooms
	       1. Large, well-lit
	       2. Good acoustics
	     B. Dressing rooms
	       1. Adequate lockers
	       2. Showers
	     C. Pool
	       1. Clean
	       2. Lanes divided
	       3. Heated
	     D. Jacuzzi and sauna
	       1. Large
	       2. Well-maintained

Alicia

III. Element or part #2
  A. Support topic
  B. Support topic
      1. Specific support
      2. Specific support
  C. Support topic
IV. Element or part #3
  A. Support topic
  B. Support topic
  C. Support topic
      1. Specific support
      2. Specific support
V. Conclusion

III. Equipment and classes
  A. Equipment
      1. Weight machines
      2. Stair machines
      3. Bicycles
      4. Rowing machines
  B. Classes
      1. High and low impact aerobics
      2. Step aerobics
      3. Yoga
IV. Staff and amenities
  A. Staff
      1. Well-trained
      2. Experienced
      3. Helpful
  B. Amenities
      1. Child care
          a. Trained staff
          b. Adequate toys and equipment
      2. Snack bar
          a. Healthy foods
          b. Power drinks

Sample Thesis Statements for Analysis and Division

Analysis

The thesis or topic sentence for analysis often states an opinion about the subject and names the parts to be analyzed.

EXAMPLES

The tone, imagery, and rhythm all contribute to the impact of "The Love Song of J. Alfred Prufrock." (literary analysis)	The writer will analyze the use of tone, imagery, and rhythm in the poem "The Love Song of J. Alfred Prufrock."
Music plays a key role in establishing the mood of *The Piano*.	The writer will analyze the role played by music in the movie *The Piano*.
The role of the hero in a traditional western movie is clear-cut.	The writer will analyze the role of the hero in traditional western movies.

Division

The thesis or topic sentence for division names the subject and its component parts.

Our local government is divided into three primary components: the commissioners, the staff, and the volunteer committees.	The writer will divide local government into three component parts.
A reputable builder will provide a potential customer with a quote that contains a completion schedule and a breakdown of the costs of permits, fees, materials, and labor.	The writer will divide a construction bid into its component parts.
Blueprints for a typical house are divided into materials lists, exterior elevations, foundation plans, framing schedules, and electrical diagrams.	The writer divides the blue-prints for a house into their component parts.

Transitions

Transitions used in analysis and division can vary widely, but analysis often makes use of transitions that relate to sequence and/or addition.

Sequence

afterward	eventually	next
at last	finally	soon after
at the same time	first, second, third, etc.	subsequently
at this point	in the end	then
by this time	meanwhile	to begin with

Addition

also	in addition
as a matter of fact	in fact
besides	likewise
for instance	moreover
furthermore	similarly

Tips on Planning Analysis or Division

Analysis

1. Brainstorm a list of some of the component parts of your subject.

2. Decide which elements seem most interesting or important, and select a limited number for your analysis.

3. Develop each element for your analysis by examining the role it plays in your subject. How does it function in the whole? How does it affect the whole?

Division

1. Choose a subject that lends itself to division, one that can be broken down into component parts.

2. Make a list of the component parts of your subject, making sure there is no overlap in the parts.

3. If you are writing an essay, decide how you will divide your subject into paragraphs. If there are many parts to your subject, see whether the parts can be divided into larger categories that could be discussed in paragraphs. For example, if you were dividing a political party's platform into its parts, you might be able to divide the parts into economic policy, social policy, and foreign policy.

PITFALLS

1. *Avoid obvious or purposeless analysis or divisions.* Keep your audience and purpose in mind when choosing a subject. Remember that analysis and division are supposed to clarify a complex subject. Therefore, choose a subject that needs explanation or clarification. For example, dividing table utensils into forks, knives, and spoons would bore readers because you aren't telling them anything they don't already know.

2. *Avoid incomplete divisions.* Make sure the sum of the parts equals the whole in division, and make sure not to leave out components. For example, you would confuse your reader if you divided the components of a good restaurant into service, atmosphere, and price—but left out food.

3. *Avoid overlapping parts in a division.* Each part of a division should be unique. For example, if you divided the parts of an action movie into the actors, the plot, the special effects, the music, and the stars, you would run into trouble because the actors and stars are overlapping categories.

Analysis

1. Analyze one or more elements of a good restaurant, hotel, or club.

2. Analyze one or more elements of a certain type of movie (horror, sci-fi, western, comedy, etc.).

3. Analyze one or more elements of a performance you have attended (ballet, opera, rock concert, etc.).

4. Analyze one or more parts of your school, city, county, or state government to show how the system is or is not working.

5. Analyze a specific TV, magazine, or Internet ad to determine its audience, purpose, tone, style, message, or content.

6. Analyze the function of one or more parts of a system you have studied or are familiar with (an engine, an aquarium, a sports team, a musical instrument, a weather system, a disease, a natural or manmade phenomenon, etc.) in order to help your reader understand the system better.

8. Analyze the role of one or more elements in a TV news show, game show, soap opera, or science program.

9. Analyze one or more elements of your favorite music television video to show how it or they make the video interesting.

10. Analyze one or more elements of a specific commercial to show how the advertiser used it or them to appeal to the audience.

Division

1. Divide a good restaurant, hotel, or club into its component parts.

2. Divide a certain type of movie (horror, sci-fi, western, comedy, etc.) into its component parts.

3. Divide a certain type of performance (ballet, opera, rock concert, etc.) into its component parts.

4. Divide the federal government into its branches, or divide one branch of the government (legislative, executive, judicial) into its parts.

5. Divide your local government into its component parts.

6. Divide the parts of a cell, leaf, flower, insect or other nature phenomenon into its component parts.

7. Divide the parts of some object you know well (sailboat, radio, television set, golf course, aquarium, terrarium, binoculars, etc.) into its parts in order to help your reader understand that object better.

8. Divide a network news show into its component parts.

9. Divide a music television video into its component parts.

10. Divide a commercial for a specific type of product (used cars, aspirin, dog food, beer, etc.) into parts.

Writing Process Prompts for Analysis and Division

1. Choose a subject for your analysis or division.

2. Determine your purpose, audience, and tone.

   Purpose: _____

   Audience: _____

   Tone: _____

3. Write a tentative main idea or thesis statement.

   _____

   _____

4. Generate the elements or parts of the analysis or division.

   1. _____

   2. _____

   3. _____

   4. _____

   5. _____

   (Add more as needed.)

5. For a paragraph, outline your paragraph using the following paragraph outline, changing it to fit your topic. Add as many supports and specifics as you need for your topic. (Then skip to prompt 7.)

Topic sentence: Subject of analysis or division _____

_____

    I. Element or part #1 _____

      A. Supporting detail_____

      B. Supporting detail_____

   II. Element or part #2_____

      A. Supporting detail_____

      B. Supporting detail_____

  III. Element or part #3_____

      A. Supporting detail_____

      B. Supporting detail_____

6. If you are writing an essay, examine the list to determine whether you can group or break the parts or elements into logical divisions around which to structure your paragraphs. Next, outline your body paragraphs, developing one for each major element or part of your analysis or division. Add as many supports and specifics as you need for your topic. Use the following essay outline, changing it as needed to fit your topic

    I. Introduction _____

      Thesis: Subject of analysis or division _____

      _____

   II. Element or part #1_____

      A. Support topic_____

      B. Support topic_____

      C. Support topic _____

  III. Element or part #2_____

      A. Support topic_____

      B. Support topic_____

      C. Support topic _____

  IV. Element or part #3_____

      A. Support topic_____

      B. Support topic_____

      C. Support topic _____

   V. Conclusion_____

- Use a technique such as brainstorming, freewriting, listing, clustering, or dividing to generate ideas for your introduction. How can you get your reader's attention?

- Generate ideas for your conclusion. Can you refer back to something in your introduction to conclude your paper? Can you restate the main points of your essay?

7. Working from your outline, write a draft of your paragraph or essay.

8. Get feedback on your writing.

9. Revise your writing using the feedback you received or using the Revision Checklist on page 62 (for paragraphs) or page 82 (for essays).

10. Edit your writing using the Editing Checklist on page 65 (for paragraphs) or page 87 (for essays).

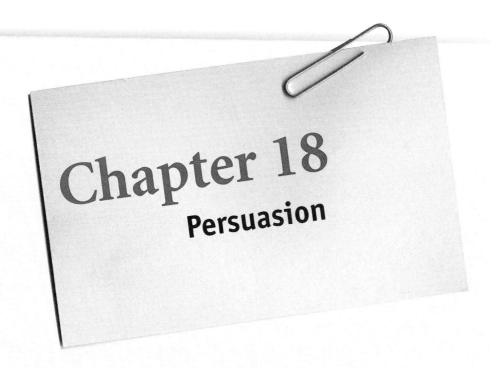

Chapter 18
Persuasion

Persuasion is really a purpose not a pattern, and all the rhetorical patterns can be used to help persuade a reader. In persuasion, the writer attempts to convince the reader to share an opinion or point of view on an issue. Facts, statistics, examples, testimony from authority, and logical reasoning can all be used to support an opinion. In formal arguments, the writer not only presents evidence to support his or her opinion but also refutes the opposition. To refute the opposition means to show why the opposite side of an argument (the logic or evidence used by those who oppose your position) is not valid. Persuasion is useful in many college classes because many assignments require you to present evidence to support your opinion or point of view.

Examples of Persuasion

PEER EXAMPLE

Paragraph

> ❝I argued against corporal punishment primarily by showing that it has negative effects.❞

Put Away the Paddle

Corporal punishment should not be used in secondary schools. First, corporal punishment aggravates antisocial behavior. Most parenting books advise parents to teach their children to solve conflicts using words rather than resorting to physical violence. When schools resort to physical punishment to resolve problems, they teach children it is acceptable to solve problems by hitting. Second, corporal punishment blocks the opportunity for communication between teacher and student. Many students who are behavior problems in school are acting out because of real or perceived injustices at home or in society. The teacher may be the only person in the student's life who is able and willing to help him. If, however, the teacher resorts to paddling, any chance at communication and positive growth is lost. Finally, corporal punishment instills fear rather than respect. Respect comes from the fair and even-handed use of authority, not from punitive measures that rob an individual of dignity. A faculty or an administration that uses paddling to solve discipline problems is relying on brute force and fear rather than on respect. Corporal punishment is worse than useless; it aggravates the very problems it is intended to solve.

PEER EXAMPLE

Essay

Put Away the Paddle

Corporal punishment is once again being accepted in many high schools. In an age when students are less orderly and less disciplined than ever before, parents and teachers perceive paddling as an effective way to instill orderliness in the student body. However, it is only a good solution for an authority too callous or too frustrated to examine the problem and come up with constructive solutions. Our school administrations must not abdicate their responsibility to model constructive problem-solving behavior. Corporal punishment is counterproductive because it aggravates antisocial behavior in the student, breaks down communication between teacher and student, and instills fear rather than respect.

Corporal punishment aggravates antisocial behavior. Most parenting books advise parents to teach their children to solve conflicts using words rather than resorting to physical violence. Surely, solving problems with words rather than force is a value we wish to instill in our children if we wish them to be nonviolent members of society. However, when schools resort to physical punishment to resolve problems, they teach children that it is acceptable to solve problems by hitting. Not only is corporal punishment a bad example, but it aggravates the problem because it makes the student angrier than he was in the first place. As a result, the student will become even more rebellious against a system he sees as unfair and hypocritical. Additionally, other students may see the student who was paddled as a kind of hero or martyr to authority, thus gaining the student the attention and respect of his peers.

In addition to aggravating antisocial behavior, corporal punishment blocks the opportunity for communication between teacher and student. Many students who are behavior problems in school are acting out because of real or perceived injustices at home or in society. The teacher may be the only person who can be objective and helpful to the student. Rather than recommending that the student be paddled or doing the paddling himself, the teacher should sit down with the student and attempt to discover the reasons for the inappropriate behavior. The teacher may be the only person in the student's life who is able and willing to help him. These are the hardest years of the student's emotional life, the years in which he will establish his emotional identity and his relation to society. The teacher is in an excellent position to help him grow. If, however, the teacher resorts to paddling, any chance at communication and positive growth are lost.

Finally, corporal punishment instills fear rather than respect. Everyone would agree that students need to learn respect for authority if they are to be productive, nonviolent members of society. Respect, however, comes from the fair and even-handed use of authority, not from punitive measures that rob an individual of dignity. It is impossible to respect someone or something that treats you unfairly or with disrespect, and it would be impossible to respect someone who is paddling you. Paddling is the most primitive way of saying, "I can enforce my power over you with disrespect." Nothing can come from this attitude but continued discord. A faculty or an administration that uses paddling to solve discipline problems is relying on brute force and fear rather than on respect.

Corporal punishment is worse than useless; it aggravates the very problems it is intended to solve. Paddling a secondary school student compounds the anger and alienation in a young person who is living through the most difficult and crucial years of his life. It robs the teacher of the opportunity to help the student by modeling constructive problem-solving strategies, and it instills fear of authority rather than respect for authority. A school system that relies on paddling is abdicating its responsibility

How Is Persuasion Organized?
Arguments are structured around the evidence or reasons the writer presents to prove the opinion.

PARAGRAPH OUTLINE	PEER EXAMPLE

Topic sentence: Opinion
   I. Main topic #1
     A. Supporting detail
     B. Supporting detail
  II. Main topic #2
     A. Supporting detail
     B. Supporting detail
 III. Main topic #3
     A. Supporting detail
     B. Supporting detail
	Topic sentence: Corporal punishment should not be used in secondary schools.
	   I. Aggravates antisocial behavior
	     A. Parenting books recommend using words, not force
	     B. Schools teach bad lesson with paddling
	  II. Blocks opportunity for communication
	     A. Students who act out may be suffering
	     B. Teacher in a position to help
	     C. Paddling destroys possibility of communication
	 III. Instills fear rather than respect
	     A. Respect comes from fairness, not punishment
	     B. Faculty that uses paddling relies on brute force, not reason

ESSAY OUTLINE	PEER EXAMPLE

I. Introduction
     Thesis: Opinion
  II. Main topic #1
     A. Support topic
       1. Specific support
       2. Specific support
     B. Support topic
     C. Support topic
	I. Thesis: Corporal punishment is counterproductive because it aggravates antisocial behavior in the student, breaks down communication between teacher and student, and instills fear rather than respect.

III. Main topic #2
   A. Support topic
   B. Support topic
      1. Specific support
      2. Specific support
IV. Main topic #3
   A. Support topic
      1. Specific support
      2. Specific support
   B. Support topic
   C. Support topic
V. Conclusion

II. Aggravates antisocial behavior
   A. Advice of parenting books
      1. Teach talking, not hitting
      2. Social importance of problem solving
   B. Schools model bad behavior
   C. Makes students angrier
      1. May become heroes
      2. Reinforce inappropriate behavior
III. Blocks communication
   A. Students acting out for reason
   B. Teacher could be helpful
      1. Talk to student
      2. Investigate problem
   C. Difficult years for teenagers
      1. Establishing identity
      2. Relation to society
   D. Teachers could help student grow
   E. Opportunity lost if paddling used
IV. Instills fear rather than respect
   A. Students should learn respect
      1. Respect comes from fairness
      2. Not disrespect
   B. Paddling is disrespectful
   C. Continued discord
V. Conclusion

Sample Thesis Statements for Persuasion

The thesis should state an opinion (a statement of belief, point of view, feeling, or attitude that can be discussed or argued about). A blueprinted thesis lists the major support areas (the reasons why the opinion is true). The list of supports in a blueprinted thesis should be parallel. The elements should be in the same form: all nouns, all prepositional phrases, all verb phrases, etc.

 **EXAMPLES**

Smokers should stop smoking because smoking damages their health, their appearance, and their pocketbook. (blueprinted thesis)	This blueprinted thesis announces the opinion, that smokers should kick the habit, and the three major reasons why smokers should quit. Notice that the list of reasons is parallel because each element is a noun.
Students who plagiarize should be expelled from college because they hurt the institution, they hurt other students, and they hurt themselves. (blueprinted thesis)	This blueprinted thesis states the reasons why students who plagiarize should be expelled. Again notice the parallelism in the list of major details: all are independent clauses that begin with *they hurt*.
Fairhope College should computerize its registration process in order to save time, money, and frustration. (blueprinted thesis)	This blueprinted thesis states the reasons why Fairhope College should computerize registration. The major details are parallel: all are nouns.
Return of the Swamp Monster is a terrible movie.	The thesis states a clear opinion, but does not list supports.

Transitions

Use transitions appropriate for the rhetorical patterns and ideas used to support the opinion.

Tips on Planning Persuasion

In writing a persuasive paragraph or essay, the writer states the idea or belief he or she is trying to convince the reader to share and then backs that idea up with supports, evidence, or reasons why that belief is valid.

1. Decide on the opinion you want your specific audience to share.

2. Formulate a tentative thesis statement.

3. Generate ideas to support your opinion. Focus on the reasons why your opinion is true. Examine each of the rhetorical patterns in Chapters 8 through 17 to see which might be useful in helping to prove your thesis.

4. In a formal argument essay, you may be required to refute the opposition case. To do so, generate a list of supports for the opposition and think of reasons why the points are not valid.

PITFALLS

1. *Avoid factual topics.* If a topic is either true or false, the answer can be looked up or researched, but there is no purpose for argument. For example, there would be no point arguing that the Denver Broncos won the Super Bowl in 1999 because the statement is either true or false, and no amount of arguing will alter the facts.

2. *Avoid obvious topics.* If everyone would agree with a statement, then there is little point in building a careful argument to support it. For example, since most people would agree with the statement that smoking damages a person's health, you would have to work very hard to get an audience's attention with this argument. (You can do it, but you have to find a way to make an argument that your audience has not already heard many times.) A more interesting and controversial topic for a general audience would be the statement that smoking should be banned in the workplace or in public places.

3. *Avoid oversimplification.* Don't oversimplify a complex problem or you will lose credibility. For example, if you argue that the planet's pollution problems could be solved if we all recycled, you will lose your audience's trust—most people know that our pollution problems cannot be solved so easily.

4. *Avoid unfair arguments.* Don't distort the truth or mislead your audience, and don't unfairly characterize the opposition or its case. For example, it would be unfair to characterize the opposition as a bunch of fools or dismiss their case as flimsy or ridiculous without presenting evidence.

Writing Topics

1. Argue for or against attendance requirements at your school.

2. Argue for or against requiring students to pass a skill test before graduation from high school or before continuing to the junior year of college.

3. Argue for or against strict penalties for academic dishonesty.

4. Argue for or against immigration quotas.

5. Argue for or against providing convicted criminals with educational opportunities.

6. Argue for or against raising or lowering the drinking, driving, or voting age.

7. Argue for the legalization of something that is currently illegal or the criminalization of something that is currently legal.

8. Persuade someone to change his or her behavior in some way.

9. Argue that home schooling is or is not a sound way to educate children.

10. Argue that women should or should not serve in the military.

Writing Process Prompts for Persuasion

1. Determine the opinion you want your audience to share.

2. Determine your specific purpose, audience, and tone.

   Specific purpose: _____

   Audience: _____

   Tone: _____

3. Write a tentative main idea or thesis statement.

   _____

   _____

4. Generate a list of reasons why your opinion is true.

5. Generate specific details for each support and a clear statement of how your support proves the opinion.

6. For a paragraph, outline your paragraph using the following paragraph outline, changing it to fit your topic. (Then skip to prompt 8.)

Topic sentence: Opinion or point of view_____

_____

    I. Support #1 _____

      A. Supporting detail_____

      B. Supporting detail_____

   II. Support #2 _____

      A. Supporting detail_____

      B. Supporting detail_____

  III. Support #3 _____

      A. Supporting detail_____

      B. Supporting detail_____

7. If you are writing an essay, examine the list to determine whether you can break the ideas you have generated into logical divisions around which to structure your paragraphs. Outline your body paragraphs, developing one for each major point or reason why your opinion is valid. Use the following essay outline, changing it as needed to fit your topic.

    I. Introduction _____

      Thesis: _____

   II. Major idea or support #1_____

      A. Support topic_____

      B. Support topic_____

      C. Support topic _____

  III. Major idea or support #2_____

      A. Support topic_____

      B. Support topic_____

      C. Support topic _____

  IV. Major idea or support #3_____

      A. Support topic_____

      B. Support topic_____

      C. Support topic _____

   V. Conclusion_____

- Use a technique such as brainstorming, freewriting, listing, clustering, or dividing to generate ideas for your introduction. How can you get your reader's attention? Do you need to provide background information to help your reader understand your argument?

- Generate ideas for your conclusion. Can you refer back to something in your introduction to conclude your paper? Can you restate the main points of your essay?

7. Working from your outline, write a draft of your paragraph or essay.

8. Get feedback on your writing.

9. Revise your writing using the feedback you received or using the Revision Checklist on page 62 (for paragraphs) or page 82 (for essays).

10. Edit your writing using the Editing Checklist on page 65 (for paragraphs) or page 87 (for essays).

Part VI

Writing Elements and Skills

Introduction

All the writing you do, in fact every sentence you write in letters, e-mails, and school papers, requires you to use many different skills. You must choose the appropriate words and spell them correctly, combine the words into clauses and phrases, and connect all the parts so that they make sense and read smoothly. This section of *Writer's Resources* covers the elements and skills you need to write college-level sentences.

Chapters 19 and 27 will introduce you to the parts of sentences and familiarize you with the grammatical vocabulary used by writers and their teachers to explain sentence structure. In Chapters 23, 31, and 32 you will learn to choose appropriate words and vary and combine sentences. The skills chapters will introduce you to all the individual skills necessary to write without making English errors.

All of the concepts and skills in this part of *Writer's Resources* will help you become a better writer. You should read the chapters in the order as assigned by your instructor, and you should complete all exercises and practices—they will help you make the concepts and skills part of your working knowledge of the written word.

Chapter 19
Parts of Speech

In English, words can be classified into the eight **parts of speech**. You should become familiar with the parts of speech in order to understand the proper grammatical structure of sentences and to use words in prescribed ways.

Nouns

A **noun** is a word that names a **person**, **place**, **thing**, or **idea**.

Examples: Faye, baseball player, home, lake, Singapore, space

There are several kinds of nouns:

- **Proper nouns** name particular persons, places, things, and ideas. They are always capitalized: *Will Rogers, White House, Renaissance.*

- **Common nouns** name general persons, places, things, and ideas. They are not capitalized: *singer, cafeteria, park.*

- **Concrete nouns** name things that can be seen, heard, smelled, tasted, or touched: *wall, music, smoke.*

- **Abstract nouns** name things that cannot be seen, heard, smelled, tasted, or touched: *love, fear, death.*

- **Collective nouns** name a group or collection. Many collective nouns are singular: *class, team, family, company or business.*

A noun can be **singular** (referring to one person, place, or thing) or **plural** (referring to more than one). The most common way to make a noun plural is to add *-s* (or *-es*, for most nouns ending in *o, x, z, sh, ch, ss,* or *y*).

> one chair → two chair**s**
>
> one beach → many beach**es**
>
> a street → some street**s**
>
> the box → no box**es**

Some nouns have **irregular plurals**.

> one child → two or more child**ren**
>
> one man → two or more m**en**
>
> one woman → two or more wom**en**
>
> one person → two or more **people**

Pronouns

Pronouns take the place of nouns. The noun to which the pronoun refers is called the **antecedent**.

> Antecedent   Pronoun
>
> The **doctor** sent me a bill for the services **she** provided

> Antecedent   Pronoun
>
> The **campers** lost **their** way in the woods.

- **Personal pronouns** refer to specific people or things.

  > Singular: I, me, you, he, she, him, her, it
  > Plural: we, us, you, they, them

- **Possessive pronouns** indicate ownership.

  > Singular: my, mine, your, yours, her, hers, his, its
  > Plural: our, ours, your, yours, their, theirs

- **Pronoun case** refers to the form of a pronoun. The case of a pronoun shows how that pronoun is used in the sentence; it indicates the pronoun's relation to the other words in the sentence. If the pronoun is used as a subject, use the subjective case. If the pronoun is used as an object, use the objective case.

	Subjective Case	Objective Case	Possessive Case
Singular	I	me	my/mine
	you	you	your/yours
	he/she/it	him/her/it	his/her/its
Plural	we	us	our/ours
	you	you	your/yours
	they	them	their/theirs

Subjective case

S V

I like to study early in the morning.

Objective case

S   V   O

Dad asked **me** to go fishing.

Possessive case

Her brother loves to polish **his** boots.

- **Reflexive pronouns** are formed by adding *-self* or *-selves* to personal pronouns. Reflexive pronouns indicate that the doer and receiver of the action are the same.

> Singular: myself, yourself, himself, herself, itself
> Plural: ourselves, yourselves, themselves
>
> ---
>
> I taught **myself** to play bridge.

A reflexive pronoun is called an **intensive pronoun** when it emphasizes its antecedent.

George **himself** rose to rebut the charges.

The boys decided their punishment **themselves**.

Writers should avoid using **nonstandard forms of reflexive pronouns**. These forms are always errors.

The boy picked **hisself** (himself) up when he fell.

The birds splashed water on **theirselves** (themselves).

My brother and his friend congratulated **themself** (themselves) on their win.

- **Relative pronouns** introduce dependent clauses and refer to a noun or pronoun that comes before them.

> who, whom, whose, which, that, whoever, whomever, whatever
>
> ---
>
> My brother is the one **who** won the race.
>
> Mary is the woman **whom** I interviewed for the assignment.
>
> The second test, **which** I passed, was harder than the first.
>
> *Crime and Punishment* is the book **that** is overdue at the library.

- **Interrogative pronouns** take the place of a noun in a question.

> who, whom, whose, which, what
>
> ---
>
> **Who** won the game last night?
>
> **Whom** did Mary play in the championship?
>
> **What** did you buy at the store?

- **Demonstrative pronouns** identify or point to nouns. They may function as **adjectives** that describe nouns or as **pronouns** that replace nouns.

> Singular: this, that
> Plural: these, those
>
> ---
>
> *Adjective*
> **This** shirt is stained.
>
> *Pronoun*
> **This** is my sister.

- An **indefinite pronoun** functions as a noun, but it does not refer to any particular person or thing.

Indefinite Pronouns

all	everybody	nothing
another	everyone	one
any	everything	several
anybody	few	some
anyone	many	somebody
anything	neither	someone
both	nobody	something
each	none	
either	no one	

Take special notice of **agreement** with indefinite pronouns. Most indefinite pronouns are *singular* and must take a singular verb. However, some indefinite pronouns are plural and take a plural verb. A few indefinite pronouns may be either singular or plural depending on the noun or pronoun to which they refer. Chapter 25 covers more information and practice on subject-verb agreement.

Singular indefinite pronouns and singular verbs:

   Everything in my kitchen **has** its place.

   Everyone in the class **does** her own work.

Plural indefinite pronouns and plural verbs:

   Both of my sisters **are** studying for their exams.

   Several candidates **present** their platforms tonight.

Singular or plural indefinite pronouns and their corresponding verbs:

   Singular: **None** of the money **is** missing

   Plural: **None** of the books **are** missing.

- **Phrasal**, or **reciprocal**, **pronouns** refer to individual parts of a plural antecedent.

  Phrasal Pronouns

  each other

  one another

Each other is generally used when the antecedent is two people. *One another* is used when the antecedent is more than two people.

Juan and Maria helped **each other** over the creek.

The three girls answered **one another's** questions.

Verbs

A **verb** is a word that expresses an action or a state of being.

Action

That child **plays** quietly.

State of Being

The child **feels** happy.

There are three kinds of verbs:

- **Action** (expresses an action): talk, strike, fight.

  The dean **talks** on the telephone frequently.

- **Linking** (links the subject to a noun or adjective): is, are, was, were, be, been, feel, look, seem, become, smell, sound, taste.

  The weather **is** beautiful.

- **Helping or auxiliary** (links subject to a verb): is, are, was, were, am, been, being, was, could, might, will, would, shall, should, did, must, can, may, have, has, had, do.

  Helping verb + action verb
  I **could have gone** to the store after work.

There are three main forms of the verb: the **present, past,** and **past participle**. While most verbs form the past tense and past participle by adding *-ed* to the verb, many common verbs have irregular past tense and past participle forms. See Chapter 26 for a list of irregular verbs.

Present	Past	Past Participle
walk	walked	walked
do	did	done
go	went	gone

The **form of the verb** changes according to its **tense** (present, past, future, present perfect, past perfect, future perfect); **number** (singular or plural); **voice** (active, passive); and **mood** (indicative, imperative, subjunctive).

From the three main verb forms comes the tense of the verb, which indicates the time of the action or state of being of the subject. There are six different tenses: present, past, future, present perfect, past perfect, future perfect. See Chapter 26 for more on verb tenses.

The verb must agree with its subject in **number**. A singular subject must take a singular verb, and a plural subject must take a plural verb. *Verbs usually have a different ending in the third-person singular of the present tense.*

	Singular	**Plural**
First-person	I walk	We walk
Second-person	You walk	You walk
Third-person	She walks	They walk
	He walks	
	It walks	

The **voice** of the verb can be **active** (subject is acting) or **passive** (subject is being acted upon.) See Chapter 26 for more on active and passive voice.

Active voice
Jerry **throws** the ball.

Passive voice
The ball **is being thrown** by Jerry.

The **mood** of the verb is the tone or attitude with which a statement is made.

- **Indicative** (used to make statements and ask questions).

    Citizens **should vote** this Tuesday.

- **Imperative** (used to give command or directions).

    Vote this Tuesday.

- **Subjunctive** (used to express wishes and requests or to express conditions contrary to fact).

    I wish it **were** Tuesday.

Verbs can also take different forms called verbals. **Verbals** are words that come from a verb but act as another part of speech.

- **Infinitives** (verb form introduced by *to*).

    My ambition is **to become** an engineer.

- **Gerunds** (verb form ending in *-ing* that acts as a noun).

    Eating is my brother's favorite activity.

- **Participles** (verb form usually ending in *-ing* or *-ed* that acts as a verb or an adjective).

    Built in 1890, the bank should be preserved.

Prepositions

A **preposition** explains the relationship between its *object* (the noun or pronoun that follows it) and another word in the sentence. Many prepositions explain time or space relationships.

Prep   Prep

After eating, the cat leaped **onto** the table.

(*After* explains the relationship of the word *eating* to the word *cat*. *Onto* explains the relationship of the word *leaped* to the word *table*.)

Common Prepositions

about	behind	in	outside of
above	below	in addition to	over
according to	beneath	inside	since
across	beside	in spite of	through
after	besides	instead of	throughout
against	between	into	to
along	beyond	like	toward
along with	by	near	under
among	despite	of	until
around	down	off	up
as	during	on	upon
as far as	except	on account of	with
at	for	on top of	within
before	from	out	without

The preposition and its object together form a **prepositional phrase**. A prepositional phrase can appear anywhere in a sentence. Note, however, that the object of a prepositional phrase cannot be the subject of the sentence.

        S   Prep Phrase V
The people **in the class** are talking.

Prep Phrase   S   V
In the class, people are talking.

    S   V   Prep Phrase
People are talking **in the class**.

Adjectives

An **adjective** describes or modifies a noun or pronoun.

     A   N   A   A   N
A **lazy** river curved through a **majestic, colorful** canyon.

The **articles** *a, an,* and *the* are adjectives that modify a noun. *A* is used before a word that begins with a consonant or consonant sound. *An* is used before a word that begins with a vowel or silent *h*.

a boy, a doctor, an apple, an A grade

In addition to describing a noun, an adjective can compare nouns (**comparative**) or show that a noun is the best (**superlative**). For most adjectives of one syllable, add *-er* to form the comparative and *-est* to form the superlative.

Comparative
The Tigers are **better** than the Red Sox.

Superlative
The Tigers are the **best** team.

For most adjectives of more than one syllable, add *more* to form the comparative and *most* to form the superlative.

Comparative
Beth's answer was **more** thoughtful than Xian's.

Superlative
Beth's answer was the **most** thoughtful.

Adjectives that end in *-y* usually form the comparative and superlative by dropping the *-y* and adding *-ier* or *-iest*.

Beth's answer was the **most** thoughtful.

Jean was **prettier** than Mary, and Wanda was **prettiest** of all.

Some adjectives are **irregular**.

Adjective	Comparative	Superlative
good	better	best
bad	worse	worst

Adverbs

An **adverb** modifies or describes a verb, adjective, or other adverb. Many adverbs end in *-ly*.

         V   Adv

The dog barked **fiercely**.

     Adv   Adj   Adv   Adv

The **fiercely** obedient dog sat **really attentively** by the man's side.

Many descriptive words can be used as either adjectives or adverbs, and you must be careful not to confuse them. Be particularly careful with *real/really* and *good/well.* Remember that *real* and *good* are adjectives and can only describe nouns. *Really* and *well* are adverbs and describe verbs, adjectives, and other adverbs.

           Adv   Adj

The mailman was **really** afraid.

    V Adv

He did **well** on the test.

Conjunctions

A **conjunction** joins words or groups of words. The two most common types of conjunctions are coordinating conjunctions and subordinating conjunctions.

Coordinating conjunctions join a word to a word, a phrase to a phrase, or a clause to a clause: **f**or, **a**nd, **n**or, **b**ut, **o**r, **y**et, **s**o

    Note: FANBOYS is a helpful mnemonic for remembering the coordinating conjunctions.

We usually vacation in winter **or** summer. (joins two words)

In the morning, we went down the path **and** into the woods. (joins two phrases)

I like English, **but** I hate math. (joins two independent clauses)

Subordinating conjunctions show the relationship between clauses. They connect a dependent clause to an independent clause.

Subordinating Conjunctions		
after	in order that	until
although	since	when
as	so that	where
because	that	whereas
before	though	while
if	unless	

Ind Clause   Dep Clause

I am going fishing with Tom **because** tomorrow is my day off.

Conjunctive adverbs also join clauses.

Common Conjunctive Adverbs

therefore, however, moreover, also, then, for example

Conj Adv

I don't feel well today; **therefore**, I will stay home from work today.

Interjections

An **interjection** communicates a strong emotion and is separated from the rest of the sentence by a punctuation mark such as a comma or an exclamation point.

Common Interjections

wow, yikes, watch out, hey, ouch, OK

Watch out! You're going to hit that tree.

Hey, that piece of pie is mine!

Chapter 20
Spelling

Spelling is an important skill. Misspelled words are not only distracting to the reader but may also be confusing—in fact, a misspelling can entirely change your meaning

Your spelling will improve if you

- Remember a few common spelling rules.

- Familiarize yourself with the most frequently misspelled words.

- Keep a record of your spelling errors.

- Use a computerized spellchecker when possible.

Common Rules for Spelling

The following rules have to do with particular combinations of **vowels** (*a, e, i, o, u,* and sometimes *y*) and **consonants** (all letters except vowels) and the rules for adding **endings** (such as *-ing, -ed*). In general, the pronunciation stays the same when word endings are added.

Rule 1

Use *i* before *e* except after *c*.

believe	receive
reprieve	deceive
friend	conceive

When the word makes a long *a* (*ay*) sound, use *e* **before** *i*.

neighbor	eight
weight	freight

Exceptions:

either	height	neither	weird
foreign	leisure	seize	

Rule 2

For a single-syllable word in which a vowel comes before a final consonant, **double** that **consonant** when adding an ending that begins with a vowel (such as -*ing, -ed, -er, -est*).

The last consonant is doubled to preserve the sound of the vowel.

bat + ed = batted	sit + ing = sitting
pen + ed = penned	run + er = runner
rob + ing = robbing	slim + est = slimmest

For multisyllable words in which the final syllable is stressed and a vowel comes before the final consonant, **double the final consonant** when adding an ending that begins with a vowel (such as -*ing, -ed, -er, -est*).

control + ed = controlled	begin + er = beginner
permit + ed = permitted	admit + ing = admitting
prefer + ed = preferred	commit + ing = committing
refer + ed = referred	patrol + ing = patrolling

Rule 3

Drop the final *e* on a word when adding an ending that begins with a vowel.

believe + er = believer	rake + ing = raking
like + able = likable	move + ed = movable

Keep the final *e* when adding an ending that begins with a consonant.

achieve + ment = achievement

rare + ly = rarely

like + ness = likeness

Exceptions:

argue + ment = argument

judge + ment = judgment

true + ly = truly

Rule 4

Drop the final *y* and add *i* when adding an ending if there is a consonant before the *y*.

pretty + er = prettier   reply + ed = replied

funny + est = funniest   happy + ness = happiness

try + ed = tried   beauty + ful = beautiful

rely + able = reliable

Keep the final *y* when adding an ending if there is a vowel before the *y*.

delay + ed = delayed

donkey + s = donkeys

play + er = player

For words ending in *y*, keep the final *y* when adding *-ing*.

Examples:

rely + ing = relying

reply + ing = replying

try + ing = trying

Exceptions:

lay + ed = laid

pay + ed = paid

say + ed = said

Frequently Misspelled Words

You can improve your spelling significantly by studying the following two lists of frequently misspelled words. Try to remember the spelling by looking at the bold letters that show what's unusual or tricky about the spelling of these one hundred words.

List 1: Everyday Words

across	finally	receive
actually	forty	regard
against	fourth	remember
a lot (two words)	forward	roommate
all right (two words)	friend	safety
almost	generally	science
although	grateful	sense
always	guard	sentence
among	happiness	several
answer	height	since
around	hungry	shining
article	interest	shoulder
attack	laid	simply
before	library	sophomore
beginning	likely	source
believe	marriage	speech
breath	meant	stopped
breathe	mere	stories
business	naturally	straight
careful	neither	strength
carried	niece	strict
clothes	ninety	studying
coming	ninth	supposed
dealt	paid	themselves
destroy	personal	therefore
dining	personnel	together
during	planned	truly
easily	poison	until
effect	possible	using
exercise	probably	view
experience	proving	writing
favorite	quiet	yield
field	really	

List 2: Academic Words

absence	equipped	pleasant
absorption	especially	practical
accomplishment	excellence	preparation
achievement	expense	proceed
acquire	experiment	procedure
amount	explanation	professor
annual	familiar	quantity
apparent	February	recognize
appearance	fulfill	recommend
appreciate	further	relative
argument	government	relieving
arrangement	independent	representative
attendance	intelligence	restaurant
attitude	involve	response
benefited	jealous	ridiculous
boundary	knowledge	sacrifice
category	laboratory	satisfied
ceiling	license	scenery
cemetery	liveliest	schedule
completely	luxury	separate
convenience	magazine	significance
curious	mathematics	succeed
decision	mechanics	surprise
dependent	medicine	suspense
description	morally	syllable
development	necessary	symbol
difference	neighbor	technique
disappoint	noticing	temperature
disease	operate	tendency
divide	opinion	theories
enemy	particular	variety
entertain	pastime	vegetable
environment	permitted	weird

Some Other Easy Ways to Improve Your Spelling

1. Correct spelling is becoming much easier to accomplish with the **spell checker** in your computer's word processing program and mechanical spell checkers for handwritten work. Be sure to use the spell checker before you finish writing a document. However, be aware that a spell checker cannot catch words that sound similar but are spelled differently or misspellings that are themselves words.

2. It's a good idea to keep a list of your common errors to study before writing. You will not always have a dictionary or spell checker handy, and you should know the spelling for common words in your vocabulary. Use the **personal error list** in the appendix at the end of this book to record your spelling errors.

Chapter 21
Problem Words

Words that **sound alike** or **have similar spellings** can cause problems for writers. Although there are many groups of **problem words**, the two lists in this chapter contain some of the most common word groups that give writers problems.

There are two easy ways to remember the differences between the words in these groups:

1. **Use a memory hook:** an easy way to remember something because it hooks your memory.

2. **Remember an example** for each word that illustrates the difference between the words.

List 1

Accept means "take" or "receive what is offered." With *accept*, think of acceptance.

I accept your invitation.

Except means "what is left out or excluded." Remember that the x in *except* means "not."

Everyone is here except Joaquin.

An means "one" or "any" and is used in front of words that begin with a vowel or silent *h*.

An airline pilot must fly for an hour before taking a break.

And means "plus."

Jean and Takela went to the store.

Its is the singular possessive pronoun meaning "belonging to it." Remember that *its* has lost its apostrophe (').

The car lost its antennae.

It's is the contraction of *it is* or *it has*. Remember that *it's = it'(i)s*.

It's a beautiful day.

Know means "to have knowledge of."

I know how to sew very well.

No means "zero."

There is no water in the dry well.

Passed is the past tense of the verb *to pass. Passed* ends in *-ed* because it's a verb.

I have passed the test.

Past is an adverb meaning "by" or "beyond," or an adjective or noun meaning "time that has already gone by."

The bus went past the bus stop every day this past week.

Peace means "tranquillity." Remember "P*eace* on *E*arth!"

There was peace after the war.

Piece means "a part of something." Remember "p*iece* of p*ie*."

A piece of thread is hanging from your sleeve.

Principal is an adjective meaning "main" or "most important," or a noun meaning "main person or thing."

    The principal road into town is Main Street.

Principle is a noun meaning "rule" or "law." Remember "princip*le* = ru*le*."

    One principle of math is addition.

Right can refer to something that is due to a person by law. Remember that "mi*ght* does not make ri*ght*."

    My neighbor has a right to park in the driveway to his house.

Write means "put words on paper." Remember that the *w* in *w*rite looks like a scribble.

    Please write your name clearly.

Steal means "rob." Remember ste*al* = illeg*al*.

    A robber could steal the bicycle.

Steel refers to a hard metal. Remember that the *ee* in *steel* is doubled to make it strong like the metal.

    The part for the machine was made of steel.

Suppose means "assume." No *d* means that *suppose* is a verb in the present tense.

    I suppose I will go to the dance unless I am sick.

Supposed to means "ought to" or "should." *Supposed to* is always preceded by a form of "*to be*" and followed by "*to*" plus a verb.

    Children are supposed to respect their parents.

Than is used to make comparisons. Remember: th*an* = comp*a*rison.

    Jackie is taller than Raphael.

Then means "for a moment in time." Remember: th*en* = tim*e*.

    First, we will go to the movie; then we will go to eat.

Their is a possessive pronoun meaning "belonging to them."
Remember: their = heir.

The neighbors should cut their lawn.

There can mean a place. Remember: there = not here.

There is a car over there in the parking lot that looks brand new.

They're is the contraction of *they are*. Remember: they're = they are.

The children are quiet because they're watching a movie.

Thorough means "complete" or "entire." Remember that *thorough* has
an *o* for *complete*.

The house needs a thorough cleaning.

Through can mean "in one side and out the other" or "finished."

The last person went through the door after the movie was through.

Throw means "launch" or "send."

The mayor will throw out the first ball at the baseball game.

Threw is the past tense of the verb *throw*.

The pitcher threw the last pitch.

To is either a preposition that indicates direction or a part of the infinitive verb form (to be, to go, to do).

I am going to the store to buy groceries.

Too means "excessively," "extremely," or "also." Remember too = too
many o's.

It's too hot to play outside.

Two is the number.

Two boys are fishing on the bridge.

Use to means "utilize" and is present tense.

That wood I will use to make a fire.

Used to means "having the habit" and is past tense. It always includes
to + verb (used to eat).

The mailman used to arrive before lunch.

Weather means "outdoor air conditions."

> The rainy weather is almost over.

Whether indicates alternatives.

> I don't know whether I can come or not.

Woman is the opposite of "man" in the singular form.

> One woman left already.

Women is the plural form of "woman."

> Two women are staying to hear the last speaker.

Would have, could have, should have, and **must** have are verb phrases; have is a helping verb. The contraction forms are **would've, could've, should've,** and **must've**.

> The garbage should have been taken out last night.

> The garbage should've been taken out last night.

Would of, could of, should of, and **must of**: The *of* that follows the verbs begins a prepositional clause. (*Note:* This construction is very rare; use of any of these phrases is almost always an error.)

> You would, of all people, be the first to know my secret.

Your is the possessive pronoun meaning "belonging to you."

> Your uncle just called.

You're is the contraction of *you are*.

> You're the most interesting person that I know.

Exercise 1

Circle the correct words in each sentence.

1. We past/passed a soft drink machine an/and stopped to get a drink.

2. The neighbors use to/used to park they're/their/there cars over they're/their/there by the pool.

3. When she went thorough/through the rain she got a thorough/through soaking.

4. They're/Their/There trying to/too/two hard for them to fail the writing/righting exam.

5. The truck should of/should have past/passed the car to avoid an/and accident.

List 2

Advice is a noun that means "a recommendation."

My father has given me good advice about my finances.

Advise is a verb that means "counsel."

The doctor will advise you to stop smoking.

Affect is a verb that means "influence" or "bring about a change." Remember *affect* is an action.

The temperature can affect plants.

Effect is a noun that means "result." Remember *effect* is a result.

One effect of exercising is weight loss.

All ready means that everyone or everything is prepared. Remember that if the sentence makes sense without *all*, write *all ready*.

My children are all ready for school.

Already means "before," "previously," or "by this time." Remember that if the sentence does not make sense without *all*, write *already*.

Dinner has been served already.

All together means that everything or everyone is together. Remember that if the sentence makes sense without *all*, write *all together*.

> The camping gear is all together in the closet.

Altogether means "completely" or "entirely." Remember that if the sentence does not make sense without *all*, write *altogether*.

> I have altogether too much work to do tonight.

Bare means "uncovered" or "just enough."

> There is barely time to reach the airport before our plane leaves.

Bear means the wild animal or "to carry", "hold up," or "endure."

> I can't bear the thought of school starting again after our vacation.

Blew is the past tense of *blow*.

> The wind blew all night long.

Blue is the color. Remember that "blue" = color or hue.

> Her eyes are blue.

Brake means a device to stop movement.

> The car's brakes needed to be replaced.

Break means an interruption.

> I must take a break before I continue working.

By is a preposition.

> My sister will stop by our apartment with cookies.

Buy means "purchase."

> You need to buy milk.

Capital means "main" or "most important."

The capital city of New York is Albany.

Capitol means the government building. Remember that capit**ol** = d**o**me.

Congress meets in the Capitol in Washington.

Choose means "pick out"; it is present tense. Remember "choose has two o's to choose from."

I will choose a new car.

Chose is the past tense of *choose* and is pronounced with a long *o*.

The dinner I chose last night gave me food poisoning.

Complement is a verb meaning "make complete" or a noun meaning "something that completes or makes perfect."

The blue shirt complements your tan slacks.

Compliment is a verb or a noun meaning "praise."

My teacher gave me a compliment about my paper.

Fair means "just," "good," "blond," "pale," or "carnival." *Fair* is used for all meanings except money.

It's not fair when someone takes advantage of an elderly person.

Fare means the ticket price.

The movie fare was only five dollars.

Hear means to perceive by ear. Remember hear = ear.

I can't hear you when you are in the next room.

Here means location. Remember here = not there.

Please come here right now.

Hole means an opening.

> The workman used a shovel to dig the hole.

Whole means entire or complete.

> I can't believe that you ate the whole pie.

Lay means "place or put." If you can substitute *place* or *put* for *lay*, then *lay* is correct.

> Please lay the book on the table.

Lie means "recline."

> My grandfather always lies down before dinner.

Loose is an adjective meaning "not tight," or a verb meaning "set free."

> The door knob is loose and wobbles when I turn it.

Lose is a verb meaning "suffer loss." Remember lose = lost.

> People can lose a lot of money gambling.

Stationary means "not movable."

> The car was stationary when it was hit by the bus.

Stationery means writing paper. Remember station**ery** = pap**er**.

> The letter came on blue stationery.

Weak means the opposite of strong.

> A muscle can be weak after an injury.

Week means seven days.

> The meeting is next week.

Exercise 2

Circle the correct words in each sentence.

1. By the time she blew/blue out the candles, she was all ready/already out of breath.

2. Exercising on the stationary/stationery bike complemented/complimented the weightlifting the athlete was doing for conditioning.

3. The setback was hard to bare/bear, but he was all together/altogether sure he could win.

4. The table was bare/bear before the waiters began to lay/lie the dishes down for the meal.

5. Don't loose/lose any more time taking shortcuts because we are all ready/already late for the appointment.

Review Exercise 1

Underline incorrect problem words in each sentence.

1. I could of changed my answer, but I was all together sure that I choose the right one.

2. That women over their use to be my neighbor before she got married.

3. When I get a brake from my job, I will build a house made of steal and glass that will stay stationery in any kind of weather.

4. Over spring break, I visited our nation's capitol, Washington, D.C.

5. The women in the last row past her test even though she didn't study.

6. Though it wasn't lose and comfortable, I choose to wear the shirt my grandmother gave me to the picnic.

7. The plane and train rides at the amusement park were a hole lot of fun even though they remained stationery.

8. The principle reason I want to lay down for a rest is that I am suppose to stay up late tonight to study.

9. The dog's owner choose it's name from a comic strip.

10. The school's principle bearly had time to finish his speech before the band started playing.

Proofread the paragraph and correct any errors with problem words.

This passed weekend, my friend Jeremy and I decided to take a trip too an amusement park that I use to go to when I was a child. When we got there, I told Jeremy I wanted to ride the roller coaster. Since Jeremy likes to ride a roller coaster less then I do, he said that I should go on it by myself. Maybe I should of taken his advise, but I told him, "Know way! Your coming too because its to scary alone." Jeremy was fine while the ride was stationery, but as soon as it began too move, Jeremy began screaming at the top of his lungs. When the ride was over, Jeremy said that it had been altogether to long. Jeremy choose to sit the next ride out, so I had to go on it alone. When that ride was over, Jeremy had all ready decided that we should go shopping for souvenirs. I bought a teddy bear, and Jeremy chose to get a cup with his name on its side. I had to lend him money for the tax because he said that all of his lose change had fallen out of his pockets on the roller coaster. While we were shopping, the whether began to get cloudy, so I thought that we should have some lunch and wait for the sun to come out again. However, Jeremy said he couldn't bare to eat right after the roller coaster. Their was a man doing magic tricks, an we stopped to watch him. I was just about to complement him on his trick when it started to rain, and the hole crowd ran indoors accept for the magician. When the rain finally stopped, I was starving, and I convinced Jeremy to go for a peace of pizza. Our day at the amusement park was a lot of fun, and Jeremy and I are already planning to go back next weak.

Chapter 22
Capitalization

Capital letters announce to the reader that a word has special importance. You probably know many of the rules for capitalization, but this chapter will acquaint you with all the rules and give you practice testing your knowledge.

Sentence Beginnings

- Capitalize the **first word of a sentence**.

Proper Nouns

Names of specific people, places, and things are considered proper nouns, and all proper nouns should be capitalized.

People

- Proper names of people should be capitalized.

    Don Jordan, Lin Ying, LaToya Jones

- Proper titles are capitalized if they are used to replace someone's name.

    Are we going shopping on Friday, Mother?

    Please, Professor, don't give us more homework.

- Do not capitalize titles if they are not used to replace someone's name in a sentence. (If a word like *my* or *the* comes before the title, the title is not replacing a proper name.)

    I told my uncle that I would come.

- The pronoun *I* is considered a proper name and should be capitalized.

    Juan and I will return soon.

Places

- Proper names of specific geographic features and proper place names should be capitalized.

    Mount Everest, Arctic Ocean, Lake Superior, Banff National Park, Tiananmen Square, Namib Desert

    Do not capitalize places that are not proper names.

    the lake, the desert, an ocean, a mountain

- Names of cities, counties, states, regions, countries, continents, and planets should be capitalized.

    Budapest, Dekalb County, Illinois, the South, Romania, North America, Venus

    Prepositions are not capitalized in proper names unless they are the first or last word of the name.

    United States of America

- Directional words ending in *-ern* are not capitalized.

    western, northern, southern, eastern

Things

- Proper names of institutions, businesses, and federal agencies should be capitalized.

    Central High School, First National Bank, University of Tennessee, Holiday Inn, Environmental Protection Agency, Chicago Bulls

- Proper names of buildings and historical monuments should be capitalized.

    Statue of Liberty, Parthenon, Kennedy Center, Sistine Chapel

- Names of holidays should be capitalized.

    Fourth of July, Thanksgiving, Flag Day, Black History Month

- Days and months are capitalized.

    Monday, Tuesday, Saturday, January, March, December

- Names of seasons are not capitalized.

    spring, summer, fall, winter

- Names of specific school courses should be capitalized.

    Fundamentals of Algebra, College Composition

- Subject names that are not part of a course title are not capitalized.

    math, writing, history

- The first word, last word, and all important words in the titles of books, poems, articles, chapters, academic papers, songs, journals, and magazines should be capitalized. Prepositions, conjunctions, and articles are not capitalized unless they are the first or last word of the name.

    Journal of Education, Paradise Lost, The Grapes of Wrath, Working Woman

- Specific historical events and any eras or periods in history should be capitalized; however, centuries should not be capitalized.

    the Civil War, the Renaissance, the Roaring Twenties, the twenty-first century

- Nationalities and languages should generally be capitalized. Some phrases using a nationality, however, have made their way into common use and may not be capitalized; check with a dictionary and use the term consistently throughout your writing.

    Swedish, English, Swiss cheese, French pastries

- Abbreviations for agencies, organizations, trade names, and radio and television stations should be written in all-capital letters.

    KCAZ, WFHB, TVA, NASA, NFL

- Capitalize only the words of animal and plant names that refer to a specific place or person.

    German shepherd, Bermuda grass, cardinals, blue whales, roses, oak trees

Quotes

- The first word of a quoted sentence should be capitalized.

  He replied, "Nothing is wrong."

Review Exercise

Correct all capitalization errors.

1. My brother dan is a dentist and lives in new mexico.

2. The new york giants are going to win a football championship soon.

3. Most people thought that forrest gump was a funny movie.

4. Of all the planets, mars is closest to earth.

5. The southern part of florida is where i live.

6. Two doctors live in my neighborhood, which is called evergreen heights.

7. She is no longer speaking to her father or aunt julia.

8. On labor day, we might take a trip and go to the mountains.

9. My school, meridian senior high school, has been rated as one of the top high schools in the state.

10. The internal revenue service, which is called the irs, is investigating my boss.

Chapter 23
Word Choice

Words are the most basic element in how we communicate, yet most of us don't spend much time thinking about the words we choose. We often use the first word that comes to mind. Sometimes our choice effectively expresses our ideas, and sometimes it doesn't. In writing, perhaps even more so than in speaking, it's important to choose the best words. This chapter will make you aware of some of the issues surrounding word choice.

The words you select should be concrete and specific enough to create a picture in the reader's mind, appeal to the senses, create images, express your intended meaning, and have the right emotional associations.

You should choose vocabulary that is appropriate for your topic so that your reader will have confidence you know what you're talking about, and you should avoid language that might turn readers off or leave them cold—such as worn-out expressions and slang. This means you have a lot of decisions to make about which words fit and which do not. Writing is hard work, but the more aware you are of words, the better chance you'll have of picking language that is clear and precise.

Deciding which words to choose is important in two stages of the writing process—drafting and revising. In your first draft, you want to choose concrete, specific language that you are familiar with—nothing fancy, just clear language that communicates your meaning. When you are revising, you can go back and focus on language again. Take a look at your nouns and verbs; are they concrete and specific enough? Take a look at your vocabulary; is it appropriate for the topic? Get rid of slang, clichés, and unnecessary words and expressions. Start thinking about the language you use, and be aware of the language used in the essays you read. Nine times out of ten, what makes writing work, what makes it effective, is the language the author chooses.

This chapter will make you aware of some of the issues surrounding word choice: use of **concrete, specific language**; awareness of **denotation** and **connotation**; **appeal to the senses**; and use of **appropriate vocabulary**. We also caution you about **Pitfalls** to avoid: **unfamiliar synonyms, slang, clichés**, and **wordiness**.

Clear Language

Abstract and Concrete Words

Words can be divided into abstract or concrete. We know concrete words through our senses. You can see, touch, taste, hear, or smell a flower or a car. Abstract words, in contrast, we know through our minds. You can't touch or see abstractions like love and loyalty. We have to use abstract words to convey concepts like beauty and truth, but when we want to create a picture in the reader's mind, we should choose specific, concrete words.

If you are describing ideas and concepts, then abstract language is appropriate, as in the first examples below. However, if you are trying to help the reader see what you are describing, abstract language won't do the trick. In the concrete examples, the specific, concrete language creates a picture that helps the reader see the scene.

Examples:

Abstract

The men **fought** because they were **loyal** to their leader.

Their cowardice in the face of **adversity** was not something they were **proud** of.

Concrete

The woods behind my house are **densely packed** with **underbrush** and **tangled** with **wild grapes**.

The **grassy dune** where the **battle** took place was littered with the **mangled bodies** of **soldiers and horses**.

Exercise 1

Identify the following words as abstract or concrete.

1. chair
2. knowledge
3. doll
4. entertainment
5. intimidating
6. fire truck
7. cup
8. authority
9. beautiful
10. grass

General and Specific Words

Concrete words vary from **general** to **specific**. General nouns, even if they are concrete, won't help the reader see a picture of what you have in mind. After all, there are all kinds of cars, flowers, and bridges.

General	Specific
car	Rolls-Royce
flower	tulip
bridge	Golden Gate Bridge
shark	great white shark
cake	German chocolate cake

Very specific nouns communicate a clear image of what the writer has in mind.

Very General			Very Specific
tree	oak	red oak	Southern Red Oak
people	students	college students	college scholarship students
humans	children	toddlers	hyperactive toddlers

General	More Specific
She has a dog.	She has a dachshund.
We drove our car.	We drove our Mustang convertible.
The animals went wild.	The gorillas, cheetahs, and polar bears went wild.

Identify the following words as general or specific.

Exercise 2

1. movie
2. alligator
3. food
4. Mount Everest
5. tulip

6. waffles
7. actor
8. bluebird
9. dog
10. boat

Vivid Adjectives

Even when we use specific nouns, we sometimes need adjectives to create a more specific picture of what we have in mind. When appropriate, use **vivid adjectives** to describe nouns, other adjectives, and adverbs.

Specific Nouns	Noun Phrases with Vivid Adjectives
Rolls-Royce	white convertible Rolls-Royce
tulip	white convertible Rolls-Royce
great white shark	ten-foot, thousand-pound great white shark

Example:

To generate a clear picture of the dog in the following sentences, we have added increasingly specific words.

She has a **dog**.

She has a **long-haired dog**.

She has a **long-haired dachshund**.

She has a **long-haired dachshund with a white patch over one eye**.

Comma Usage with Adjectives

Coordinate Adjectives

Commas are needed between **coordinate adjectives**; these are adjectives that modify the noun separately (that is, each adjective modifies the noun directly). To determine whether a set of adjectives is coordinate, try either rearranging them or placing the word *and* between them.

Example:

She is a sweet, affectionate child.

In the sentence above, the adjectives are coordinate; they can be rearranged, and you can place *and* between them. It sounds just as good to say, "She is an affectionate, sweet child," or "She is a sweet and affectionate child."

Cumulative Adjectives

Commas are not needed between **cumulative adjectives**, which are adjectives that do not modify the noun separately.

Example:

He lived in a large brick house.

You don't need commas between the adjectives *large* and *brick* in the sentence above. They can't be rearranged, and you can't place and between them because it wouldn't sound right to say, "He lived in a brick large house," or "He lived in a large and brick house."

Place commas where needed in the following sentences.

Exercise 3

1. I bought a blue velvet dress for the prom.
2. My cousin is a tall handsome basketball player.
3. I've always been afraid of large growling dogs.
4. I love my yellow Mustang convertible.
5. My mother is an honest loving woman.

Specific Verbs

Like nouns, verbs vary from **general** to **specific**. General verbs tend to be weak, whereas specific verbs communicate an image to the reader and are therefore powerful.

Specific verbs help create an image of an action, just as specific nouns help create an image of people, places, and things. Specific verbs are known as strong verbs.

General Verbs	Specific Verbs
walk	stroll, stride, amble, glide, slink, creep
say	yell, scream, whisper, growl, snarl, chatter
eat	devour, nibble, gulp, inhale

> *When I revised my paragraph, I tried to use specific strong verbs that were right for the topic I was writing about.*

Luxury Ride

The interior of the new Supra minivan **is designed** for the driver's safety and comfort. When a motorist **enters** the vehicle, she **is offered** choices for adjusting the seat's height, distance from the steering wheel and lower back support, which **ensures** that every driver **is** properly **positioned** to operate the vehicle without straining, stretching, or hunching down. In front of the driver of a minivan, there's a beautifully displayed instrument panel with a digital display that **is lit** in bright colors for easy reading. Moreover, the console next to the driver **anticipates** her needs with its cup holders and organizer tray for tapes or CDs. When the van **is moving**, a computerized voice **warns** of unlocked doors or seat belts that are not fastened, which **puts** a driver at ease when carrying a van load of kids. The driver **can** even **control** the mirror on the passenger door to get a better look at the lanes of traffic, and the mirror on the back gate **allows** the driver to feel confident when backing into a parking space. The Supra's interior **makes** driving a pleasure.

To Be and *To Have*

The verbs *to be* and *to have* are general verbs. Often, more specific verbs can be used in their place.

Examples:

Weak
Mr. Tirkenhaas *is* the manager of the Steak House.

If your writing often uses the verbs *to be* and *to have*, try to find a more specific verb to fit a situation.

Strong
Mr. Tirkenhaas *manages* the Steak House.

Weak
The restaurant *has* a wide selection of desserts.

When you can replace *to be* or to *have* with another verb, your sentence will be stronger and more effective.

Strong
The restaurant *offers* a wide selection of desserts.

Identify the following verbs as general or specific:

Exercise 4

1. squint
2. exclaim
3. say
4. see
5. whisper

6. yell
7. slouch
8. shiver
9. feel
10. want

Circle the most appropriate verb from the two choices in each set of parentheses.

Exercise 5

A Difficult Destination

My girlfriend, Marianella Rolla, *stays* (lives, belongs) at the end of a long, winding dirt road that takes me forever to travel. There are so many potholes and tree roots that I must *go* (creep, move) along at under ten miles per hour so I don't *harm* (snap, hurt) an axle. It is even worse after a hard rain when puddles *are in* (hide, obscure, fill) the potholes and make me *go* (crawl, move) along the shoulder of the dirt road, or else my truck and I might *get wet* (bog down, drown). When the weather is dry, I have to be careful that my truck's tires don't *move* (slide, turn) in the loose sand and get stuck. Nighttime *is* (presents, has) the worst danger of getting lost because I can't *find* (see, locate) the landmarks that tell me where I am, and there is no street sign for the dirt lane that *goes* (leads, moves) into her driveway. Picking up my girlfriend for a date *is* (presents, makes) a real challenge!

Colorful Adverbs

When appropriate, use **colorful adverbs** to describe verbs, adjectives, and other adverbs.

Examples:

He rode along the mountain trail.

He rode **recklessly** along the mountain trail.

He rode **lightheartedly** along the mountain trail.

He rode **cautiously** along the mountain trail.

Notice how each adverb creates a completely different image

She stepped in front of the men.

She stepped **rudely** in front of the men.

She stepped **confidently** in front of the men.

She stepped **quickly** in front of the men.

The modifying adverb gives you more information about the action.

Exercise 6

Write a sentence by selecting a word from the list of descriptive words to replace each symbol and bold word or phrase.

1. The ♦ **child made a sound** ♦.

Adjective	child	made a sound	Adverb
spoiled	toddler	squealed	contentedly
hyperactive	baby	cooed	angrily
precocious	infant	murmured	softly
hungry	waif	yelled	happily
sleeping	whined	incessantly	
fussy			
sun-burned			

2. The ♦ **car went down** the ♦ **road**.

Adjective	car	went	down	Adjective	road
dusty	jeep	skidded	across	rain-slick	highway
shiny	limousine	slid	over	crowded	interstate
rusty	truck	flew	on	dusty	dirt road
huge	semi	rumbled	through	muddy	city street
sleek	dragster	accelerated		reflective	track

Create your own sentences by substituting specific nouns, vivid adjectives, strong verbs, and colorful adverbs.

1. The tree moved in the wind.

   _____

   _____

2. The clouds were in the sky.

   _____

   _____

3. The animal crossed the road.

   _____

   _____

4. The instructor gave an assignment.

   _____

   _____

5. The man caught the ball.

   _____

   _____

Denotation

Choose words that have the right **denotation**, or literal meaning. If you're not absolutely sure the word you have in mind is the right one, look it up in the dictionary. Nine times out of ten, you're better off choosing a word you are familiar with rather than one you think sounds sophisticated.

Circle the correct word in each sentence. Use a dictionary if you need to.

Exercise 7

1. The instructor is liable/likely to put anything on the exam.
2. Sonia looked real/really tired after the hike.
3. Chocolate cake is my favorite dessert/desert.
4. Jeremy wasn't conscious/conscience of the fact that he had hurt Alicia's feelings.
5. My brother Ernie refunded/refurbished his money.

Connotation

Choose words that have the right **connotation**, or emotional association. Words come with their own baggage; they have many shades of meanings. For example, it sounds a lot worse to say someone is a liar than to say he or she takes liberties with the truth.

Examples:

Positive Connotation	Negative Connotation	
slender	skinny	Describing a person as skinny sounds negative, whereas slender sounds attractive.
full	cluttered	When my wife tells me that my dresser drawer is cluttered, I know I have to straighten it up.
hurry	rush	While most of us are in a hurry in the morning, we know that being in a rush can cause accidents.
sociable	chatterbox	I'll never forget the look on my daughter's face when I remarked that she was a little chatterbox at the dance. I should have said that she was sociable.

Exercise 8

Circle the word that does not have a negative connotation.

1. The garbage had begun to rot/decompose.

2. The teacher's dress was colorful/gaudy.

3. The job applicant was dressed in disorganized/a casual manner.

4. During the performance, the auditorium was practically empty/deserted.

5. The man takes pride in having an antiseptic/a clean apartment.

Writing Style

Appeal to the Senses

Descriptive writing appeals to the **senses** (sight, touch, hearing, smell, and taste) and creates images or mental pictures.

> In describing my grandmother's rocking chair, I tried to use as much specific detail as possible and to appeal to as many of the senses as possible.

Memaw's Rocker

My grandmother's rocking chair **sits empty** [sight] in the corner of the living room. The **simple, unpainted cane rocker** [sight] would be of little interest to an antique dealer, but I wouldn't part with it for the world. The seat is cupped slightly from years of use: afternoons and evenings when she sat **shelling peas, darning socks, or knitting sweaters** [sight]. The arms are **sanded smooth** [touch] from the constant motion of her thin arms. The chair is silent now, but if I close my eyes, I can still hear the **squeak of the rockers** against the pine floor and hear the **click of her knitting needles** [sound]. They were sounds that always comforted me and made me feel as if everything were right with the world. Even today, I can't look at the rocker without seeing Memaw **smiling** at me over the **rim of her glasses** [sight] and hearing her say she loves me.

Figurative Language

Good writers use **figurative language** to help readers see what they are describing. Figurative language employs figures of speech—such as similes, metaphors, and personification—that compare or identify one subject with another.

A **simile** is a comparison that uses *like* or *as*.

Examples:

He eats like a pig.

Her look penetrated like an X ray.

The sailboat glided through the water like a swan.

A **metaphor** is a comparison that likens two things without using *like* or *as*.

Examples:

He is a pig.

Her look X-rayed me.

The sailboat was a feather in the wind.

Personification is to give human characteristics to something nonhuman.

Examples:

Money talks.

The sails inhaled and exhaled with each gust of wind.

The trees sighed in the wind.

PEER
EXAMPLE

Dan

Clearwater Lake

Clearwater Lake is a small lake nestled in the Adirondack Mountains. The glassy lake is ringed with aspen, larch, birch, and fir trees, and in the fall, **the mountainsides are on fire** [metaphor] with brilliant oranges, reds, and yellows. I arrive at the lake early, with **mist still clinging to the surface of the water like smoke** [simile].

Appropriate Vocabulary

Choose vocabulary that is appropriate for the subject and audience. Using the right vocabulary can go a long way toward convincing your audience that you know what you are talking about.

PEER
EXAMPLE

Beth

> When I wrote this paragraph, I wanted to show the negative health effects of smoking during pregnancy. I wanted the writing to sound authoritative, so I used medical terminology that doctors use.

What a Drag

While cigarettes create health problems for all smokers, babies are put at great health risk by their smoking mothers. First, smoking can cause damage to the **fetus** by **reducing oxygen** that reaches the **unborn** child in the **mother's uterus**. During **childbirth**, smokers are more likely than nonsmokers to suffer **heart and lung complications** due to their **impaired breathing capabilities**, and often the **stress from childbirth** causes injuries to babies. At birth, the babies of mothers who smoke weigh an average of 25 percent less than other newborns, and **low birth weight** weakens the babies' **resistance to disease**. Also, newborns may suffer **respiratory ailments** from their mothers' cigarette smoke. Finally, because the milk of mothers is **contaminated by nicotine**, a **stimulant that overexcites the heart**, many affected newborns **show signs of high blood pressure**. In conclusion, the surgeon general, **the nation's top health authority**, warns on every pack of cigarettes about the dangers of smoking during pregnancy.

Within each set of parentheses, circle the most appropriate word or phrase to replace the italicized word or phrase.

Exercise 9

A Good Deal

Cut-rate (discount, cheap) stores meet a lot of our needs today. First of all, the *stuff* (merchandise, things) *you* (people, consumers,) can *get* (buy, grab) is *cheap* (inexpensive, less). For example, there are *places* (stores, buildings) that *have* (sell, give) *stuff* (products, things) for the house that *you* (people, shoppers) use every day—such as razors, cereal, and soap. These items can be *had* (purchased, gotten) for less than half of the cost at a *regular* (full-priced, real) store. *Factory-reject* (Defective, Factory-seconds) clothing stores are a real bargain, too. *You* (customers, someone) can *get* (see, find) *fancy clothes from designers* (fancy threads, designer wear) for *cheap* (less, nothing). Finally, *cut-rate* (discount, secondhand) auto parts stores are a great way to save because these places have things like oil, headlights, and batteries for less than a gas station charges. Try cut-rate *places* (stores, digs) to save money.

Write a paragraph using one of the following prompts. Try to use specific, concrete language that appeals to the senses.

WRITING PRACTICE 2

1. Describe one location in winter and summer. Try to give the reader a picture of the place in each season.

2. Describe an image from a magazine. (Turn in the picture with your description.)

3. Describe one location at different times of the day. (a stadium before, during, and after a game; downtown at midnight and at rush hour, etc.)

4. Describe the place you most like to spend time. Use words that make the reader want to spend time there, too.

5. Write a paragraph that develops one of the following topic sentences. Imagine the place and what might go on there.

> John Deerfield Memorial Stadium was filled with excited fans.
>
> The volcano erupted at 2:00 a.m.
>
> The mountain path disappeared into a thicket of trees.
>
> The desert shimmered with heat.

PITFALLS

Take care to avoid pitfalls such as using unfamiliar synonyms, slang, clichés, and wordiness in your writing.

Pitfall 1: Unfamiliar Synonyms

Avoid using **unfamiliar synonyms** (words that have the same or similar meaning).

Words listed in a thesaurus as synonyms are not always interchangeable because each word has its own shade of meaning and its own associations. Too often, writers use words they aren't familiar with because they think they should use language that sounds impressive or sophisticated. More often than not, they choose words that have the wrong meaning or the wrong associations.

Example:

The president of the company appeared before the **laborers** (workers) and admitted that the company had **obfuscated** (hidden) its financial difficulties.

The writer tries to use sophisticated vocabulary but winds up changing the meaning of the sentence. Most workers would resent being called *laborers*, which usually means workers who perform manual labor. *Obfuscated* means "confused" or "clouded," which has the effect of hiding, but in the context of the sentence, *hidden* is the clearer word.

Pitfall 2: Slang

Avoid **slang** (informal words that have a specific meaning to a group of people) and **profanity** (language that is disrespectful or vulgar). Slang may be colorful, but it is generally considered inappropriate for most writing. One of the problems with slang is that the writer runs the risk of the audience not understanding the intended meaning.

Examples:

anyways	dis (disrespect)
awesome	dude
bad	far out
bro (brother)	gross
bummed	gnarly
cool	hood (neighborhood)

Pitfall 3: Clichés

Avoid **clichés**, expressions that have been used so much they have lost their freshness. Many clichés are similes, figures of speech that use *like* or *as* to compare two things. Others are simply phrases that we've become so familiar with that they no longer help us see an image.

Examples:

cold as ice	poor as a church mouse
dumb as an ox	pretty as a picture
go out on a limb	read him like a book
happy as a clam	red as a rose
hot as hell	sink your teeth into
mad as a hornet	strong as a bear
open-and-shut case	

Pitfall 4: Wordiness

Avoid **wordiness**, the use of words that do not contribute to meaning. Often writers end up using more words than they need. When we speak, we tend to use lots of extra words. In writing, it's best to be concise.

Examples:

Wordy

In my opinion, if politicians were **being absolutely** honest **and straightforward about the actual facts of** where they get their money, **the people who** vote **for them** would understand whose voice is most important **and who gets listened to.**

In this sentence, the bold words are not needed. They are either understood (*in my opinion, actual facts*) or redundant, meaning they repeat the meaning of the words around them (*being absolutely, and straightforward, and who gets listened to*). The phrase the people who vote for them is a lot of words that simply mean "voters."

Concise

If politicians were honest about where they get their money, voters would understand whose voice is most important.

Exercise 10

Eliminate slang, clichés, and wordiness from the following sentences.

1. It goes without saying that Rico is the best man for the job.

2. An amazingly high number of citizens of the United States are overweight.

3. I absolutely agree with you that your brother is a sly dog who cannot be trusted any further than you can throw him.

4. Some people who go out to restaurants feel that they need to get their money's worth by eating the whole entire meal even if they feel full to the point of not wanting to eat any more.

5. Last time I went to the beach, I ran into a totally cool dude, and we surfed some awesome waves.

For each italicized word or phrase, circle the most appropriate choice within the parentheses ([delete] means that the best choice is simply to cut the italicized word).

Sleep

Sleep is an *extremely* ([delete]/really) important and *very* ([delete]/really) troubling part of *the lives each of us lives every day* (our lives/our everyday lives). The *person who is like most people* (average person/regular Joe) spends more than 220,000 hours *in bed* ([delete]/in his own bed) asleep *from the time he is born until the time he dies* (in his lifetime/his whole entire lifetime). Some people sleep nine to ten hours *each and every night* ([delete]/a night), while others need as few as three hours of sleep *each night of the week* ([delete]/every night). Some of us take naps, and some find napping to be *very* ([delete]/way) difficult and *somewhat* ([delete]/kind of) disorienting. Sleep is *so* ([delete]/very) necessary to restore our vitality, reduce stress, and regenerate. Unfortunately, *in actual fact* ([delete]/in reality), many people have trouble sleeping *really well*, ([delete]/getting some serious Zs) and Americans spend *so* ([delete]/many) many millions *and millions* ([delete]/upon millions) of dollars on sleep aids every year. Experts *who understand people who have trouble sleeping* ([delete]/who are knowledgeable about this subject) estimate *with an educated guess* ([delete]/roughly) that *each and every* (every/every single) night *close to* ([delete]/approximately) one in three people *or so* ([delete]/thereabouts) has *some type of problem or trouble* (trouble/some kind of difficulties) sleeping.

For each italicized word or phrase, circle the most appropriate vocabulary from each set of parentheses.

Lots of Bikes for Free

Teenagers in one town are doing something *really cool* (awesome, productive) and helping many *people who live there* (townspeople, folks) get around. These teens are fixing up old bicycles that are *ditched* (dumped, discarded) around town. Then each of the bikes is put back on the busy streets for *people* (residents, people who reside there) to use. All the bikes can be spotted *as easy as pie* (no problem, easily) because they are painted a bright fluorescent color. When *a person* (a person who rides the bike, bicyclist) is *done* (finished, completed) using a bike, she just *dumps* (places, throws) it on a curb for the next *person* (guy, citizen) who comes along and needs a quick ride. The bikes are popular with lots of schoolkids and even elderly people on their way to one of the churches in town.

There are many *good things* (benefits, perks) to this program. Teenagers get mechanical training. Some of the volunteers have gained job training that has gotten them a job that pays well. Also, the *cops* (heat, police) like this program because there are few thefts of bikes anymore since there is a free bike available almost everywhere. One of the *best things* (advantages, perks) is that most old bicycles are being recycled instead of *trashing* (corrupting, cluttering), city streets or being thrown away and clogging the town dump. Most important, this town and its citizens feel a sense of community.

Chapter 24
Identifying Subjects and Verbs

A **sentence** is a group of words that contains a **subject** and a **verb** and expresses a complete thought. Subjects and verbs are the building blocks of the sentence. To avoid run-ons, sentence fragments, and subject–verb agreement errors in your writing, you should be able to identify subjects and verbs.

Subjects

The **subject** is who or what the sentence is about.

       S   V

My **neighbor** walks his dog every morning.

               S   V

In the summer, the **bugs** are terrible.

Finding the Subject

To find the subject of the sentence, ask who or what the sentence is about.

    S

Jake and Sabrina dance well together.

Who or what is the sentence about?

  S

We will study tonight.

Who or what is the sentence about?

    S

There is a **dog** in the yard.

Who or what is the sentence about?

The **simple subject** is the subject without modifying words like adjectives.

S

The uninvited **guest** at the party liked the idea.

Subjects can be **nouns** (persons, places, or things); **pronouns** (I, she, they); or **gerunds** (verbs ending in -*ing* that act as nouns).

S

My **friends** went on a trip.

S

I don't like spinach.

S

Swimming is great exercise.

A **compound subject** is two or more words that tell who or what the sentence is about.

S

Jake and Sabrina dance well together.

Problems with Identifying the Subject

In **command sentences**, the subject is *implied*.

Imp S

(You) Open the door.

Imp S

(You) Turn left at the corner.

The subject follows the verb in sentences that begin with *there* or *here*.

S

There is a funny **bug** on the window.

The subject is not found in a prepositional phrase (a preposition followed by its object).

P P   S   P P

After eating, the **cat** leaped on the table.

Common Prepositions

about	behind	in	outside of
above	below	in addition to	over
according to	beneath	inside	since
across	beside	in spite of	through
after	besides	instead of	throughout
against	between	into	to
along	beyond	like	toward
along with	by	near	under
among	despite	of	until
around	down	off	up
as	during	on	upon
as far as	except	on account of	with
at	for	on top of	within
before	from	out	without

To find the subject of the sentence, cross out the prepositional phrases and ask who or what the sentence is about.

PP   S   PP
~~In the morning~~, **James** drops me ~~off at school~~.

Cross out each prepositional phrase and circle the subject.

Exercise 1

1. Around midnight during finals week, students with a need to stay up all night go out in search of coffee.

2. The all-night diner down the street from my apartment becomes crowded from midnight until midmorning.

3. Over the next few days, some students with research to complete will live in the library.

4. Except for a Saturday-night break, Bill and Lisa studied every day in the last week.

5. With little sleep and lots of coffee, I am worried about my performance on the final exam.

Verbs

The **verb** tells the subject's action or state of being. The verb usually comes after the subject. Note, however, that the verb is not necessarily the next word after the subject, nor does it always follow the subject.

Finding the Verb

To find the verb, ask what the subject is doing or what word expresses the state of being of the subject.

      S   V

Everyone at the meeting **likes** the idea.

What is everyone doing?

      S   V

Mrs. Jones **was** late for the meeting.

What word tells the state of being of Mr. Jones?

                          S   V

Satisfied with her work, the scientist **has returned** to her office.

What words tell what the scientist is doing or her state of being?

The **three classes of verbs** are *action verbs, linking verbs*, and *helping verbs.*

    Action verbs tell what the subject is doing.

      S V

The car **rolled** down the hill.

Linking verbs link the subject to words that describe or identify the subject.

    S   V

I really **feel** tired today.

Common Linking Verbs

is, feel, look, seem, become, smell, sound, taste, appear

Helping verbs, called **auxiliaries**, help the main verb. The helping verb plus the main verb make a **verb phrase**, which expresses the complete action or state of being of the subject.

      S   V

The moon **has come** out from behind the cloud.

Common Auxiliaries

Forms of *to be*	Forms of *to do*	Forms of *to have*	Others
am	does	have	will/would
is	do	has	shall/should
are	did	had	may/must/might
was			can/could
were			need to/ought to
been			

Problems with Identifying the Verb

The **present participle** is not complete by itself and needs a helping verb.

> Incomplete Verb
> The man **walking** down the street.

> Complete Verb
> The man **was walking** down the street.

The past participle is not complete by itself and needs a helping verb.

> Incomplete Verb
> The damage **done** by the fire.

> Complete Verb
> The damage **was done** by the fire.

The main verb of the sentence is not found in a **dependent clause** (a group of words beginning with a subordinating conjunction or a relative pronoun).

>   S   D C   V
> The man who was mowing his lawn **was** injured.

>   D C   S   V
> When the rain stopped, the children **went** out to play.

A subject can have a **compound verb** (more than one verb).

>   S   V   V
> Christopher **swims** twenty laps and **runs** three miles every day.

Review Exercise 1

Circle the subject and underline the verb of each sentence. You may cross out the prepositional phrases to help in your identification.

1. Once during a storm, I stood under a tree.

2. It saves money.

3. Get a tutor for English.

4. There are many new homes in this subdivision.

5. My mom and dad understand, but they miss me.

6. I am worried that my girlfriend back home will forget me.

7. Gardens need care and attention.

8. Have you ever eaten a fresh carrot?

9. There are many dogs and cats in my neighborhood.

10. Some families on my street own a dog and a couple of cats.

Review Exercise 2

Circle the subject and underline the verb of each sentence. You may cross out the prepositional phrases to help in your identification.

1. The books that I ordered have arrived

2. The best runners in my class run five miles every day.

3. During the spring, birds from South America fly north.

4. Studying for most students takes up to two hours for each hour spent in class.

5. The car that my parents gave me is old and has many parts that need replacing.

6. The neighbors who live next door water their plants every day.

7. Speaking two languages can be useful when traveling.

8. Once in a while, my brothers and I like to go camping without our parents.

9. There are many ways to travel to Europe.

10. A trip can cost a lot and take a lot of planning.

Chapter 25
Subject–Verb Agreement

Making subjects and verbs agree is a crucial skill because subject–verb agreement errors are major writing errors. The rules are fairly simple, but there are several areas in which writers commonly make errors. Be sure to complete both exercises at the end of this chapter to ensure that these errors are not part of your writing.

Subject–Verb Agreement Rules

Subjects and verbs must **agree** in number. A singular subject takes a singular verb, and a plural subject takes a plural verb.

   S   V

Joe takes his lunch to work every day.

The singular subject *Joe* agrees with the verb *takes*.

   S   V

They take binoculars to view the wildlife.

The plural subject *they* agrees with the verb *take*.

Telling the difference between singular and plural subjects is usually easy (though see the section below on problem subjects): most nouns that end in *-s* or *-es* are plural, and it's easy to tell singular pronouns (like *he*) from plural ones (like *they*). Telling the difference between singular and plural verbs can be trickier.

In the present tense, the singular and plural forms of the verb are identical in both the first and second person: they take no ending. In the third person, however, singular verbs take an *-s* or *-es* ending, and plural verbs take no ending.

	Singular	**Plural**
First person	I work	We work
Second person	You work	You work
Third person	He works	They work
	She works	Students work
	It works	
	A student works	

The following easy-to-remember formula may help you remember the correct endings for verbs:

I and *you* take a verb with no ending.

"*Single subject*" begins with *s*, and the verb needs an *-s* ending.

"*Plural*" doesn't begin with *s*, so the verb needs no *-s*.

Problem Subjects

Indefinite Pronouns

Most **indefinite pronouns**, commonly used as the subject of a sentence, are singular and take a verb with an *-s* ending.

Singular Indefinite Pronouns

Ending in –*one*	Ending in –*body*	Ending in –*thing*	Other
anyone	anybody	anything	each
everyone	everybody	everything	either
no one	nobody	nothing	neither
someone	somebody	something	

Example:

S   V

Everything seems fine.

Singular or Plural Words

Some subjects can be **either singular or plural** depending on the meaning of the sentence.

Subjects That Can Be Singular or Plural			
a lot	any	more	none
all	lots	most	some

Example of singular:

S   V

A lot of energy **goes** into studying.

Example of plural:

S   V

A lot of students **enjoy** college.

Collective Nouns

Collective nouns are words that refer to one whole made up of parts. Most collective nouns are singular and take a verb with an -s ending.

Common Collective Nouns		
audience	crowd	group
band	faculty	jury
class	family	team
committee		

Example:

S   V

The **class meets** on Monday.

However, some collective nouns can be either singular or plural depending on how they are used. When the members of a collective noun are thought of as individuals, the noun is considered plural and therefore takes a verb with no ending.

S   V

The **number** of tickets being printed **is** very large.

S   V

A **number** of those tickets **are** misprinted.

Fields of Study
Fields of study are singular subjects and take a verb with an -*s* ending.

Fields of Study		
history	music	politics
home economics	news	statistics
mathematics	physics	

S   V

Mathematics requires logic to understand.

Compound Subjects
Compound subjects (two or more subjects joined by *and*) are plural; they take a verb with no ending.

S   S   V

Mary and **Jason walk** home together every day.

When subjects are joined by *or* or *nor*, however, the verb agrees with the **closest subject**.

S   S   V

The woman **or** her **children answer** the phone.

S   S   V

The children **or** their **mother answers** the phone.

S   S   V

Neither the children **nor** their **mother answers** the phone.

S   S   V

Neither the mother **nor** her **children answer** the phone

Gerunds
A **gerund** (an -*ing* word used as a subject) is singular and takes a verb with an -*s* ending.

S   V

Running takes energy.

Problem Verbs

Compound Verbs

Both verbs in a **compound verb** should agree with the subject.

      S   V   V

The letter carriers **stop** at mailboxes and **deliver** mail.

Irregular Verbs

Irregular verbs—such as *to be, to do,* and *to have*—can cause confusion. Sometimes, *I be, he be,* and *they be* are used in speaking; however, these forms are not standard English and should be avoided in writing.

To be	Singular	Plural
First person	I am	we are
Second person	you are	you are
Third person	he is	they are
	she is	
	it is	

To do	Singular	Plural
First person	I do	we do
Second person	you do	you do
Third person	he does	they do
	she does	
	it does	

To have	Singular	Plural
First person	I have	we have
Second person	you have	you have
Third person	he has	they have
	she has	
	it has	

Problem Sentence Structures

Confusion about subject–verb agreement can occur when the structure of a sentence is unusual or complicated. That is why it is important to be able to identify the subject and the verb (see Chapter 24).

Prepositions

Be careful not to confuse an **object of a preposition** with the **subject of the sentence**. This confusion can arise when a prepositional phrase comes at the start of the sentence or between the subject and the verb. (As explained in Chapter 24, the subject of a sentence is never found in a prepositional phrase.)

S   P P   V

The **men** in the car **drive** carefully.

Reversed Order

The subject usually comes after the verb in a question or in a sentence that begins with *there* or *here* (see Chapter 24). Even though the usual order is **reversed**, the basic subject–verb agreement rule still applies.

V   S

There **is** a **cat** on the car.

V   S

Here **are** some **napkins**.

V   S

What **are** your **feelings**?

V   S

Where **is** my **pen**?

Dependent Clauses

A **dependent clause** may also come before the subject or between the subject and the verb in a sentence. Still, the verb must agree with the subject; do not confuse the subject of the clause for the subject of the sentence. (Dependent clauses are discussed further in Chapter 27.) When a verb follows a **relative pronoun** in a dependent clause, the verb must agree with the **antecedent**, the word the relative pronoun refers to in the sentence.

Examples:

S   V

The **chores** that drive me crazy **are** mopping the floors and washing dishes.

S   D C   V

The **woman** who does the alterations **is** out sick today.

Underline the correct verbs.

1. Is/are the newspaper here yet?

2. Christopher swims/swim twenty laps and runs/run three miles every day.

3. During recess, the class is/are in the field.

4. College for most students requires/require time and demands/demand commitment.

5. Taking a test after staying up late with friends is/are risky.

6. John or his friends waters/water the plants every day.

7. Speaking two languages is/are useful in some jobs.

8. Economics happens/happen to be my major.

9. There appears/appear many ways to get there from here.

10. The pinball machine that steals/steal my quarters isare in the game room.

Review Exercise 1

Correct any subject–verb agreement errors.

1. Poodles with bows around their neck makes me laugh.

2. A good teacher offers the students a clear example and help the students understand the material.

3. The hand movements that are used by the referee confuses me.

4. One of my roommates who admire movie stars hangs their pictures all over the house.

5. Politics in most towns are discussed in the newspaper.

6. There is a lot of adventurous rides at the theme park that remind me of my childhood.

7. Because I have such a limited budget, the prices at the mall really annoys me.

8. Although neither my friends nor my brother have ever stolen anything in our lives, the security guards who patrol the mall always follow me.

9. Cars with only one air bag doesn't help the passenger at all.

10. When classes at school ends for spring break, I hop in my car and leave town as fast as I can.

Review Exercise 2

Chapter 26
Verb Tenses

The past tense of the verb indicates that the action or state of being existed before the present moment. Verb tense is signaled in several ways. The past participle verb form uses a helping verb, usually *has/have/had* or *was/were*. The past tense and past participle forms of verbs can be a problem for writers.

Luckily, many verbs are regular; these should not give you much trouble. However, many others are irregular; these are much more difficult because their forms change. You should review the correct forms and practice using them.

In addition, the past participle can be used in a number of ways, and it is important to know how and when to use it. Once you have learned about verbs in the present and past tenses, you will be ready to edit your writing for verb shifts.

Forming the Past Tense and Past Participle

Regular Verbs

To form the past tense or past participle of **regular verbs**, add *-ed* to the verb.

> walked, talked, returned

When adding the *-ed* ending to verbs, pay attention to the spelling rules.

- If the verb ends in *e*, drop the extra *e*.

    > imagined, fired, filed

- If the word is one syllable and a vowel comes before the final consonant, double that consonant.

    > stopped, dripped

Irregular Verbs

There is no set pattern to form the past or past participle of **irregular verbs.** You must memorize the forms.

Some irregular verbs keep the **same form** in the present tense, past tense, and past participle.

Irregular Verbs That Do Not Change Forms		
bet	hurt	shut
burst	let	slit
cast	put	split
cost	quit	spread
cut	read	wet
hit	set	

Present: The canoes **cost** only $10 each per day.

Past: Yesterday, the two canoes **cost** $20.

Past participle: The canoes have **cost** only $40 for the two days.

Most irregular verbs, however, take **different forms** in the present tense, past tense, and past participles.

Present	**Past**	**Past Participle**	**Present**	**Past**	**Past Participle**
arise	arose	arisen	buy	bought	bought
awake	awoke	awakened	cast	cast	cast
bear	bore	born	catch	caught	caught
beat	beat	beaten	choose	chose	chosen
become	became	become	cling	clung	clung
begin	began	begun	come	came	come
bend	bent	bent	cost	cost	cost
bet	bet	bet	creep	crept	crept
bind	bound	bound	cut	cut	cut
bite	bit	bitten	dare	dared	dared
bleed	bled	bled	deal	dealt	dealt
blow	blew	blown	dig	dug	dug
break	broke	broken	do	did	done
bring	brought	brought	draw	drew	drawn
build	built	built	dream	dreamed/	dreamed/
burn	burned	burned/burnt		dreamt	dreamt
burst	burst	burst	drink	drank	drunk

Present	Past	Past Participle	Present	Past	Past Participle
drive	drove	driven	meet	met	met
eat	ate	eaten	pay	paid	paid
fall	fell	fallen	quit	quit	quit
feed	fed	fed	read	read	read
feel	felt	felt	ride	rode	ridden
fight	fought	fought	ring	rang	rung
find	found	found	rise	rose	risen
fling	flung	flung	run	ran	run
fly	flew	flown	see	saw	seen
forget	forgot	forgotten	seek	sought	sought
forgive	forgave	forgiven	sell	sold	sold
freeze	froze	frozen	send	sent	sent
get	got	gotten/got	shake	shook	shaken
give	gave	given	shave	shaved	shaved
go	went	gone	shine	shone	shone
grind	ground	ground	shoot	shot	shot
grow	grew	grown	show	showed	shown/showed
hang	hung/hanged	hung/hanged	shrink	shrank	shrunk
have	had	had	shut	shut	shut
hear	heard	heard	sing	sang	sung
hide	hid	hidden	sink	sang	sunk
hit	hit	hit	sit	sat	sat
hold	held	held	sleep	slept	slept
hurt	hurt	hurt	slide	slid	slid
keep	kept	kept	slit	slit	slit
know	knew	known	speak	spoke	spoken
lay	laid	laid	speed	sped	sped
lead	led	led	set	set	set
leave	left	left	spend	spent	spent
lend	lent	lent	spin	spun	spun
let	let	let	split	split	split
lie (to relax)	lay	lain	spread	spread	spread
light	lit/lighted	lit/lighted	spring	sprang	sprung
lose	lost	lost	stand	stood	stood
make	made	made	steal	stole	stolen
mean	meant	meant	stick	stuck	stuck

Present	Past	Past Participle	Present	Past	Past Participle
sting	stung	stung	throw	threw	thrown
strike	struck	struck	understand	understood	understood
string	strung	strung	wake	woke	woke
swear	swore	sworn	wear	wore	worn
sweep	swept	swept	weave	wove	woven
swim	swam	swum	wed	wed	wed
swing	swung	swung	weep	wept	wept
take	took	taken	wet	wet	wet
teach	taught	taught	win	won	won
tear	tore	torn	wind	wound	wound
tell	told	told	wring	wrung	wrung
think	thought	thought	write	wrote	written

Present: I often **go** on a trip.

Past: Last week, I **went** on a trip.

Past participle: I have **gone** on a trip every summer.

Note: Good dictionaries list the past tense forms of irregular verbs.
  One of the most irregular verbs is *to be.* It has different forms for different persons in the past tense.

To be	Singular	Plural
First person	I was	we were
Second person	you were	you were
Third person	he was	they were
	she was	
	it was	

Write the correct form of the verb in the space.

Exercise 1

1. to run

The horse _____ from the stable when the dog barked.

I have _____ every day this week.

2. to bet

My friend _____ me that he would get an A on the French exam.

She has _____ on the lottery.

3. to take

I _____ the coat to the cleaners.

They have _____ a part-time job.

4. to choose

Miranda _____ to wear a red dress to the party last night.

I have _____ an excellent school for my child to attend.

5. to have

The motorist _____ to blow her horn to get the pedestrian's attention.

We have _____ a hard time paying our bills.

6. to find

Yesterday I _____ a quarter.

The jury has _____ the man innocent.

7. to eat

Someone _____ the whole pie before I got home.

We have _____ at the same restaurant for many years.

8. to draw

The child _____ a picture for her mommy.

She has _____ many pictures of the dog.

continues

continued

9. to bite

Yesterday I _____ my tongue.

My dog has never _____ a mailman.

10. to hurt

Yesterday I _____ my leg.

The defeat has _____ the team's chances for the title.

Using the Part Participle

The Present Perfect Tense

The **present perfect tense** expresses an action that began in the past and is continuing in the present. The present perfect tense is made with the present tense of *to have* and the past participle.

I **have gone** to the same school for two years.

The present perfect tense can also describe an action that has just been completed or an action that was completed at an undetermined time in the past.

The same postman **has delivered** our mail for years.

The Past Perfect Tense

The **past perfect tense** is used to emphasize that an action occurred in the past before another past action or point in time. It is always used when *already* or *just* is in a sentence in which one action occurred in the past before another past action. The past perfect tense is made with the past tense of *to have* and the past participle.

I **had** already **been** in college for two years before I decided on my major.

I **had** just **become** a recreation major when I met my future husband.

Underline the correct verb form.

Exercise 2

1. The sandhill cranes arrived / have arrived last weekend.

2. Most days this week I went / have gone out at dusk to watch these stately birds.

3. During all these years, I saw / have seen them in my yard twice.

4. Yesterday the birds flew / have flown away because a tractor was plowing nearby.

5. I have took / had taken many pictures already before I got the best one, the flock of birds rising above the trees with the sun dawning behind them.

The Passive Voice

In the **passive voice**, the subject of the sentence receives the action of the verb. The passive voice is made with a form of the verb *to be* and the past participle.

This seat **is taken** by my husband.

The dinner **was paid** for by Bill.

The explanation **will be given** by the president's spokesman.

(Notice that the passive voice takes the emphasis away from who or what is doing the action and puts the emphasis on who or what is receiving the action.)

In most writing, the **active voice** is preferable to the passive voice because it communicates clearly and directly the subject completing the action. However, the passive voice is acceptable when the doer of the action is unknown or unimportant.

The crime **was committed** at 11:31 p.m.

(No one knows who committed the crime.)

The explosion **was recorded** on videotape.

(Who recorded the videotape is unknown or unimportant.)

Using the Past Participle as an Adjective

The past participle form of the verb may be used as an adjective (a modifier).

> a piece of **broken** glass
>
> some **fried** chicken
>
> a **closed** book

Avoiding Shifts in Tense

Avoid shifting tenses within a piece of writing unless the time of the action changes. For example, if the actions took place in the past, remain consistent in using past tenses for verbs; if the actions are taking place in the present, remain in the present throughout the writing.

> *Tense shift:*
>
> When I **asked** the grocer about the vegetables, he **says** to me that they **came** in fresh that morning.

> *Consistent tense:*
>
> When I **asked** the grocer about the vegetables, he **said** to me that they **came** in fresh that morning.

Review

To form the past or past participle of **regular verbs**, add *-ed* to the verb.

- There is no set pattern to form the past or past participle of **irregular verbs**.

- The **present perfect** tense expresses an action that began in the past and is continuing in the present. This tense can also describe an action that has just been completed or an action that was completed at an undetermined time in the past.

- The **past perfect** tense expresses an action that occurred in the past before another action or point in time in the past.

- In most writing, the **active voice** is preferable to the **passive voice**.

- The past participle form of the verb is also used as an **adjective** (a modifier).

- **Avoid shifting tenses** within a piece of writing.

Correct all verb errors in the following sentences. Rewrite sentences in the passive voice to put them in the active voice. (Note: Some verbs are correct and should not be changed.)

1. Tennis was play by our team at a local club.

2. I have hitted tennis balls with my friends all summer.

3. I have been playing with my brother until he went away to camp.

4. I were playing with a racket that was stringed incorrectly.

5. My racket was broken by me when I smash an overhead shot.

6. After the game, I layed the racket in my car.

7. I have replace my broke racket with a new one.

8. Since I have began playing tennis, I've became a pretty good player.

9. I have played racquetball before I took up tennis.

10. I had hopes of becoming good at racquetball, but I stop playing when I hurted my wrist.

Chapter 27
Sentence Types

The sentence is the building block for all writing. Understanding the basic structure of the sentence will help you in writing paragraphs. This structure includes the parts of the sentence and how those parts can be put together.

A sentence contains a **subject** and a **verb** and expresses a **complete thought**. The subject of the sentence is the person, place, thing, or idea the sentence is about. The verb is what the subject does (action) or is (state of being). When the subject and the verb, along with the words around them, express a complete thought, the word group can stand alone as a sentence.

    S   V

Mr. Magruder works late every Friday.

Clauses

The subjects and verbs in a sentence are contained in word groups called **clauses**. Clauses are the primary parts of a sentence; putting them together in different ways creates different sentence structures.

An **independent clause** is a group of words that contains a subject and a verb and expresses a complete thought. An independent clause can stand alone as a sentence. In fact, every sentence contains at least one independent clause.

The robins have migrated south already.

A **dependent clause** includes a subject and a verb but does not express a complete thought. It usually begins with a **subordinating**

conjunction or a **relative pronoun**. A dependent clause cannot stand alone as a sentence. To complete its meaning, it must be joined to an independent clause. Some sentence types contain one or more dependent clauses.

Subordinating Conjunctions

after	even though	until
although	if	when
as	since	whereas
because	though	whether
before	unless	while

Relative Pronouns

that	whoever
which	whom
whichever	whomever
who	whose

D C   I C   D C
Because the air is cool, I enjoy the springtime even though it often rains.

I C   D C
I love the lamp that she bought at the antique store.

Phrases

Sentences may also contain **phrases**, which are groups of words that act together in a sentence but do not include both a subject and a verb. There are many kinds of phrases that can add information to sentences; these include:

- Noun phrases (a noun and its modifiers): *The small green tugboat* chugged along.

- Verb phrases (a verb and its modifiers): Jordan *always talks and laughs.*

- Prepositional phrases (a preposition and its object): The ad was *on the last page.*

- Verbal phrases (a phrase beginning with a gerund, an infinitive, or a participle): *Walking home* takes me ten minutes.

Sentence Types

Writers can combine clauses to create four different sentence types.

Simple

A **simple sentence** contains one independent clause.

      I C

Jacob walked to the store.

Compound

A **compound sentence** contains two or more independent clauses joined together by a comma and a coordinating conjunction, a semicolon, or a semicolon and a conjunctive adverb.

    I C   C C   I C

Jacob walked to the store, but he got a ride home.

    I C   I C

Jacob walked to the store; he got a ride home.

    I C   Conj Adv   I C

Jacob walked to the store; however, he got a ride home.

Complex

A **complex sentence** contains one or more dependent clauses and an independent clause.

      D C   I C

Although Jacob walked to the store, he got a ride home.

    I C   D C

Jacob walked to the store although he got a ride home.

Compound-Complex

A **compound-complex sentence** contains at least one dependent clause and at least two independent clauses.

      D C   I C   I C

Although Jacob walked to the store, he got a ride home, so he wasn't late for dinner.

Sentence Purposes

All sentences, no matter what type, can be classified according to purpose. There are four basic purposes.

Declarative

Declarative sentences make a statement. They *declare* something about a person, place, thing, or idea.

Martin bowls on Friday night.

Interrogative

Interrogative sentences ask questions and end in a question mark. (*Interrogative* is related to *interrogate*, which means to question.)

When does Martin bowl?

Imperative

Imperative sentences give commands. Usually the subject *you* is implied or understood, and not written.

Don't go bowling, Martin.

(The subject *you* is understood.)

Exclamatory

Exclamatory sentences express a strong emotion or surprise and end in an exclamation point. (*Exclamatory* is related to *exclaim*.)

Martin bowled a perfect game!

Chapter 28
Sentence Fragments

Sentence fragments are parts of sentences that are punctuated as if they were complete sentences. We use sentence fragments all the time in our speech. We also see fragments in advertising and in some published books and articles, where writers use them on purpose, for specific effects. However, in most academic and business writing, sentence fragments are major English errors.

A **sentence fragment** is a group of words that does not express a complete thought. (The reader is left asking questions about a fragment.) There are many types of sentence fragments, but most are missing either a subject, a verb, or both. Fragments that do contain a subject and a verb may not express a complete thought, as in dependent clauses. To correct a fragment, a writer must either add words to the fragment or connect the fragment to a sentence.

Fragment: Walked his dog at five o'clock every day. (Who walked his dog?)

Sentence: My **neighbor** walked his dog at five o'clock every day. (A subject is added.)

Fragment: The final exam given on Friday. (What about the final exam?)

Sentence: The final exam given on Friday **was** easy. (A verb is added.)

Fragment: In the summer. (What happens in the summer?)

Sentence: In the summer, students sometimes **work** part-time. (A subject and a verb are added.)

Missing-Subject Fragments

A common type of fragment is one that is missing a subject. It may contain a noun, but that noun does not act as the subject of a complete sentence.

$$V$$

Have plans for the party on Friday.

(Who has plans?) To correct this fragment, add a subject.

S V

I have plans for the party on Friday.

Exception: Remember that the subject *you* is understood in **imperative sentences** (see Chapter 27). Although the subject is not written in the sentence, the reader understands that the verb refers to you.

S   V

(**You**) Take a break after you move those boxes.

Missing-Verb Fragments

Another type of fragment is one in which there is a subject but no verb.

S

The little **boy** with curly black hair.

(What is the little boy doing?) To correct this fragment, add a verb.

S   V

The little **boy** with curly black hair **pulled** his wagon down the walk.

Fragments also occur when the verb for the sentence is not complete. Present participles (verbs ending in *-ing*) and past participles are not complete verbs. To correct this kind of fragment, add a helping verb or a complete verb.

S

Fragment: The **student** working on his term paper.

S   V

Sentence: The **student** working on his term paper **was** late to class.

S

Fragment: The **apples** fallen on the ground.

S   V

Sentence: The **apples have fallen** on the ground.

Missing-Subject-and-Verb Fragments

Phrases lack a subject and a verb; unless they are attached to an independent clause, they are fragments. Add a subject and a verb to make phrases into sentences.

Fragment: From morning until night.

Sentence: **I work** from morning until night.

Fragment: Walking home after dark.

Sentence: Most **people don't enjoy** walking home after dark.

Dependent-Clause Fragments

Even though they contain a subject and a verb, dependent clauses are always fragments because they do not express a complete thought. Dependent-clause fragments are corrected by removing words or adding words to make a complete thought. Often, dependent-clause fragments can be joined to an independent clause.

Fragment: Because Mr. Pastorelli caught a cold last week.

Sentence: Because Mr. Pastorelli caught a cold last week, **he missed** work.

Fragment: The woman who lives down the street.

Sentence: The **woman** who lives down the street **is** friendly.

> To identify fragments in your writing, look at each word group for the subject and the verb. Then make sure that the word group is a complete thought and can stand alone as a sentence.

Exercise 1

Identify each word group as a sentence (S) or fragment (F). Then make each fragment into a complete sentence on the blank that follows it; add words as needed to make the sentence complete.

_____1. Being the mail carrier in my neighborhood.

_____

_____2. There are dogs barking all the time.

_____

_____3. Bitten on the leg by a mean German shepherd.

_____

_____4. Because you never know if a barking dog will bite or not.

_____

_____5. Dogs are not the only problem.

_____

_____6. One yard that is a real challenge because of the poison ivy climbing up the mailbox.

_____

_____7. The leaves of the plant, which sting if you touch them.

_____

_____8. Another hassle for the letter carrier is neighbors who park in front of their mailbox.

_____

_____9. The carrier can't deliver the mail.

_____

_____10. The problems delivering mail in my neighborhood safely.

_____

Correct the fragments in the following paragraph. You may either add subjects and verbs or connect the fragments to other sentences.

Exercise 2

The Perfect Houseplant

African violets are the perfect houseplant. Ever blooming, with single, semi-double, or double flowers in lots of colors. African violets also charm admirers with their green or variegated foliage of smooth, velvety, or deeply creased leaves. Discovered in 1890 by Baron Walter von Saint Paul while hiking in Africa. Easy to grow with the right temperature and sunlight. They like temperatures in the 70s. Also, indirect sunlight or the fluorescent lighting from overhead lights. Many gardeners like to start new plants from old ones. Two methods. Division of plants that produce offspring and leaf cuttings that grow new plants. A very inexpensive plant to grow and a very enjoyable indoor hobby!

Chapter 29
Run-ons

Run-ons consist of two or more independent clauses that are run together without proper punctuation. (See Chapter 27 for a discussion of independent clauses.) Because they make writing difficult to understand, run-ons are major English errors. Readers expect to see a complete thought between ending punctuation marks. When writers omit those marks or fail to add connectors, readers become confused.

Types of Run-ons

A **fused sentence** incorrectly joins or fuses two independent clauses together without any punctuation.

       S   V   S   V

The **sun is shining we are going** to the beach.

A **comma splice** incorrectly joins or splices together two independent clauses with only a comma.

       S   V   S   V

The **sun is shining, we are going** to the beach.

To identify a run-on, first identify the subject and the verb in a word group that ends with a period. If there is a second subject and verb that can be separated from the first subject and verb to make two complete sentences, the word grouping is a run-on. If the word group cannot be divided into two complete thoughts, it is not a run-on.

Ways to Correct Run-ons

- Separate the independent clauses with a period, and start the second with a **capital letter**.

  The sun is shining. We are going to the beach.

- Join the two independent clauses with a **comma** and a **coordinating conjunction**.

  The sun is shining, so we are going to the beach.

- Join the two independent clauses with a **semicolon**, a **transition word**, and a **comma**.

  The sun is shining; therefore, we are going to the beach.

- Join the two independent clauses with a **semicolon**.

  The sun is shining; we are going to the beach.

- Join the two clauses with a **subordinating conjunction**.

  Because the sun is shining, we are going to the beach

Exercise 1

Directions: Identify each word group as a <u>S</u>entence or a <u>R</u>un-on. In the blanks, use one of the five ways of correcting run-ons listed above.

_____1. My hometown offers residents many advantages, for example it has lots of parks and playgrounds.

_____

_____

_____2. He plays the lottery regularly, he wants to win a million dollars.

_____

_____

_____3. Last weekend, Nancy learned to use a compass because she doesn't want to get lost in the woods.

_____

_____

_____4. I enjoy going home my family is glad to see me.

_____

_____

_____5. I can never find a place to park unless I arrive at 7:30 a.m. for my 10:00 a.m. class.

_____

_____

_____6. Some bosses let employees off for tests, however some bosses do not.

_____

_____

_____7. The class is required to attend two cultural events, also there are three major exams.

_____

_____

_____8. The coffee was cold, and the toast was burned.

_____

_____

_____9. The messenger picked up a package at the post office, later she delivered a package downtown.

_____

_____

_____10. I graduate in June, which is five years from when I began school.

_____

_____

Exercise 2

Correct the run-ons in the following passage.

Future Movie Stars

My friends Jane and Carol are moving to California within a few weeks. They have always been interested in motion pictures, they hope to become movie stars. The two women studied acting in college, therefore they believe that they can find careers in the movie industry. When they arrive in Hollywood, California, they expect to work part-time as waitresses or office assistants while they audition for acting parts. Jane read a book about going to Hollywood that advised actors to get an agent, but Carol is afraid that an agent will cost too much money. Fortunately, Carol has a contact at one of the movie studios he said he would help them. Maybe someday I will see them on the big screen, then I can brag about my good friends.

Chapter 30
Sentence Combining

Good writers vary the structure of their sentences in order to include lots of information and to keep their readers' interest. **Sentence combining** is the process of building compound, complex, and compound-complex sentences from simple sentences. (These four sentence types are discussed in Chapter 27.) Sentence combining is especially useful in generating strong support in paragraphs.

Sentence combining is a three-step process:

1. Generate two or more ideas expressed in simple sentences (independent clauses).

   Original sentences:

   Emil's Café offers soft lighting and romantic music. This restaurant is a favorite place to take a date.

2. Combine the ideas into one sentence that expresses the relationship between the ideas.

   Combined sentences:

   Emil's Café offers soft lighting and romantic music, so this restaurant is a favorite place to take a date.

3. Use **coordination** and **subordination** to combine ideas into a variety of sentence structures.

   Combined sentences:

   Emil's café offers soft lighting and romantic music; therefore, this restaurant is a favorite place to take a date.

   Because Emil's café offers soft lighting and romantic music, this restaurant is a favorite place to take a date.

Coordination

Writers use **coordination** to combine two or more ideas of equal importance, giving each idea equal weight.

Original sentences:

Renovating my house is exciting. Remodeling can be expensive and tiring.

Combined sentences using coordination:

Renovating my house is exciting, but remodeling can be expensive and tiring.

Renovating my house is exciting; however, remodeling can be expensive and tiring.

Coordinating Conjunctions

A simple way to coordinate two ideas is to use a **comma** and a **coordinating conjunction** to create a compound sentence.

Original sentences:

I like to play tennis. I enjoy swimming.

Combined sentences:

      I C   C C   I C

I like to play tennis, **and** I enjoy swimming.

To choose the conjunction that most clearly shows the relationship between the ideas, the writer must know the meaning of each coordinating conjunction.

And adds two ideas that are similar.

I like English, and I love to write.

But contrasts two ideas.

I like English, but I hate math.

For means "because."

I must leave the party now, for I have to get up early tomorrow.

Nor negates both ideas.

I don't like English, nor do I like to write.

Or offers the ideas as equal choices.

I must leave the party now, or I will never get up early tomorrow.

Yet limits or contrasts two ideas.

I enjoy dancing, yet I'm not a very good dancer.

So suggests results.

Emil's Café offers soft lighting and romantic music, so this restaurant is a favorite.

Choose the appropriate conjunction (*for, and, nor, but, or, yet, so*) to combine the ideas.

Exercise 1

1. Football is popular throughout the United States, _____ hockey isn't.

2. Jack doesn't like spinach, _____ does he like tuna.

3. Dave sees a lot of movies, _____ he runs the projector at the local theater.

4. It's raining outside, _____ let's take a walk later.

5. We can eat dinner now, _____ we can wait until after the show.

Compound Predicates

Ideas can be coordinated using a **compound predicate** (two verb phrases). To do this, we add a coordinating conjunction and drop the subject of the second sentence. Note that in this method of coordination, we do not use a comma.

Original sentences:

I love to cook. I hate to wash dishes.

Combined sentences:

Verb Phrase   Verb Phrase

I love to cook but hate to wash dishes.

Exercise 2

Choose the appropriate conjunction (*for, and, nor, but, or, yet, so*) to combine the ideas.

1. John works at a supermarket. He brings home sale items sometimes.

   John works at a supermarket _____ brings home sale items sometimes.

2. Computers cost businesses a lot of money. They save a lot of workers time and energy.

   Computers cost businesses a lot of money _____ save a lot of workers time and energy.

3. The best team in the league will go to the championship game. It will play the best team from the other conference.

   The best team in the league will go to the championship game _____ will play the best team from the other conference.

4. Air bags are offered on many new cars. They make the cars more expensive.

   Air bags are offered on many new cars _____ make the cars more expensive.

5. Many people go to their parents' home for Thanksgiving. Many people cook at home on this holiday.

   Many people go to their parents' home for Thanksgiving _____ cook at home on this holiday.

Conjunctive Adverbs and Transitional Expressions

Independent clauses can be coordinated using a **semicolon (;)** and a **conjunctive adverb** or **transitional expression**.

Original sentences:

Emil's Café offers soft lighting and romantic music. This restaurant is a favorite place to take a date.

Combined sentences:

I C   Conj Adv   I C

Emil's Café offers soft lighting and romantic music; **therefore**, this restaurant is a favorite place to take a date.

To combine ideas into compound sentences using semicolons and conjunctive adverbs or transitional expressions, writers must understand the relationship between the ideas and choose a word or phrase that expresses that relationship.

To add two related ideas	
also	in addition
as a matter of fact	in fact
furthermore	moreover

Example:

What we eat can affect our ability to fight colds; **moreover**, foods high in copper, zinc, and protein can help our immune system fend off the common cold.

To contrast two related ideas or to limit an idea	
conversely	on the contrary
however	on the other hand
nevertheless	otherwise

Example:

I love driving fast in my sports car; **on the other hand**, I don't like getting pulled over by the police.

To show that one idea is a consequence of the other	
accordingly	for this reason
as a result	therefore
consequently	

Example:

Our immune system weakens as we get older; **consequently**, people over the age of sixty-five should take care to eat foods that help strengthen the immune system.

To show repetition or illustration of an idea in fact	
for example	in other words
for instance	indeed

Example:

Yogurt is a proven disease fighter; **for example**, studies have shown that women who eat yogurt every day get fewer yeast infections than women who do not eat yogurt.

Exercise 3

Circle the conjunctive adverb or transitional expression that shows the relationship between the ideas.

1. One can find lots to do at a county fair; (nevertheless, accordingly, indeed), the rides provide an exciting and spine-tingling experience.

2. The United States has never had a woman president; (however, therefore, for example), England has had women as its monarch and its prime minister.

3. Mark earned an honors degree in engineering; (otherwise, as a result, for instance), he was able to get a job with NASA.

4. A Mercedes is the car I want; (furthermore, nevertheless, for this reason,), it is too expensive for my budget.

5. The newspaper is a primary source of news about world events; (also, on the contrary, accordingly), the newspaper provides news about local events.

Subordination Strategies

Writers use **subordination** to combine a main idea and a related but less important (or subordinate) idea. Subordination combines a **dependent clause** or **phrase** with an **independent clause**.

Original sentences:

Emil's Café offers soft lighting and romantic music.

This restaurant is a favorite place to take a date.

Combined sentences:

D C

Since Emil's Café offers soft lighting and romantic music, this restaurant is a favorite place to take a date. I C

I C   D C

Emil's Café is a favorite place to take a date **because** it offers soft lighting and romantic music.

Subordinating Conjunctions

The most common way to subordinate ideas is to use a **subordinating conjunction** to turn an independent clause into a dependent clause.

Original sentences:

Renovating my house is exciting. Remodeling can be expensive and tiring.

Combined sentences:

D C   I C

Although renovating my house is exciting, remodeling can be expensive and tiring

To combine sentences using subordinating conjunctions, writers must understand the relationship between the ideas and choose a subordinating conjunction that expresses that relationship. Subordinating conjunctions show the following relationships between ideas.

One idea is a contrast of the other

although	whereas
even though	while
though	

Example:

Though it's late, I'm not tired at all.

One idea is a consequence of the other

as
because
since

Example:

Because my favorite team is playing this weekend, I want to go to the game.

One idea is a condition of the other

if	unless

Example:

If I have to do chores around the house, I would like to do the ones I enjoy like washing the car.

> **One idea is related in time to the other**
>
> | | |
> |---|---|
> | after | until |
> | as | when |
> | before | while |

Example:

Sometimes I play games on my computer **while** I am talking on the phone.

Exercise 4

Circle the subordinating conjunction that shows the relationship between the ideas.

1. I know a lot about computers (though, since, unless) my father works for a computer maker.

2. (Even though, Because, If, Before) the movie starts in an hour, let's eat dinner now.

3. (Although, Since, Unless, While) my aunt works as a maid, her own house is a mess.

4. (While, Because, If, After) Napoleon was defeated at Waterloo, he ended his days in exile.

5. (Even though, As, If, Before) I should pass Basic Writing, I will take College Composition.

Relative Pronouns

Two ideas can sometimes be combined using a **relative pronoun** (*who, that,* or *which*). The relative pronoun is used to make one idea into a dependent clause in order to define a word or phrase in the other idea (the independent clause.)

Original sentences:

My neighbor owns a store in town. The store sells lawn mowers and lawn maintenance supplies.

Combined sentence:

My neighbor owns a store in town **that** sells lawn mowers and lawn maintenance supplies.

When subordinating a clause using a relative pronoun, choose the appropriate relative pronoun to refer back to the noun in the main clause. The relative pronoun should follow the noun to which it refers. Also, use commas to set off relative clauses that express nonessential (or nonrestrictive) information—that is, any information that does not restrict the meaning of the sentence.

Who takes the place of people.

Which takes the place of things.

That usually takes the place of things or people when the clause is essential (or restrictive).

Examples:

My boss, who is a kind man, lets me go home early sometimes.

My house, which is located on Cherry Street, is painted green.

The computer that was advertised in the newspaper wasn't expensive.

Circle the appropriate relative pronoun to combine these sentences.

Exercise 5

1. Our new car already has a scratch on it. We bought it last week.

   Our new car, (who, that, which) we bought last week, already has a scratch on it.

2. I like my geography professor. She has traveled all over the world.

   I like my geography professor, (who, that, which) has traveled all over the world.

3. A house was burglarized last night. It is on the next block.

   A house (who, that, which) is on the next block was burglarized last night.

4. I just bought a new computer. I use it for school.

   I just bought a new computer, (who, that, which) I use for school.

5. I just talked to Marina Federov. She is my best friend.

   I just talked to Marina Federov, (who, that, which) is my best friend.

Appositives

Two ideas can sometimes be combined using an **appositive**, a group of words that defines or explains a given word or phrase. When two ideas are combined using an appositive, one idea defines a word or phrase in the other idea.

Original sentences:

Mr. Hernandez is very nice. He is my teacher.

Combined sentence:

Appositive

Mr. Hernandez, **my teacher**, is very nice.

Exercise 6

Fill in the blanks with words from the second sentence that can be used to form an appositive in the first sentence.

1. That telephone call was from Jose. He's the top student in my math class.

   That telephone call was from Jose, _____.

2. My car is in the parking lot. It's an old blue station wagon with a dent in the fender.

   My car, _____, is in the parking lot.

3. A major health problem for teenagers is bulimia. Bulimia is an eating disorder.

   A major health problem for teenagers is bulimia, _____.

4. I loved my first home. It was a two-story Victorian townhouse.

   I loved my first home, _____.

5. The neighbors' dog always chases cats. It is a golden retriever.

   The neighbors' dog, _____, always chases cats.

Verbal Phrases

Two ideas can sometimes be combined by making one idea into a **verbal phrase** beginning with an **infinitive verb**, a **present participle**, or a **past participle**.

Infinitive phrase

Original sentences:

I wanted to get a job. I had to cut my hair.

Combined sentence:

To get a job, I had to cut my hair.

Present participial phrase

Original sentences:

Juanita was getting a cold. Juanita left work early.

Combined sentence:

Getting a cold, Juanita left work early.

Past participial phrase

Original sentences:

The worker was tired of her job. The worker told her boss that she was quitting.

Combined sentence:

Tired of her job, the worker told her boss that she was quitting.

Note: Using verbals correctly can be tricky because the verbal must refer to a subject that performs the action of the verbal.

Mistake: Running up the hill, my heart was pounding.

(Who is running up the hill?)

Correction: Running up the hill, I could feel that my heart was pounding.

(The subject closest to the verbal must be the one running up the hill.)

Use words in the first sentence to form a verbal phrase for the second sentence.

Exercise 7

1. The waitress was carrying a platter of food. The waitress didn't see the customer bent over tying his shoe.

   _____, the waitress didn't see the customer bent over tying his shoe.

2. The waitress had to keep the platter from falling. The waitress stumbled to an empty table and set the platter down.

   _____, the waitress stumbled to an empty table and set the platter down.

3. She was done for the day. She counted her tips.

   _____, she counted her tips.

continues

continued

4. The waitress was tired from all the work. The waitress still had to walk home.

   _____, the waitress still had to walk home.

5. The waitress was unlocking her door. She remembered that she had forgotten to pick up her tips.

   _____, she remembered that she had forgotten to pick up her tips.

Using Coordination or Subordination

Understanding the relationship between two or more given ideas is the key to combining those ideas into strong sentences. The three most common relationships are **addition of similar ideas, contrast of opposing ideas,** and **consequence of resulting ideas**. Below are the conjunctions used to show these relationships.

	Addition	Contrast	Consequence
Coordinating conjunctions	and	but yet	so for
Subordinating conjunctions	along with in addition to while	even though although though	because since
Conjunctive adverbs and Transitional Expressions	moreover furthermore in addition also	however in contrast nevertheless	therefore as a result consequently
Relative pronouns	that which who		

Combine the following pairs of sentences according to the directions following each pair. Refer to the chart of connectors to choose an appropriate connecting word and sentence pattern.

Exercise 8

1. Susan loves the beach. She lives on the coast.
   Use a coordinating conjunction in a compound sentence.

   _____

   Use a coordinating conjunction in a compound predicate.

   _____

   Use a conjunctive adverb or transitional expression.

   _____

   Use a subordinating conjunction.

   _____

   Use a relative clause.

   _____

   Use an appositive.

   _____

   Use a verbal phrase.

   _____

2. Mrs. Hall loves her husband. He is a lazy bum.
   Use a coordinating conjunction in a compound sentence.

   _____

   Use a conjunctive adverb or transitional expression.

   _____

   Use a subordinating conjunction.

   _____

   Use a relative clause.

   _____

   Use an appositive.

   _____

continues

continued

3. Miss America is very beautiful. She has shown a lot of talent as a pianist.

   Use a coordinating conjunction in a compound sentence.

   _____

   Use a coordinating conjunction in a compound predicate.

   _____

   Use a conjunctive adverb or transitional expression.

   _____

   Use a subordinating conjunction.

   _____

   Use a relative clause.

   _____

4. His attempt at cooking dinner was a disaster. They went out to eat.

   Use a coordinating conjunction in a compound sentence.

   _____

   Use a conjunctive adverb or transitional expression.

   _____

   Use a subordinating conjunction.

   _____

5. The employee wanted a day off. He was afraid to ask his boss.

   Use a coordinating conjunction in a compound sentence.

   _____

   Use a coordinating conjunction in a compound predicate.

   _____

   Use a conjunctive adverb or transitional expression.

   _____

   Use a subordinating conjunction.

   _____

   Use a relative clause.

   _____

Chapter 31
Sentence Variety

Good writers vary their sentences. Effective communication takes place when the reader is paying attention to each new sentence and not getting bored by repeated patterns. Imagine listening to a teacher who began every sentence throughout an entire class period with the words *Students will…* The repeated words at the beginning of every sentence would probably turn you off and maybe even annoy you. Similarly, a paragraph or an essay that repeats the same pattern in a number of sentences puts off readers. Learning sentence variety techniques will give you strategies to make each sentence fresh.

Writers use sentence variety strategies both while writing and while revising. The strategies are fairly simple, yet they create powerful results. In this chapter, you will examine revised paragraphs to learn how writers can improve sentence variety. In addition, you will practice these strategies so that you will be ready to use them in your own writing.

There are four basic sentence variety strategies:

1. Vary the beginnings of sentences.

2. Vary the length of sentences.

3. Vary the placement of important information in sentences.

4. Vary the sentence structures.

We will look at each one in turn, but before we do, let's look at an overall example of revision to achieve sentence variety.

Beth

> I eventually received a high grade on this paragraph about the supermarket after I revised my paragraph using the sentence variety guidelines. Read my first draft below, and then see how I followed my instructor's comments to improve the presentation of my ideas.

*Don't overuse 'supermarket.'
Vary the first word of sentences.*

Good Start!

One-Stop Shop

Combine simple sentences to use different sentence types

All important information comes at the end of your supports. Vary the placement so information sometimes comes at the beginning.

The supermarket has become a one-stop shopping center for the entire family. The supermarket still sells the usual groceries. What's new is the variety of choices from around the world. There are Italian olive oils and pastas, Asian noodles, and South American plantains. The supermarket's bakery bakes everything from breads to donuts and birthday cakes. Supermarkets have become our primary drugstore because we can fill prescriptions while we shop. Many supermarkets stock videos, flowers, and even perfumes. Most supermarkets provide stamps, check cashing, and photo processing. Now a lot of stores house a deli that makes sandwiches and salads for busy workers on the go. Shopping is becoming a pleasure at supermarkets these days.

Use transitions to improve the flow of ideas

> My teacher liked the content of my paragraph because it provided a lot of factual information. However, she pointed out that most sentences were long and began with the subject *supermarkets*. Also, the important information came at the end of each sentence. These repeated patterns made the paragraph sound monotonous. My instructor showed me ways to improve the sentence variety, and I received a much higher grade on the revision below.

I avoided starting sentences with the same words & I used synonyms for supermarket.

One-Stop Shop

I placed important information at the beginning of the sentence.

I tried to use different sentence types.

I used a transition to make sentences flow.

The modern American supermarket has become a one-stop shopping center for the entire family. While the neighborhood supermarket still sells the usual groceries, what's new is the variety of choices from around the world such as Italian olive oils and pastas, Asian noodles, and South American plantains. The store bakery bakes everything from breads to donuts and birthday cakes, and because we can fill prescriptions while we shop, supermarkets have become our primary drugstore. Videos, flowers, and even perfumes are a few of the expanded lines of merchandise that grocery stores stock. Also, most stores provide stamps, check cashing, and photo processing, and they house a deli that makes sandwiches and salads for busy workers on the go. Shopping is becoming a pleasure at supermarkets these days.

Vary Sentence Beginnings

One of the easiest ways to get variety in your sentences is to change the way they begin. In general, avoid starting two consecutive sentences with the same words. The following sections give you some techniques for varying sentence beginnings.

Use a Synonym

Use a **synonym** (a word with a similar meaning) for repeated words at the beginning of sentences.

> Example:
> (The words in bold are synonyms for *writing letters*.)

> **Writing letters** to send by electronic mail is a great way to communicate with friends around the world. **Composing messages** on the computer can also improve one's writing ability because one has the support of a spell check and grammar check program. **Corresponding** is fast and cheap with e-mail.

Use a Transition

Use a **transition** (such as a conjunctive adverb or transitional expression—see Chapter 30) to begin the sentence.

> Example:
> (The transitions change the beginning of sentences and show the relationship between the sentences.)

> Writing letters to send by electronic mail is a great way to communicate with friends around the world. **For instance**, writing letters on the computer can also improve one's writing ability because one has the support of a spell check and grammar check program. **Furthermore**, writing letters is fast and cheap with e-mail.

Rearrange the Sentence

Rearrange the sentence so that it starts with different words. Use information from the sentence to create an introductory element from a dependent clause, prepositional phrase, or infinitive phrase (the word *to* plus a verb).

> *Original sentence:*

> Writers can also improve their writing ability **because** they have the support of a spell check and grammar check program.

> *Rearranged sentence:*

> **Because** they have the support of a spell check and grammar check program, writers can also improve their writing ability.

Original sentence:

Writing letters is fast and cheap **with** e-mail.

Rearranged sentence:

With e-mail, writing letters is fast and cheap.

Original sentence:

Writers use e-mail **to communicate** with friends around the world.

Rearranged sentence:

To communicate with friends around the world, writers use e-mail.

Use a Pronoun

Use a **pronoun** (*he, she, it, they,* etc.) that takes the place of the subject of the previous sentence.

Example:

Writers have a fast and cheap method of communication with e-mail. **They** use e-mail to communicate with friends around the world.

Combine Two Sentences

Combine two sentences to avoid repetitive wording. For example, use a compound sentence or a complex sentence.

Original sentences:

Writing letters is fast and cheap with e-mail. Writing letters electronically is becoming very popular.

Compound sentence:

Writing letters is fast and cheap with e-mail, **so** writing letters electronically is becoming very popular.

Complex sentence:

Because writing letters is fast and cheap with e-mail, writing letters electronically is becoming very popular.

Rewrite the following paragraph using the strategies for varying sentence beginnings. Make sure that no more than two sentences begin with the word *laughter*.

The Gift of Laughter

Laughter has many health benefits. Laughter stimulates the immune system. Laughter activates germ-killing T-cells and speeds up the manufacture of new immune cells. Laughter makes us feel good and have a better sense of well-being by pumping extra adrenaline into our bloodstream and bringing on a rush of endorphins, the body's natural painkillers. Laughter greases the mental gears and stimulates creative thinking. Laughter exercises the heart, the lungs, and the muscles in our upper body and back. Most important, laughter reduces or eliminates stress. Laughing a hundred times a day may definitely keep the doctor away.

Vary Sentence Length

The second sentence variety strategy is to vary sentence length. **Alternate** long sentences with short ones. If all the sentences are short, use sentence combining (described in Chapter 30) to make some longer ones. If all the sentences are long, break some up. Your writing should have a rhythm to it, just as music has rhythm. Following a long sentence with a shorter one keeps your writing from sounding monotonous.

PEER EXAMPLE

Alicia

“ When I read this first draft of my paragraph out loud, it sounded choppy. Then my teacher pointed out that most of the sentences in my paragraph are short. ”

Eating Out and Spending Less

Paying attention to the bill when dining out can keep the cost down. Diners should avoid the bar. Drinks raise the bill substantially. Choosing à la carte items is expensive. Meals that include salad or soup are usually cheaper. Don't allow the waiter to top off the wineglasses. This encourages more drinking. Substitutions to specials can be costly. Ask the price of a different vegetable or side dish before ordering. Dessert and coffee can add 25 percent to the bill. Think about skipping them. Diners can save a lot of money by being aware of what they order.

66 In this final draft of my paragraph, I combined most of the short sentences into longer ones; however, I left a few short sentences to create variety for the longer ones. Now the writing seems to flow better. 99

Eating Out and Spending Less

Paying attention to the bill when dining out can keep the cost down. Diners should avoid the bar because drinks raise the bill substantially. Choosing à la carte items is expensive, but diners can save money if they order meals that include salad or soup. The waiters should not be allowed to top off wineglasses because this encourages more drinking. Since substitutions to specials can be costly, alert consumers will ask the price of a different vegetable or side dish before ordering. Also, skipping dessert and coffee can often save 25 percent of the bill. Diners save money by being aware of what they order.

WRITING PRACTICE 2   Try rewriting this paragraph so that short and long sentences alternate.

Barcelona

Barcelona is a fascinating city. This city is home to Portuguese, Jewish, and Moroccan communities. These cultures give Barcelona an international air. The museums in Barcelona include the Picasso Museum and the Miró Foundation. In fact, the city has a very artistic feel to it. An important Spanish architect, Antonio Gaudi, built many buildings in Barcelona. He is renowned for his bizarre imagination and modern designs. The city is also blessed with special treasures. There are bullfights, cable car rides across the harbor, and church services at the cathedral. Of special interest to Americans is the Plaza del Rey. Christopher Columbus announced his discovery of the New World there. Barcelona has a lot to offer.

Vary the Placement of Important Information

The third sentence variety strategy is to vary the placement of important information in sentences. If the important information is always at the end of the sentence, the reader will pay attention only to the sentence endings. Placing important information at the beginning, middle, and end of different sentences will keep the reader alert. However, in certain rhetorical patterns such as classification, repetition of a pattern of support within a paragraph is sometimes necessary.

Tony

> I wasn't aware that I had fallen into a boring pattern in this first draft. Then, my instructor pointed out that I use the same pattern to present information about each kind of meditation. First I name and define a type of meditation, and then I explain it in a second sentence.

Kinds of Meditation

There are three basic kinds of meditation. Passive meditation happens when we just sit and observe the movement of our breath. This type of meditation develops our concentration. Openness meditation focuses on being open to the sensations we experience in our bodies. We become aware of sights, sounds, and feelings in our body. Creative meditation helps us use our imagination to unlock creative energy. In this meditation, we imagine experiences such as unlocking doors or taking a sauna that will relax us and allow us to realize our potential. Each kind of meditation is useful for different purposes.

> To improve the variety of the sentences, I put the important information about open meditation at the beginning of the sentence. I also changed the pattern of development in the last two types of meditation and included examples in the third type.

Kinds of Meditation

There are three basic kinds of meditation. Passive meditation happens when we just sit and observe the movement of our breath. This type of meditation develops our concentration. Being open to the sensations we experience in our bodies is the focus of openness meditation. Sights, sounds, and feelings in our body are the object of our attention. When we use our imagination to unlock creative energy, we are using creative meditation. We imagine experiences such as unlocking doors or taking a sauna that will relax us and allow us to realize our potential in this meditation. Each kind of meditation is useful for different purposes.

WRITING PRACTICE 3   Try rewriting the sentences so that the important information is not always at the end of the sentence.

Parents Matter

Parents play a vital role in helping their children do well in school. First, parents set an example by the way they relate to their own work. Kids learn to value hard work when they observe their parents succeed through persistence. Parents can also make the job of learning fun by incorporating educational activities into everyday life at home. For example, parents can foster good reading skills in their children by reading frequently to them from the time they are toddlers until they are teenagers. Finally, the parents' view of learning influences how kids view their education. Students will value their hard work to develop good skills if parents value the kids' hard work more than the grades they get. The attitudes of parents about learning affect their kids' performance in school.

Vary the Sentence Structure

The fourth and final sentence variety strategy is to mix the four sentence structures (described in Chapter 27 and reviewed in the box below) in paragraphs. Sometimes you will have to combine sentences to form these structures (see Chapter 30).

The Four Sentence Structures

- **Simple sentence**

  Independent clause.

- **Compound sentence**

  Independent clause, coordinating conjunction + independent clause.

  Independent clause; independent clause.

  Independent clause; transition, independent clause.

- **Complex sentence**

  Independent clause + dependent clause.

- **Compound/complex sentence**

  Two independent clauses + one or more dependent clauses.

Rewrite the following paragraph to improve the variety in sentence structure.

At the Fair

The county fair entertains the entire family. Many people bring their kids to enjoy the carnival rides. Teenagers especially like the bumper cars and roller coaster. Grownups test their skill by trying to win prizes at the rifle shoot or basket throw. Some people get a kick out of the sideshows. The fortune-teller always has something interesting to say about romance or money. Townsfolk eventually get hungry. They start looking for their favorite junk food such as hot dogs, hamburgers, cotton candy, or candied apples. Of course, people-watching is a popular activity too. Teenagers like to be seen with their dates. Adults get a chance to meet friends' families and see how much the kids have grown. The fair is a community event we all look forward to.

Chapter 32
Commas

Knowing how to use commas correctly is an important skill for writers. Examine any piece of good writing, especially academic writing, and you will see commas in many of the sentences. Writers use commas to organize information. They also use commas to add information to sentences and to create sentence variety in paragraphs.

Most teachers and students rank commas as the most difficult punctuation mark to use correctly. In this chapter, you will learn a number of important rules through easy-to-remember formulas and examples. In addition, you will get practice using the rules and avoiding common errors.

Dates and Addresses

Use commas between items in **dates** and **addresses**.

> My grandfather was born on Friday, June 7, 1902, in Atlanta, Georgia, of Irish immigrants.

Misuses

Don't separate the month from the year if the day is not given.

> Incorrect: The last time to apply for the scholarship is May, 2003.

> Correct: The last time to apply for the scholarship is May 2003.

Series

Use commas to set off items in a **series**. A series is a list of at least three items. The items may be single words, phrases, or clauses.

> The flag is red, white, and blue.

> I enjoy walking on the beach, sitting on the sand, and swimming in the water.

Although some grammarians now consider the comma before the final *and* to be optional, using the last comma makes the series clear to the reader.

Misuses

Don't use commas when there are only two items in a list.

> Incorrect: I like coffee, and donuts for breakfast.

> Correct: I like coffee and donuts for breakfast.

Don't use commas when *and* or *or* joins each item.

> Incorrect: I enjoy a warm bath, and a soft bed, and a good night's sleep.

> Correct: I enjoy a warm bath and a soft bed and a good night's sleep.

Don't use a comma after the last item in the series.

> Incorrect: Red, white, and blue, are my favorite colors.

> Correct: Red, white, and blue are my favorite colors.

Compound Sentences

Use a comma between **two independent clauses** joined by a **coordinating conjunction** (see Chapters 27 and 30). The comma comes after the first independent clause and before the conjunction.

> **Formula**
> Independent clause, coordinating conjunction + independent clause.

> Examples:
> I love my job at Shands Hospital, and I hope I can work there for a long time.

> Rock climbing is exciting, yet it is also dangerous.

Key words

Coordinating conjunctions: **for, and, nor, but, or, yet, so**

(Remember *fanboys* to memorize these key words.)

Misuses

Do not use a comma before a coordinating conjunction that does not join two *independent* clauses. (This is the most common comma error.)

               S   V   V

Incorrect: Sarah **borrowed** my car, and **drove** her mother home.

(The word group following the conjunction is not an independent clause because it does not have a subject.)

Correct: Sarah borrowed my car and drove her mother home.

In general, do not use a comma between word groups that are not joined by a coordinating conjunction.

Incorrect: Computers are very useful, because they can perform calculations quickly.

Correct: Computers are very useful because they can perform calculations quickly.

Incorrect: My neighbor always catches the bus, at 8:00 in the morning.

Correct: My neighbor always catches the bus at 8:00 in the morning.

Do not use a comma before *so that*. (*So* is a coordinating conjunction, but *so that* introduces a dependent clause, not an independent one.) This can be tricky when the *that* is left out, which often happens in informal writing.

Incorrect: I am on a diet, so (that) I can lose weight.

Correct: I am on a diet so (that) I can lose weight.

> To use the compound sentence comma rule correctly, identify the subject and the verb in each clause to make sure that the coordinating conjunction joins two independent clauses.

Exercise 1

Add commas where needed. (Some sentences may not need any commas.)

1. We chose to drive on the turnpike for we needed to get home quickly.

2. Joe and Ted play football together and help each other with their homework each night.

3. Our dog can run hard to catch a cat yet will only walk slowly when he is called back home.

4. My car broke down so I had to take it to a mechanic.

5. I exercise regularly so I can stay in good condition.

Introductory Elements

Use a comma after most **introductory elements.** An introductory element is either a dependent clause or a phrase that introduces an independent clause. Most introductory elements begin with verbals, prepositions, or subordinating conjunctions.

Formula
Dependent clause or phrase, independent clause.

Remember that an introductory element is a sentence fragment that introduces a complete thought (sentence).

Verbal Phrases

Verbal phrases begin with present participles (such as *going, buying, seeing*); past participles (such as *gone, bought, seen*); or infinitives (such as *to go, to buy, to see*).

Examples:

Present Participial Phrase   IC
Sleeping on the job, I missed an important call from my boss.

           Past Participial Phrase   IC
Built in the 1890s by a timber baron, the mansion was the grandest building in town.

     Infinitive Phrase   IC
To see the latest results, the scientists met in the laboratory.

Prepositional Phrases
Prepositional phrases begin with a preposition.

Example:

Prepositional Phrase   IC

On the first day of the term, the professor informed her class of her attendance policy.

Dependent Clauses
Dependent clauses begin with a subordinating conjunction.

Subordinating conjunctions				
after	before	when	although	even though
though	whereas	as	if	unless
whether	because	since	until	while

Examples:

Dependent Clause   IC

Although it was raining, they took a walk anyway.

Dependent Clause   IC

Since it was raining, they decided not to have a picnic.

Dependent Clause   IC

If the rain didn't stop soon, they would have to go inside.

Misuses
A comma is usually not needed if the dependent clause **follows** the independent clause.

Example:

IC   DC

Incorrect: You'll have to pay for gas, if you drive my car.

Correct: You'll have to pay for gas if you drive my car.

Exercise 2

Add commas where needed. (Some sentences may not need any commas.)

1. Whenever I go to the computer lab I always forget to remove my disk from the computer.

2. After winning the football game the players went to a celebration party.

3. Talking to a friend helps when you are sad and blue.

4. To succeed in business the business owner must make lots of contacts in the community.

5. Since the roads were icy the weather service issued a warning not to drive.

Interrupters

Commas are used to set off **interrupters**, which are single words or groups of words that change the flow of a sentence. Interrupters include the following:

- Small words at the beginning of sentences.
- Names in direct address.
- Transitions.
- Appositives.
- Nonrestrictive elements.

The various rules regarding interrupters cover words, phrases, and clauses at the beginning, in the middle, or at the end of a sentence.

Small Words

Use a comma after certain **small words** at the beginning of a sentence. Such words are *Yes, No, Oh, Well, Hey,* and *Hi.* These words are not used often in formal writing, although they are common in informal writing such as letters, memos, and e-mail.

Formula
Small word, sentence.

Examples:

Yes, this rule is easy to learn.

Well, the Patriots will have a chance to beat the Giants next year.

Misuse

This rule applies only when the small word actually functions as an interrupter, not when it is part of the subject.

Incorrect: No, students have registered yet.

(*No* is part of the subject of the sentence; it's not an interrupter coming before the sentence.)

Correct: No students have registered yet.

Direct Address

Direct address means communicating directly to the person or group being named. Names or titles can be placed anywhere in the sentence and should be separated from the rest of the sentence by commas when they interrupt the flow of the sentence.

Formula
Name or title, sentence.
Sentence, name or title.
Sentence beginning, name or title, sentence ending.

Examples:

Sir, your order will take two weeks to deliver.

Please complete the assignment by Friday, students.

Your appointment, Andre, is on Thursday at noon.

Misuse

Do not use commas to set off a name or title unless the person is in fact being directly addressed. When writing *about* a person or group of people, do not use commas to set off the name or title.

Incorrect: I think, Mr. Jordan, is the best athlete ever.

Correct: I think Mr. Jordan is the best athlete ever.

Transitions

If a **transition** can be removed from a sentence without changing the meaning of the sentence, it is an interrupter. These interrupters can be **conjunctive adverbs** or **transitional expressions** (see Chapter 30), and they can be placed anywhere in the sentence. **Interrupting transitions** should be separated from the rest of the sentence by commas.

Formula
Transition, sentence.
Sentence, transition.
Sentence beginning, transition, sentence ending.

Examples:

Moreover, he had trouble reading the test because he didn't have his eyeglasses.

The design is flawed because it allows no wheelchair access, **for example.**

The reason, **however**, for the delay was the severe thunderstorm.

Misuses
A transition that is a *necessary* word in the sentence should not be separated by commas. If the transition cannot be removed from the sentence without changing the meaning of the sentence, it is a necessary part of the sentence and not an interrupter.

Incorrect: My best friend is, also, my neighbor.

(*Also* is a necessary word and not an interrupter in this sentence.

Correct: My best friend is also my neighbor.

Exercise 3

Add commas where needed. (Some sentences may not need any commas.)

1. My father's wish in any event was for me to attend college.
2. The rules prohibit running on the pool deck also.
3. The students passed the test as a result of their hard work.
4. Thus the tide rose and lifted the boat off the shoal.
5. Consequently it's time to take stock of our priorities.

Appositives

Use commas to set off an **appositive**, a word or group of words that defines or explains the word or phrase that comes before it. Usually an appositive comes immediately after the word or phrase it defines. An appositive must be the same part of speech as the word it defines.

Formula
Sentence, appositive.
Sentence beginning, appositive, sentence ending.

Examples:

App

I like George, **my next-door neighbor**.

App

My mother's native land, **Colombia**, is located in South America.

Recognizing Appositives

Because an appositive phrase must be the same part of speech as the word it renames, the appositive and its referent are interchangeable. In other words, the sentence should make sense either without the appositive or with only the appositive.

> Washington, D.C., the nation's capital, is beautiful in April when the cherry trees bloom.

> Read the sentence without the appositive: "Washington, D.C., is beautiful in April when the cherry trees bloom." Then read the sentence without the word or phrase the appositive defines. "The nation's capital is beautiful in April when the cherry trees bloom." Since both sentences mean the same thing, the phrase *the nation's capital* is clearly an appositive.

Misuse

The most common error with appositives occurs when the writer fails to end the appositive with a comma.

> Incorrect: Bill, my next-door neighbor is a great golfer.

> Correct: Bill, my next-door neighbor, is a great golfer.

> (Don't forget the final comma to define where the appositive ends.)

Add commas where needed. (Some sentences may not need any commas.)

Exercise 4

1. The plane crashed because its altimeter a gauge that measures altitude was malfunctioning.

2. The golden retriever one of the most popular dogs in America is known for its obedience and gentle disposition.

3. Our study group met at Joe's Deli a popular snack shop in order to plan our class presentation.

4. The traffic light on the corner of Main Street was stuck on green.

5. I always enjoy going to class when my favorite instructor Ms. Taylor gives the lecture.

Nonrestrictive Elements

Use commas to separate information that is **nonrestrictive**, or nonessential to the meaning of the sentence. Nonrestrictive information is not necessary to understand the meaning of the word or phrase that the information is modifying or explaining. This rule governs when to use commas to separate information that modifies or explains a word or phrase in a sentence. The nonrestrictive comma rule is one of the hardest to learn because it is not always easy to tell whether a certain word or word group is necessary in a given sentence.

> My family's first house, which was in Vermont, had a fireplace.

> The information inside the commas interrupts the flow of the sentence. It is not necessary to understand what house the sentence is about since there is only one house that was "my family's first house." Commas *should* separate this nonessential information.

> Our history teacher, who is from Vermont, told us about New England's rich history.

> The information inside the commas interrupts the flow of the sentence. It is not necessary to understand what teacher is being written about. Commas *should* separate this nonessential information.

Restrictive Elements

Do *not* use commas to separate **restrictive** information in a sentence; this is information that is essential to the meaning of the sentence. Restrictive information limits (that is, restricts) the meaning of the word or phrase it modifies and is therefore necessary to the meaning of the sentence.

> The teacher who is from Vermont has not yet arrived at the teachers' conference.

> The clause *who is from Vermont* is restrictive; it provides essential information that is necessary to understand which teacher, out of all the teachers at the conference, has not yet arrived. The clause *should not* be separated by commas from the rest of the sentence.

Recognizing Nonrestrictive versus Restrictive Information

One good test of whether or not information is essential to a sentence is to take the information out. If the meaning of the sentence changes, then the information is essential and therefore should not be separated by commas.

> All students who have not paid their fees will be dropped from the course.

Who have not paid their fees is necessary information; it tells which students will be dropped from the course. Commas should *not* separate this essential information.

Newspapers will not print stories that have not been checked twice.

That have not been checked twice is necessary information to identify which stories will not be printed. Commas should *not* separate this essential information.

Misuses

Writers make comma errors when they are not sure whether a word or phrase is restrictive or nonrestrictive. Here are some ways to help decide whether commas are needed:

1. If the information begins with *that*, then the information usually is restrictive and no commas are needed.

   Incorrect: The building, that was condemned last week, burned down yesterday.

   The clause *that was condemned last week* identifies which building burned down and is necessary information, so no commas should separate it from the rest of the sentence.

   Correct: The building that was condemned last week burned down yesterday.

2. If the information describes a noun that needs no identification or clarification, then the information is nonrestrictive.

   Incorrect: The firefighters surrounded the burning building which was condemned last week.

   The clause *which was condemned last week* is not necessary to identify the building, so this is extra information that must be separated by commas.

   Correct: The firefighters surrounded the burning building, which was condemned last week.

Exercise 5

Place commas where needed. (Some sentences may not need any commas.)

1. The students received their awards which were foot-high trophies.

2. My mother who likes to crack jokes is crazy.

3. El Indio Restaurant located on 15th Street is great.

4. My exercise class which is in the gym starts at 9:00.

5. The English class that begins at 9:00 is in the auditorium.

Review Exercise 1

Add commas where needed. (Some sentences may not need any commas.)

1. New Jersey is one of the most populous states and although it is not a large state in land area New Jersey has a great deal of variety.

2. Because of its beautiful beach and scenic boardwalks the Jersey shore is a popular vacation spot and it is always crowded in peak tourist seasons.

3. In the northern part of the state many people commute to jobs in New York City New York.

4. The airport in Newark New Jersey is always crowded at rush hour even though it is very spacious but it is often less congested than Kennedy International on Long Island which is busy twenty-four hours a day.

5. There is a rivalry nevertheless between New York and New Jersey.

6. According to native New Yorkers anyone not from New York City is to be pitied.

7. Some New Yorkers think that their city is the most important place on earth and maybe they are right.

8. Yes David the five boroughs of New York are Manhattan Brooklyn the Bronx Staten Island and Queens.

9. Although New York was founded by Dutch settlers there is not much Dutch influence visible today.

10. Certainly it is very interesting to live in New York City one of the largest cities in the world.

Add commas where needed.

A Good Sport

Racquetball one of the fastest-growing sports in America is an easy game
to learn. It can be played on a court of three or four walls but according
to the best players the four-wall game is the most challenging. In the game
of four-wall players can also use a fifth wall which is the ceiling and if the
players are very good the game will consist of high lobs kill shots and Z
shots. Of course even beginners have fun playing racquetball but are
more likely to receive injuries. With so many racquets and players in such
a small area it's easy to get hit and eye injuries are the most serious.

Chapter 33
Apostrophes

Apostrophes give writers trouble for two reasons. First, apostrophes don't appear as often as periods and commas, especially in formal writing in which contractions are not used. Second, a missing or misplaced apostrophe doesn't affect the sound of a sentence the way other misused punctuation does, so writers have a harder time detecting apostrophe errors. This chapter will make you aware of when and how to use apostrophes.

Contractions

Use an apostrophe to indicate missing letters in a **contraction**, a combination of two words in which some letters have been left out.

Examples:

there's = there is

we'll = we will

can't = cannot

it's = it is *or* it has

you're = you are

Possession

Use an apostrophe to show a **possessive relationship**, that is, to show ownership.

> Examples:
>
> Jack's car = the car that belongs to Jack
>
> an author's viewpoint = the viewpoint of an author
>
> some neighbors' yards = the yards of some neighbors
>
> the men's club = the club of the men

Determining Possession

The most important step to using possessive apostrophes correctly is to determine if there is a possessive relationship between words in a phrase. A common mistake is to put an apostrophe in a word that is plural but not possessive. Not every word that has an *s* at the end should have an apostrophe. You must check carefully for a possessive relationship. Once you are aware that you are using a possessive phrase, the rules for where to put the apostrophe are easy (we cover these in the following sections).

Test for ownership by converting the form of the phrase from **owner(?) + object** to **the object of the owner(?).** If the restated phrase makes sense and shows the relationship of ownership, an apostrophe is needed. (You can perform this check in your head, without writing down the words.)

> Examples:
>
> Bill's friend = friend of Bill (apostrophe needed)
>
> Horses raced = raced of horse (no apostrophe needed)

Another test for possession is to ask whether the second word or group of words belongs to the word before it.

> Examples:
>
> Bill's friend: *Friend* belongs to *Bill*, so there is a possessive relationship.
>
> horses raced: *Raced* doesn't belong to *horses*, so no apostrophe is needed to show possession.

Word Order in a Possessive Phrase

Remember that the object owned must immediately follow the owner. The only words that might come between the owner and the object are adjectives that describe the object.

Examples:

Bill's dear old friend = dear old friend of Bill

the lawyer's detailed defense = detailed defense of the lawyer

Placement of the Apostrophe in Possessive Phrases

There are only three basic rules for the placement of the apostrophe in possessives:

> If the owner is singular, add an *-s* after the apostrophe. If the owner is plural and therefore already has an *-s* at the end, the apostrophe comes after the *-s* ending. For irregular plural words that have no *-s* ending, add the *-s* after the apostrophe, as you would do for a singular owner.

Singular Owner

To make a singular word possessive, add **'s**.

Examples:

a day's work   summer's heat

an essay's thesis   a book's title page

Note that this rule holds true even if the singular owner is a word that ends with *s*.

Examples:

Mr. Bliss's daughters

Russ's car

the class's field trip

Add apostrophes where needed.

Exercise 1

1. Mrs. Smiths daughter was married yesterday.

2. I want to visit Jacksonvilles beautiful beaches.

3. Februarys weather is always the worst of the winter.

4. It is someone elses fault, not mine.

5. Larry Joness old dog barked all night.

Plural Owners

To make a regular plural word possessive, add an apostrophe after the final **s**.

Examples:

three weeks' pay

cities' mayors

doctors' conference

Exercise 2

Add an apostrophe where needed.

1. The two boys bikes are in the garage.

2. Three hours wait was too long.

3. Two dollars difference is not much.

4. Some families homes have been damaged in the storm.

5. Most companies employees receive sick leave.

Determiners

Avoid mistakes with possessive apostrophes by paying attention to determiners that signify plural owners (*some*, *all*, *many*, *most*, *few*) and determiners that signify singular owners (*a*, *an*, *one*).

Examples:

Some kids' parents will chaperone the school dance.

A kid's parents will chaperone the school dance.

Pronouns that refer to possessive phrases can also help writers determine whether the owner is singular or plural.

Examples:

The student's teacher told **him** to study hard for the test.

The students' teacher told **them** to study hard for the test.

Add an apostrophe where needed.

Exercise 3

1. A dogs best friend is its owner.
2. Many cars air conditioners break in the summer.
3. The girls friends told her not to worry.
4. The neighbors dog got out of their yard.
5. I left our neighbors paper on her doorstep.

Irregular Plural Owners

Some plural words do not end with an s. With irregular plural owners, add **'s**. The most common irregular plurals are *children, women, men,* and *people.*

Examples:

children's toys	people's reaction
men's boots	women's salaries

Add an apostrophe where needed.

Exercise 4

1. The mens talent was obvious to everyone.
2. The womens paintings were displayed in the main gallery.
3. Most policemens jobs include talking to the public.
4. The childrens balloons were distributed at the birthday party.
5. Peoples opinions can change as they get older.

Possessive Pronouns

Despite the word *possessive* in their name, do not use apostrophes with possessive pronouns.

Possessive Pronouns

its	ours
hers	theirs
his	yours

Examples:

The tire lost its hubcap.

Shall we take my car or yours?

Letters and Numerals

To avoid confusion, use an apostrophe to make letters and numerals plural.

Examples:

Many of my instructors have Ph.D.'s.

My son is writing his 3's and 9's backwards.

Follow directions carefully to make A's.

Exceptions: Apostrophes are generally not used with all-capital acronyms, with single capital letters where misreading is not likely, or with plural decades.

Examples:

I have many CDs in my collection.

He got all Bs and Cs on his last report card.

My mother loves the music of the 1960s.

I was born in the 80s.

Review Exercise 1

Read the following passage to find apostrophe errors. Add apostrophes where needed, and cross out any incorrect apostrophes.

Cooking

Cooking is not one of my hobbies', and I didnt bother to learn when I was young because it was always my parent's job to make meals. I dont have a microwave oven, so I always have to drag out pots' and pans' just to heat my leftovers. Its' not very convenient for me since Im a student with little time to spare for leaning over my stove's burners. Whats even more difficult is that not one of the burners works completely. Each one has at least one malfunctioning heat level, so when I want to boil water for rice and then to simmer rice for flavor, I have to move the pan from one burner to another. What a pain cooking can be sometime's! To be honest, I lack the patience and the know-how needed for good cooking skills'. My two favorite cookbooks' pages are yellowed from age, grease, and use, but they didn't get that way because I have used them. Ive never understood how my mother and father could spend an entire days' work for one single meal, but I have to admit, those meals were usually pretty fancy and quite delicious creation's. I remember one time when my father cooked his famous mushrooms in wine sauce side dish. The dish's flavor is "tangy but tasty" as my father says. Usually, it's my family's favorite, but one time he added too much lemon juice. When we dug into the mushrooms, our lips puckered, and our eyes' watered because Dad's mushrooms were so sour! It's that kind of simple yet embarrassing mistake that discourages me from learning how to cook.

Chapter 34
Pronoun Agreement

Pronouns are words that take the place of nouns. Pronouns cause problems in writing when the incorrect pronoun is used or when it isn't clear what noun the pronoun refers to. Pronoun errors can create misunderstandings for the reader and are particularly important in official papers. For example, imagine an accident report that misidentifies who is at fault because a wrong or unclear pronoun is used.

Many people misuse pronouns in their speech. Therefore, writers have difficulty identifying pronoun errors because the errors do not sound wrong. In order to learn how to use pronouns correctly, students need to pay particular attention to the rules and not rely on their ear to tell them what is correct.

Below are the personal pronouns. Other types of pronoun include relative pronouns, reflexive pronouns, and interrogative pronouns.

	Subjective case	Objective case	Possessive case
Singular	I	me	my/mine
	you	you	your/yours
	he/she/it	him/her/it	his/her/its
Plural	we	us	our/ours
	you	you	your/yours
	they	them	their/theirs

Antecedents

Pronouns take the place of nouns (see Chapter 19). The noun to which the pronoun refers is called the **antecedent**, a Latin word meaning "what precedes."

Examples:

Antecedent   Pronoun

The **employee** filled out **her** time card incorrectly.

Antecedent   Pronoun

Our **college** registers **its** students by phone.

Antecedent   Pronoun

Our **neighbors** lost **their** dog.

A pronoun must **agree in number** with its antecedent. If the antecedent is **singular**, any pronouns referring to the antecedent must also be singular.

Examples:

My favorite **restaurant** raised **its** prices last week.

The **girl** took **her** mother's hand.

The **boy** grabbed **his** coat.

If the antecedent is **plural**, any pronouns referring to the antecedent must also be plural.

Example:

The **lawyers** take money from **their** clients.

Avoiding Sexist Language

Pronoun use is changing to **avoid sexist language**. Always using *he* to refer to an unspecified individual is considered sexist.

A **student** left **his** umbrella in the auditorium.

Here are some options for avoiding sexist language when referring to an unknown singular antecedent:

Use *his or her.*

A **student** left **his or her** umbrella in the auditorium.

Use *his/her.*

A **student** left **his/her** umbrella in the auditorium.

Alternate *he* and *she*.

A **student** left **his** umbrella in the auditorium.

Another **student** left **her** book in the auditorium.

Use an article instead of a pronoun.

A **student** left **an** umbrella in the auditorium.

Change the antecedent to a plural.

Some **students** left **their** umbrellas in the auditorium.

Each of these alternatives requires careful practice to avoid sounding awkward. Because there is no single accepted solution to the problem of how to refer to an antecedent that may be male or female, it is best to consult with your instructors for their preferences.

Agreement Errors

Pronoun **agreement errors** occur when the wrong pronoun is used. The most common error is the use of *a plural pronoun* with *a singular antecedent*.

Incorrect: **Everyone** must turn in **their** test.

Everyone is a singular noun. Therefore, the plural pronoun *their* doesn't match the noun it refers to. The pronoun must agree in number (singular or plural) with the noun.

Correct: **Everyone** must turn in **his or her** test.

Incorrect: A **student** forgot **their** book bag.

The word *student* is a singular noun, and *their* is a plural pronoun. The pronoun must agree with the noun.

Correct: A **student** forgot **his or her** book bag.

Cross out any incorrect pronouns and write a correct pronoun above.   # Exercise 1

1. A shopper left their umbrella in the store.

2. The lost dog was returned to their owner.

3. The students who passed their tests received awards.

4. The Air Force requires their recruits to attend six weeks of basic training.

5. The cup had a crack in its side.

Problem Antecedents

Compound Antecedents

Compound antecedents joined by *and* are plural.

Example:

Sarah and Julie decided to try **their** luck at the game.

With compound antecedents joined by *either…or* or *neither…nor*, the pronoun should agree with the nearest antecedent.

Examples:

Neither my sister nor her **friends** can find **their** tickets to the play.

Neither my friends nor my **sister** can find **her** ticket to the play.

Exercise 2

Cross out any incorrect pronouns and write a correct pronoun above.

1. The dog and cat played with its toys while the children watched.

2. Either the employees or the boss will contribute their ideas to the debate.

3. The explorer and his friends celebrated their accomplishments.

4. Neither the teacher nor the students were certain of their exact location.

5. Either the sheriff or the campers will become famous for his courage.

Indefinite Pronouns as Antecedents

Indefinite pronouns refer to nonspecific nouns (see Chapter 19). They themselves can serve as antecedents to personal pronouns. Most indefinite pronouns are singular, but some are plural. Writers must pay careful attention to agreement between indefinite pronoun antecedents and the pronouns that refer to them.

another	both	no one	several
any	each	nobody	some
anybody	everybody	none	somebody
anyone	many	nothing	someone
anything	neither	one	something

Singular examples:

Everybody should know **his/her** license number.

Someone forgot **his or her** book.

No one is bringing **his or her** family to the party.

Plural examples:

Many lost **their** books.

Few are chosen to lead **their** country.

A few indefinite pronouns may be **either singular or plural** depending on the noun or pronoun to which they refer.

Examples:

None of the money has lost **its** markings.

None of the books are missing **their** pages.

Cross out any incorrect pronouns and write a correct pronoun above.

Exercise 3

1. Everyone chose their favorite poem to read to the class.

2. Nobody remembered to bring her umbrella.

3. One of the visitors forgot their book.

4. Each of the members of the department wanted the chance to bring their suggestions up at the meeting.

5. Any of the students needing help with their essays should let their teacher know as soon as possible.

Collective Nouns as Antecedents

Most **collective nouns**—words that refer to one whole made up of parts (see Chapter 25)—are singular and, when they serve as antecedents, must take a singular pronoun.

Examples:

A **business** just moved **its** operations into the building next door.

The **team** elected **its** best player as captain.

The **school** and **its** principal were featured in the newspaper.

Exercise 4

Cross out any incorrect pronouns and write a correct pronoun above.

1. The IRS expects all tax returns sent to their office to be post-marked by April 15.

2. Rangehill Community College registers its students using the latest automated phone registration system.

3. The team celebrated their victory.

4. The jury filed back into the room to announce their verdict.

5. Ryan's Steak House flame-broils their steaks.

Avoiding Shifts in Number

While it's important to check for pronoun agreement within a sentence, it is also important to be consistent from sentence to sentence. Do not shift from singular subjects to plural subjects or vice versa within a paragraph.

Incorrect:

A **dentist** can be scary. **They** almost always have needles next to **their** examination chair.

Do not shift from singular *dentist* to plural *they*. Remain consistent in using plural subjects or singular subjects.

Correct:

Dentists can be scary. **They** almost always have needles next to **their** examination chair.

OR

A **dentist** can be scary. **She** almost always has needles next to **her** examination chair.

Avoiding Shifts in Person

Pronouns are classified according to **person**: first person (*I, me, we*); second person (*you*); and third person (*he, she, it, they*). Do not shift from one person to another within a sentence or paragraph.

Incorrect: **I** like golf because **you** can enjoy nature while **you** exercise.

Do not shift from *I* to *you* when the same person is clearly meant. Remain consistent in using the same person.

Correct: **I** like golf because **I** can enjoy nature while **I** exercise.

Limiting Use of the Second Person

Although the second-person pronoun, *you*, is useful when giving instructions or getting the readers' attention, in most academic writing it is considered vague. Its use should be limited to specific kinds of writing.

Vague: **You** should pay **your** fees before **your** classes are canceled.

It is not clear who the *you* in this sentence is. Be specific in naming who the subject is.

Improved: A **student** should pay **his or her** fees before **his or her** classes are canceled.

OR

Students should pay **their** fees before **their** classes are canceled.

Related Agreement Errors

When correcting pronoun errors, correct any related errors (such as verb errors).

Incorrect: **Every** student should pay **their** fees before **they lose their** classes.

If an incorrect pronoun is used with a verb, sometimes the verb ending must be changed if the pronoun is corrected. Be sure to make pronoun subjects agree with their verbs.

Correct: **Every** student should pay **her** fees before **she loses her** classes.

Cross out any incorrect pronouns and write a correct pronoun above. Make sure to correct any related verbs also.

Review Exercise

1. Someone left their book in my car.
2. The football team lost their last football game.
3. Many of the students took their tests.
4. Every student who wants to pass their test must study.
5. All of the teachers agreed that they would grade on a curve.
6. Each roommate should do his share of the housework.
7. Neither my brother nor my friends have their license.
8. A student should do their homework every day.
9. Mary and Bob lost their favorite book.
10. Someone took the car, and they didn't return it.

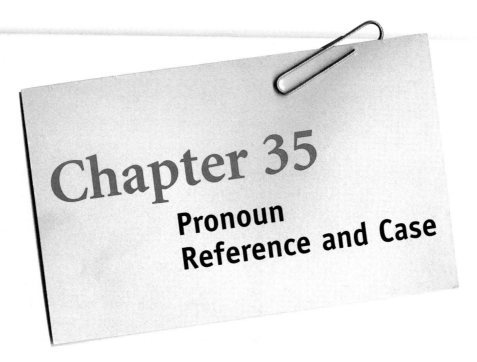

Chapter 35
Pronoun Reference and Case

Unclear pronoun references and errors in pronoun case are even more common in our everyday speech than pronoun agreement errors are. Writers must avoid these pitfalls with pronouns so that the reader can get a clear and correct understanding of their ideas.

Pronoun Reference

A pronoun should refer clearly to its **antecedent** (see Chapter 34).

Examples:

John lent me **his** bicycle.

The **boys** decided to return **their** library books.

Ambiguous Pronoun Reference

In a sentence that contains more than one noun, writers must be careful to avoid **ambiguous pronoun reference**—that is, constructing the sentence so that the pronoun can refer equally well to either the subject or another noun in the sentence.

Examples:

Ambiguous	Clear
Doctors always tell patients if **they** need a vacation.	Doctors always tell **patients** if the **patients** need a vacation.
(Does the pronoun *they* refer to the doctors or the patients? Since there are two plural antecedents, we can't be sure.)	One way to correct an ambiguous pronoun is to restate the noun.
	Doctors always tell the **patient** if **he or she** needs a vacation.
	Another option is to reword the sentence, avoiding the ambiguous reference.

Ambiguous	Clear
Jose told Keith that **he** didn't like math.	Jose told Keith that **Jose** didn't like math.
(Does the pronoun *he* refer to Jose or Keith? Since both antecedents are singular, we can't be sure.)	One way to correct an ambiguous pronoun is to restate the noun.
	Jose told Keith, "**I** don't like math."
	Another option is to reword the sentence, avoiding the ambiguous reference.

Exercise 1

Correct the unclear pronouns.

1. Janet told Ruby that she was late for work.

2. A veterinarian will tell a client if he or she needs to medicate his or her pet.

3. Antonio explained to his teachers why he had been late for class.

4. Juan asked Mario if he could join the team.

5. The girls waved to the boys when they saw them at the mall.

Vague Reference

The pronouns *it, this, that,* and *which* should refer to a single noun, not an entire idea.

Examples:

Vague	Clear
My aunt fell down the stairs and broke her leg, **which** was unfortunate.	Unfortunately, my aunt fell down the stairs and broke her leg.
What does the pronoun *which* refer to?	OR
Because it doesn't refer to any of the nouns in the sentence, but to an entire idea, the reference is vague. The only way to correct the error is to rewrite the sentence.	My aunt fell down and broke her leg; her accident was unfortunate.
My brother wrecked my car. **This** caused our argument.	My brother wrecked my car. This **accident** caused our argument.
What does the pronoun *this* refer to? It cannot refer to *wrecked* because *wrecked* is a verb. Because there is no noun for the pronoun to refer to, the reference is vague.	OR
	My **brother** and I got into an argument because **he** wrecked my car.

Exercise 2

Identify the pronoun as clear or vague.

1. Reading romance novels is a pastime that I enjoy.

2. Not studying caused me to fail the class, and it was a big mistake.

3. After my brother wrecked my car, I had to take it to the shop for repairs.

4. I overslept and missed the bus, which caused me to be late for class.

5. The city commission spends too much time arguing. This causes citizens to feel alienated.

Implied Reference

Avoid using a pronoun for which no antecedent exists; an **implied reference** is usually unclear. The noun must be mentioned first before a pronoun can refer back to it.

Examples:

Implied	Clear
If a student's car won't start, **they** will jump start it for her.	If a student's car won't start, the campus police will jump start it for her.
To whom does *they* refer? Only the student has been mentioned in the sentence.	When *the campus police* replaces *they,* there is no question about who will help the student.
As soon as an employee makes one little mistake, **they** are right there to notice.	As soon as an employee makes one little mistake, her boss is right there to notice.
To whom does *they* refer? No antecedent is mentioned. *They* might refer to bosses, peers, or inspectors.	When *her boss* replaces *they,* we know who "is right there to notice."

Exercise 3

Identify the pronoun reference as correct or implied.

1. Before a suspect can be arrested, they have to read him his rights.

2. At a car dealership, sales representatives are offered a commission on their sales.

3. A customer shouldn't believe a word they tell him during a sales pitch.

4. The test was unfair because he asked questions that were not covered in class or in the book.

5. When I take my car to the garage, the mechanics always make me feel incompetent when they explain what is wrong.

Pronoun Case

Like nouns, pronouns can function as either subjects or objects in a sentence. How the pronoun functions in a sentence determines its form, or **case**.

Subjective Case

Pronouns in the **subjective case** perform the action.

Subjective Case Pronouns

Singular	Plural
I	we
you	you
he/she/it	they

Examples:

    S   V

They play golf on Sundays.

    S   V

She studies every night.

Objective Case

Pronouns in the **objective case** receive the action or complete a thought. The object pronoun tells who or what was affected by the action.

Objective Case Pronouns

Singular	Plural
me	us
you	you
him/her/it	them

Examples:

       Obj

Sam met **him** at the park.

       Obj

She gave **us** a present.

After Prepositions

A pronoun may also serve as the object after a preposition. Use the objective case when a pronoun follows a preposition.

Examples:

Obj

Sarah is standing **by him**.

Obj   Obj

Between you and **me**, Sam prefers pistachio ice cream.

Tests to Determine Case

Two easy tests can help writers decide whether to use subjective or objective case.

Test 1

Ask yourself whether the pronoun is performing the action or receiving the action.

Examples:

Lauren's dad and (**he or him?**) are going to the baseball game.

Lauren's dad and the other person are performing the action in the sentence, so the subjective-case pronoun (*he*) should be used.

S   S

Lauren's **dad** and **he** are going to the baseball game.

S

The officer thanked Bill and (**I or me ?**).

In this sentence, the officer is performing the action. Bill and the speaker are receiving the action. The objective-case pronoun (*me*) is correct.

Obj   Obj

The officer thanked **Bill** and **me**.

Test 2

When the pronoun is connected by a conjunction to a noun, temporarily remove the other noun from the sentence. (In order to read the sentence with the other noun removed, you may have to change the verb.) Your ear should tell you which pronoun case is correct.

Examples:

Lauren's dad and (**he or him?**) are going to the baseball game.

Remove *Lauren's dad and.* Which sounds better: *He is going* or *Him is going?* Your ear should tell you that the subjective-case pronoun (*he*) is correct.

S　　　S

Lauren's **dad** and **he** are going to the baseball game.

The officer thanked Bill and (**I or me ?**).

Remove *Bill and* from the sentence. Now, which sounds better: *The officer thanked I* or *The officer thanked me?* Your ear should tell you that the objective-case pronoun (*me*) is correct.

Obj　　　Obj

The officer thanked **Bill** and **me**.

Choose the correct pronoun for each sentence.

Exercise 4

1. Susan and _____ used to ride our bikes on Saturday. (I, me)

2. Carly, please stand by Jeff and _____. (he, him)

3. There are many reasons for Margaret and _____ to be mad. (I, me)

4. Ellen and _____ studied chemistry. (she, her)

5. Don't laugh at Ed and _____. (they, them)

Comparisons and Pronoun Case

In **comparisons** using *than* or *as,* complete the clause to find the correct pronoun.

Examples:
Are you as hungry as (**he or him**)?

The subjective pronoun (*he*) should be used because the complete clause is *Are you as hungry as **he is?***

You talked to Tyrone more than (**I or me?**).

The objective pronoun should be used if the writer means *You talked to Tyrone more than **you talked to me.*** However, the subject pronoun should be used if the speaker means *You talked to Tyrone more than **I did.***

In formal writing, it is a good idea to complete the comparison. Incomplete comparisons can be confusing, and a mistake in pronoun case can give the reader the wrong idea.

Exercise 5

Choose the correct pronoun. If you cannot tell which pronoun is correct, complete the comparison in a way that makes sense.

1. Doreen donated more money to the church than _____. (I/me)

2. My sister is taller than _____. (I/me)

3. I wish I could be as smart as _____. (he/him)

4. My friends studied as hard as _____. (they/them)

5. Debbie was in love with Mark more than _____. (he/him)

Pronouns within an Appositive

A pronoun in an **appositive** (an interrupter that renames the word that comcs before it—see Chapter 32) should use the same case as the noun it renames.

Examples:

The two hosts, Terry and **I**, scheduled the party.

Terry and I renames the subject, *hosts*, so the subjective case must be used.

An award was given to the winners, Blake and **her**.

Blake and her renames the direct object, *winners*, so the objective case must be used.

Exercise 6

Choose the correct pronoun.

1. The two recent graduates, LaDona and (he/him), will be applying for that job.

2. Masako gave the American girls, Jane and (she/her), a very interesting lecture on Japanese customs.

3. The two top students, Brad and (I/me), are allowed to leave class early.

4. Everyone likes my children, Brian and (he/him).

5. The relay team, Sharon, Chandra, Kelly, and (I/me), came in first place at the track meet.

Who/Whom

Who/whoever and *whom/whomever* are **relative pronouns**. Relative pronouns relate or refer back to nouns, and they introduce a set of words (a subordinate clause) that helps describe or tell about those nouns (see Chapters 19 and 30).

Who and *whoever* are subjective-case pronouns like *I, you, he, she, we,* and *they.*

Example:

Shannon is the woman **who** won the race.

> *Who* refers back to the noun *woman. Who* is also the subject of the subordinate clause and therefore takes the subjective case.

Whom and *whomever* are objective-case pronouns like *me, you, him, it,* and *them.* One way to remember that *whom* and *whomever* are object-case pronouns is to associate the *m* in each word with the *m* in *him* and *them.*

Examples:

The counselor **whom** I requested was not available.

> *Whom* refers back to *counselor. Whom* is also the object of the subordinate clause (think, *I requested whom,* which is equivalent to *I requested him*).

Test 1

Tests for *Who* or *Whom*

Determining whether to use *who* or *whom* can be tricky. Writers must first identify the subordinate clause and then determine whether the pronoun functions as the *subject* or *object* of the clause.

Examples:

                          S   V

Jose Rodriguez is the man **who rescued** the child.

In the subordinate clause, *rescued* is the verb and *who* is its subject.

                            Obj   S   V

Mr. Rodriguez is a hero **whom we all admire**.

In this clause, *admire* is the verb, and *we* is its subject, so *whom* is the object.

Test 2

Writers can also rearrange the subordinate clause in normal sentence order (subject-verb-object) to help determine the case of the relative pronoun.

Examples:

$$\overset{S}{\qquad} \overset{V}{\qquad} \overset{Obj}{\qquad}$$

Jose Rodriguez is the man **who rescued** the **child**.

Mr. Rodriguez is a hero whom we all admire.

$$\overset{S}{\qquad} \overset{V}{\qquad} \overset{Obj}{\qquad}$$

we all admire whom

Test 3

Another test is to substitute a different subject- or object-case pronoun for the relative pronoun. If *he, she,* or *they* fits, use *who* or *whoever.* If *him, her,* or *them* fits, use *whom* or *whomever.*

Examples:

Travis is the student (**who or whom?**) made an A.

Since *he made an A* sounds better than *him made an A*, use the subjective-case relative pronoun, *who.*

Travis is the student who made an A.

Patrick, (**who or whom?**) the president mentioned, has designed our Web site.

First, rearrange the subordinate clause in subject-verb-object order: the president mentioned (he or him?). *Him* sounds better, so *whom* is correct.

Patrick, **whom** the president mentioned, has designed our Web site.

The above tests also can be used when the relative pronoun follows a preposition.

Examples:

$$\overset{Prep}{\qquad} \overset{Obj}{\qquad}$$

Victor is the student **for whom** the test was hard.

The test was hard for *him*; therefore, use the objective-case *whom.*

$$\overset{Prep}{\qquad} \overset{S}{\qquad} \overset{V}{\qquad}$$

The madman yells **at whoever is** in the room.

Although *at* is a preposition and seems to indicate that the object pronoun whomever should be used, the verb *is* needs a subject, so the subjective-case *whoever* must be used.

Choose the correct pronoun.

Exercise 7

1. (Whoever/whomever) wins the contest will be crowned king.

2. John married Pam, (who/whom) I met yesterday.

3. I will negotiate with (whoever/whomever) you elect as your captain.

4. Jake is the athlete (who/whom) I most admire.

5. Jessica and Parker, (who/whom) are best friends, always study together.

6. Please face the person to (who/whom) you are speaking.

7. I have no idea about (who/whom) you are talking.

8. Do not ask for (who/whom) the bell tolls.

9. I will give a prize to (whoever/whomever) walks in the door next.

10. Sh'lane is tired of listening to (whoever/whomever) wants to dominate the conversation.

Who and *Whom* in Questions

In questions, if the pronoun functions as a subject, use *who* or *whoever*; if the pronoun functions as an object, use *whom* or *whomever*.

Examples:

S   V
Who is at the door?

In this question, *who* is the subject for the verb *is*.

Obj   S   V
Whom did the group elect as their leader?

In this case, *group* is the subject and *elect* is the verb. *Whom* is the object. The word order in questions must sometimes be rearranged into normal sentence order (subject-verb-object) in order to determine whether the pronoun is functioning as a subject or object.

Exercise 8

Choose the correct pronoun.

1. (Who/Whom) will you vote for?

2. (Who/Whom) won the contest last year?

3. (Who/Whom) do they suspect?

4. (Who/Whom) will have to do that job?

5. (Who/Whom) is calling?

Review Exercise

Cross out each incorrect pronoun and write in the correct one. (Not every pronoun is incorrect.)

1. I like to eat at Chaucer's because they offer excellent vegetarian food.

2. The poet, who is internationally known, recently won a major prize.

3. The police said that they were looking for Ed and me.

4. The two students with perfect attendance records, Catherine and I, were recognized at the awards ceremony.

5. Sally hopes to be accepted into the cosmetology program because she wants to learn it.

6. Pam lied to me about the girl who stole my purse. This was wrong.

7. Tom is jealous because Bill and me have always shared our deepest secrets.

8. Please save some ice cream and cake for Elizabeth and me.

9. My aunts and uncles took different roads to the beach, but they arrived late.

10. The photographer whom I selected was expensive.

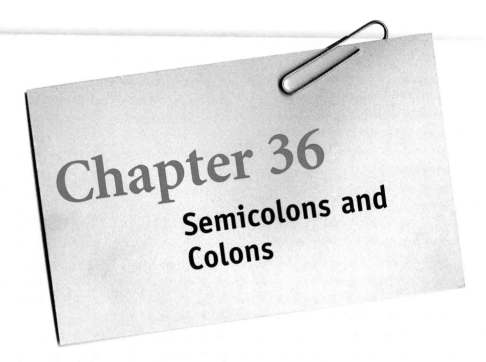

Chapter 36
Semicolons and Colons

Semicolons and colons are not used as often as periods and commas. However, they are important because they give writers options that other punctuation marks do not. Also, they are used primarily after independent clauses, and their misuse can create serious English errors.

Semicolons

With Independent Clauses

Typically, writers use a coordinating conjunction and a comma to join two independent clauses. However, writers sometimes choose to use a **semicolon (;)** to connect two independent clauses when the relationship between the two clauses is clear and no connecting word is needed to show the relationship.

Formula
Independent clause; independent clause.

Examples:

           IC   IC

Some movies are long and boring; others are short and exciting.

           IC   IC

One boy excelled in math; his twin did better in English.

Each of the independent clauses or sentences expresses a complete thought. Because the clauses are closely related, they can be joined with a semicolon.

Misuses

Do not use a semicolon between an independent clause and a dependent clause or phrase.

DC   IC

Incorrect: Because Bob moved away; Maria got the job.

The semicolon in this sentence is incorrect because one part of the sentence is a dependent clause and the other is an independent clause. The correct punctuation between this fragment and sentence is a comma.

Correct: Because Bob moved away, Maria got the job.

Do not use a semicolon between two independent clauses joined by a coordinating conjunction (*for, and, nor, but, or, yet, so*). Instead, use a comma before the coordinating conjunction.

Incorrect: Sue wanted a new car; but she couldn't afford it.

Correct: Sue wanted a new car, but she couldn't afford it.

Exercise 1

Identify the following sentences as correct (C) or incorrect (I) in their use of punctuation.

1. The rain began at 9:00; it didn't stop until well after midnight.

2. Although I have always been a fan of light shows; this one was a disappointment.

3. Class is generally over by 3:00; so I arranged to meet my friends at 3:30.

4. My first date with Jim was lots of fun; our last date was not.

5. My son was very sick; he had a temperature of 102.

With Conjunctive Adverbs or Transitional Expressions

When joining two independent clauses with a **conjunctive adverb** or a **transitional expression** (see Chapter 30), use a semicolon before the adverb or transitional word and a comma after it. The semicolon must be placed before the conjunctive adverb or transition in order to end the first independent clause.

Formula

Independent clause; conjunctive adverb, independent clause.
Independent clause; transition, independent clause.

Common conjunctive adverbs

accordingly	finally	meanwhile	specifically
also	futhermore	moreover	still
anyway	hence	nevertheless	subsequently
besides	however	next	then
certainly	indeed	nonetheless	therefore
consequently	instead	otherwise	thus
conversely	likewise	similarly	

Common transitional expressions

after all	for instance	in other words
as a matter of fact	in addition	on the contrary
as a result	in conclusion	on the other hand
for example	in fact	

Examples:

IC   Conj Adv   IC
The band will lead the parade; next, the floats will follow.

                    IC   Conj Adv
Water conservation can be practiced at home; for instance, your garden's soil should be made of materials that hold water. IC

Misuses

If the conjunctive adverb or transition is merely interrupting the flow of one sentence (not joining two independent clauses), do not use a semicolon. Simply use commas to set off the conjunctive adverb or transition from the rest of the sentence when it serves as an interrupter (see Chapter 32).

Incorrect: The problem; however, was easily solved.

Correct: The problem, however, was easily solved.

When placing a semicolon in sentences with conjunctive adverbs or transitions, make certain that the semicolon is placed where a period could be used to separate the two independent clauses. Generally, the semicolon follows the first independent clause.

Incorrect: John was certain he wanted to learn French, therefore; he enrolled in an introductory French class.

Correct: John was certain he wanted to learn French; therefore, he enrolled in an introductory French class.

Exercise 2

Identify the following sentences as correct (C) or incorrect (I) in their use of punctuation.

1. My sailboat was damaged in the storm; as a result, I had to pay for repairs.

2. The newest fad among elementary school children is virtual pets, as a matter of fact, half of my daughter's second grade class owns a computerized pet.

3. The Olympics have always been my favorite sporting event, therefore; I was excited to get tickets.

4. I have learned a great deal by studying the rulebook; however, practice is what has made me a croquet champion.

5. Algebra; for example, is my hardest course.

With Items in a Series

Use semicolons between **items in a series** when one or more of the items use commas. Each comma goes with the information about the item, so semicolons must be used to separate the items.

> **Formula**
> A, a; B, b; and C, c.

Examples:

The tour includes visits to Helsinki, Finland; Riga, Latvia; Warsaw, Poland; and Kiev, Ukraine.

Ms. Smith introduced Mr. Bradley, a lawyer; Dr. Elliot, a surgeon; and Ms. Lathrop, an accountant.

Exercise 3

Identify the following sentences as correct or incorrect in their use of punctuation.

1. My favorite vacation destinations are Fairbanks, Alaska; Seattle, Washington; and Washington, D.C.

2. He ordered shrimp cocktail for an appetizer, steak, baked potato, and broccoli with cheese for dinner, and strawberry shortcake for dessert.

3. My brother's three favorite baseball teams are the Florida Marlins, who won the World Series last year; the New York Yankees, who won the year before; and the Atlanta Braves, who won three years ago.

4. In my family, I most respect my mother, Lenora Jones; my father, Isaac Jones, and one of my brothers, Jacob Jones.

5. Most workers in the company get the day off on July 4, Independence Day, December 25, Christmas, and Thanksgiving Day.

Colons

To Introduce a List
Use a colon after an independent clause that introduces a list.

Formula
Independent clause: A, B, C.

Examples:

          IC   A,   B,   C.

We sold many items at the garage sale: old clothes, dishes, and books.

The family visited three states: Maine, Vermont, and New Hampshire.

Misuse
Do not use a colon after an incomplete sentence that introduces a list.

Incorrect: The family visited: Maine, Vermont, and New Hampshire.
Correct: The family visited Maine, Vermont, and New Hampshire.

Incorrect: Maine is famous for delicacies such as: lobster, maple syrup, and wild blueberries.
Correct: Maine is famous for delicacies such as lobster, maple syrup, and wild blueberries.

After *Following/As Follows*
Use a colon after an independent clause that includes the words *the following* or *as follows*.

Formula
Independent clause . . . as follows: . . .
Independent clause . . . the following: . . .

Examples:

The test will include the following punctuation skills: commas, semicolons, and colons.

My plans are as follows: get my college degree, find a good job, and have a family.

continued

To make a basic piecrust you need the following: flour, salt, shortening, and cold water.

The dictionary defines an ecosystem as follows: "An ecological community and its environment considered as a unit."

Exercise 4

Identify the following sentences as correct or incorrect in their use of punctuation.

1. There are three hard courses I'm taking this term: French, algebra, and statistics.

2. My friends are always nagging me to: quit my job, try out for the baseball team, and go out with them more often.

3. My coach defines good sportsmanship as follows: trying hard and respecting your opponent.

4. My favorite dishes are: chicken pot pie, spaghetti, and pizza.

5. I most enjoy water sports such as: swimming and water skiing.

Review Exercise

Identify the following sentences as correct (C) or incorrect (I) in their use of punctuation.

1. I like attending a community college; moreover, it costs less than a university.

2. My favorite courses are: math, science and psychology.

3. My roommate is from Milwaukee; and he knows how to ski.

4. Always remember to pack: a toothbrush, a comb, and a book.

5. When my mother visits at Thanksgiving; we cook together.

6. I haven't seen or heard from him; but I think he is coming today.

7. My car overheats; therefore, I put water in the radiator daily.

8. A car phone is great for emergencies; for example, when my car breaks down on the highway.

9. My three favorite teachers are my chemistry teacher, Mr. Blass; my French teacher, Ms. Leclerc; and my English teacher, Ms. Jones.

10. I've had to give up my three favorite foods: peanut butter, chocolate cake, and ice cream.

Chapter 37
Modifiers

Modifiers are words or phrases that explain, describe, or limit one or more other words in a sentence. The word *modifier* can be used for many of the parts of speech and parts of sentences we have discussed in the preceding chapters: adjectives, prepositional phrases, dependent clauses, and so on. Mistakes with modifiers can create confusion about the meaning of a sentence. Writers sometimes make these mistakes when they are not paying attention to word order.

Examples of modifiers:

The doctor owns a **green** Jaguar.

Crossing the finish line, the runner looked exhausted.

The prize was awarded to the boy **in the front row**.

Whether they come before or after, modifiers should be placed as close as possible to the word or words they modify.

Examples:

Exhausted after the race, *Renata* collapsed at the finish line.

I sent the *letter* **in a pink envelope** to the woman.

Julio was the **only** *one* who voted.

Misplaced Modifiers

Modifiers that modify the wrong word or words because of their placement are called **misplaced modifiers**. To avoid confusion, place the modifier as close as possible to the word, phrase, or clause it describes.

Incorrect: He gave ice cream to the children covered with chocolate.

Are the children covered in chocolate? The phrase *covered in chocolate* is supposed to modify *ice cream* not *children*. To correct the error, place the modifier next to the word it describes.

Correct: He gave ice cream **covered with chocolate** to the children.

Incorrect: The woman walked down the stairs **wearing the slinky black gown**.

The phrase *wearing the slinky black gown* incorrectly modifies the words *the stairs*. To avoid confusion, place the modifier as close as possible to the word it describes.

Correct: The woman **wearing the slinky black gown** walked down the stairs.

Exercise 1

Underline the misplaced modifier and draw an arrow to the word it should explain, describe, or limit.

1. The horse won the race with the white mane.

2. The woman sold the bicycle to her friend with bad brakes.

3. The woman ran after the bus in the blue dress.

4. The police car chased the speeder with flashing lights.

5. He read the announcement about the meeting in the paper.

Limiting Modifiers

Limiting modifiers usually come before the word or words they modify. Different placements of these modifiers *change the meaning* of the sentence.

Limiting Modifiers	
almost	merely
even	nearly
every day	never
frequently	only
hardly	scarcely
just	

Examples:

Different placements of the modifier *only* completely change the meaning of the sentences.

Mario **only had** three dollars in his pocket. (Mario had nothing else in his pocket.)

Mario had **only three** dollars in his pocket. (Mario had no more than three dollars in his pocket.)

Only Mario had three dollars in his pocket. (Mario alone had three dollars in his pocket.)

Mario had three dollars in his **only pocket**. (Mario had no more than one pocket.)

Don't place limiting modifiers in front of a verb unless they are intended to modify the verb.

Incorrect: I **almost** cooked all the potatoes.

This sentence is unclear because it could mean that I partially cooked all of the potatoes or that I started to cook all of the potatoes but changed my mind and cooked only some of them. Placing the modifier in front of the phrase it modifies makes it clear that I cooked some of the potatoes but not all of them.

Correct: I cooked **almost** all the potatoes.

Incorrect: The doctor **only** spoke with me for five minutes.

This sentence is unclear because *only* modifies *spoke*, which could mean that the doctor didn't do anything but speak or that he spoke with *only me* and no one else. Placing the modifier in front of *five minutes* makes it clear that the amount of time I had with the doctor was limited.

Correct: The doctor spoke with me for **only** five minutes.

Squinting Modifiers

Generally, limiting modifiers are placed before the word or words they modify. However, if doing so means that the modifier is placed between two words such that it could describe either one, the sentence will be unclear. Modifiers that have such placement are sometimes called squinting modifiers.

Examples:

Incorrect: He told her **every day** to say her prayers.

In this sentence *every day* could modify how often he tells her or how often he'd like her to say her prayers. This is a squinting modifier. Even though limiting modifiers generally come before the word they modify, it may be necessary to place the limiting modifier after the word it modifies in order to avoid confusion.

Correct: He told her to say her prayers **every day**.

Incorrect: Going to rock concerts **frequently** damages one's hearing.

In this sentence *frequently* could modify how often one goes to rock concerts or how often one damages one's hearing. In this case we can put the modifier before the word it modifies to make the sentence mean frequent attendance at rock concerts damages one's hearing.

Correct: **Frequently** going to rock concerts damages one's hearing.

Exercise 2

Underline the limiting modifier and tell whether it is correct (C) or incorrect (I) in its placement.

1. The teacher told Yasmin regularly to study. _____

2. When the whistle blew, we jumped almost out of our shoes. _____

3. My father travels frequently for business reasons. _____

4. He told her to exercise regularly. _____

5. He bicycles to school often with a backpack. _____

Split Infinitives

In general, do not **split** parts of an **infinitive** (*to* plus the base form of the verb: *to be, to go, to dance, to think*) with a modifier.

Incorrect: I like to **frequently** exercise.

The modifier *frequently* splits the infinitive *to exercise*. Placing the modifier after the infinitive corrects the sentence.

Correct: I like to exercise **frequently**.

Dangling Modifiers

Some modifiers are incorrect because what they modify has been left out of the sentence. If a modifier has no word to describe, it is called a **dangling modifier**. Dangling modifiers can be corrected by adding a subject after the modifier or rewriting the modifying phrase to include a subject.

Incorrect: **Running down the street**, my heart was pounding.

What does *Running down the street* modify? Who was running down the street? A heart can't run down the street. One way to correct the dangling modifier is to change the subject of the independent clause to say who was running down the street. Another way to correct the dangling modifier is to rewrite the modifying phrase to include a subject.

Correct: **Running down the street, I** felt my heart was pounding.

Correct: **As I was running down the street**, my heart was pounding.

Incorrect: **Using a telephoto lens**, the pictures of the soccer match turned out beautifully.

What does *using a telephoto lens* modify? Pictures can't use a telephoto lens. Who was using a telephoto lens? One way to correct the dangling modifier is to change the subject of the independent clause to express who was using the telephoto lens. Another way to correct the dangling modifier is to rewrite the modifying phrase to include a subject.

Correct: **Using a telephoto lens, Leslie** took beautiful pictures of the soccer match.

Correct: **Because Leslie was using a telephoto lens**, the pictures of the soccer match turned out beautifully.

With Verbal Phrases

Often, a dangling modifier occurs when a sentence begins with a verbal phrase:

- A present participial phrase (a phrase that begins with a verb ending in -*ing*).

- A past participial phrase (a phrase that begins with a past tense verb).

- An infinitive phrase (a phrase that begins with *to* + a verb).

Incorrect: **Dancing at the club**, the music was too loud.

Correct: **Dancing at the club**, I thought that the music was too loud.

Correct: **When I was dancing at the club**, the music was too loud.

Incorrect: **Defeated by their enemy**, the war was lost.

Correct: **Defeated by their enemy**, the soldiers lost the war.

Correct: **When the soldiers were defeated by their enemy**, the war was lost.

Incorrect: **To fly an airplane**, instructions are needed.

Correct: **To fly an airplane**, a pilot needs instructions.

Correct: **In order for a pilot to fly an airplane**, instructions are needed.

Exercise 3

Underline the modifier in each sentence and tell whether it is correct (C) or incorrect (I).

1. Caught in my headlights, the deer froze in the road. _____

2. To excel in sports, practice is required. _____

3. Running to catch up, my heart was pounding. _____

4. Exhausted by the long hike, the camper collapsed by the fire. _____

5. Waking at 2:00 a.m., the night was silent. _____

With Imperatives

In an imperative sentence (one that gives a command—see Chapter 27), a modifier may describe the implied subject (you). In this case, no dangling modifier occurs.

Examples:

To run a business successfully, (you) emphasize good customer service.

To run a business successfully correctly modifies the implied *you*, which is the subject of a command sentence.

Circle the modifier in each sentence and tell whether it is correct (C) or incorrect (I).

Exercise 4

1. After tilling the soil, plant the seeds. _____

2. When taking a dog for a walk, a leash is needed. _____

3. To win an election, votes are needed. _____

4. Before crossing the street, look both ways. _____

5. In order to arrive early, set the alarm for 6:00 a.m. _____

Circle the modifier in each sentence and tell whether it is correct (C) or incorrect (I).

Review Exercise 1

1. Crossing the finish line, the runner collapsed. _____

2. After studying for four hours, the test was easy. _____

3. The car was pulled over by the police with a missing license plate. _____

4. Although frightened by the storm, my dog crept out from under the bed. _____

5. The dog crossed the road with a limp. _____

6. Exhausted by a day in the park, the toddler fell asleep. _____

7. Unraveling the loose thread, my dress came apart. _____

8. To avoid a ticket, do not speed. _____

9. I said on Saturday I will go fishing. _____

10. The backpack was left on the table that was stained with dirt. _____

Circle the modifier in each sentence and tell whether it is correct (C) or incorrect (I).

Review Exercise 2

1. While channel surfing, the TV remote control broke. _____

2. Yelling at the top of their lungs, the cheerleaders welcomed the team. _____

3. My trainer advised me regularly to work out. _____

4. After talking with my friends, the decision was made to run for office. _____

continues

continued

5. The bird was given shelter in the animal refuge with a broken wing. _____

6. While skiing in Vale, I broke a leg. _____

7. I had trouble competing in the race with a bruised ankle. _____

8. Caught in the thunderstorm, the campers were frightened. _____

9. On Monday, my teacher said she would not accept late homework. _____

10. Having finished the main course, dessert was ordered. _____

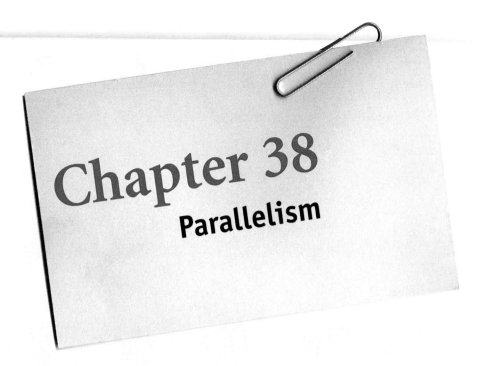

Chapter 38
Parallelism

In math, parallel lines run side by side. In writing, **parallelism** means using the same grammatical forms to express similar ideas. Being able to identify the parts of speech (see Chapter 19) is an important part of understanding different grammatical forms. Parallelism is particularly important in the thesis statement of essays. If a thesis statement lists the ideas the essay will develop, the ideas must be expressed in parallel structures.

Items in a Series

To be parallel, **items in a series** must all be expressed in the same grammatical form.

> Incorrect: The workers in the warehouse **pushed, pulled,** and **had to carry** the boxes.

In this series, the last item is not parallel with the first two members of the series because a different verb form is used. To correct the error, the same form of *carry* should be used.

> Correct: The workers in the warehouse **pushed, pulled,** and **carried** the boxes.

>   Adj Adj   V
> Incorrect: Yolanda is **pretty, tall,** and **acts** friendly.

In this sentence, two items in the series are adjectives and one is not. To balance the series, change the last item to an adjective.

>   Adj Adj   Adj
> Correct: Yolanda is **pretty, tall,** and **friendly**.

Exercise 1

Identify the parallelism as correct (C) or incorrect (I).

1. My father is proud, intelligent, and acts brave. _____

2. My grandmother loves weaving, knitting, and sewing. _____

3. Jack is strong, agile, and fast. _____

4. Julie is brunette, slender, and has brown eyes. _____

5. The seagulls squawk, flap, and soar. _____

Pairs

Use parallel constructions for **pairs**—that is, for words joined by the coordinating conjunctions (*for, and, nor, but, or, yet, so*).

Incorrect: She likes **spicy pumpkin pies** and **cakes that are chocolate and delicious**.

The second item in this pair does not follow the same grammatical form as the first item. To correct the error, put the second member of the pair into the same grammatical structure as the first.

> Adj Adj N   Adj Adj N
Correct: She likes **spicy pumpkin pies** and **delicious chocolate cakes**.

Incorrect: I like **to cook**, but I don't like **cleaning up**.

In this sentence the first verb phrase includes the infinitive *to cook*, but the second verb phrase includes a gerund, *cleaning*. Using the same verb form for each will help the sentence follow a pattern.

> Inf   Inf
Correct: I like **to cook**, but I don't like **to clean up**.

Use parallel construction in pairs joined by **correlative conjunctions** (*both…and, either…or, neither…nor, not only…but also, and whether…or*).

Examples:

> Gerund Phrase   Gerund Phrase
Either **going for a ride** or **lying in the sun** is my idea of a good time.

> N   N
I like neither the **taste** nor the **texture** of this cake.

> Adj   Adj
My current job is both **stressful** and **demanding**.

                    Prep Phrase   Prep Phrase
Not only am I late **for my appointment**, but also I am **out of breath**.

            Noun Clause   Noun Clause
Whether **you drive a car** or **you take a bus**, you should leave early.

Identify the parallelism as correct (C) or incorrect (I).

Exercise 2

1. Either I will graduate with honors or I will take a job. _____

2. Not only is this food unattractive, but also bad service. _____

3. Neither my answers nor the way I explained myself satisfied the teacher. _____

4. Not only was my hair cut too short but also it was not even. _____

5. When I met Clara, both my instinct and my intuition told me she was honest. _____

Comparisons

As with series and pairs, the different parts of a comparison must be parallel.

> Incorrect: I prefer **to make** Christmas presents rather than **buying** them at a store.

This sentence is awkward because an infinitive form, *to make*, is used in the first part of the comparison and a gerund form, *buying*, is used in the second part of the comparison. The sentence becomes parallel when two infinitive forms or two gerund forms are used.

> Correct: I prefer **to make** Christmas presents rather than **to buy** them at a store.

> Correct: I prefer **making** Christmas presents rather than **buying** them at a store.

Exercise 3

Identify the parallelism as correct (C) or incorrect (I).

1. I enjoy snowboarding more than to hike.

2. Riding a bicycle to school is actually faster than driving a car.

3. The police usually prefer that motorists remain in their car during a traffic stop rather than getting out to meet the officer.

4. Some computers are faster than other computers.

5. There is more rain this winter than the rainfall last winter.

Phrases and Clauses

Recall from Chapter 27 that **phrases** are groups of words that are missing a subject or a verb or both, while **clauses** contain a subject and a verb. Independent clauses express a complete thought, and dependent clauses do not express a complete thought. Pairs and series of phrases and clauses in sentences should have similar grammatical structures. You should balance a phrase with a phrase and a clause with a clause.

Prep Phrase   Prep Phrase

My mother likes to vacation **at the beach** and **in the mountains**.

Inf Phrase

My seventh-grade teacher would not allow us **to chew gum** or
Inf Phrase
to wear shorts.

Clause   Clause

I don't want to go to the game **because it is raining** and **because I am tired**.

Clause   Clause

No matter **how much I study** or **how hard I work**, I still have difficulty in algebra.

Parallel Words

When writing sentences that include series and pairs, you should balance an article with an article, a preposition with a preposition, and a subordinating conjunction with a subordinating conjunction.

Examples:

I'd like **a** milkshake, **a** hot dog, and **a** piece of apple pie.

Ann is looking for a bike **with** hand brakes and **with** a basket

I was given the scholarship **because** I was the first eleventh grader to win a National Science Foundation award and **because** I was an A student.

One way to tell whether items are parallel is to organize them in a table. If the same grammatical forms appear in each column, then the items are parallel.

Examples:

Phrase   Phrase

My grandfather owns **a new blue car** and **an old red truck**.

To check for parallelism in these phrases, take each word and place in into a table. The words in each phrase should match for each part of speech for the phrases to be parallel.

Art	Adj	Adj	Noun
a	new	blue	car
an	old	red	truck

Example:

Clause   Clause

My mother informed me **that I could not watch TV** and **that I was grounded for a week**.

A clause depends on the rest of the sentence for meaning, but it contains a subject and verb. In this case, the subjects are repeated for each of the verb phrases.

Conjunction	Pronoun	Verb Phrase
that	I	could not watch TV
that	I	was grounded for a week

Exercise 4

Identify the parallelism as correct (C) or incorrect (I).

1. I promise to be a good husband and that I will clean the apartment. _____

2. The puppy is energetic and behaves well. _____

3. The campers returned tired yet happy. _____

4. I will be glad to go to the play with you on Friday but not paying for it. _____

5. My father told me that I should go to college or get a job. _____

Review Exercise 1

Identify items that have correct parallelism, and fix the faulty parallelism in the items that are incorrect.

1. This weekend I will either clean the garage or play tennis.

2. For my graduation, I received a blue pickup truck and a pen that was gold.

3. Traffic congestion is a problem in many large cities but not in areas that are rural.

4. The woods are lovely, dark, and deep.

5. Kennedy Space Center is known for its historic spacecraft and hangars that are huge.

6. The workers fought for better pay and greater job security.

7. Scientists blame global warming for the increasing frequency of killer tornadoes and flooding that is severe.

8. The meal was attractive, nutritious, and inexpensive.

9. Ashley decided that she would invite the neighbors to dinner and to make pot roast.

10. Our instructor said our paper had to be typed, documented, and that it should be double-spaced.

Identify items that have correct parallelism and fix the faulty parallelism in the items that are incorrect.

1. The city should close the downtown area to traffic in order to reduce noise, congestion, and crime.

2. Ewen was so upset about his grade that he refused to talk, eat, or sleeping.

3. Consistency, not creativity, is my strong point.

4. My mother asked me to be home by ten and not riding with anyone who had been drinking.

5. My son can punt, pass, and kick a football.

6. Urban sprawl affects the air quality, soil quality, and water quality.

7. Staying out late and to miss class are problems for students.

8. Claudia admires Michael Jordan for his talent and because he works hard.

9. Karen likes to fish, but not hunting.

10. I like neither the pay nor the hours.

Chapter 39
Editing for English Errors

Editing means reading a piece of writing a number of times to check for English errors. As explained in Chapters 4 and 5, it follows the drafting and revision stages in the writing process. In many ways, editing is one of the most challenging tasks for any writer.

Effective editing is developed through practice. You have been taking the first important steps by learning the rules for using proper grammar and punctuation. Now you are ready to put your individual skills together in the complex task of finding different errors in a piece of writing. This chapter is meant to help you develop a step-by-step routine for this difficult task. You can practice the routine on the editing exercises provided in this chapter, and then you will put your skills to work when editing your own writing.

The Art of Editing

Effective editing takes place in a step-by-step process that you use every time you write. The key to successful editing is to read your paper over a number of times, looking for only one kind of error at a time. This way, you are less likely to become overwhelmed or confused.

Editing Plan

Read the piece of writing over five to ten times, looking for one error at a time.

1. Check each word group that ends in a period to make sure it is a complete sentence. (Identify the subject and the verb, and make sure the word group makes complete sense.)

2. Make sure that subjects and verbs agree, and that the verb tenses are correct and consistent.

3. Check for correct capitalization.

4. Use your dictionary or spell checker to look up the spelling of any words you are not sure about.

5. Check for any problem words—that is, for words that sound alike or are close in spelling to other words.

6. Verify your use of commas; make sure you know what rule you are using and why the comma fits the rule.

7. Check for contractions and possessive phrases that need apostrophes.

8. Be sensitive to pronouns in the writing. Does each pronoun have a clear antecedent? Does it agree with that antecedent?

9. Edit for modifiers and parallelism.

10. Look for any missing words or letters by reading backward; read slowly from the last sentence to the first.

Tips for Effective Editing

- All writers, including authors, make errors. Assume that there are errors in any piece of writing you do. Careful editing is necessary for every writer.

- Slow down your reading while editing. Many, if not most, errors we make are the result of thinking and writing rapidly. When we read over something we have just written, we have a tendency to read it very quickly because we know what it says already. However, to find mistakes, we need to slow down our eye. Many writers try reading the writing from the last sentence to the first.

- It's crucial to read the writing over a number of times in order to catch errors. Every time you write or take a writing skills test, use the Editing Plan given above to check for errors. The editing process gets easier and more effective with practice.

- Keep a list of errors you make in your writing and review the list before writing. When editing, concentrate on looking for errors you have made in the past.

Basic Editing Practice

The passage below contains ten to fifteen errors. Correct all errors, and underline the corrections. You may need to add words. Edit for the following kinds of errors:

run-ons
fragments
verb errors
capitalization
problem words

Exercise 1

Back to School

The summer has passed, and now college is already starting again.

The school year use to begin at the end of September, now the term starts

in the middle of august. I don't know how I am suppose to keep a tan

when I have to start back to school so early.

The principal benefit of starting classes is meeting new classmates.

Attending classes are great. Because I make so many new friends and

have a different date every night. The only problem with my courses is all

the homework that is gave to me. For example, their is homework in my

science class every night, I have problems to solve in math 101 every

evening to. Its unbelievable how much time I have spent in the lab doing

experiments. I am already looking forward to thanksgiving.

Exercise 2

The passage below contains ten to fifteen errors. Correct all errors, and underline the corrections. You may need to add words. Edit for the following kinds of errors:

run-ons
fragments
verb errors
capitalization
problem words

Audrey Arroyo Exercise Hour

Many television viewers in my hometown enjoy the Audrey Arroyo Exercise Hour, which is on television every saturday morning. Ms. Arroyo help people loose weight and have fun while exercising. She teaches the principals of physical fitness and the way to eat well to. She always present healthful recipes. Sometimes with the help of a guest. My friends and I watch her and laugh because she do such crazy things to get her point across. She will lay on the floor and hold her legs above her head until she barely has the strength to speak. She should of been an actress because she is so good at dramatizing what she teaches. Audrey dresses up like a Policewoman to teach about watching what we eat, the audience is suppose to learn from her skit. The hole show is pretty silly, but everyone agree that its fun to watch with friends.

Intermediate Editing Practice

The passage below contains ten to fifteen errors. Correct all errors, and underline the corrections. You may need to add words. Edit for the following kinds of errors:

Exercise 3

run-ons	problem words
fragments	commas
verb errors	pronouns
capitalization	apostrophes

A New Frontier

My little nissan truck has been a good by for me, after owning an old six cylinder american truck. First of all they get great gas mileage, over thirty miles per gallon on the highway. It has a four-cylinder engine and a five-speed transmission, and because of these performance features my truck is both economical and fun to drive. Another attractive feature of this line of trucks are the automatic locks on both of the doors. I like my trucks compact looks it's racing wheels, and its chrome bumpers. The low price tag was my trucks biggest advantage. I still cant believe that I could find such a great truck.

Exercise 4

The passage below contains ten to fifteen errors. Correct all errors, and underline the corrections. You may need to add words. Edit for the following kinds of errors:

run-ons	problem words
fragments	commas
verb errors	pronouns
capitalization	apostrophes

A Fine Food Place

Mamma lou's is one of the best places to eat in town. When diners go to this restaurant they will find a wide variety of food to chose from. Along with the menus variety the waiter or waitress is almost always friendly. This restaurant serves a full course dinner. Which includes a meat dish with two vegetables and a dessert, for under ten dollars. If customers want one of Mamma Lou's specialties their fried chicken with rice is suppose to be the best in town, I believe that it's true. This restaurants entertainment includes a juke box and a television. With great food friendly service, and enjoyable entertainment its hard to beat Mamma Lou's.

Advanced Editing

The passage below contains ten to fifteen errors. Correct all errors, and underline the corrections. You may need to add words. Edit for the following kinds of errors:

Exercise 5

run-ons	pronouns
fragments	apostrophes
verb errors	semicolons and colons
capitalization	parallelism
problem words	modifiers
commas	

The Natives

Thousands of years before Columbus ever set sail, North America and South America was inhabited by native people called Indians. Unlike europeans who usually saw theirselves as masters over all creation the Indians think of themselves as brothers and sisters of other creatures and as sons and daughters of the earth. Thus, when spring came, they walked softly on the ground, since they didn't want to disturb the earth. Afraid of hurting the earth, the plow was not used by Indians. For thousands of years, they live by fishing and hunting, later, they farmed and used tools and weapons of stone, shell, or made of wood. The Indians many languages were complex; in fact, they might have spoke any one of 15,000 different languages and none of these are related to any European languages. From the northern to the southernmost tip of South America: Indians have existed in harmony with nature for centuries.

Exercise 6

The passage below contains ten to fifteen errors. Correct all errors, and underline the corrections. You may need to add words. Edit for the following kinds of errors:

run-ons	pronouns
fragments	apostrophes
verb errors	semicolons and colons
capitalization	parallelism
problem words	modifiers

River of Grass

Although it was described as a vast and dismal swamp for many years; the Florida Everglades are today consider a unique and beautiful natural wonder. The Indians called it "Pa-hay-o-kee," which means grassy water, and that is indeed what visitors see as they gaze across the miles and miles of long grass. The Everglades, however, contain more then just grass, in fact, thousands of plants and animals thrive there. Throughout the Everglades, there is small and large "hammocks" or islands. Which provide a foothold for plants such as: palmettos, mangroves, and coontie, and provide homes for such animals as alligators, flamingos, and wildcats.

The coontie, a foot-tall green plant that resembles a fern, has been use by the Indians of the area for centuries. They grate and squeeze the roots and sift them into flour to make a stew. According to legend, when the Indians once prayed to their god to ease the famine, he sent down his little boy to walk along the edge of the Everglades, and wherever his heels made a mark the coontie grew for the Indians to eat. Later, the white men used it to make starch, and called it arrowroot.

The alligator is well suited to the Everglades because an alligators eggs must have heat and moisture to incubate. Matting together masses of wet weeds, the nest is prepared by the female alligator. Later, she lays her eggs, covers them, and she leaves them to incubate in the sun for eight weeks. When the babies begin to squeak in their shells, she returns to uncover them and free the tiny alligators. The coontie and the alligator are only two of the many natural wonders of the Everglades.

Part VII

Readings

Special Topics

Introduction/Conclusion: The author gets the reader interested in the topic by telling a story that exemplifies or illustrates how easy it is to slip into the habit of telling white lies to children in order to control their behavior in public. The story helps parents relate the topic to their own lives. The thesis is not introduced until paragraph 8, the end of the introductory narrative, and then it is not overtly stated but rather implied. The conclusion returns to the anecdote used in the introduction.

Rhetorical Patterns: Cause/Effect and Example

The author examines the reasons parents tell white lies (paragraphs 9, 11, 12); the negative effects of white lies (paragraphs 9, 10, 14–16); and the positive effects of telling the truth (paragraph 17–21).

The author also uses examples throughout the essay to illustrate her points (paragraphs 1–7, 13–16, 18, 20).

Why White Lies Hurt
Grace Bennett

"Where's my doll? We lost Baby!" cried five-year-old Ariel Rosen of Millwood, New York. Ariel, her mom Shari, my daughter Anna, and I were standing in line at a bagel place. Shari had apparently left Ariel's doll at our local community center, where the girls had just finished a late morning class. Now all hell threatened to break loose.   1

Then, as I watched, Shari pulled a cellular phone from her purse, pretended to dial the center, and embarked[1] on a make-believe conversation with the "lady at the desk."   2

"You see my daughter's doll on the table? Oh, good. We'll come pick it up in a little while. Thank you. Bye! . . . You see, Ariel, they'll hold Baby for us until later." Ariel smiled broadly. Her whole body seemed to relax. Satisfied with her mom's fib, she was content enough now to sit down to lunch.   3

"That sure did the trick!" I commented.   4

"I'm the queen of white lies." Shari smiled, but she looked slightly embarrassed. "Anyway, I know exactly where we left the doll. I'm not worried about finding it later."   5

"Oh, you don't have to explain," I told her. "I've used white lies with Anna."   6

In fact, most parents can empathize[2] with another mother's or father's decision to tell a "little white lie" to avoid an unpleasant scene with their preschooler, particularly in public. "It's important to pick your battles," more than one parent told me. And telling an occasional untruth seems like a small price to pay for family harmony.   7

[1] set off, began

[2] understand or share feelings

8   The experts, however, could not disagree more. The ones I spoke with are not terribly willing to cut us harried,[3] tired souls much slack when it comes to sacrificing[4] honesty for some form of short-term relief.

[3] tormented, hurried
[4] giving up

The Habit of Flying

9   "We make the decision to lie, not because we're bad, but because it's expedient[5] or convenient.[6] Lying saves us money, time, or a headache," notes Bettie Youngs, Ph.D., Ed.D., a family counselor in Del Mar, California, and the author of *Stress and Your Child: Helping Kids Cope With the Strains and Pressures of Life* (Fawcett Book Group). "But what you're doing when you tell a white lie is pulling the wool over your child's eyes. It's OK on a rare occasion if your child doesn't find out about the deception. Trouble is, if you get into the habit of telling lies, eventually you lose track of what it is your child does or doesn't know."

[5] suitable for getting the desired results
[6] easy

10   Worse, your child may eventually come to feel that telling you a little white lie is justifiable.[7] "No, Mom, I don't see the blue shirt you want me to wear," she may yell out, when the blue shirt is right there in front of her. She prefers the red and would rather not argue about it. "You may unwittingly[8] set up a cycle of mutual[9] disrespect," notes Dr. Youngs.

[7] excusable

[8] without intention
[9] shared

11   Many parents rationalize[10] that a small fib protects their child from unnecessary stress, that saying there are no more cookies spares her the upset of realizing Mom just doesn't want her to have one. Dr. Youngs calls this a cop-out. "Parents today take far too seriously the idea that their children should always be emotionally comfortable," she says. "But actually, the child who's really most comfortable is the one who has a parent with some backbone."

[10] make an excuse

12   Parents use white lies to overprotect their children from reality, adds William Damon, Ph.D., director of the Center for the Study of Human Development at Brown University in Providence and the author of *Greater Expectations: Overcoming the Culture of Indulgence in Our Homes and Schools* (Free Press). "It's our job as parents to introduce kids to the true story of what life is like," Dr. Damon argues. "Especially with pre-schoolers, you need to send the message that everything they want or ask for will not automatically be granted—because that's not the way the world works."

13   Dr. Damon grants that telling a white lie can be overwhelmingly tempting. In fact, he's done it himself. On an outing, his two young children were insisting on yet another fast-food meal. "I couldn't bear the thought, and told them the place was closed," recalls Dr. Damon. Today he regrets not telling the truth. "Yes, it temporarily gets the kids off your back," he admits. "Ultimately,[11] though, you're doing your child a disservice.[12] Our real job as parents is to help prepare a child to meet reality, not avoid it."

[11] in the end
[12] harm, injury

Getting Caught

White lies also have an uncanny[13] way of backfiring when you 14 least expect them to. When that happens, notes Dr. Damon, you lose precious credibility.[14] "A child needs to trust that what a parent says is genuine,"[15] he says. "If a parent has a history of saying things that turn out not to be true, there is a risk that a breakdown in communication between the parent and child may follow."

[14]believability

[15]real, true

It's also hard to look a preschooler in the eye when you've been 15 caught red-handed. Sarah Craig of Springfield, Oregon, found this out—in her church, of all places. Sarah volunteers as a teacher in a Sunday school classroom of two-year-olds, and her five-year-old daughter, Janie, attends a class for preschoolers. One day, Janie wanted to go with her mom to the two-year-old class. "I told her I wasn't teaching it, thinking that she'd go willingly to her own class," explains Sarah. "When she refused, I ended up taking her with me anyway. We were in the class for about five minutes when Janie asked me, "Mom, why did you tell me you weren't teaching the two-year-old class when you really are?"

"I was very embarrassed," Sarah admits. "I think Janie perma- 16 nently cured me of telling white lies that day!"

[16]an act of refusal or denial

Parents need to remember that "children can take rejection,[16] 17 and they can learn to respect limits," says Dr. Youngs. "It's up to us to teach children the boundaries[17] of correct behavior. The sooner we start, the sooner they develop self-control."

[17]limits

In Janie's case, Sarah's truthful answer to her daughter might 18 have been, "I can't take you to class with me because it's my job to pay attention to the two-year-olds. If you're there, I might have a hard time doing that."

Why Honesty Pays Off

[18]that can be defended as right

[19]prevent

The bottom line, says Dr. Youngs, is that there is never any jus- 19 tifiable[18] reason to lie, even to a very young child. For every white lie you are tempted to tell, there is a morally superior—and honest—response to opt for instead. Sure, it may not always avert[19] the whining and carrying-on you were hoping to avoid, but take comfort in the fact that with each effort at truthfulness, you teach your child important life lessons.

[20]demanding loudly

Say, for instance, your child is clamoring[20] for a toy. You can 20 avoid a scene with a line like, "Sorry, I don't have any more money in my wallet right now." Or you can simply be honest and say, "I'm afraid not. We can't afford to buy something new every time you want us to. We have occasions for giving things. Or maybe it's possible for you to do something special to earn it."

In this way, you can help your child begin to understand not 21 only that your spending has limits, but also that new possessions are not available on demand.

22   No one's suggesting that you should beat yourself up over using an occasional white lie, says Dr. Damon. But when I told my friend Shari all that I'd learned, she and I felt duly chastened.[21] We agreed to try harder to resist the impulse to resort to fibbing, or at least not resort to it right away. Dr. Damon, by the way, was sympathetic to our struggle. "Kids grow up in an imperfect world," he says. "Part of that world is parents just doing the best they can." You bet.

[21]chastised, corrected

Comprehension Questions

1. According to the author, what is the main motive people in general have for lying?

    A. personal benefit

    B. economic gain

    C. convenience

    D. guilt

2. Why is the habit of telling white lies to children damaging?

    A. They will discover the deception and lose respect.

    B. They will learn to tell white lies themselves.

    C. It doesn't help them learn to deal with reality.

    D. All of the above.

3. How should a parent respond when her child cries for a toy or a piece of candy in a store?

    A. She should tell the child she doesn't have enough money in her wallet.

    B. She should tell the child she can't afford to buy everything the child wants.

    C. She should tell the child that there are special occasions for giving or suggest that the child do something to earn the desired object.

    D. B or C.

4. There are often justifiable reasons to lie to a child. (T/F)

5. Why is it not a good idea to tell your child white lies to protect him from stress?

    A. Your child won't learn to deal with reality.

    B. Your child will be emotionally comfortable.

    C. Your child will have trouble in school.

Discussion Questions

1. How effective is the introductory anecdote used by the author?

2. Why do people tell white lies to children?

3. How does telling white lies to children affect their ability to deal with reality?

4. What effects can the habit of telling white lies have on the relationship between parents and children?

5. What are the benefits of being honest with a child?

Journal Topic

1. Describe a situation in which you or someone you know used a white lie with a child. How might you handle such a situation differently after reading this article?

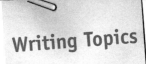
Writing Topics

1. Discuss the negative effects of lying to children.

2. Agree or disagree with the author's contention that parents should not lie to children.

3. Think of other situations in which people commonly tell white lies. Discuss whether other kinds of white lies have negative effects.

4. Argue that using a white lie in a certain situation had positive or negative effects.

5. Classify types of white lies.

6. Compare and contrast two types of white lies.

Special Topics

Rhetorical Patterns: Notice how the author incorporates narration, example, and cause and effect in telling the story of how one community took a stand against racism. The story focuses on one person in the town, Tammie Schnitzer, in order to show how the events affected the townspeople. The author uses dialogue to dramatize the events, and he explores both the causes and the effects of the townspeople's actions.

Not in Our Town!
Edwin Dobb

1   As Tammie Schnitzer came to a stop at the intersection near the synagogue[1] in Billings, Mont., she noticed something on the stop sign. She got out of her car to take a closer look, and a shiver shot down her spine. A sticker showed a swastika[2] over a Star of David[3] and the words "Want more oil? Nuke Israel."

2   Suddenly Tammie recalled a conversation with her husband, Brian, when they began dating years earlier. "There's something I have to tell you," he had said gravely.[4] "I'm Jewish." Tammie was amused that he would make such a fuss over a difference that could never impede[5] their relationship. Before marrying Brian, a physician who had come to Montana to work with the Indian Health Service, Tammie, a Billings native, converted to Judaism. Now on that morning in May 1992 she saw how life as a Jew could be very unpleasant.

3   The display of raw hate unnerved Tammie. She felt vulnerable and worried about their three-year-old son, Isaac, and eight-month-old daughter, Rachel. Then the 33-year-old homemaker came up with an idea. She called Wayne Schile, publisher of the *Billings Gazette*, to talk about the problem of hate groups in their community. "What problem?" Schile replied.

4   A few days later Tammie visited Schile. "This problem," she said, handing over hate literature that had been circulated in Billings. Schile was stunned.

5   In the months that followed, Tammie returned often to Schile's office with the latest hate literature. Finally, in October, the *Gazette* ran a front-page story on local skinheads, detailing their attitudes toward minorities and their links to the Ku Klux Klan.

Vicious[6]

6   For most of the 85,000 residents of Billings, the story was a revelation of organized hate in their midst. But Wayne Inman, chief of the Billings Police Department, knew through informants that a group of angry young men and their hangers-on, most of them

[1] a place of worship for Jews
[2] an emblem of Nazi Germany
[3] an emblem of Judaism

[4] with great seriousness
[5] stop the flow of

[6] savage and cruel

poorly educated and underemployed, were followers of the KKK, and he worried about what might come next.

On January 18, 1993, leaflets were placed on cars during an 7 interfaith Martin Luther King Day observance at the First United Methodist Church. The fliers insulted a number of minorities, including the town's small community of about 120 Jews.

Inman called a press conference. "I can't do anything about 8 this filth," he said, "because no crime has been committed. But the community can, and should, before it's too late."

Then Inman told a story. Before coming to Billings, he had 9 been the assistant police chief in Portland, Ore., where seemingly harmless leafleting had escalated[7] to vicious crimes: minorities were assaulted, their property was vandalized. Finally, in the fall of 1988, three skinheads beat an Ethiopian man to death with base-ball bats. "Only then," Inman said, "did the people of Portland acknowledge the problem."

"Silence is acceptance," Inman continued. "These people are 10 testing us. And if we do nothing, there's going to be more trouble. Billings should stand up and say, 'Harass[8] one of us and you harass us all.'"

In response, leafleting increased. Then one September morning, 11 Brian Schnitzer drove to the Jewish cemetery to help pick up litter. Unlocking the gate, Brian discovered that most of the headstones were tilted or lay face down. Someone had vandalized the small bur-ial ground.

"This is not a teen-age prank," Inman later told reporters. 12 "This is a hate crime, pure and simple, directed at Jews."

Meanwhile the leafleting attacks became personal. Uri Barnea, 13 the music director of the Billings Symphony, who had emigrated[9] from Israel, was singled out by name in fliers. On November 27, a bottle was hurled through his glass-paneled front door.

"I'm Scared."

On the evening of December 2, a stranger stole[10] into the 14 Schnitzers' yard after Brian and Tammie had each driven away to attend meetings. Looking in a window of a well-lit room, the stranger could not have failed to notice Isaac's toys and the child-size bed. Nor could there have been doubt about the Schnitzers' religion. Resting on the chest of drawers was a menorah, the can-delabrum Jews display during Hanukkah,[11] the eight-day Festival of Lights. The banner on the window proclaimed "Happy Hanukkah."

The intruder heaved a cinder block through the window. Glass 15 exploded as the concrete bounced across the bed and landed on the floor. Luckily, Isaac was in the rec. room playing with Rachel and their sitter.

---

[7] intensified, increased

[8] bother, disturb

[9] moved (from one's home country)

[10] entered stealthily, sneaked

[11] Jewish holiday commemorating the rededication of the Temple of Jerusalem

16   When Tammie returned, Brian led her into Isaac's room. Her legs went weak, and she began to cry. Recalling the vandalism of storefronts that preceded the roundup of Jews in Germany in 1938, Tammie wondered, *Is this another Kristallnacht, the night of the broken glass?* "I'm scared, Brian," Tammie said. "Whoever did this waited until we left. They were watching us."

17   They discussed restricting the children's activities. But gradually Tammie's worry turned to anger. *Why should my children have to live in fear? Only one force could protect Isaac and Rachel, she realized—the community. Would anyone care enough to help them?*

18   The next day Tammie called Schile. "You're setting yourself up for more trouble," Schile warned. "I don't care," Tammie said. "This is a quality of life issue, not a Jewish issue." That evening, the Schnitzers observed the beginning of the Sabbath. They huddled in a corner of the kitchen, far from windows, and lit the ceremonial candles.

Royal Example

19   The following morning, Margie MacDonald sat reading about the Schnitzers in the Gazette. As executive director of the Montana Association of Churches, she worked to educate religious leaders about the dangers of allowing bigotry[12] to go unchallenged.

[12]intolerance of religious or racial differences

20   One passage caught MacDonald's eye. The night of the attack, a police officer had suggested that Brian and Tammie take down their Hanukkah decorations. "How do I explain that to my children?" Tammie had asked. "I shouldn't have to do that."

21   MacDonald envisioned the people of Billings shielding the Schnitzers and every other victim of religious intolerance. Then she remembered the story of King Christian of Denmark. When the Nazis informed him that all Jews would be forced to display the yellow Star of David on their coats, the king responded that he would be first to wear it, and all Danes would follow his lead. The Nazis withdrew the order.

22   Now MacDonald reasoned, *What if instead of the Jews removing menorahs[13] from their windows, Christians placed menorahs in theirs?* She contacted the Rev. Keith Torney, pastor of the First Congregational Church. "Margie, that's a great idea," he said.

[13]ceremonial candleholders

23   That Saturday afternoon, Torney called the pastors of several other churches, asking if they would distribute paper menorahs. The response was enthusiastic. Pastors reproduced the candelabrum and encouraged congregants[14] to display it in their homes.

[14]members of a congregation

24   Torney gave out 300 paper menorahs at his church. And in his sermon that Sunday he said: "We dare not remain silent as our Jewish sisters and brothers are threatened: I will put a menorah in my window and in my heart, for what happens to Jews also happens to me. You must decide what your response will be."

On Wednesday, December 8, the *Billings Gazette* ran an edito-   25
rial under the headline "Show the Vandals That Hatred Has No
Place in This Season of Love and Light," urging readers to place
menorahs in their windows.

A 68-year-old member of Torney's congregation decided to   26
place a menorah on a window where it would be seen clearly from
the street. As she taped it to the glass, a neighbor begged her to take
it down. "Don't you know what's going on?" the neighbor said.

"Yes," the woman replied. "That's exactly why I'm putting it up."   27

"Leave Our Babies Alone."

Rick Smith, manager of Universal Athletics, placed a message   28
on the reader board outside his store: "Not in our town! No hate,
no violence. Peace on earth." Ron Nistler, principal of Billings
Central Catholic High School, proclaimed on the school's elec-
tronic sign: "Happy Hanukkah to our Jewish friends."

Reaction among Jews to the sudden outpouring of support   29
was mixed. Many feared the Schnitzers' efforts to draw attention to
anti-Semitism [15] in Billings would only further incite bigots. [16] Thus,
it was a divided congregation that greeted Samuel Cohon, Beth
Aaron Synagogue's new student rabbi. The rift [17] dividing his community preoccupied Cohon as he planned a vigil [18] to precede [19]
Sabbath services on December 10, the third night of Hanukkah.

At 6:30 p.m. on that chilly Friday, about 200 people, mostly   30
Christians, gathered across the street from the synagogue. As candles were distributed and lit, a small constellation [20] of flames took
shape around a pickup truck on which Rabbi Cohon and the
Schnitzers stood. Cohon lit a menorah and blessed it, saying that it
symbolized the human spirit. "You cannot stifle [21] it."

Then Tammie stepped forward to speak. She said that the   31
block that smashed her son's window was aimed at everyone who
is a victim of prejudice. Just then a few skinheads arrived, glower-
ing [22] at the crowd. Staring at one of the young men, Tammie
declared, "Leave our babies alone!"

Rabbi Cohon quoted British statesman Edmund Burke's   32
observation on empathy [23]: "The only thing necessary for the triumph of evil is for good men to do nothing." Then he led his congregants into the synagogue. The skinheads wandered off. But just
in case, a few good people stayed to keep watch during the service.

The next morning's Gazette featured a front-page story about   33
the vigil, a full-page color reproduction of a menorah and a statement urging readers to display it.

But the following day the paper carried unsettling news: small-   34
caliber bullets had shattered windows at Central Catholic High
School, near the sign that extended holiday greetings to Jews. The
incident was a first in a weeklong spree of hate crimes.

[15] opposition to Jews

[16] people who hate others
because of their religion
or race

[17] a division in a group
caused by a difference of
opinion

[18] a period of watchfulness

[19] come before

[20] configuration (as in a
constellation of stars)

[21] suffocate

[22] scowling

[23] understanding and
identification with
someone else's feelings
or situation

Scare Tactics

35   Late Sunday night, two families received anonymous phone calls: "Go look at your car, Jew lover." The homeowners found their cars' roofs stomped on and windshields shattered. Four other residents discovered their cars similarly damaged. None of the victims was Jewish but all had exhibited paper menorahs.

36   Two nights later, vandals broke three windows that displayed menorahs at First United Methodist. The same evening, the glass doors at the Evangelical United Methodist Church were shattered.

37   "The hate groups are trying to silence us through scare tactics," Chief Inman declared. "We can't allow it. For every act of vandalism, I hope 100 people will put menorahs in their windows. It's impossible for a small group of bigots to intimidate thousands of citizens who stand together. Tammie Schnitzer reinforced his remarks: "This is not a Jewish issue. It's a human issue." Then two local businesses announced they would distribute menorahs at all of their outlets in the area.

38   This time the entire town was aroused. Soon the nine-candle symbol could be seen everywhere—on office windows, in homes and apartments, on cars and trucks, in restaurants and stores, schools and other public buildings-thousands in all. One night just before Christmas, Tammie Schnitzer took Isaac and Rachel for a drive around Billings. She wanted them to see that they lived in a community that stood by its children. Tammie pointed out the menorahs that hung in windows ringed by bright colored lights. "Gosh," Isaac said, "are all these people Jewish?" "No, Isaac," Tammie replied, "they're your friends."

Comprehension Questions

1. The hate group in Billings, Montana, was linked to
    A. the Ku Klux Klan.
    B. a foreign government.
    C. another hate group in Ohio.
    D. the Nazis.

2. The hate group in Billings, Montana,
    A. killed an Ethiopian man.
    B. distributed hate literature.
    C. dug up graves.
    D. beat up citizens.

3. Who was the prominent townsperson who had a bottle thrown through his front door?

    A. the police chief

    B. the mayor

    C. the school superintendent

    D. the music director of the symphony

4. What is a menorah?

    A. a candleholder

    B. a cross

    C. a fountain

    D. a star

5. What famous person identified himself as a Jew in order to protect the Jews of his country?

    A. the King of England

    B. the President of Israel

    C. the King of Denmark

    D. the Prime Minister of Germany

Discussion Questions

1. What were the events that led the people of Billings to realize that there were hate groups in town?

2. Discuss how the individuals, churches, and businesses in Billings responded to the harassment of their Jewish citizens.

3. Why was the town's display of menorahs effective in protecting people like the Schnitzers?

4. Explain the meaning of the quote "The only thing necessary for the triumph of evil is for good men to do nothing." What do you think would have happened if no one had protested the hate group's actions in Billings?

5. Discuss how the hate group's actions actually encouraged the residents of Billings to love and accept one another.

Writing Topics

1. Explain how we can eliminate hate crimes in our culture. You may wish to consider how education, the legal system, and religion could play a part in eradicating prejudice.

2. Write a cause/effect essay or two paragraphs recounting the events that led the people of Billings to discover a hate group in their town and the effects the hate group had on the town.

3. After the police chief of Billings said, "Silence is acceptance" (paragraph 10), residents of Billings decided to take a stand against the tactics of hate groups. Discuss their response and its effectiveness. Could their actions serve as an example to other communities?

4. Have you or has anyone else in your community experienced a hate crime? Or have you ever experienced discrimination based on your age, race, sex, nationality, dress, hair, weight, or some other factor? Describe an incident of hate or of discrimination that you have witnessed, and tell how you responded.

5. Discuss a controversy your town has experienced recently. Explain what caused the controversy, how people reacted, and what the results were. What were your feelings about the controversy?

Special Topics

Rhetorical Patterns: The author attempts to persuade the reader that friends are important to a person's physical and mental well-being by examining the beneficial effects of close friendships.

Audience: Although the author's topic applies to everyone, he directs his comments specifically to older Americans.

Evidence from Authority: Throughout the article, the author makes reference to scientific studies and experts in the field to support his claims. He quotes gerontologist Rosemary Blieszner (paragraph 2); a Stanford University School of Medicine study (paragraph 2); psychology professor Blair Justice (paragraph 3); and Robert Milardo, professor of family relationships at the University of Maine (paragraph 8).

Introducing Evidence: Notice that for each study or authority cited, the author identifies the source with name, title, and affiliation; puts the selected words in quotation marks; and uses tag phrases such as *according to* or *says* to identify the speaker. Even when the author does not use direct quotes, but rather paraphrases (puts the source's ideas into his own words), he uses tag phrases to identify the source. Notice the punctuation used with quotations (commas and periods inside quotation marks) and tag phrases (commas before, after, or around the tag phrase, depending on where it is placed).

Friends as Healers
Old Friends Are Good For You, Physically, Mentally, and Emotionally

R. Daniel Foster

The hunger for friendship begins in childhood and stays with us throughout our lives. Close friends are particularly important because they know our assets[1] and our flaws and think we're just great anyway. Often these friendships are highly dynamic,[2] moving through the years from tranquillity to occasional discord,[3] from intense support to lesser involvement, and back again.   1

"People who maintain a safety net of friends can protect themselves against the losses that come with age," says gerontologist[4] Rosemary Blieszner of Virginia Polytechnic Institute and State University. "The qualities that people mention in studies—confiding problems and needs, building trust, addressing problems that come up—are foundations for friendships that contribute to physical and mental health." Confiding in someone may offer big payoffs in terms of health, experts say. A Stanford University School of   2

[1] valuable or desirable qualities

[2] possessing energy; changeable

[3] disagreement

[4] scientist who studies the aging process

Medicine study, published in 1989, compared two groups of women with metastatic[5] breast cancer: those who attended regular support meetings, and those who toughed it out on their own. The pain levels among those who attended meetings were significantly lower than their counterparts'. The meetings also helped alleviate[6] stress and depression. The best news? Survival rates for the supported women were nearly twice as high.

3   "The willingness to disclose our deepest feelings to another person has an effect on the central nervous system that affects the cardiovascular[7] and immune[8] systems," says Blair Justice, associate dean of academic affairs and professor of psychology at the University of Texas–Houston School of Public Health.

4   When we don't confide our problems, Justice says, the body and brain work overtime to suppress[9] emotions. Disclosing our feelings is an act of release, which reduces stress hormones that dampen[10] immune response and hike blood pressure. "It's very stressful on the body to constantly repress feelings," says Justice.

5   How many friends do you need before your health improves? "Much benefit can be had from a warm, close relationship with just one other person," Justice says. "Quality is more important than quantity."

6   And the quality is often highest when it comes from a woman, Blieszner says. "Both men and women feel closer to females who give support. Women are more relational[11] and listen to problems and give feedback. They have deeper relationships. Some use the expression, 'Men have side-by-side friendships; women have face-to-face friendships.' Men's friendships are activity based; women want to talk about things. That's true across all ages."

7   In fact, husbands rely almost exclusively on their spouses to fulfill intimacy needs. Wives do not. In surveys, men routinely list their spouses as being their best friends.

8   While men may feel their greatest support from women friends, cross-gender[12] friendships prove to be the hardest to maintain. "Opposite-gender friends can promote jealousy between close partners," says Robert Milardo, professor of family relationships at the University of Maine.

9   "The boundaries between intimate friendship and a sexual component can become blurred. That can be difficult if one friend is married." There is much, it seems, that conspires[13] to keep the sexes from becoming friends.

10   After three decades of research, the evidence is clear: Good friends are critically important to successful aging. Friends can be "more important to the psychological well-being of older adults than even family members are," according to Blieszner's research.

[5] spreading from one part of the body to another

[6] reduce

[7] of the heart and blood vessels
[8] of the system that fights infection
[9] keep down
[10] reduce

[11] focused on relationships

[12] different-sex

[13] plots

[14]assigned or set by birth

She notes that older adults can more easily receive moral support from people their own age. Although family relationships are meaningful and family members provide important support such as health care, relationships that are built from scratch, rather than ascribed,[14] retain more importance in terms of mental and emotional health.

"With families, old power relationships are still there, and old baggage," says Blieszner. "But friends are age peers. They're chosen relationships." And what could be more valuable than a hand-picked support network of friends to enrich your life? "The bottom line is: Friends are essential to everyone's life," Blieszner says. "Everyone needs friends."

11

Comprehension Questions

1. Which of the following are characteristics of friendships?

   A. They remain unchanged through the years.

   B. There are never any disagreements.

   C. They move through periods of disagreements and greater and lesser involvement.

2. In a 1989 Stanford University School of Medicine study, survival rates were twice as high for women who

   A. exercised regularly.

   B. participated in support groups.

   C. took medication to reduce pain.

   D. had strong family support.

3. How does disclosing one's feelings benefit the body?

   A. It strengthens the immune system.

   B. It reduces stress hormones.

   C. It reduces high blood pressure.

   D. All of the above.

4. The more friends a person has, the healthier he or she is likely to be. (T/F)

5. In regard to the well-being of older adults, friends can be more important than family members. (T/F)

Discussion Questions

1. What effects can friendship have on an individual's chances of surviving an illness?

2. What are some of the beneficial effects of friendship?

3. According to the author, how are men's and women's friendships different?

4. Why are cross-gender friendships difficult to maintain?

5. Why are friends more important than family members to one's mental and emotional health?

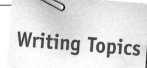

Writing Topics

1. Describe the beneficial physical, mental, emotional effects of friendship.

2. Agree or disagree with the author's claim that everyone needs friends.

3. Compare and contrast two different kinds of friendships (male/female, childhood/adult, etc.) or friendships at different ages (elementary school, high school, college, etc.).

4. Analyze the effects friendships have had on you.

5. Classify types of friends.

Special Topics

Use of Metaphor: In paragraph 1, notice how the author uses the metaphor of music to describe the changes in a runner's life.

Growing Through a Phase
Jeff Galloway[1]

[1] Jeff Galloway has written many books on running and is an expert on training for and running marathons.

[2] without change

[3] difficult

Our running life isn't static,[2] a single note played over and over. It is growth and movement, an evolution from our "birth" as runners to the fullest development of our potential; a melody full of lulls and surges, silences and crescendos. After those first labored[3] steps, every runner goes through stages, enduring a few "growing pains" along the way. But if you're open to each of these phases, you can continue to benefit from the positive elements of each one as you move on to more rewarding running experiences.   1

The Beginner

[4] characterized by much sitting and little movement

[5] not able to be perceived

[6] beginner

[7] enthusiasm

[8] grow or prosper

Perched on the edge of a new, vigorous life, the beginning runner is primarily a sedentary[4] person. He or she is impatient with the slow process of weight loss and the almost imperceptible[5] increase of running pace. The novice[6] wants results, now! Filled with exuberance,[7] beginners often push too hard, get injured or tired, and quit, only to restart a dozen times.   2

Beginners thrive[8] on joining running groups. Though they sometimes struggle to "just get out there," novices eventually learn to enjoy the relaxed feeling running brings. When they start to sense a clearer, more focused mental state on their running days, they're on the verge of entering the next phase.   3

The Jogger

Though the jogger may sometimes lack the motivation to start a run, he feels secure with the habit of running. While most beginners need a specific benefit from each run, the jogger finds satisfaction in the act itself and seldom describes runs as "boring."   4

Joggers have begun to feel like part of the running community and may enjoy identification with a particular running event. They rarely have a training plan and usually abandon special schedules because of the conflicts of work and home life.   5

[9] mystical

As joggers enter the next phase, some become competitive and train hard for faster times or challenging events. Others bypass competitive urges and discover the transcendental[9] quality of the "Runner" phase.   6

The Competitor/The Athlete

7 There's a competitive streak, often hidden, in all of us. Controlled and directed, it can motivate us, stimulating strengths that would otherwise stay submerged.[10] The negative compulsion[11] of the competitor is an obsessive[12] pursuit[13] of personal records or age-group awards.

8 If the competitor can break free from this preoccupation[14] with ego boosts, he'll strive to bring out his best on any given day. This marks entry into the world of the athlete, who pushes through tiredness and discomfort, developing the capacity[15] to deal with adversities[16] in races and in other areas of life.

9 As a competitor, you learn how to choose events and develop racing techniques. Once you mature into an athlete, however, you appreciate your ability to rise to the challenge and use current personal resources to maximize potential on that day.

10 Competitors know exactly where they rank in the pecking order—and yearn[17] for the next level. The athlete finds success in every running experience.

The Runner

11 It is possible to have it all. This phase balances the elements of fitness, commitment, competition and mental invigoration[18] with the demands of career and family. Runners have a life apart from running, yet appreciate how running enhances[19] each area of their lives.

12 Intuitively,[20] the runner combines strength, speed, form and endurance with motivation and willpower. The running experience itself confers[21] so much satisfaction that each run becomes a natural expression of who the runner is and what he stands for. The runner appreciates the chemistry of a group but loves the transcendental quality of a solitary[22] run.

13 As a runner, you can relive the enjoyment of each stage—the beginner's excitement and the jogger's glow of fitness; moments of the competitor's ambition, balanced by the athlete's quest for personal excellence. And for the runner, it's possible, on parts of every run, to transcend[23] the physical experience, letting your mind soar[24] into creative and intuitive visions.

[10]hidden, as if underwater
[11]strong impulse
[12]excessive
[13]act of striving for or following
[14]concern
[15]ability
[16]setbacks

[17]strongly desire, long

[18]stimulation

[19]makes richer
[20]understood by instinct rather than reason
[21]brings, gives

[22]performed alone

[23]go beyond
[24]rise above, fly

Comprehension Questions

1. According to the author, the life of a runner
    A. can remain unchanging for years.
    B. includes growth and movement.
    C. usually peaks at age thirty.
    D. is most difficult in the beginning stage.

2. In which stage in a runner's life does the runner usually join a running group?

    A. the beginner stage

    B. the jogger stage

    C. the competitor stage

    D. the runner stage

3. Which stage in a runner's life is characterized by learning racing techniques?

    A. the beginner stage

    B. the jogger stage

    C. the competitor stage

    D. the runner stage

4. Which stage includes the enjoyment of all the other stages?

    A. the beginner stage

    B. the jogger stage

    C. the competitor stage

    D. the runner stage

5. According to the author, running can be enjoyable on

    A. a physical level.

    B. a mental level.

    C. a social level.

    D. all levels.

Discussion Questions

1. Why does the author believe that a runner goes through different stages?

2. What are the four stages of a runner's life, and what marks each stage as different from the other stages?

3. How does the fourth stage, the runner, combine all of the other stages?

4. How are the stages the author classifies similar to stages in other sports or learning activities?

5. What stages have you gone through in learning to write?

1. Classify the different stages of a runner's life.

2. Classify the stages that you have gone through in some sport or hobby or skill that you have perfected.

3. Contrast a jogger and an athlete according to the author's definition of these two stages.

4. Compare the beginning stages of running and those of some other sport that you have participated in.

5. Explain why you enjoy a particular sport of hobby.

Special Topics

Introduction/Conclusion: Goleman opens his essay with a story (narrative example) of a man who is happy with himself and with his life and who is therefore a success. Goleman then contrasts this happy individual with a young man of high IQ who is unhappy and maladjusted. By opening with two contrasting examples, Goleman not only gets the reader's attention, but goes a long way toward convincing the reader that traditional intelligence is not as important as emotional intelligence in determining someone's success in life.

Rhetorical Patterns: The author makes use of several rhetorical patterns in this excerpt from his book *Emotional Intelligence*. He defines emotional intelligence by listing its characteristics or component parts and by giving examples of each. He also helps define the term by contrasting it with high IQ to show the reader how emotional intelligence differs from traditional intelligence as measured on tests.

What's Your Emotional IQ?
Condensed from *Emotional Intelligence*
Daniel Goleman

1 It was a steamy afternoon in New York City, the kind of day that makes people sullen[1] with discomfort. I was heading to my hotel, and as I stepped onto a bus, I was greeted by the driver, a middle-aged man with an enthusiastic smile.

2 "Hi! How're you doing?" he said. He greeted each rider in the same way.

3 As the bus crawled uptown through gridlocked traffic, the driver gave a lively commentary: there was a terrific sale at that store…a wonderful exhibit at this museum…had we heard about the movie that just opened down the block? By the time people got off, they had shaken off their sullen shells. When the driver called out, "So long, have a great day!" each of us gave a smiling response.

4 That memory has stayed with me for close to 20 years. I consider the bus driver a man who was truly successful at what he did.

5 Contrast him with Jason, a straight A student at a Florida high school who was fixated on getting into Harvard Medical School. When a physics teacher gave Jason an 80 on a quiz, the boy believed his dream was in jeopardy.[2] He took a butcher knife to school, and in a struggle the teacher was stabbed in the collarbone.

6 How could someone of obvious intelligence do something so irrational[3]? The answer is that high I.Q. does not necessarily predict who will succeed in life. Psychologists agree that I.Q.

[1] moody and resentful

[2] danger

[3] lacking reason

contributes only about 20 percent of the factors that determine success. A full 80 percent comes from other factors, including what I call emotional intelligence.

7   Following are some of the major qualities that make up emotional intelligence, and how they can be developed:

1. Self-awareness.

8   The ability to recognize a feeling as it happens is the keystone of emotional intelligence. People with greater certainty about their emotions are better pilots of their lives.

9   Developing self-awareness requires tuning in to what neurologist[4] Antonio Damasio, in his book *Descartes' Error*[5], calls "somatic markers"—literally, gut feelings. Gut feelings can occur without a person being consciously aware of them. For example, when people who fear snakes are shown a picture of a snake, sensors on their skin will detect sweat, a sign of anxiety, even though the people say they do not feel fear. The sweat shows up even when a picture is presented so rapidly that the subject has no conscious awareness of seeing it.

10   Through deliberate effort we can become more aware of our gut feelings. Take someone who is annoyed by a rude encounter for hours after it occurred. He may be oblivious to[6] his irritability and surprised when someone calls attention to it. But if he evaluates his feelings, he can change them.

11   Emotional self-awareness is the building block of the next fundamental of emotional intelligence: being able to shake off a bad mood.

2. Mood Management

12   Bad as well as good moods spice life and build character. The key is balance.

13   We often have little control over when we are swept by emotion. But we can have some say in how long that emotion will last. Psychologist Dianne Tice of Case Western Reserve University asked more than 400 men and women about their strategies for escaping foul moods. Her research, along with that of other psychologists, provides valuable information on how to change a bad mood.

14   Of all the moods that people want to escape, rage seems to be the hardest to deal with. When someone in another car cuts you off on the highway, your reflexive[7] thought may be, That jerk! He could have hit me! I can't let him get away with that! The more you stew, the angrier you get. Such is the stuff of hypertension[8] and reckless driving.

15   What should you do to relieve rage? One myth is that ventilating[9] will make you feel better. In fact, researchers have found that's

[4] branch of medicine specializing in the nervous system

[5] The French philosopher Rene Descartes (1596–1650) is famous for the statement "I think, therefore I am."

[6] unaware of

[7] involuntary or automatic

[8] high blood pressure

[9] releasing

one of the worst strategies. Outbursts of rage pump up the brain's arousal system, leaving you more angry, not less.

A more effective technique is "reframing," which means consciously reinterpreting a situation in a more positive light. In the case of the driver who cuts you off you might tell yourself: Maybe he had an emergency. This is one of the most potent ways, Tice found, to put anger to rest.

16

Going off alone to cool down is also an effective way to defuse[10] anger, especially if you can't think clearly. Tice found that a large proportion of men cool down by going for a drive—a finding that inspired her to drive more defensively. A safer alternative is exercise, such as taking a long walk. Whatever you do, don't waste the time pursuing your train of angry thoughts. Your aim should be to distract yourself. The techniques of reframing and distraction can alleviate[11] depression and anxiety as well as anger. Add to them such relaxation techniques as deep breathing and meditation and you have an arsenal[12] of weapons against bad moods. "Praying," Dianne Tice also says, "works for all moods."

17

3. Self-motivation

Positive motivation—the marshaling[13] of feelings of enthusiasm, zeal and confidence—is paramount[14] for achievement. Studies of Olympic athletes, world-class musicians and chess grandmasters show that their common trait is the ability to motivate themselves to pursue relentless[15] training routines.

18

To motivate yourself for any achievement requires clear goals and an optimistic, can-do attitude. Psychologist Martin Seligman of the University of Pennsylvania advised the MetLife insurance company to hire a special group of job applicants who tested high on optimism, although they had failed the normal aptitude[16] test. Compared with salesmen who passed the aptitude test but scored high in pessimism, this group made 21 percent more sales in their first year and 57 percent more in their second.

19

A pessimist is likely to interpret rejection as meaning I'm a failure; I'll never make a sale. Optimists tell themselves, I'm using the wrong approach, or that customer was in a bad mood. By blaming failure on the situation, not themselves, optimists are motivated to make that next call. Your predisposition to a positive or negative outlook may be inborn, but with effort and practice, pessimists can learn to think more hopefully. Psychologists have documented that if you can catch negative, self-defeating thoughts as they occur, you can reframe the situation in less catastrophic[17] terms.

20

[10]to take the fuse out of, make less explosive

[11]relieve

[12]storehouse

[13]gathering as if for battle
[14]of primary importance
[15]harsh, without a break

[16]ability

[17]disastrous

4. Impulse Control.

21   The essence of emotional self-regulation is the ability to delay impulse in the service of a goal. The importance of this trait to success was shown in an experiment begun in the 1960s by psychologist Walter Mischel at a preschool on the Stanford University campus. Children were told that they could have a single treat, such as a marshmallow, right now.

22   However, if they would wait while the experimenter ran an errand, they could have two marshmallows. Some preschoolers grabbed the marshmallow immediately, but others were able to wait what, for them, must have seemed an endless 20 minutes. To sustain themselves in their struggle, they covered their eyes so they wouldn't see the temptation, rested their heads on their arms, talked to themselves, sang, even tried to sleep. These plucky kids got the two-marshmallow reward.

23   The interesting part of this experiment came in the follow-up. The children who as four-year-olds had been able to wait for the two marshmallows were, as adolescents, still able to delay gratification[18] in pursuing their goals. They were more socially competent[19] and self-assertive, and better able to cope with life's frustrations. In contrast, the kids who grabbed the one marshmallow were, as adolescents, more likely to be stubborn, indecisive[20] and stressed. The ability to resist impulse[21] can be developed through practice. When you're faced with an immediate temptation, remind yourself of your long-term goals—whether they be losing weight or getting a medical degree. You'll find it easier, then, to keep from settling for the single marshmallow.

[18]reward

[19]capable

[20]unable to make a decision

[21]sudden desire

5. People Skills

24   The capacity to know how another feels is important on the job, in romance and friendship, and in the family. We transmit and catch moods from each other on a subtle,[22] almost imperceptible[23] level. The way someone says thank you, for instance, can leave us feeling dismissed, patronized[24] or genuinely appreciated. The more adroit[25] we are at discerning[26] the feelings behind other people's signals, the better we control the signals we send.

25   The importance of good interpersonal skills was demonstrated by psychologists Robert Kelley of Carnegie-Mellon University and Janet Caplan in a study at Bell Labs in Naperville, Ill. The labs are staffed by engineers and scientists who are all at the apex[27] of academic I.Q. tests. But some still emerged[28] as stars, while others languished.[29]

[22]not obvious

[23]hard to perceive or notice

[24]treated as a protected inferior

[25]skillful

[26]perceiving, figuring out

[27]height

[28]became visible

[29]became weak or weary

What accounted for the difference? The standout performers 26
had a network with a wide range of people. When a non-star
encountered a technical problem, Kelley observed, "He called
various technical gurus and then waited, wasting time while his
calls went unreturned. Star performers rarely faced such situations because they built reliable networks before they needed
them. So when the stars called someone, they almost always got
a faster answer."

No matter what their I.Q., once again it was emotional intelli- 27
gence that separated the stars from the average performers.

Comprehension Questions

1. According to the author, IQ contributes what percentage of the
   factors that determine success?

   A. 80

   B. 50

   C. 20

   D. 10

2. What characteristic is the keystone of emotional intelligence?

   A. the ability to recognize a feeling as it happens

   B. strong family bonds

   C. regular physical exercise

3. One of the best ways to defuse anger is to

   A. express or vent it.

   B. repress it.

   C. reframe the situation.

4. Studies of world-class athletes and musicians show that they share

   A. superior intelligence.

   B. an ability to motivate themselves.

   C. similar upbringings.

5. Youngsters who were able to delay gratification as four-year-
   olds were _____ as adolescents.

   A. frustrated

   B. socially and emotionally well adjusted

   C. emotionally stressed

Discussion Questions

1. How does the author define success? Do you agree with him?

2. What qualities contribute to emotional intelligence?

3. How does awareness of one's emotions contribute to emotional intelligence?

4. What are some ineffective and effective ways to defuse anger?

5. How does the ability to delay gratification affect achievement?

Journal Topic

1. Which of the qualities Goleman discusses do you have? Which are you lacking? How could you build on your strengths and control your weaknesses in order to develop your emotional intelligence?

Writing Topics

1. Select three qualities that contribute to emotional intelligence, explain them, and give examples from the article or from your own experience.

2. "If you believe you can or if you believe you can't, you're right." Would Goleman agree or disagree? Why?

3. How could the qualities Goleman discusses affect a student's success in school?

4. How important do you think emotional intelligence is in life? Argue that it is or is not important.

5. Discuss the best ways to manage anger. What are some common triggers of anger, and how can they be defused?

Special Topics

Introduction: Notice how the author of this article, which originally appeared in a Chicago newspaper, gets the reader's attention in the first few paragraphs by telling of Jordan's failures. Often writers begin with the unexpected in order to get the reader interested.

Jordan Is Never Afraid of Failure
Bob Greene,[1] *Chicago Tribune*

[1] Chicago Tribune columnist Bob Greene is the author of two books about Michael Jordan: *Hang Time: Days and Dreams With Michael Jordan* and *Rebound*.

[2] This article was written in June 1998 after Michael Jordan and the Chicago Bulls had won their fourth world championship.

[3] the second of the two things mentioned

[4] without a hit as a batter

The best lesson anyone can take from Michael Jordan's life—the lesson that comes the closest to explaining why he is who he is, and why he has accomplished what he has accomplished—made itself evident during the brief period of his adulthood when no one thought he was any good. 1

During this week's victory celebrations,[2] during the endless replays of the basket-steal-basket sequence in which Jordan won the championship for the Bulls—during these moments when everyone is saying, once again, that he is the best in the world—I found myself thinking about the moments of Jordan's failure. 2

They came during the time when people were making fun of him—during his attempt to play baseball. I have been fortunate enough to see Jordan at close range during days of triumph and cheers, and also during days of apparent humiliation. There haven't been many of the latter.[3] But those days—the days when he was no good—provide the answer to why the brilliant days are so often his. 3

That baseball summer—the summer that followed the murder of his father, the summer Jordan in essence ran away from basketball—there was a minor-league batting instructor named Mike Barnett who was assigned to the Birmingham Barons, Jordan's team. 4

And this is what would happen just about every day: Barnett would be in his room at the Holiday Inn, or wherever the Barons were staying. Early in the morning, following a night game in which Jordan may have gone hitless,[4] Barnett's phone would ring. The caller—Jordan, from another room—would always greet Barnett with some variation of the same question: "Is it too early for us to go over?" Meaning: Jordan wanted to work. Meaning: Jordan would like Barnett to go with him, hours before anyone else, to the local minor-league ballpark. 5

The two men would go to the ballpark and, as the sun climbed higher in the sky, would work for hours in the heat. Jordan wouldn't be making it to the majors—everyone knew that by now. He would never be good enough. He could quit baseball now and no one in the world would blame him. Go home, enjoy your millions 6 of dollars, and decide whether you want to return to basketball. That would be the logical way out.

7   But the Southern League season wasn't over, and Jordan wasn't going to concede⁵ defeat yet. Instead, sweat pouring down his face, soaking through his clothes, he worked and worked and worked at trying to get better at something at which he had already been declared a failure. To witness that day after day—to sit in an empty ballpark while Jordan and Barnett spent hour after hour at this task—was something to see. The best and the truest Jordan.

⁵ admit

8   Why? Because this is the kind of thing that gets you to where you dream. The great moments—the moments the world cheers, whether you are an athlete or a businessman or an artist—are not the moments that count. The moments that count are the ones when it's just you, and people have stopped believing in you, and the work you put in comes with no guarantee that there will ever be a reward. The work you are putting in may very well be wasted.

9   But there is no waste in that kind of work—that's the secret. Far from being wasted, that is the kind of work, those are the kind of moments, that define you. I would watch Jordan missing the ball as he swung, then adjusting his swing, then dribbling the ball weakly through the empty infield. His minor league teammates— most of them more skilled than he—were still asleep, or sitting by the motel pool.

10   And he wouldn't go back to his room. He wouldn't leave. Instead he would ask Mike Barnett if they could work longer—if they could keep practicing in the sun. No one in the seats, no real prospect of becoming good enough, Jordan had an assignment to be here: an assignment from himself. "I think I'm getting this," he would say to Barnett with a hopeful sound in his voice.

11   Meaning: Keep working with me. I don't want to stop. The cheers this week, the championship trophy? They start somewhere. The cheers are loud on the day of victory, but they begin in moments of doubt when a whisper could break the silence.

12   I'm no good? Then I'll try to be better. I have no chance? Maybe not—we'll see. I think I'm getting this. I think I'm getting this. Is it too early to go over? Let's work.

Comprehension Questions

1. According to the author, what is the best lesson Michael Jordan teaches?

    A. Basketball is a great sport.

    B. Money isn't everything.

    C. Working hard to improve one's skills defines a person's excellence.

    D. Being famous can be rewarding.

2. Along with playing basketball professionally, Michael Jordan also played which sport as a professional?

    A. golf

    B. tennis

    C. football

    D. baseball

3. The person Jordan worked with, according to the author, was a _____.

    A. lawyer

    B. director

    C. coach

    D. trainer

4. Jordan called Mike Barnett early each morning to request _____.

    A. batting practice

    B. a massage

    C. a report

    D. a video

5. While Michael Jordan practiced with Mike Barnett, who was usually watching?

    A. no one

    B. his teammates

    C. his kids

    D. television cameras

Discussion Questions

1. What does the author think is the secret to Michael Jordan's success?

2. Why did Jordan work so hard at a sport in which he would never succeed to the degree that he did in basketball?

3. Why does the author think Michael Jordan is "the best and truest" when he is practicing a sport at which he will never succeed?

4. Explain the author's statement that "the cheers are loud on the day of victory, but they begin in moments of doubt when a whisper could break the silence."

5. What lessons does Michael Jordan teach us about how to live successfully? How might you use his example to succeed in college?

Writing Topics

1. Choose someone you know and admire, and explain how this person's actions are a good example of how to succeed in life.

2. Discuss an experience you have had learning a skill. Describe what you did to improve and how this experience has affected your work habits.

3. Choose three habits you have that have helped you to succeed in school, work, or your personal relationships.

4. Explain how some of your ways of coping with challenges have hurt your performance in the past.

5. Choose a famous celebrity (other than Michael Jordan) and explain why this person is a good or bad role model.

Special Topics

Negative definition: Paragraphs 2–7 introduce characteristics of non-violent resistance by explaining what nonviolent protest is not in order to clarify what nonviolent resistance is.

Classification: Paragraph 8 classifies three different kinds of love.

Definition: Paragraphs 9–13 define agape.

Related readings: "Martin Luther King" by Jack E. White.

Pilgrimage to Nonviolence
Dr. Martin Luther King Jr[1]

[1] Dr. Martin Luther King Jr. (born January 15, 1929; died April 4, 1968) was the winner of the 1964 Nobel Peace Prize.

[2] a protest movement started in Montgomery, Alabama, when Rosa Parks refused to give up her seat on a city bus.

[3] elements

[4] Hindu nationalist leader Mohandas K. Gandhi (1869–1948) led India to independence from Great Britain through the use of nonviolent protest. He believed in the importance of moral principles in public life and called his autobiography *The Story of My Experiment with Truth*. Both a politician and a highly religious man, Gandhi saw a strong link between the weapons of truth and nonviolence in seeking justice for the poor and powerless. Gandhi was a role model for King.

[5] not active

[6] lessen the pride or dignity of

Since the philosophy of nonviolence played such a positive role in the Montgomery Movement[2], it may be wise to turn to a brief discussion of some basic aspects[3] of this philosophy. 1

First, it must be emphasized that nonviolent resistance is not a method for cowards; it does resist. If one uses this method because he is afraid or merely because he lacks the instruments of violence, he is not truly nonviolent. This is why Gandhi[4] often said that if cowardice is the only alternative to violence, it is better to fight. He made this statement conscious of the fact that there is always another alternative: no individual or group need submit to any wrong; there is the way of nonviolent resistance. This is ultimately the way of the strong man. It is not a method of stagnant passivity. The phrase "passive[5] resistance" often gives the false impression that this is a sort of "do-nothing method" in which the resister quietly and passively accepts evil. But nothing is further from the truth. For while the nonviolent resister is passive in the sense that he is not physically aggressive toward his opponent, his mind and emotions are always active, constantly seeking to persuade his opponent that he is wrong. The method is passive physically, but strongly active spiritually. It is not passive non-resistance to evil, it is active nonviolent resistance to evil. 2

A second basic fact that characterizes nonviolence is that it does not seek to defeat or humiliate[6] the opponent, but to win his friendship and understanding. The nonviolent resister must often express his protest through noncooperation or boycotts, but he realizes that these are not ends themselves; they are merely means to awaken a sense of moral shame in the opponent. The end is the creation of the beloved community, while the aftermath of violence is tragic bitterness. 3

A third characteristic of this method is that the attack is directed against forces of evil rather than against persons who happen to 4 be doing the evil. It is evil that the nonviolent resister seeks to defeat, not the persons victimized by evil. If he is opposing racial injustice, the nonviolent resister has the vision to see that the basic tension is not between races. As I like to say to the people in Montgomery, "The tension in this city is not between white people and Negro people. The tension is, at bottom, between justice and injustice, between the forces of light and the forces of darkness. And if there is a victory, it will be a victory for justice and the forces of light. We are out to defeat injustice and not white persons who may be unjust."

5   A fourth point that characterizes nonviolent resistance is a willingness to accept suffering without retaliation,[7] to accept blows from the opponent without striking back. "Rivers of blood may have to flow before we gain our freedom, but it must be our blood," Gandhi said to his countrymen. The nonviolent resister is willing to accept violence if necessary, but never to inflict[8] it. He does not seek to dodge jail. If going to jail is necessary, he enters it "as a bridegroom enters the bride's chamber."

6   One may well ask: "What is the nonviolent resister's justification for this ordeal to which he invites men, for this mass political application of the ancient doctrine of turning the other cheek?" The answer is found in the realization that unearned suffering is redemptive.[9] Suffering, the nonviolent resister realizes, has tremendous educational and transforming possibilities. "Things of fundamental importance to people are not secured[10] by reason alone, but have to be purchased with their suffering," said Gandhi. He continues: "Suffering is infinitely more powerful than the law of the jungle for converting the opponent and opening his ears which are otherwise shut to the voice of reason."

7   A fifth point concerning nonviolent resistance is that it avoids not only external physical violence but also internal violence of spirit. The nonviolent resister not only refuses to shoot his opponent but he also refuses to hate him. At the center of nonviolence stands the principle of love. The nonviolent resister would contend[11] that in the struggle for human dignity, the oppressed people of the world must not succumb[12] to the temptation of becoming bitter or indulging[13] in hate campaigns. To retaliate in kind would do nothing but intensify[14] the existence of hate in the universe. Along the way of life, someone must have sense enough and morality enough to cut off the chain of hate. This can only be done by projecting the ethic of love to the center of our lives.

8   In speaking of love at this point, we are not referring to some sentimental or affectionate emotion. It would be nonsense to urge men to love their opponents in an affectionate sense. Love in this

[7] hitting back in revenge

[8] impose, cause

[9] a cause of redemption (saving, rescuing)
[10] guaranteed

[11] assert
[12] yield, give in
[13] allowing to participate
[14] make more extreme

[15]from the Greek
   philosopher Plato

[16]longing

[17]pertaining to a sense of
   beauty

[18]happening without an
   apparent cause

[19]unbiased

[20]difference

[21]twisted out of shape

[22]commonality

connection means understanding, redemptive good will. Here the Greek language comes to our aid. There are three words for love in the Greek New Testament. First, there is eros. In Platonic[15] philosophy eros meant the yearning[16] of the soul for the realm of the divine. It has come now to mean a sort of aesthetic[17] or romantic love. Second, there is philia, which means intimate affection between personal friends. Philia denotes a sort of reciprocal love; the person loves because he is loved. When we speak of loving those who oppose us, we refer to neither eros nor philia; we speak of a love which is expressed in the Greek word agape. Agape means understanding, redeeming good will for all men. It is an overflowing love which is purely spontaneous,[18] unmotivated, groundless, and creative. It is not set in motion by any quality or function of its object. It is the love of God operating in the human heart.

9   Agape is disinterested[19] love. It is a love in which the individual seeks not his own good, but the good of his neighbor (I Cor. 10:24). Agape does not begin by discriminating between worthy and unworthy people, or any qualities people possess. It begins by loving others for their sakes. It is an entirely "neighbor-regarding concern for others," which discovers the neighbor in every man it meets. Therefore, agape makes no distinction[20] between friend and enemy; it is directed toward both. If one loves an individual merely on account of his friendliness, he loves him for the sake of the benefits to be gained from the friendship, rather than for the friend's own sake. Consequently, the best way to assure oneself that Love is disinterested is to have love for the enemy-neighbor from whom you can expect no good in return, but only hostility and persecution.

10   Another basic point about agape is that it springs from the need of the other person—his need for belonging to the best in the human family. The Samaritan who helped the Jew on the Jericho Road was "good" because he responded to the human need that he was presented with. God's love is eternal and falls not because man needs his love. St. Paul assures us that the loving act of redemption was done "while we were yet sinners"—that is, at the point of our greatest need for love. Since the white man's personality is greatly distorted[21] by segregation, and his soul is greatly scarred, he needs the love of the Negro. The Negro must love the white man, because the white man needs his love to remove his tensions, insecurities, and fears.

11   Agape is not a weak, passive love. It is a love in action. Agape is a love seeking to preserve and create community. It is insistence on community even when one seeks to break it. Agape is a willingness to sacrifice in the interest of mutuality.[22] Agape is a willingness to go to any length to restore community. It doesn't stop at the first mile, but it goes the second mile to restore community. It is a willingness to forgive, not seven times, but seventy times seven to restore

community. The cross is the eternal expression of the length to which God will go in order to restore broken community. The resurrection is a symbol of God's triumph over all the forces that seek to block the community. The Holy Spirit is the continuing community creating reality that moves through history. He who works against community is working against the whole of creation. Therefore, if I respond to hate with a reciprocal[23] hate, I can do nothing but intensify the cleavage[24] in broken community. I can only close the gap in broken community by meeting hate with love. If I meet hate with hate, I become depersonalized[25], because creation is so designed that my personality can only be fulfilled in the context of community. Booker T. Washington[26] was right: "Let no man pull you so low as to make you hate him." When he pulls you that low he brings you to the point of working against community; he drags you to the point of defying creation, and thereby becoming depersonalized.

12   In the final analysis, agape means a recognition of the fact that all life is interrelated. All humanity is involved in a single process; and all men are brothers. To the degree that I harm my brother, no matter what he is doing to me, to that extent I am harming myself. For example, white men often refuse federal aid to education in order to avoid giving the Negro his rights; but because all men are brothers they cannot deny Negro children without harming their own. They end, all efforts to the contrary, by hurting themselves. Why is this? Because men are brothers. If you harm me, you harm yourself.

13   Love, agape, is the only cement that can hold this broken community together. When I am commanded to love, I am commanded to restore community, to resist injustice, and to meet the needs of my brothers.

14   A sixth basic fact about nonviolent resistance is that it is based on the conviction that the universe is on the side of justice. Consequently, the believer in nonviolence has deep faith in the future. This faith is another reason why the nonviolent resister can accept suffering without retaliation. For he knows that in his struggle for justice he has cosmic companionship. It is true that there are devout believers in nonviolence who find it difficult to believe in a personal God. But even these persons believe in the existence of some creative force that works for universal wholeness. Whether we call it an unconscious process, an impersonal Brahman,[27] or a Personal Being of matchless power and infinite love, there is a creative force in this universe that works to bring the disconnected aspects of reality into a harmonious whole.

[23]experienced by both sides

[24]division

[25]not recognized as a person

[26]Booker T. Washington (1856–1915) was an African American educator and reformer, and first president of Tuskegee Institute. He believed education was the key that would allow African Americans to achieve political and social equality. His autobiography is entitled *Up from Slavery*.

[27]Bhrama is the Hindu god of creation

Comprehension Questions

1. King states that nonviolent resistance is "not a method for cowards" because

    A. it advocates armed resistance.

    B. it does resist evil.

    C. it is used by those who are brave.

    D. it is used by those without guns.

2. The purpose of nonviolent resistance is

    A. to overthrow those in power.

    B. to humiliate people who do evil.

    C. to break down a community.

    D. to create a community based on love.

3. According to King, nonviolent resisters should attack

    A. those who do evil.

    B. the forces of evil.

    C. the police.

    D. the racists.

4. King and Gandhi both believed that more powerful than force or the law of the jungle is

    A. prayer.

    B. money.

    C. suffering.

    D. action.

5. At the heart of nonviolent resistance stands the principle of

    A. hate.

    B. power.

    C. fairness.

    D. love and understanding.

Discussion Questions

1. Explain King's statement that nonviolent resistance "is passive physically, but strongly active spiritually."

2. Explain why King writes that suffering "has tremendous educational and transforming possibilities."

3. Why does King write that "at the center of nonviolence stands the principle of love"?

4. King classifies different kinds of love. Why is agape the most important kind of love for the nonviolent resister?

5. Discuss how nonviolent resistance can help create a "beloved community."

Writing Topics

1. Classify three kinds of love according to King.

2. Define nonviolent resistance and give examples.

3. How do the beliefs King professes in this article demonstrate his greatness as an American leader? (You may want to refer to the article "Martin Luther King," by Jack E. White, p. 544.)

4. Use an encyclopedia or the Internet to research the biography of Martin Luther King Jr., and write a report recounting his life and achievements.

5. Do you believe that all men and women are brothers and sisters? King states, "Because men are brothers. If you harm me, you harm yourself." Is violence ever justified in righting a wrong?

Special Topics

Rhetorical Patterns: Patrick Mazza builds his argument on cause and effect, factual evidence, and evidence from authorities.

Cause and Effect: Mazza goes to great lengths to establish a scientific cause-and-effect relationship between global warming and increased incidences of El Niño–related weather patterns. Because the weather patterns he discusses are complex, he explains them in detail. His careful use of cause-and-effect reasoning is central to his argument.

Evidence from Authority: Throughout the article, the author makes reference to scientific studies and experts in the field to support his claims. Notice that each time a study or an authority is introduced, the author identifies the source with name, title, and affiliation; puts his or her words in quotation marks; and uses tag phrases such as *according to* or *says* to identify the speaker. Even when the author does not use direct quotes, but paraphrases or puts the source's ideas into his own words, he uses tag phrases to identify the source. Notice the punctuation used with quotations (commas and periods inside quotation marks) and tag phrases (commas before, after, or around phrase, depending on where it is placed).

Refutation of Opposition: In paragraph 8, Mazza acknowledges critics and proceeds in paragraphs 9–10 to refute them. In paragraph 20, he acknowledges the opposition's case by conceding that the scientific community is "far from a consensus on the relationship between ENSO and global warming." He then argues (in paragraphs 21–22) that the scientific method should not govern policy in the case of global warming.

The Invisible Hand

As human activity warms the earth, El Niño grows more violent.
Are we doing this to ourselves?
Patrick Mazza

[1] "Acts of God" are what people call the calamities[1] the world suffered at the hands of El Niño last winter. Freak tornadoes killed more than three dozen people in Florida. Thirty-five-foot waves battered[2] the California coast, while a numbing[3] procession of torrential rains brought widespread flooding and mud slides, driving hundreds of people from their homes and causing up to $1 billion in damage. Hundreds more were killed in Peru and Ecuador by floods and slides, and thousands left homeless. Canada and the northeastern United States were hit by a catastrophic[4] ice storm, which knocked out power to 4 million people. Brazil and Indonesia, on the other hand, are tinder dry[5]; 12 million acres of their precious

[1] disasters

[2] pounded
[3] causing numbness

[4] causing catastrophe or sudden disaster
[5] dry as material used for starting fires

rainforest burned last year. "This was the year the world caught fire," concluded a report by the World Wildlife Fund.

2   But it may not be fair to blame these disasters on the Deity. We now know that human activity—mostly the burning of fossil fuels[6]—is warming the earth. The Intergovernmental Panel on Climate Change, a gathering of 2,000 of the world's top climatologists,[7] has declared that "the balance of evidence suggests a discernible[8] human influence on global climate."

3   How will that influence manifest[9] itself? Warmer air temperatures, ironically,[10] may ultimately[11] not be the most significant aspect[12] of global warming. According to the U.S. Global Change Research Program, "Widespread increases in the intensity of the hydrologic cycle[13] may have more immediate and far-reaching ecological[14] and socioeconomic impacts[15] than elevated[16] temperature alone."

4   And one of the most intense manifestations[17] of that hydrologic cycle is the weather pattern known as El Niño. Every four to seven years, a band of water 2 to 10 degrees warmer than the surrounding ocean bulges[18] toward the pacific coast of South America, spawning[19] enormous storms, altering[20] currents, changing wind patterns, and causing droughts[21] all around the world. Because it often appears around Christmas, it's called El Niño, "The Child."

5   The system that arrived in March 1997 came only two years after a five-year El Niño, the longest ever documented[22]. The new system gathered power at record speed until its force exceeded that of 1982/83, previously the most powerful El Niño on record. With the ocean's heat valve[23] shifting into overdrive[24] at the same time the planet is experiencing the warmest year on record, we naturally have to ask: Have we brought this on ourselves? Are we parents to The Child?

6   Typically, El Niño is followed by its cooling counterpart, La Niña. But over the past two decades a hothouse Pacific has generated[25] five El Niños, and only one La Niña of any size. "You can think of El Niño and La Niña as the ticktock," notes University of Washington climate-ocean scientist Richard Gammon. "Lately we've been having more ticks than tocks."

7   Meteorologists[26] call this ticktock the El Niño Southern Oscillation, or ENSO. Pioneer El Niño researcher Kevin Trenberth was the first to nail down ENSO's four- to seven-year cycle; he is now trying to determine whether there is a connection between the unprecedented[27] string of El Niños since 1976 and the fact that they coincided[28] with the ten hottest years on record. As the head of the climate analysis section at the National Center for Atmospheric Research, Trenberth and fellow NCAR scientist Timothy Hoar have applied statistical[29] methods to the seeming skew[30] in the cycle over the past 20 years. They concluded that such

[6] coal, gas, oil

[7] scientists who study weather patterns

[8] noticeable, recognizable

[9] show

[10] the opposite of what one might expect

[11] in the end

[12] part

[13] water cycle of precipitation and evaporation

[14] having to do with living things and their environments

[15] effects on society and economy

[16] raised

[17] effects, something that becomes manifest or apparent

[18] bumps, swollen areas

[19] creating, producing

[20] changing

[21] long periods without rain

[22] recorded

[23] mechanism for releasing heat

[24] a gear that at a certain speed automatically reduces an engine's fuel consumption without reducing speed

[25] produced

[26] scientists who study weather and weather forecasting

[27] without precedent or previous example

[28] occurred at the same time

[29] analysis of facts or numbers

[30] swerve or bend

[31]followed by looking at numerical data

[32]scientists who study the ocean

[33]personal stories

[34]count

[35]cylindrical sections of the earth taken with a hollow drill

[36]edge of overflowing

[37]mechanism for releasing heat

[38]too large amount

[39]noticeable

[40]to change from a gas to a liquid

[41]rise up

an odd sequence would occur naturally only once every 2,000 years. "Is this pattern of change a manifestation of global warming [or] a natural variation?" Trenberth and Hoar wrote in the peer-reviewed *Geophysical Research Letter.* "We have shown that the latter is highly unlikely."

"Something is going on," Trenberth says. "I think El Niños are being changed by global warming."   8

Some scientists have found Trenberth's conclusions less persuasive because El Niño has been statistically tracked[31] for only the past 120 years. Even so, Trenberth points out, "If you take the first 20 years and compare it with the second 20 years, and the third, fourth, and fifth, they don't look greatly at odds with one another. It's only in the last 20 years that things seem to have been different."   9

Attempting to lengthen the historical record, Oregon State University oceanographers[32] William Quinn and Victor Neal have studied anecdotal accounts[33] by Spanish explorers and colonists. Doing so has allowed them to tally[34] eight very strong ENSOs from 1525 to 1982. Since 1728 very strong ENSOs appeared about every 42 years; before that, only one was detected. Quinn and Neal concluded that the 1982/83 event was the most powerful in nearly 500 years. The 1997/98 El Niño, apparently even stronger, followed only 14 years later—the briefest time between very strong El Niños, they say, in five centuries.   10

Ice cores[35] provide physical evidence of climate change in the same period. This data stretches back thousands of years, notes Nicholas Graham, a climate-ocean researcher at Scripps Oceanographic Laboratory, but recent warm temperatures have melted away the evidence of the past several decades. "This suggests very strongly that the temperatures in the mid-nineteen seventies to early nineties were the warmest in the last five hundred years."   11

According to the IPCC, global warming has raised world ocean temperatures by one degree in the past century. The world's warmest patch of ocean is the tropical Pacific; when its heat reservoir fills to the brim,[36] El Niño acts as the discharge valve.[37] "The climate system is a giant heat engine," explains Nathan Mantua, a climate researcher at the University of Washington who focuses on the Pacific. "An excess[38] of energy comes in at low latitudes relative to the high latitudes; winds and currents try to wipe out this imbalance." The workings of this engine shape the earth's standard weather patterns. The most prominent[39] effect of solar energy striking the earth is not to heat the atmosphere but to evaporate water from the surface of the ocean. The warm, moist air rises to form clouds, where water condenses[40] and falls back as cooling rain. The heat that evaporated the water continues to ascend,[14] and is carried for thousands of miles by high winds.   12

13   The tropical western Pacific is the hottest stretch of open ocean on Earth—"the warm pool" scientists call it. In normal years, heat rises from the region, creating a low pressure zone. Rising in the atmosphere, it blows east until it descends[42] off the coast of South Africa, creating a high-pressure zone. In an effort to achieve equilibrium,[43] the atmosphere pumps surface winds west along the equator back toward the warm pool—the famous trade winds. The winds push warm water west, allowing cool water to rise to the surface in the east. This upwelling of nutrient-rich water is crucial[44] to South American fisheries[45]; though upwelling areas cover only one-tenth of one percent of the earth's oceans, they account for 40 percent of the commercial fish catch.

14   This normal cycle, however, cannot dissipate[46] all the excess[47] heat in the tropical Pacific. When too much accumulates,[48] El Niño kicks in. The warm pool's system of clouds and heavy rainfall expands[49] toward the central Pacific, blunting[50] the trade winds. Consequently, the warm water piled up in the western Pacific rushes east until it hits the coast of South America, blocking the cool upwelling and collapsing fisheries.

15   In addition to disrupting the trade winds, El Niño's storm track is powerful enough to divide the jet stream, which normally courses[51] over the Pacific Northwest. During El Niño one branch blows farther north, while the other is drawn south across vast expanses of heat pumping warm ocean, where it picks up abnormally large amounts of water. In North America, this leaves the Northwest warmer and drier, California and the Southwest sodden[52] and cooler. The storms that walloped California grew strong on El Niño's heated waters, and the powerful southern branch of the jet stream energized[53] a low—pressure zone in the Southeast, giving rise to Florida's killer tornadoes.

16   While El Niño blows cold and wet in California, it causes drought in India, Southeast Asia, Brazil, and parts of Africa. Besides devastating agriculture, the disruption of normal rain patterns sets the stage for huge fires such as those last year in Australia, Indonesia, and Amazonia. Should El Niño conditions persist, entire regions could see their natural features radically altered[54] and economies shaken to their root.

17   A rule of thumb is that every 2-degree increase in temperature puts 6 percent more water vapor into the air. And according to the U.S. Global Change Research Program, more water vapor in the atmosphere means "a significant increase in the energy available to drive storms and associated weather fronts."

18   From 1973 to 1993, notes Trenberth, atmospheric moisture over the United States increased by 5 percent per decade. In 1995

[42]comes down
[43]balance, equal pressure

[44]of great importance
[45]fishing grounds, businesses based on catching and selling fish
[46]to break up, scatter, or reduce
[47]extra
[48]collects, gathers together
[49]extends, spreads out
[50]making blunt or dull, slowing down

[51]moves

[52]soaked with water
[53]fueled, gave energy to

[54]changed

the National Climatic Data Center found that precipitation[55] over temperate[56] regions of the Northern Hemisphere had increased 10 percent over the past century, while extreme rain and snowstorms have gone up 20 percent.

Other studies have connected warmer tropical oceans with the retreat of mountain glaciers around the world. (At the current rate of retreat, there will be no glaciers left in Glacier National Park in 30 years.) The National Oceanic and Atmospheric Administration's Climate Diagnostics Center reports that its research "strongly suggests that the recent observed changes in freezing-level heights are related to a long-term increase in sea surface temperature in the Tropics." 19

[57]continuing

[58]gases that cause the greenhouse effect, a trapping of heat in our atmosphere

[59]declining

[60]toothed wheel that allows movement in only one direction; move up

[61]agreement

[62]statement that cannot be attacked or penetrated

If global warming continues, El Niño–like weather may become the norm. A computer simulation run by Gerald Meehl and Warren Washington of NCAR shows El Niño–like conditions persisting[57] as greenhouse gases[58] increase. With a doubling of the amount of carbon dioxide in the atmosphere, their model shows trade winds slackening[59] while the eastern Pacific warms, increasing rainfall and kicking on the heat machine. And, Meehl warns, should El Niño become the norm, global warming might also ratchet[60] up the ENSO cycle to an even more intense level. 20

Washington and other researchers caution that science is far from a consensus[61] on the relationship between ENSO and global warming. While El Niños and ocean temperatures "are increasing in a way ... consistent with the idea that climate change is making El Niño more intense," says Nathan Mantua, "it's not quite a bulletproof statement[62] at this time." 21

[63]computer-generated models

The scientific method demands not only that theory be backed by solid evidence, but that the evidence hold up under repeated experiments. For climate scientists, those experiments are conducted using computer simulations.[63] While some modes show an ENSO-climate change connection, many do not. In fact, the first success in predicting El Niño didn't come until 1986. A number of models accurately forecast the next ENSO in 1991, but of seven major models, not one predicted the extreme magnitude of the 1997/98 event. 22

[64]imitating

[65]different scientific disciplines or fields; *venue* is a legal term referring to the county in which a crime occurs

"Computer models used for global climate change don't do a great job of simulating[64] natural variability," Mantua notes. "The models that do, don't do a good job on global climate change." Part of the difficulty is that studies of El Niño and global warming are, for the most part, taking place in separate scientific venues.[65] "The El Niño people are really meteorologists who work in forecasts out from two weeks to a month to a season," says Richard Gammon. "The climate people are coming at it from a much longer perspective. There's not enough communication between those two groups. Most scientists are in their own very small corner of the sandbox." 23

24   Public policy should not necessarily wait for scientific consensus, however. "The level of proof scientists need is much higher than what you would think is important in public policy," says Gammon. "If you knew with even seventy percent certainty that something bad was going to happen, as a civil servant you would ring the bell."

25   If humans are indeed influencing El Niño, it brings the disruptive potential of global warming into immediate focus. Our response, says Trenberth, comes down to a value judgment: "How much we pay attention to the future generations and what kind of stewards[66] we are to the planet."

[66]keepers or guardians

Patrick Mazza *edits* Cascadia Planet, *a Pacific Northwest bioregional Web site at* www.tnews.com. *A longer version of this article, "El Niño's Growing Ferocity: Ocean in the Greenhouse?" is available from the Atmosphere Alliance, 2103 Harrison Ave., N.W., Suite 2615, Olympia, WA 98502; (360) 352-1763; e-mail* atmosphere@olywa.net.

Printed by *Sierra*, May/June 1998, pp. 69–95.

Comprehension Questions

1. The most significant effect of global warming is

   A. warmer temperatures.

   B. an increase in the intensity of hydrologic cycle.

   C. an increase in the numbers of forest fires.

2. Scientists at NCAR have concluded that the increase in frequency and intensity of El Niños in the past 20 years is highly unlikely to be caused by

   A. the melting of polar ice caps.

   B. natural variations in the cycle.

   C. global warming.

3. Which of the following have scientists used to lengthen the historical record of El Niño occurrences?

   A. studying account by Spanish explorers and colonists

   B. studying ice cores

   C. studying tree cores

   D. both a and b

4. A two-degree rise in temperature puts how much more water vapor into the air?

   A. 2%

   B. 6%

   C. 15%

Discussion Questions

1. How does Mazza use his first paragraph to get the reader's attention?

2. How does El Niño influence storm patterns?

3. How does global warming influence El Niño?

4. Why does the author argue that public policy should not wait for scientific consensus?

5. How effective is Mazza's argument? What did you find most persuasive about his argument?

Writing Topics

1. How does global warming affect weather patterns?

2. Analyze the causes and effects of El Niño.

3. Agree or disagree with the author's contention that global warming is fueling the increasing intensity of El Niño–related changes in weather patterns and storms.

4. How well does the author argue his case? You might want to examine how effectively he uses facts, sets up rhetorical patterns, cites authorities, and acknowledges and refutes the opposition.

5. Using Internet resources as well as this article, examine the causes, effects, and/or solutions to global warming.

Special Topics

Examples: Notice how the use of examples throughout the essay helps the author communicate his ideas about what makes happy families different.

Why Happy Families Are Different

John E. Obedzinski, M.D[1]

1 The couple in my office looked bewildered[2]. Well-educated, they had raised their children according to the most "progressive" thinking. Emphasizing feelings rather than behavior, the parents allowed the kids to express themselves openly and loudly, offered them an equal voice in family decisions and gave them freedom to pick their clothes, friends and TV shows. They sprang to their children's defense when the kids collided with school authorities, and absolved[3] them of household chores.

2 Sitting with the couple were the results of all that dedicated effort—a sullen,[4] arrogant[5] 15-year-old boy and a totally self-absorbed 13-year-old girl. The four of them were the opposite of the strong, loving family the parents believed their attitudes were helping to build.

3 I had heard this tale at the Center for Families and Children many times. Not all the parents I'd dealt with had pursued[6] the feel-good approach, of course. Others had followed an earlier model of child rearing, in which parents cracked the whip and made all the decisions for their kids. They had their own set of problems with rebellious children.

4 Then I thought of the strong families I knew—the truly happy, resilient[7] families who always seemed able to weather the ups and downs of life with equanimity.[8] How did these families thrive[9] when others flopped?

5 In part, they did it by not following set philosophies, feel-good or authoritarian. Indeed, their family-building tactics often flew right in the face of conventional[10] wisdom. Here I have tried to define what makes these families work.

6 *Children know their place.* A happy family is not a democracy in which everyone has an equal vote, or where kids operate with total freedom. Parents wield[11] a benign[12] authority, listening to their children's ideas and taking account of their feelings, but reserving the right to make final decisions. Moreover, kids feel comfortable knowing who's in charge.

7 One day my teen-age daughter Erika told her mother she wanted to drop piano lessons, saying she was tired of practicing.

[1] John E. Obedzinski is a behavioral pediatrician at the Center for Families and Children in Corte Madera, California, and a clinical assistant professor of behavioral pediatrics at the University of California, San Francisco.

[2] puzzled, confused

[3] set free, released from

[4] showing ill humor by a dark quietness

[5] making pretensions of being superior

[6] followed

[7] able to recover easily

[8] an even temper, calmness

[9] be successful

[10] ordinary

[11] exercise, possess

[12] gentle, not harmful

Her mother listened, then made a parental decision. She told Erika to stick it out for three months. Then if she still wanted to quit, she could. That was six years ago. Last September Erika went off to college—to study music.

Parents talk kid language. We often forget that children are   8
not miniature adults. They speak differently, think differently, react differently.

One day a friend and his son were preparing lunch. "Is there   9
any soup?" the boy asked. "I don't see any," the father said. "But is there any soup?" the boy repeated. After three repetitions, the father got the message. To the more literal-minded child, "I don't see any" meant that the soup was simply out of sight and his father should move a few cans until he could see it.

Of course, some kids act like hair-splitting lawyers. "You told   10
me not to throw the ball in the living room," a boy may say. "You never told me not to throw it in the dining room." But he knows full well that the spirit of the order was "Don't throw the ball indoors." Young kids live in the here and now. They don't see the consequences of their actions the way their parents do. That's why what the parent says may be dodged by the child or at least may take a while to be absorbed.[13]

Some of my colleagues[14] estimate, not wholly jokingly, that a   11
young child must be reminded 2,000 times before a given lesson sinks in. That can be annoying. But parents in strong families recognize that constant repetition is at the heart of learning. And it is more important to make directions and the reasons for them clear than it is to convince a child of their justice.

They're not always happy. Strong families recognize that the   12
sun may not shine every day. Thus, when Mom gets sick, Dad is transferred or a greater tragedy occurs, family ties prepare them to withstand the deluge.[15]

One of my neighbors was laid off from his job at a telecommu-   13
nications firm. He went right home to his wife and their two college-age children to map strategy. Together, they decided to launch a family business. They refinanced their home, the son and daughter increased their college loans, the wife switched from a part-time to a full-time job, and the husband enrolled in a training course for the new business. The firing was viewed as a family challenge.

They don't believe in "quality time." Instead of reserving a spe-   14
cial time to "be with the children," as popular advice suggests, parents make it clear that they're always available. And if that means parents must sometimes set aside other pressing chores, so be it. Once I was summoned from a university conference by a call from my older daughter, then about four. We had just moved to a home

[13]taken in, digested
[14]associates, partners

[15]flood (of overwhelming events)

in the country with a stream on the property. Alarmed, I hurried to the phone. "The salmon are running!" Mariska told me. She wanted someone to share her excitement. Such special moments simply can't be scheduled.

15   *They value tradition.* Happy families observe their own time-honored rituals. These are an important source of strength for those who share them. Grace before meals is such a tradition. So is a "quiet hour" after dinner. A family I know declared Friday "Pizza Night," when kids were free to bring friends to share dinner and soft drinks.

16   Many treasured rituals revolve around holidays. In my family, with its Eastern European background, we always decorated eggs for Easter. It was a time-consuming process, and when my daughters reached their teens I suggested abandoning it. The girls wouldn't hear of it. The tradition had come down from their grandparents, and they were determined to keep it alive.

17   *They make mistakes.* No one succeeds 100 percent of the time. In happy families, the fact is admitted, and it doesn't immobilize[16] or traumatize[17] them. Kids are allowed to make choices, including poor ones. Parents may review how a decision might have been made differently, but then the case is closed. Kids aren't reminded of past mistakes.

18   Many parents are fearful that their slightest misstep will damage their kids irreparably. Not so with parents in strong families. They know they aren't perfect, and they're not afraid to admit it. "I'm sorry I lost my cool" goes a long way toward preserving family unity.

    They fight. Of course happy families argue. But they don't resort to name calling and dredging[18] up the past. And they have a method for straightening out relationships when things have gone sour.

19   One approach we've found helpful is what we call the "volcano technique." Each family member has the right to erupt like Vesuvius[19] when he or she has a gripe. They can spout hot lava for five minutes, describing whatever has made them angry, but not personally attacking another family member. Others are obliged to listen and then get their chance to respond. By that time the steam has usually gone out of the volcano as well as the listeners.

20   Sometimes, though, a disagreement is more basic, about the household budget or attitudes toward child rearing. Yet families can remain strong if they acknowledge[20] such differences and try to accommodate[21] them.

21   In one family I know, the husband is a workaholic. His wife doesn't like it, and occasionally she explodes. But she also recognizes that his work habits are their only major difference. He understands her frustration and tries to make up for it by reserving an occasional weekend for family activities and by taking

[16]paralyze
[17]upset

[18]digging

[19]a famous volcano

[20]admit, recognize
[21]adjust to

[22] competition for attention by brothers and/or sisters

[23] firmly established over time

[24] person whom one knows

[25] sorrowfully
[26] glum, sullen

[27] small weaknesses

[28] foresee

work-free vacations. The conflict has not gone away, but both have learned to deal with it in ways that don't undercut the relationship.

They compete. Unrestrained sibling rivalry[22] can be dangerous. Yet when competition is channeled, it teaches kids how to win and lose.

23

Ski champions Phil and Steve Mahre are examples of the outcome of family competition. Each twin pushed the other until both won Olympic medals. All the while, they assisted each other, too, passing along tips that would help the other achieve his best. Recently I saw a photo of the two, now 37 and retired from competitive skiing. They were facing each other across a chessboard, still competing.

24

The children work. In a strong family, everyone works—including the kids. Chores needn't be strenuous or time-consuming, but they should be regular. When my daughters were young, we were inveterate[23] campers. Their task was to clear the dishes after meals. They didn't relish the job at first, but eventually it gave them a feeling of contributing to the fun. As they grew older, they made the transition to clearing the dishes at home too.

25

They laugh at one another. An acquaintance[24] and his wife stopped at a dress shop while traveling with their friends Gerry and Jan. While the two women inspected fashions, the men stood off to the side, waiting. Jan caught a glimpse of her husband, who was glumly staring at the floor. "Gerry's wearing his shopping face," she said, smiling. Gerry ruefully[25] grinned back. The dour[26] expression he wore while Jan was shopping was obviously a long-standing, yet affectionate, family joke.

26

A sense of humor is a trademark of the happy family. They can laugh at one another's quirks and foibles,[27] but the humor is never malicious. Children aren't allowed to mock each other, and they don't hit each other's weak spots. Humor unites them.

27

When parents sadly tell me that they have followed all the rules without success, I remind them of a quotation from the general semanticist Alfred Korzybski: "The map is not the territory." A map shows you the routes to your destination, but it doesn't reveal the surprises you may encounter—potholes, detours, rainstorms.

28

In the same way, we often carry a "map" of a model family in our heads. But, like the highway that's unexpectedly closed for repairs, family life often doesn't match what we expect. Strong families know they can't anticipate[28] all the twists in the road. Their secret includes flexibility, rooted in love and understanding.

29

Comprehension Questions

1. Another way of describing the families that the author thinks are happy would be to describe those families as

    A. strong and resilient.

    B. free of fighting.

    C. valuing each individual's happiness.

    D. feeling good about themselves.

2. The author believes that families

    A. need to follow his philosophy of how to be happy.

    B. need to feel good to be happy.

    C. need to follow rules set by parents.

    D. need to be flexible in dealing with issues and problems.

3. The author's purpose is to explain

    A. what makes happy families succeed.

    B. how to make kids happy.

    C. how to make parents happy.

    D. what happiness means.

4. What does the author mean when he says that happy families make mistakes?

    A. Families are happier making mistakes than being perfect.

    B. Mistakes are expected and don't ruin family members' feelings for one another.

    C. Happy families learn to be happy by making mistakes.

    D. Mistakes are part of life and should be enjoyed.

5. Happy families are successful because they

    A. allow family members the freedom to act how they want.

    B. allow competition so that the best members can direct the others.

    C. exhibit love and understanding in their interactions.

    D. follow the guidelines designed by the author.

Discussion Questions

1. The author states that happy families demonstrate flexibility. In the examples the author gives of happy families, how do these families exhibit such flexibility?

2. Are the happy families always happy? If not, what does the author mean by the label "happy families"?

3. Explain what the author means when he states that happy families "laugh at one another."

4. Which characteristics of happy families that the author discusses have you seen in your family or a family you have observed?

5. Discuss examples of happy families that you have seen portrayed on television. Which characteristics discussed in the essay do they exhibit?

Writing Topics

1. Define a "happy family" according to the author.

2. Summarize three to five guidelines for happy families, and give examples of each.

3. Using your family, a family you know, or one from television, analyze how this family fits the definition of a happy family.

4. Choose three characteristics that you think are most important for a happy family, and explain why they are so important.

5. Argue that families usually have a difficult time following the guidelines given in this article, and explain why this is so.

Special Topics

Rhetorical Patterns: Each of the famous people interviewed describes and gives examples of what he or she considers to be a hero. The numerous examples help define the notion of what a hero is. In addition to the use of example, the author uses comparison/contrast (heroes and celebrities, true heroes and state-mandated heroes) to help define what a hero is and is not.

Who Are Our Heroes?

Some Prominent Americans Share Their Ideas on Heroism and
Tell Whom They Admire
Ponchitta Pierce

What is a Hero? Today the term is applied to everyone from the founding fathers to movie stars to classical composers. We asked prominent Americans in many fields, some of whom are seen as heroes themselves, to give their views. They don't always agree, but all have strong opinions on whom we should admire—and why.

1   Daniel Boorstin, 80—a historian, Pulitzer Prize[1]–winning author and former Librarian of Congress[2]—finds heroes in the past. "Read history, read books," he said, "not just newspapers and magazines. The temptation to make your contemporaries[3] into heroes is the temptation to see them as divine. That is what happened with Hitler."

2   Today's world may have heroes, he added, but they are now overshadowed by celebrities. "The hero is known for achievements," Boorstin explained, "the celebrity for well-knownness. The hero reveals the possibilities of human nature. The celebrity reveals the possibilities of the press and media. Celebrities are people who make news, but heroes are people who make history. Time makes heroes but dissolves celebrities."

3   Boorstin's heroes include Thomas Jefferson, Abraham Lincoln and William James, the psychologist and philosopher. "They symbolize the receptive, open mind," he said. "They considered that mankind is capable of things that have not been revealed in the past."

4   Richard Parsons, 47, president of Time Warner, believes people discover their heroes early in life, largely through personal experience. "You don't sit down with a child and say, 'Look let me tell you what heroes are about.'" he said. "Young people make that judgment for themselves because they know who they're attracted to, who they want to be like."

5   Parsons' father, Lorenzo, an electronics technician, has been the one constant hero of his life, even when Parsons realized his

[1] Alfred Pulitzer, publisher of *The New York World*, established this prize for outstanding achievement in drama, literature, music, and journalism. The prize has been awarded since 1917, and although the monetary award is low ($5,000 for literature, drama, music), it is considered the most prestigious American award.

[2] The Library of Congress, the national library of the United States, was established in 1800 and is the largest in the world. The Librarian of Congress is appointed by the president.

[3] people who live at the same time

[4] imitate

[5] In 1955, Rosa Parks refused to give up her seat to a white man on a crowded bus in Montgomery, Alabama. Her arrest sparked a year-long boycott of the bus system that eventually led to a Supreme Court ruling that segregation on the Montgomery buses was unconstitutional.

[6] someone involved in trying to change the status quo (the way things are)

[7] ridiculing, making fun of

[8] small weaknesses

[9] failures to be consistent

[10] acts of saying one thing and doing another

[11] pleasant to the taste

[12] the period after the stock market crash on 1929 when the United States experienced economic difficulties and many Americans were unemployed

[13] During the Cultural Revolution (1966–1969), many of China's intellectuals suffered persecution and were forced to work as laborers in rural villages.

[14] Mao Tse Tung, or Mao Zedong (1893–1976), was the founder of the People's Republic of China and the leader of the Chinese Communist Party. Mao mobilized young people into battalions of Red Guards to attack intellectuals during the Cultural Revolution.

[15] copy or be like

dad's limitations. "There is an expression," Parsons explained: "'Never get to know your hero too well.' My father was not a businessman. There were points when I realized I had to run to someone else for guidance, because he just didn't come from the world I was entering."

Jackie Joyner-Kersee, 33, a track and field star and winner of three Olympic gold medals, is seen as a hero by many. It disturbs her that this label often is given for her image alone.   6

Joyner-Kersee frequently returns to her hometown of East St Louis, Ill., to speak to young people. She tells them, "'If you think of me as your hero, it's important that you emulate[4] Jackie Joyner-Kersee the person, not the athlete you read about.' I want kids to understand my values—that I was able to accomplish my goals by working hard—and to realize that, for me to do that, I needed people who believed in me."   7

"The true sense of 'hero' is someone who really has made a difference in your life, she went on. "The person could be your parent or grandparent. They might not be great in someone else's eyes, but to you they are great." Rosa Parks,[5] the civil-rights activist,[6] is a hero to Joyner-Kersee. "Parks made people realize they do have a voice," she explained. "She proved that people can be strong if they work together."   8

But the larger-than-life heroes of the past—such as Franklin Delano Roosevelt and John F. Kennedy—may be gone today, said Jules Feiffer, 66, a political cartoonist known for satirizing[7] our foibles[8] and the author of several books and plays. With today's public nature of private lives, "we can't closet our inconsistencies[9] or hypocrisies[10] as easily as we once could," he continued. "If you're looking for a leader or hero, and you ask for one who's had no experience or temptations, then you're asking for a return to an innocence we can never go back to."   9

I. F. Stone, the journalist and philosopher, and Fred Astaire are two of Feiffer's heroes. "Stone taught me to find ways to tell the unpleasant truths and make them seem palatable,[11]" Feiffer explained. As for Astaire, he added: "During the Depression[12] he could dance his way through life and make it seem effortless. As I grew older, I realized the amount of work that went into this effortlessness. It became a standard for me."   10

Joan Chen, 34, played Empress Wan Jung in the film *The Last Emperor* and was seen on the TV show *Twin Peaks*. She grew up in Shanghai during China's Cultural Revolution,[13] when heroes such as Mao[14] were state-mandated. "In the Communist system," explained the actress, "heroes were so important. By giving us heroes the Communists wanted us to emulate[15] them."   11

12   True heroes—unlike the Communist images or U.S. celebrities—are strong in moments of choice, Chen said, and make the morally right choice. "So often we make compromises[16] in life," she explained. "Often these choices go against our principles. Heroes rise above."

13   The Burmese opposition leader Daw Aung San Suu Kyi[17] is one such person. She won the Nobel Peace Prize[18] in 1991 and recently was freed from house arrest after almost six years. Aung San Suu Kyi is a hero, said Chen, because "she took action and sacrificed a lot—physically, materially and emotionally—for the cause she steadfastly believed in."

14   Heroes guide us to achieving our dreams, said John Leguizamo, 30, the Colombian-born actor and playwright: "When you feel like the world is against you or you give up hope, you look at your heroes and say, 'They were able to do it. They had hard times and a lot of opposition, but they got through it.' Then you feel, 'I can do it too.'"

15   Leguizamo—who wrote, produced and starred in Fox TV's Latin comedy show *House of Buggin'*—said he has different heroes for different things: some for comedy, others for sports or playwriting. They're heroes for what they've accomplished, added Leguizamo, but also because they have overcome obstacles. He described Richard Pryor as one of his heroes: "Pryor took the urban experience and made it very funny, yet touching at the same time." Julio Cesar Chavez, the Mexican boxer, is another. "He came from a small town and had a dream to become the best boxer he could be." said Leguizamo. "He also gives back to his community. I respect that."

16   For Brandy Norwood, the 16-year-old pop singer whose songs "Best Friend" and "Baby" reached the top of the charts, there's no question who rates as heroes: "My parents are everything a child would want," she said. They teach me principles, morals and values, and about self-confidence. And they're with me all the time, by my side."

17   Other than her parents, Norwood admires Whitney Houston—but not because of the pop icon's fame. Rather it is for Houston's moral integrity. "Whitney is so powerful, and she carries herself as a positive woman," noted Norwood. "She doesn't have to use sex to sell records. I want to be like her in my own way."

18   At 26, Awadagin Pratt won the 1992 Naumburg International Piano Competition and became a celebrated Classical musician. While he has inspired many performers, Pratt prefers to avoid the term "hero," because he believes it has lost its meaning through overuse. He admitted, however, "At different points in my life, there were people whose work I admired and relied upon to provide me with inspiration."[19]

[16]mutually agreeable solutions that entail each party giving up some original desires

[17]Daw Aung San Suu Kyi (1945–) is the leader of the nonviolent movement for human rights and democracy in Myanmar, formerly Burma. She was placed under house arrest in 1989 but led the National League for Democracy (NLD), which she founded, to victory in the 1990 elections. In spite of the victory, the government refused to allow the elected parliament to convene.

[18]Established by Alfred Nobel, a Swedish chemist, philanthropist, and the inventor of dynamite, the Nobel Prize has been awarded each year since 1901 for outstanding contributions in the fields of physics, chemistry, medicine, literature, economics, and international peace.

[19]stimulating or creative influence

[20]The Canadian pianist, composer, broadcaster, and writer Glenn Gould (1932–1982) became famous in 1955 for his recording of the *Goldberg Variations* by Johann Sebastian Bach. He is also known for his recordings and experimental radio documentaries in which he interwove the voices of the people he interviewed.

[21]The German composer Ludwig Van Beethoven (1770–1827) is considered one of the greatest composers of the Western world. He was enormously popular and successful in his lifetime, but began to lose his hearing at the age of 28 and was virtually deaf by his late 40s.

[22]standard ways of doing things

[23]unfavorable

[24]aid, support

[25]someone who fought to abolish slavery

[26]opponents

The late classical pianist Glenn Gould[20] and the composer Beethoven[21] have affected Pratt deeply. They are heroes, he said because of their ability to maintain an independent spirit in the face of pressures to conform to the conventions[22] of their day. Pratt also admires Arthur Ashe, the tennis star who became an AIDS activist and died in 1993 from an HIV-related infection. "Ashe was a person with great dignity and character," Pratt said. "He was an activist who dealt with a lot of adverse[23] situations."   19

The poet Maya Angelou, 67—whose works include the autobiography *I Know Why the Caged Bird Sings* and "On the Pulse of Morning," the poem she read at President Clinton's inauguration—also doesn't use the word "hero." She prefers the term "hero/shero," because "hero" too often is thought of as male. "Young women and young men need to know that there are women who give encouragement and succor,[24] nourishment and insight," explained Angelou. "A hero/shero encourages people to see the good inside themselves and to expand it."   20

Angelou lists Eleanor Roosevelt, the author Pearl S. Buck and the abolitionist[25] Frederick Douglass among her heroes. "They confronted societies that did not believe in their ideas and faced hostile adversaries,"[26] she said. "At times they were angry. Anger is very good—but I have not seen any case where any of them became bitter."   21

We can develop the heroic in ourselves, Angelou continued, by seeking to do right by others. "Are you concerned about the poor, the lonely and the ill?" she asked. "Do you follow your concern with action? I try to act as I would want my hero/shero to act. I want to display courtesy, courage, patience and strength all the time. Now, I blow it 84 times a day. But I'm trying."   22

Comprehension Questions:

1. According to Daniel Boorstin, heroes and celebrities share many similarities. T/F

2. Jackie Joyner-Kersee wants to be admired because of her values and hard work, not her athletic ability. T/F

3. Joan Chen admires the state-mandated heroes she grew up with in Communist China. T/F

4. Maya Angelou admires Eleanor Roosevelt, Pearl S. Buck, and Frederick Douglass because they confronted societies that did not believe in their ideas. T/F

5. Jackie Joyner-Kersee and Jules Feiffer consider their parents heroes for giving them love, support, and values. T/F

Discussion Questions

1. How are heroes and celebrities different?

2. What are some of the most important qualities of a hero mentioned in the article?

3. Which definition of a hero do you agree with most?

4. Give examples from the article of heroes who are political figures, historical figures, and contemporary figures.

5. Do you consider the people the author interviewed to be heroes? Why or why not?

Journal Topic

1. What does a hero mean to you? Give examples of people you consider heroes and describe what makes them heroic.

1. Chose a personal, public, or historical figure and argue that he or she is a hero.

2. Give three examples of heroes and discuss why you admire these figures.

3. Select three qualities of a hero and discuss which prominent figures mentioned in the article share that vision of a hero.

4. Using examples from the article and/or your own life, discuss why and how heroes are important in our lives.

5. Define the term *hero.* You might want to discuss what the word means (and what it does not mean) and give examples. See the lesson on definition in Chapter 14 for more ideas.

Special Topics

Using the testimony of experts for support: This article employs a very strong strategy for developing its argument. It uses the words and thoughts of experts in child psychology to explain the best ways to handle divorce with children.

The use of quotes: Notice how the author quotes experts on children and divorce. The author inserts the quotes into her own sentence so that the sentence is smooth and clear.

> **Example:**
>
> As Dr. Wallerstein, a psychologist at the University of California at Berkeley, explains, "A society that makes divorce so easy has a responsibility to help families through the inevitably difficult transitions."

When the quote continues on to a second paragraph, no quotation mark ends the first paragraph, but a quotation mark does begin the next paragraph. See paragraphs 11 and 12.

Helping Children Through Divorce
Rita Rooney

[1] unavoidably

When the family breaks up, children are inevitably[1] hurt: some bear the scars all their lives. But, as a new study shows, parents can do much to lessen the pain—in several specific ways.

[2] determined, led

[3] effect

[4] ability to hold or achieve something

[5] guess, predict

[6] prove

[7] characterize

For some time now, researchers have agreed that a couple's decision to divorce or remain together should not be governed[2] by the impact[3] on their children. Though divorce obviously changes the course of a child's life, it need not alter the child's whole outlook or capacity[4] for happiness.   1

Until recently, however, professionals could only speculate[5] about the long-range effects of divorce on children. There was no real evidence to substantiate[6] how children respond, or to trace the changing relationships that typify[7] a post-divorce family.   2

[8] thorough

Then, in 1971, Doctors Judith Wallerstein and Joan Berlin Kelly began work on the California Children of Divorce Project, an exhaustive[8] ten-year study funded by a private foundation and geared to develop guidelines for divorcing families. As Dr. Wallerstein, a psychologist at the University of California at Berkley explains, "A society that makes divorce so easy has a responsibility to help families through the inevitably difficult transitions."   3

[9] first

The study began with the interviews of 60 families, with a total of 131 children. Youngsters and their parents were first seen within a year of the initial[9] separation; there were follow-up interviews a year later, again after five years, and then ten years later. To date,   4 it is the largest, most intensive continuous study of the effects of divorce on children that has been done.

5   The researchers' basic conclusion is not surprising: Divorce does indeed leave scars on children that may never heal. Even after ten years, young people in the study continued to see themselves as "children of divorce," as if such a label identified them for all time.

6   Even so, Dr. Wallerstein says, this does not mean that couples should stay bound to a marriage that has become a source of anguish[10] to one or both partners. "What it does mean," she points out, "is that parents who fail at married life owe it to their children not to fail at divorce." In other words, couples must learn to recognize the ways in which their divorce will affect their children—and handle the situation with sensitivity and love.

[10]suffering, distress

7   The first hurdle divorcing parents face with their children is breaking the news. Based on her research, Dr. Wallerstein advises that youngsters be told as soon as the decision is final, but not before. It is unfair, she contends, to drag a child through the painful deliberations[11] that precede[12] separations; but it is equally wrong for parents to announce a divorce and then continue living together, since most children will cling to a hope that the divorce won't happen.

[11]decision-making processes
[12]come before

8   If at all possible, parents should make the announcement together. Whether they tell the children individually or all at the same time is best determined by the age span involved. "If the children are close enough in age so that you can address them in the same way," Dr. Wallerstein says, "it's best to bring the whole family together. Youngsters support each other. But couples with a five-year-old and a teenager will probably want to tailor[13] the explanation for each child."

[13]adapt
[14]very important

9   The announcement itself is critical.[14] Children have to be told what the divorce will mean to them. They should be told where each family member will be living. If the house is to be sold, or they will have to change schools, say so. A child's worst fear of disruption is often much worse than the disruption itself. All in all, it's best to be candid in admitting to children that divorce will bring a temporary upheaval to the family but that in time everything will settle down.

10   The only way a child can deal with the idea of divorce is to find a reason for it. If parents do not explain, youngsters must rely on their own fantasies—which, in the end, can hurt more than the truth. Most professionals agree that it's best to be honest with children within the boundaries of their understanding. Even a parent's infidelity should not be entirely skirted.[15] While parents have to exercise some sensitivity to the issue, it's better to say up front that

[15]avoided

Daddy will be living in a new house with another woman than to have a child make his own shattering discovery.

Dr. Wallerstein also emphasizes the importance of parents telling their children, "We're sorry." "Don't be afraid of those words," she says. "Young people need to know that your separation is not an impulsive decision, that you have tried to make the marriage work and that you wish things had turned out differently. Give a child permission to be sad.   11

"Above all, make it clear that mothers and fathers may divorce but children never do. An alarming number of children are tragically torn between parents. They need reassurance that it's okay to love them both."   12

No matter how rationally parents explain the situation, however, most children will still refuse to accept the divorce. A seven-year-old, when told his parents are separating because they are not happy together, is likely to argue, "Stop being unhappy." And a teenager, confronted by a father's alcoholism, may reason, "All you have to do is stop drinking, get a job, and everything will be all right again."   13

According to Dr. Wallerstein, parents must override such objections with loving firmness, however difficult it may be for them. "Recognize the children's right to argue, but don't be drawn into the argument," she advises. "Tell them, 'I understand how you feel. If I were you, I'd feel that way, too. I wish I could take your advice, but that isn't possible.'"   14

On the basis of her research, Dr. Wallerstein believes the most important step divorced parents can take is to "finish the divorce." All too often, the issues that caused them to separate are reopened year after year. And though a man and woman who are married long enough to have children will probably always share an emotional tie, once they divorce they have to learn to keep their involvement to a minimum and to accept the fact that they are now separate and independent adults.   15

"We see couples who, whether they realize it or not, are holding on to their relationship," she says. "This can be very hurtful to children." After five years of divorce, one woman in the study continued to call her ex-husband whenever their youngster visited him. "Be sure your son takes a shower," she would charge.   16

Parents who remain separated without divorcing, or who attempt periodic but unsuccessful reconciliations,[16] cloud the issue for their children, increasing the uncertainty they already feel.   17

Though it is unlikely that any two youngsters will react in the same way to their parents' divorce, the study offers some guidelines to predictable behavior based on a child's age.   18

[16]acts of restoring a relationship

19   Not surprisingly, preschoolers are especially vulnerable to the breakup of their family. And since most divorces occur in the sixth or seventh year of marriage, it is preschoolers who most frequently have to face the crisis.

20   The common denominator among these children appears to be anxiety, a fear of being abandoned by either or both parents. To a three-year-old, going across town can be as awesome as crossing the Sahara. Young children worry that, when they go to visit Daddy, they may never get home again. Dr. Wallerstein calls this the Hansel and Gretel fantasy and suggests that mothers point out familiar landmarks along the way. "Look, there's the pretty church we saw last week" is the kind of offhand remark that may help a young child who is afraid of being "lost in the woods."

21   Even a new arrangement for being picked up at a baby-sitter's can be agonizing for a preschool child. Dr. Wallerstein talks of the value of giving the child subtle reassurance with a concrete timetable. "I'll come for you at five. We'll go home and have supper. Then we'll read a story."

22   One mother in the study noticed that her little girl was distressed each morning because she couldn't remember whether it was Mommy or Daddy who was scheduled to bring her home from kindergarten. The woman solved the problem by giving the child alternate lunch boxes—a blue on for Daddy's day, a pink one for Mommy's.

23   "Parents need to look for their own creative solutions," Dr. Wallerstein says.

24   Slightly older children—around five and a half to eight years old—tend to demonstrate more open yearning[17] for the absent parent. At this age, children feel abandoned by the parent who left—not by both parents, as younger children are apt to do. Boys, particularly, feel the loss of contact with their fathers and may be fearful of being left in the care of their mothers. Their logic is that the more powerful parent threw the weaker one out of the house, and they worry, Will I be next?

[17]longing, desire

25   This is also the age during which little girls form a strong attachment to their fathers—and what many mothers fail to realize is that this attachment extends to all fathers, not just the good ones. Children of this age protect themselves with a fantasy that Daddy will return.

26   Dr. Wallerstein urges mothers not to crush this fantasy outright, but not to reinforce it, either. Instead, respond with understanding, saying, "I know you miss your dad." And emphasize again that the child still has her father: He left Mommy, not his children. She warns fathers that their relationships with their

[18]cared for

children after divorce will not simply go along as they did before; a new bond must be formed and carefully nurtured.[18] To both mothers and fathers she stresses that nothing can be gained by destroying a child's relationship with the other parent: "The only thing that's gained is destruction of the child."

[19]asked for their opinion

As a rule, children between nine and 12 years of age express open anger at their parents' divorce, usually out of a sense of desperation. They feel powerless and want to know why they were not consulted[19] before the decision was made. Their anger is usually directed at the parent they think wants the divorce. Children of this age tend to divide the world into black and white: One parent is right, the other wrong. They identify with the parent they think of as a victim, and often turn on the parent they were closest to during the marriage because, with their limited ability to understand the complexities of adult behavior, they feel abandoned by their protector. Unfortunately, many parents feed this moral indignation[20] by establishing an unholy alliance[21] with the child that pits him or her against the other parent.   27

[20]anger
[21]partnership

[22]faced

"A youngster's anger won't go away by itself. It needs to be addressed,"[22] says Dr. Wallerstein. "But you don't have to give the child a hunting license in order to deal with his harsh judgment of the other parent."   28

Adolescents and young people of college age may be the most neglected of all children of divorce. Historically, many couples wait "until the kids are grown" to separate. Yet it is these near-adults who are usually most depressed by parental separation. They question, "What about me?" They wonder who will send them to college. Often, they are thwarted[23] in their need to establish autonomy[24] outside the family by a parent's over reliance on them. Sometimes they are overwhelmed by what is going on in the family and find it difficult to concentrate in school and maintain friendships that are crucial to normal development.   29

[23]frustrated
[24]independence

[25]awakening

If the divorce is grounded in a parent's infidelity, other problems arise. "Teenagers are preoccupied with their own burgeoning[25] sexuality," Dr. Wallerstein points out. "They find it comforting to think of their parents as too old for sex. To be confronted with the suddenly visible sexual need of a parent can be traumatic."   30

[26]dividing lines between children and adults
[27]boundary

Two important lessons for parents of adolescents seem clear. The first is that while one or both divorced parents may rely on an older child's emotional support, they must be careful not to intrude on the youngster's life outside the home. And, second, both parents must be alert to a breakdown of generational boundaries,[26] aware that young people may be pushed across the threshold[27] into adult behavior before they are able to handle the consequences.   31

32   Specifically, Dr. Wallerstein says, "Don't consult a teenager about the details of your social life or who you are dating. Parents often make the mistake of forcing young people into advisory roles they can't handle."

33   For children of any age, divorce does not end with a decree.[28] Youngsters need continuing support from both parents to balance the impact of loss in their lives. Dr. Wallerstein recommends that parents work out a visitation policy, fine-tune it and stick with it. Don't let the child fret[29] about weekend or holiday arrangements; let him know about them well in advance.

[28]legal document certifying the divorce

[29]worry

34   The biggest challenge of all for a child of divorce may be a parent's remarriage. Suddenly, there is not only a stepfather or stepmother, but possibly stepbrothers and sisters as well. Dr. Wallerstein urges couples to give new relationships time to set in. Two mistakes are common she says: A remarried mother expects her new husband to take over immediately as parent; and the new husband responds that they are *her* children, *her* problem. The same holds true for remarried fathers. What couples really need is time to get to know each other, time to define the new relationships.

35   Children are not comforted by the reassurance that, for an increasing number of people, divorce is a natural progression of family life. Knowing that several of her classmates have divorced parents is no help to a little girl mourning the loss of her father. In fact, there is growing evidence that the high incidence of divorce intensifies children's anxiety about the hazards of loving someone. Teachers report that youngsters from intact families sometimes come to school after a parental argument and want to know, "Are my folks going to get a divorce?"

36   Children need help—from the time of separation throughout adolescence. They need the understanding and wisdom of parents who recognize that, while divorce may be the only solution for *them*, it is never a decision a child accepts easily. On the whole, children in the study who fared[30] best were those who had continuing relationships with both parents and whose lives after the divorce were on a more even keel[31] than before.

[30]got along

[31]balance

37   "In other words," Dr. Wallerstein says, "children do well when the divorce solves the problems it was meant to solve."

Comprehension Questions

1. The thesis or main idea of this essay is that
   A. parents need to recognize the ways their divorce will affect their children and handle the situation with sensitivity and love.
   B. a couple's decision to divorce shouldn't be determined by the impact on their children.
   C. helping children through divorce can be easy if couples follow certain guidelines.
   D. it is the parents' responsibility to make their children happy.

2. According to the article, when announcing their divorce, couples should
   A. tell the children as soon as they know that they might want to separate.
   B. make the announcement separately.
   C. explain to the children what the divorce will mean to the children.
   D. always tell the children one at a time and never all together.

3. To "finish the divorce" means to
   A. get the legal papers completed quickly.
   B. stop the contact between the parents except when necessary.
   C. get over the emotional scars of the divorce and become friends for the children's sakes.
   D. refuse to see the other parent ever again.

4. At what years of age do children typically fear abandonment by a parent?
   A. 1–5
   B. 6–10
   C. 11–16
   D. 17–20

5. According to the essay, what may be the biggest challenge for children of divorce?
   A. a parent's infidelity
   B. a parent's remarriage
   C. fear of losing the absent parent
   D. changing households

Discussion Questions

1. At what age do you think it is the hardest for children to accept divorce? Use the essay to support your answer.

2. Which issue does the author bring up that you think is the most important consideration in helping children handle their parents' divorce?

3. Why shouldn't parents consult their older children about their new social life after the divorce? Can you think of a situation in which talking to an older child could be good for the child and parent?

4. Give examples from your own experience or families you know of guidelines that the author discusses that you agree with.

5. Explain why you disagree with one or more of the author's assertions.

Writing Topics

1. Summarize the steps that parents should take to help their children through their divorce.

2. Define a three-stage process that parents should undertake to ensure that children cope well with the divorce.

3. Using the essay for support, explain how you would handle a divorce with your children.

4. Analyze a divorce that you have experienced or observed, and explain how the participants handled the divorce well or poorly for their children.

5. Compare and contrast how parents are advised to treat their children in divorce in this essay with the way parents are advised to treat their children in John Odebzinski's article, "Why Happy Families Are Different" (p. 503).

Special Topics

Narration: Notice how, in paragraph 4, the author sets the scene of his chemistry experiments in his living room. He supplies details of the scene such as the television program his father is watching. In paragraph 5, he relates just enough of what his mother has heard and what she says to him to show how it excited him.

I Just Wanna Be Average
By Mike Rose[1]

It's popular these days to claim you grew up on the streets. Men tell violent tales and romanticize[2] the lessons violence brings. But, though it was occasionally violent, it wasn't the violence in South L.A. that marked me, for sometimes you can shake that ugliness off. What finally affected me was subtler, but more pervasive[3]: I cannot recall a young person who was crazy in love or lost in work or one old person who was passionate about a cause or idea. I'm not talking about an absence of energy—the street toughs and, for that fact, old Cheech had energy. And I'm not talking about an absence of decency, for my father was a thoughtful man. The people I grew up with were retired from jobs that rub away the heart or were working hard at jobs to keep their lives from caving in or were anchorless and in between jobs and spouses or were diving headlong into a barren[4] tomorrow: junkies, alcoholics, and mean kids walking along Vermont looking to throw a punch. I developed a picture of human existence that rendered it short and brutish[5] or sad and aimless or long and quiet with rewards like afternoon naps, the evening newspaper, walks around the block, occasional letters from children in other states. When, years later, I was introduced to humanistic psychologists[6] like Abraham Maslow and Carl Rogers, with their visions of self-actualization,[7] or even Freud[8] with his sober dictum[9] about love and work, it all sounded like a glorious fairy tale, a magical account of a world full of possibility, full of hope and empowerment. Sinbad and Cinderella couldn't have been more fanciful.[10] Some people who manage to write their way out of the working class describe the classroom as an oasis of possibility. It became their intellectual playground, their competitive arena. Given the richness of my memories of this time, it's funny how scant[11] are my recollections of school. I remember the red brick building of St. Regina's itself, and the topography[12] of the playground: the swings and basketball courts and peeling benches. There are images of a few students: Erwin Petschaur, a muscular German boy with a strong accent; Dave Sanchez, who was good in

1

[1] The author is director of the University of California–Los Angeles Writing Programs. His best-known book is *Lives on the Boundary: The Struggles and Achievements of America's Underprepared,* from which this excerpt is taken.

[2] make an idea sound romantic or adventurous

[3] spread throughout

[4] uninteresting, unfruitful

[5] brutal, cruel

[6] scientists who study the potential of humans to become fulfilled

[7] realization of one's potential

[8] Sigmund Freud (1856–1939) was the father of modern psychology and psychoanalysis.

[9] serious saying

[10] imaginary, unreal

[11] limited, meager

[12] geography

math; and Sheila Wilkes, everyone's curly-haired heartthrob. And there are two nuns: Sister Monica, the third-grade teacher with beautiful hands for whom I carried a candle and who, to my dismay, had wedded herself to Christ; and Sister Beatrice a woman truly crazed, who would sweep into class, eyes wide, to tell us about the Apocalypse.[13]

[13]the end of the world (according to the Bible)

1   All the hours in class tend to blend into one long, vague stretch of time. What I remember best, strangely enough, are the two things I couldn't understand and over the years grew to hate: grammar lessons and mathematics. I would sit there watching a teacher draw her long horizontal line and her short, oblique lines and break up sentences and put adjectives here and adverbs there and just not get it, couldn't see the reason for it, turned off to it. I would hide by slumping down in my seat and page through my reader, carried along by the flow of sentences in a story. She would test us, and I would dread that, for I always got Cs and Ds. Mathematics was a bit different. For whatever reasons, I didn't learn early math very well, so when it came time for more complicated operations, I couldn't keep up and started daydreaming to avoid my inadequacy.[14] This was a strategy[15] I would rely on as I grew older. I fell further and further behind. A memory: The teacher is faceless and seems very far away. The voice is faint and is discussing an equation written on the board. It is raining, and I am watching the streams of water form patterns on the windows.

[14]lack of ability
[15]method

2   I realize now how consistently I defended myself against the lessons I couldn't understand and the people and events of South L.A. that were too strange to view head-on. I got very good at watching a blackboard with minimum awareness. And I drifted more and more into a variety of protective fantasies. I was lucky in that although my parents didn't read or write very much and had no more than a few books around the house, they never debunked[16] my pursuits.[17] And when they could, they bought me what I needed to spin my web.[18]

[16]stripped of pretentions, put down
[17]pastimes
[18]Imagination is spun by the mind like a spider spins a web.

3   One early Christmas they got me a small chemistry set. My father brought home an old card table from the secondhand store, and on that table I spread out my test tubes, my beaker, my Erlenmeyer flask, and my gas-generating apparatus. The set came equipped with chemicals, minerals, and various treated papers— all in little square bottles. You could send away to someplace in Maryland for more, and I did, saving pennies and nickels to get the substances that were too exotic[19] for my set, the Junior Chem-craft: Congo red paper, azurite, glycerine, chrome alum, cochineal—this from female insects!—tartaric acid, chameleon paper, logwood. I would sit before my laboratory and play for hours. My father

[19]unusual

rested on the purple couch in front of me watching wrestling or *Gunsmoke* while I measured powders or heated crystals or blew into solutions that my breath would turn red or pink. I was taken by the blends of names and by the colors that swirled through the beaker. My equations were visual and phonetic. I would hold a flask up to the hall light, imagining the veils of a million atoms dancing. Sulfur and alcohol hung in the air. I wanted to shake down the house.

One day my mother came home from Coffee Dan's with an awful story. The teenage brother of one of her waitress friends was in the hospital. He had been fooling around with explosives in his garage "where his mother couldn't see him," and something happened, and "he blew away part of his throat. For God's sake, be careful," my mother said. "Remember poor Ada's brother." Wow! I thought. How neat! Why couldn't my experiments be that dangerous? I really lost heart when I realized that you could probably eat the chemicals spread across my table.

I knew what I had to do. I saved my money for a week and then walked with firm resolve past Walt's Malts, past the brake shop, across Ninetieth Street, and into Palazolla's market. I bought a little bottle of Alka-Seltzer and ran home. I chipped up the wafers and mixed them into a jar of white crystals. When my mother came home, dog tired, and sat down on the edge of the couch to tell me and Dad about her day, I gravely[20] poured my concoction[21] into a beaker of water, cried something about the unexpected, and ran out from behind my table. The beaker foamed ominously.[22] My father swore in Italian. The second time I tried it, I got something milder—in English. And by my third near-miss with death, my parents were calling my behavior cute. Cute! Who wanted cute? I wanted to toy with the disaster that befell Ada Pendleton's brother. I wanted all those wonderful colors to collide in ways that could

But I was limited by the real. The best I could do was create a toxic[23] antacid. I loved my chemistry set—its glassware and its intriguing labels—but it wouldn't allow me to do the things I wanted to do. St. Regina's had an all-purpose room, one wall of which was lined with old books—and one of those shelves held a row of plastic-covered space novels. The sheen of their covers was gone, and their futuristic portraits were dotted with erasures and grease spots like a meteor shower of the everyday. I remember the rockets best. Long cylinders outfitted at the base with three slick fins, tapering at the other end to a perfect conical[24] point, ready to pierce out of the stratosphere and into my imagination: X-fifteens and Mach 1, the dark side of the moon, the Red Planet Jupiter's Great Red Spot, Saturn's rings—and beyond the solar system to swirling wisps of galaxies, to stardust.

[20]with great seriousness
[21]mixture
[22]threateningly
[23]poisonous
[24]cone-shaped

5

6

7

8   I would check out my books two at a time and take them home to curl up with a blanket on my chaise lounge,[25] reading, sometimes, through the weekend, my back aching, my thoughts lost between galaxies. I became the hero of a thousand adventures, all with intricate[26] plots and the triumph of good over evil, all many dimensions removed from the dim walls of the living room. We were given time to draw in school, so, before long, all this worked itself onto paper. The stories I was reading were reshaping themselves into pictures. My father got me some butcher paper from Palazolla's, and I continued to draw at home. My collected works rendered[27] the Horsehead Nebula, Goofy space cruisers, robots, and Saturn. Each had its crayon, a particular waxy pencil with mood and meaning: rust and burnt sienna for Mars, yellow for the Sun, lime and rose for Saturn's rings, and bright red for the Jovian[28] spot. I had a little sharpener to keep the points just right. I didn't write any stories; I just read and drew. I wouldn't care much about writing until late in high school.

9   The summer before the sixth grade, I got a couple of jobs. The first was at a pet store a block or so away from my house. Since I was still small, I could maneuver around in breeder cages, scraping the heaps of parakeet crap from the tin floor, cleaning the water troughs and seed trays. It was pretty awful. I would go home after work and fill the tub and soak until all the fleas and bird mites came floating to the surface, little Xs in their multiple eyes. When I heard about a job selling strawberries door-to-door, I jumped at it. I went to work for a white-haired Chicano named Frank. He would carry four or five kids and dozens of crates of strawberries in his ramshackle[29] truck up and down the avenues of the better neighborhoods: houses with mowed lawns and petunia beds. We'd work all day for seventy-five cents, Frank dropping pairs of us off with two crates each, then picking us up at preassigned corners. We spent lots of time together, bouncing around on the truck bed redolent[30] with strawberries or sitting on a corner, cold, listening for the sputter of Frank's muffler. I started telling the other kids about my books, and soon it was my job to fill up that time with stories.

10   Reading opened up the world. There I was, a skinny bookworm drawing the attention of street kids who, in any other circumstances, would have had me for breakfast. Like an epic taleteller, I developed the stories as I went along, relying on a flexible[31] plot line and a repository[32] of heroic events. I had a great time. I sketched out trajectories[33] with my finger on Frank's dusty truck bed. And I stretched out each story's climax, creating cliffhangers like the ones I saw in the Saturday serials. These stories created for me a temporary community.

[25] recliner chair

[26] complicated

[27] showed, represented

[28] of the planet Jupiter

[29] shaky, ready to collapse

[30] having a pleasant odor

[31] easily changeable
[32] storehouse
[33] arcs (of rockets)

Comprehension Questions

1. What most affected the author about growing up on the streets?

    A. He had no interactions with people who were passionate about their lives.

    B. He was victimized by crime and violence.

    C. He didn't have the money for school.

    D. He never saw any natural beauty in his surroundings.

2. The subjects the author remembers best in school are

    A. physical education.

    B. shop.

    C. grammar and mathematics.

    D. science.

3. When he didn't understand the lessons he was being taught, the author

    A. misbehaved.

    B. talked to other students.

    C. raised his hand.

    D. daydreamed.

4. The author's first job was

    A. cleaning cages at a pet store.

    B. raking leaves.

    C. washing cars.

    D. selling newspapers.

5. To become popular with the boys he worked with, the author

    A. sold them lottery tickets.

    B. told them stories.

    C. did their homework for them.

    D. lent them money.

Discussion Questions

1. What does the author find wrong with growing up on the streets?

2. What events in the author's childhood helped him to escape his everyday world and develop his curiosity and imagination?

3. How did the author's parents help him develop his imagination?

4. Do you think that the author had a happy childhood? Find support for your ideas in the article.

5. How did reading open up the author's world?

Writing Topics

1. Trace the important events that take Mike Rose out of his everyday world and put him into a world of imagination.

2. Choose three events in the author's childhood and explain how they helped him develop his curiosity and imagination.

3. Identify an experience that you had while growing up that helped you develop your curiosity and imagination.

4. Explain how your parents helped or hindered your development as a child.

5. Explain your experience of school in the early grades. What do you remember of your classes? What were your strategies for dealing with the pressures of learning and socializing with the other kids?

Special Topics

Rhetorical Patterns: The author reports on a persuasive study that shows that valedictorians are successful because of their hard work and can-do attitude, not because of their intelligence.

Use of Sources: Michael Ryan reports on a study done by Professor Terry Denny of the University of Illinois and Associate Professor Karen Arnold of Boston College. Notice how tag phrases are used with each quote.

Related Articles: Several essays examine the role of motivation and attitude in achieving success and/or happiness. All agree that motivation and hard work are more important than intelligence or innate ability.

"What is Your Emotional IQ?" by Daniel Goleman

"Who Is Great?" by Michael Ryan

"Jordan Is Never Afraid of Failure" by Bob Green

Do Valedictorians Succeed Big in Life?
By Michael Ryan

[1] imitate, copy

[2] person who graduates with highest grade point average in the class

[3] hard working

They are role models—the kids whom teachers wish all their students would emulate,[1] the scholars whose hard work and achievements all parents wish their children would copy. High school valedictorians[2] are the young adults who seem the brightest, most diligent[3] and most likely to succeed.

But do they actually succeed?

[4] facing

In the summer of 1981, Prof. Terry Denny of the University of Illinois asked that question—and started a long-term study that may have found the answer: By and large they do succeed, but not without confronting[4] the same life problems we all have.

"Terry Denny spent his career studying success," said Associate Prof. Karen Arnold of Boston College, who joined Denny in January 1982 and became director of the project when he retired 1986. "Much to his surprise, he found that there was not a study of high school valedictorians." Professor Denny traveled across Illinois, attending high school graduations and selecting 81 students to participate in the Illinois Valedictorian Project, a study that has followed these high school stars from adolescence into their mid-30s.

[5] final, greatest

Denny asked the scholars about their lives, their goals, what they thought their ultimate[5] happiness might be. Arnold has continued that work, visiting the former valedictorians every few years and keeping in regular touch with them by mail. She has published her results in academic articles and a book, *Lives of Promise* (Jossey-Bass, San Francisco).

6   "As a group, they absolutely stand apart in how hard they work," Arnold told me. "I gave them standardized tests that measure motivation[6] to work hard. They knocked the top off the work scale compared to any other group." On the standardized ACT test, however, which measures some intellectual skills, the valedictorians' scores varied, ranging from just average for college-bound students up to the top percentile. They are not always the brightest kids in school. They are the hardest-working.

[6] drive, force that pushes

7   Besides giving tests, Denny also talked with each of the study subjects. "He picked students from the most diverse communities possible," said Arnold, "from little rural[7] schools to rich suburban[8] schools near Chicago to city schools." (The sample group also includes several salutatorians—the second-ranked students in their classes—as well as a few other top students.)

[7] country
[8] pertaining to neighborhoods surrounding cities

8   The first big surprise came when Denny and Arnold discovered that the valedictorians were popular. "The stereotype[9] would be that they were misfits or 'grinds' who would study all the time and never have any friends," said Arnold. Instead, many were athletes, musicians or editors of their school papers. "They had friends among the good students and the not-so-good students," added Arnold.

[9] fixed idea about group or idea that does not allow for individual variation

9   What's more, once they graduated, not all of the valedictorians chose the fast track to success. Although all sought higher education, a number enrolled in colleges that offered less challenge than they could have handled. One student rejected a prestigious[10] university and attended a community college. After he received his associate's degree, he transferred to the university he had turned down to earn a bachelor's. Within a few weeks, he thought of dropping out, convinced he couldn't do the work. But he stayed and was stunned by his success. At graduation, he was near the top of his class.

[10] well-known and highly regarded

10   "A lot of first-generation college students among the valedictorians didn't know how to parlay[11] their talents and credentials[12] into college careers," said Arnold. "Not a single rural valedictorian went to school out of state." Arnold attributed part of this problem to what she called "tacit[13] knowledge." For valedictorians from noncollege homes, top schools seemed unreachable. "Their guidance counselors should have been telling them about opportunities and encouraging them," said Arnold. Students whose parents were college-educated learned early that they could try for top schools and find financial aid.

[11] increase to something of greater value, trade up
[12] achievements
[13] understood but not spoken

11   Several valedictorians in the study compiled[14] perfect records. For many of those who didn't, getting their first "B" was a

[14] built gradually

liberating experience. "A lot of them said they couldn't wait to get it," said Arnold. "It took the pressure off."

Nearly half of the valedictorians chose career-related majors rather than focusing on liberal arts. That was due in part, Arnold explained, to a severe recession[15] while they were in high school. The students wanted to learn marketable[16] skills.

In her book, Arnold tells of two students whom she calls "Matthew" and "Nick." (Arnold used aliases[17] for all the scholars in her study, to protect their identities.) Matthew, from an affluent[18] family, attended an Ivy League school.[19] After college, he taught himself finance, became a trader and forged[20] a lucrative[21] career. Financially stable, he is now indulging[22] his intellectual interests by earning a Ph.D.

Nick, on the other hand, came from a less affluent background and decided to major in accounting to get a job that would help his family. He took courses he thought would prepare him for a career. After graduation, he landed a good job with a national firm and moved to California. He was miserable. Nick was laid off from his job and turned to his first love: teaching. He earned his certification and, now in his mid-30's, is beginning a career that will pay him much less than accounting but, he believes, will fulfill him much more.

"My advice to valedictorians," said Arnold, "would be to give yourself the luxury of doing what you love. You don't translate college into career just by the classes you take. You do it by making connections with faculty, by internships and summer jobs. Things get opened up to you in important ways."

Few of the valedictorians became "intellectuals"—people who learn for the sheer love of learning. "High school rewards generalists,"[23] said Arnold. "To be equally interested in calculus, gym, home economics and English is almost impossible, but these bright people managed to engage in all of them." She noted that some very bright students don't become valedictorians because they don't invest effort in subjects that don't interest them.

As they approach middle age, the valedictorians in the study have some impressive achievements. Almost 60% have graduate degrees: Three are doctors, six are lawyers, 10 are MBAs and 15 are Ph.D.s. But not all have progressed as far in their careers as they might have—especially, said Arnold, the first-generation college graduates, women and minorities. This is partly because of a lack of mentoring[24] at college. (Forty-five men and 36 women were study participants. There were 72 whites, two black men, three black women, three Hispanic women and one Asian man.)

Some women in the study have put their careers on hold in favor of motherhood. "They still have all their ambition and drive, and I predict they'll came back to the workforce," said Arnold.

12

13

14

15

16

17

18

[15]economic slowdown

[16]sellable, tradable for money

[17]fictional names

[18]rich

[19]any of a group of well-known northeastern colleges (whose walls were traditionally covered with ivy)

[20]shaped

[21]profitable

[22]gratifying

[23]people who are interested in many subjects

[24]counseling, role modeling

19   So far, none of the valedictorians in the study has become famous or even a leader in his or her profession. "It's too much to expect somebody from a group of 81 people to become eminent,"[25] said Arnold, "but a few of them are still on track for that." A couple of the participants are doing high-level science research, another is a partner at a prestigious law firm, and one is a social activist.

[25]famous

20   Arnold chides[26] those who take comfort in the fact that none of these valedictorians has gained fame: "It's a sour-grapes argument," she said. "It's the idea that if you just lifted a finger, you could surpass these people who've been working away all these years. That idea is not supported by evidence."

[26]scolds

21   Arnold expected that the valedictorians would have a lower rate of mental illness, emotional problems and other life difficulties than the rest of us. She was wrong. "What's different is how they react," she said. "If they have a problem, they seek help."

22   One woman was devastated by manic depression. After battling her disability, she has begun to return to a fully functional life. To the woman, conquering her illness was a foregone[27] conclusion. "Of course I can deal with this," she told Arnold. "After all, I was a valedictorian."

[27]determined in advance

Comprehension Questions

1. Which statement represents the thesis of the article?

   A. Valedictorians are role models.

   B. Valedictorians succeed but not without confronting the same life problems we all do.

   C. Professor Denny spent his career studying success.

   D. Valedictorians stand apart in how hard they work.

2. According to the article, valedictorians are

   A. the brightest kids in their class.

   B. misfits who study all the time.

   C. the hardest-working kids in their class.

   D. not athletic.

3. Once they graduated, the valedictorians in Denny and Arnold's study

   A. all chose the fast track to success.

   B. did not all go to college.

   C. all went to college out of state.

   D. all went to college.

4. What percentage of the valedictorians in Denny and Arnold's study earned graduate degrees?

    A. 40

    B. 50

    C. 60

    D. 90

5. According to the article, valedictorians

    A. have low rates of emotional and mental illness.

    B. do not seek help when they have a problem.

    C. seek help when they have a problem.

    D. give up easily when confronted with difficult problems.

Discussion Questions

1. Whom did Denny study and for how long?

2. What is the "tacit knowledge" the author refers to in paragraph 10, and how does it affect the goals of first-generation college students?

3. Compare and contrast intellectuals and valedictorians.

4. What groups of valedictorians in Denny and Arnold's study were least successful, and why?

5. Do the characteristics Denny and Arnold describe fit the valedictorians you know?

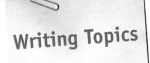

Writing Topics

1. What are the characteristics of valedictorians?

2. Are valedictorians good role models? Use examples from both the article and your life to illustrate.

3. How well did the valedictorian in your high school fit the characteristics Denny and Arnold describe?

4. Which characteristics of valedictorians do you possess, and which do you lack? Illustrate with examples from you life.

5. After reading this article and the following one (Michael Ryan's "Who Is Great?"), compare and contrast the characteristics of valedictorians and those who are great.

Special Topics

Introduction: The author gets the reader's attention by opening with three surprising examples of people whom we all recognize and yet who showed little promise early in life. The second paragraph poses several questions that the essay will answer, the last of which is really the thesis posed as a question.

Rhetorical Patterns: The author *defines* greatness by examining its characteristics and giving numerous *examples* of people from a variety of fields who are great.

Use of sources: Ryan relies primarily on the research done by Keith Simonton (paragraphs 4–17, 20–21), but also includes a 1985 Brandeis University study by Teresa Amabile (paragraphs 18–19), and cites Dr. Arnold Ludwig (paragraphs 22–23). Notice how each source is introduced and how tag phrases identify the source of each quote, fact, or idea.

Are the people we call "great" really different from you and me? Here's what experts find when they ask…

Who Is Great?
Michael Ryan

1   As a young boy, Albert Einstein[1] did so poorly in school that teachers thought he was slow. The young Napoleon Bonaparte[2] was just one of hundreds of artillery lieutenants in the French Army. And the teenage George Washington,[3] with little formal education, was being trained not as a soldier but as a land surveyor.

2   Despite their unspectacular beginnings, each would go on to carve a place for himself in history. What was it that enabled them to become great? Were they born with something special? Or did their greatness have more to do with timing, devotion and, perhaps, an uncompromising personality?

3   For decades, scientists have been asking such questions. And, in the past few years, they have found evidence to help explain why some people rise above, while others—similarly talented, perhaps—are left behind. Their findings could have implications[4] for all of us.

Who Is Great?

4   Defining who is great depends on how one measures success. But there are some criteria.[5] "Someone who has made a lasting contribution to human civilization is great," said Dean Keith Simonton, a professor of psychology at the University of California at Davis and author of the 1994 book *Greatness: Who Makes History and Why*. But he added one caveat[6]: "Sometimes

[1] Albert Einstein (1879–1955) was born in Germany but lived most of his life in the United States, where he worked as a physicist at Harvard University and formulated the theory of relativity.

[2] Napoleon Bonaparte (1769–1821) was the French military leader and emperor of France from 1804 to 1815

[3] George Washington (1732–1799) was a military leader in the Revolutionary War and first president of the United States.

[4] implied meanings

[5] bases for judgment

[6] formal warning

great people don't make it into the history books. A lot of women achieved great things of were influential but went unrecognized."

In writing his book, Simonton combined historical knowledge about great figures with recent findings in genetics,[7] psychiatry and the social sciences. The great figures he focused on include men and women who have won Nobel Prizes,[8] led great nations or won wars, composed symphonies that have endured for centuries, or revolutionized science, philosophy, politics or the arts. Though he doesn't have a formula to define how or why certain people rise above (too many factors are involved), he has come up with a few common characteristics.

A "Never Surrender" Attitude

If great achievers share anything, said Simonton, it is an unrelenting[9] drive to succeed. There's a tendency to think that they are endowed with[10] something super-normal," he explained. "But what comes out of the research is that there are great people who have no amazing intellectual processes. It's a difference in degree. Greatness is built upon tremendous amounts of study, practice and devotion.

He cited Winston Churchill, Britain's prime minister during World War II, as an example of a risk-taker who would never give up. Thrust[11] into office when his country's morale was at its lowest, Churchill rose brilliantly to lead the British people. In a speech following the Allied evacuation of Dunkirk[12] in 1940, he inspired the nation when he said, "We shall not flag or fail. We shall go on to the end…We shall never surrender." After the war, Churchill was voted out of office but again demonstrated his fighting spirit when he delivered his famous "Iron Curtain"[13] speech at Westminster College in Missouri in 1946. This time at the dawn of the Cold War,[14] he exhorted[15] the entire Western world to stand up to communism: "We hold the power to save the future," he said. "Our difficulties and dangers will not be removed by closing our eyes to them."

Can You Be Born Great?

In looking at Churchill's role in history—as well as the roles of other political and military leaders—Simonton discovered a striking pattern: "Firstborns and only children tend to make good leaders in time of crisis: They're used to taking charge. But middleborns are better as peacetime leaders: They listen to different constituencies[16] better and make the necessary compromises. Churchill, an only child, was typical. He was great in a crisis, but in peacetime he was not effective—not even popular."

Timing is another factor. "If you took George Washington and put him in the 20th century, he would go nowhere as a politician," Simonton declared. "He was not an effective public speaker, and he

5

6

7

8

9

[7] the study of genes (units on chromosomes that transmit and determine inherited characteristics)

[8] Established by Alfred Nobel, a Swedish chemist, and the inventor of dynamite, the Nobel Prize has been awarded since 1901 for outstanding contributions in science, medicine, literature, economics, and international peace.

[9] constant, unending

[10] given, granted

[11] pushed forward

[12] seaport in northern France from which the Allies retreated after an unsuccessful attempt to retake France from Germany

[13] a metaphor coined by Churchill for the post–World War II separation of the Soviet Union and its allies from the United States and its allies

[14] economic and diplomatic antagonism between countries

[15] strongly urge or warn

[16] groups of clients or voters

didn't like shaking hands with the public. On the other hand, I'm not sure Franklin Roosevelt would have done well in Washington's time. He wouldn't have had the radio to do his fireside chats."

Can You Be Too Smart?

10   One surprise among Simonton's findings is that many political and military leaders have been bright but not overly so. Beyond a certain point, he explained, other factors, like the ability to communicate effectively, become more important than innate[17] intelligence as measured by an IQ test. The most intelligent U.S. Presidents, for example—Thomas Jefferson, Woodrow Wilson and John F. Kennedy—had a hard time getting elected, Simonton said, while others with IQs closer to the average (such as Warren G. Harding) won by landslides. While political and economic factors also are involved, having a genius IQ is not necessary to be a great leader.

[17]inborn

11   In the sciences, those with "genius level" IQs do have a better shot at achieving recognition, added Simonton. Yet evidence also indicates that overcoming traditional ways of thinking may be just as important.

12   He pointed to one recent study where college students were given a set of data and were asked to see if they could come up with a mathematical relation. Almost a third did. What they did not know was that they had just solved one of the most famous scientific equations in history: the Third Law of Planetary Motion, an equation that Johannes Kepler came up with in 1618.

13   Kepler's genius, Simonton said, was not so much in solving a mathematical challenge. It was in thinking about the numbers in a unique[18] way—applying his mathematical knowledge to his observations of planetary motion. It was his boldness that set him apart.

[18]one and only, different

Love Your Work

14   As a child, Einstein became fascinated[19] with the way magnets draw iron filings. "He couldn't stop thinking about this stuff," Simonton pointed out. "He became obsessed with problems in physics by the time he was 16, and he never stopped working on them. It's not surprising that he made major contributions by the time he was 26."

[19]extremely interested

15   "For most of us, it's not that we don't have the ability," Simonton added, "it's that we don't devote the time. You have to put in the effort and put up with all the frustrations and obstacles."

16   Like other creative geniuses, Einstein was not motivated by a desire for fame, said Simonton. Instead, his obsession[20] with his work was what set him apart. Where such drive comes from remains a mystery. But it is found in nearly all creative geniuses—whether or not their genius is acknowledged[21] by contemporaries.[22]

[20]preoccupation
[21]recognized, admitted
[22]people who live at the same time

[23]American poet
(1830–1886)

[24]Irish poet and fiction
writer (1882–1941)

[25]challenging, facing

[26]central, unable to be
removed

[27]without names

"Emily Dickinson[23] was not recognized for her poetry until   17
after her death," said Simonton. "But she was not writing for fame.
The same can be said of James Joyce,[24] who didn't spend a lot of
time worrying about how many people would read *Finnegans
Wake*. Beethoven once said, when confronting[25] a musician strug-
gling to play some of his new quartets, 'They are not for you, but
for a later age.'"

Today, researchers have evidence that an intrinsic[26] passion for   18
one's work is a key to rising above. In a 1985 study at Brandeis
University conducted by Teresa Amabile, now a professor of business administration at Harvard University, a group of professional
writers—none famous—was asked to write a short poem. Each
writer was then randomly placed in one of three groups: One group
was asked to keep in mind the idea of writing for money; another
was told to think about writing just for pleasure; and a third group
was given no instruction at all.

The poems then were submitted anonymously[27] to a panel of   19
professional writers for evaluation. The poetry written by people
who thought about writing for money ranked lowest. Those who
thought about writing just for pleasure did the best. "Motivation
that comes from enjoying the work makes a significant difference,"
Amabile said.

What Price Greatness?

Many great figures have had poor personal relationships, per-   20
haps a result of their drive to excel, said Simonton. And great people, he added, often can be unbearable: "Beethoven, for instance,
was tyrannical with servants and rude to his friends. His personal
hygiene was not particularly great either. When working, he would
go for days or weeks without bathing."

Yet one common belief about greatness—that it often is   21
accompanied by mental imbalance—seems unfounded.

"Certain types of psychopathology are more common in some   22
professions than in others," explained Dr. Arnold M. Ludwig, a psy-
chiatrist at the University of Kentucky Medical Center and author
of a new book, *The Price of Greatness*. "Poets, for example, have high
rates of depression. But architects as a group are very stable. Fiction
writers and jazz musicians are more likely to abuse drugs and alcohol. But when you go outside the artistic fields, you find phenom-
enal creative achievements among scientists, social activists and
politicians. It is certainly possible for people to achieve great things
without corresponding mental illness."

Dr. Ludwig did some personal research on the issue as well. "I   23
have two children who are very creative and artistic," he said. "I

decided to find out whether they would have to be crazy if they were to grow up to be geniuses. I was happy to find out that they would not."

Comprehension Questions

1. Albert Einstein

    A. excelled in math in school.

    B. did so poorly that his teachers thought him slow.

    C. attended college at the age of thirteen.

    D. developed no early interests.

2. The author relies primarily on

    A. his own research.

    B. quotes from famous people.

    C. the research of Keith Simonton.

    D. common knowledge.

3. _____ is/are primarily responsible for greatness.

    A. Luck

    B. Intelligence

    C. Drive and passion

    D. Birth order

4. Winston Churchill

    A. was a popular leader after World War II.

    B. became a leader during World War II.

    C. was a middle child.

    D. possessed superior intelligence.

5. Many great people

    A. commit suicide.

    B. have poor personal relationships.

    C. are mentally unstable.

    D. abuse drugs and alcohol.

Discussion Questions

1. How does Keith Simonton define greatness?

2. Who might his definition leave out and why?

3. How does attitude affect greatness?

4. What role does innate intelligence as measured by IQ test play in greatness?

5. Is there a price associated with greatness? Has the price of greatness and/or fame changed over time?

Writing Topics

1. Using both the essay and your own experience, define greatness.

2. What are the characteristics of greatness?

3. What factors influence the effectiveness of political and military leaders? Use examples from the essay and from your own knowledge.

4. Argue that one or more figures not mentioned in the essay are great.

5. Are the types of people described in the essay good role models? Why or why not?

Special Topics

Rhetorical Pattern: Staples tells the story of his brother's murder, but he doesn't do so chronologically (in time order). Instead, he begins at the end of the story, with the murder, so that the reader will understand the importance of the story he is about to tell. He then jumps back to their childhood and moves chronologically up to the point of the murder.

Introduction/Conclusion: Staples begins with the shocking news of his brother's murder, and in a few short sentences, recreates the violent moment (notice the use of active verbs, *emerged, fired, fled*). He returns to the moment he hears of his brother's death in the conclusion.

A Brother's Murder
Brent Staples

1   It has been more than two years since my telephone rang with the news that my younger brother Blake—just 22 years old—had been murdered. The young man who killed him was only 24. Wearing a ski mask, he emerged[1] from a car, fired six times at close range with a massive .44 Magnum, then fled. The two had once been inseparable[2] friends. A senseless rivalry—beginning, I think, with an argument over a girlfriend—escalated[3] from posturing, to threats, to violence, to murder. The way the two were living, death could have come to either of them from anywhere. In fact, the assailant[4] had already survived multiple gunshot wounds from an incident much like the one in which my brother lost his life.

2   As I wept for Blake I felt wrenched[5] backward into events and circumstances that had seemed light-years gone. Though a decade apart, we both were raised in Chester, Pa., an angry, heavily black, heavily poor, industrial city southwest of Philadelphia. There, in the 1960's, I was introduced to mortality,[6] not by the old and failing, but by beautiful young men who lay wrecked after sudden explosions of violence. The first, I remember from my 14th year— Johnny, brash[7] lover of fast cars, stabbed to death two doors from my house in a fight over a pool game. The next year, my teenage cousin, Wesley, whom I loved very much, was shot dead. The summers blur. Milton, an angry young neighbor, shot a crosstown rival, wounding him badly. William, another teen-age neighbor, took a shotgun blast to the shoulder in some urban[8] drama and displayed his bandages proudly. His brother, Leonard, severely beaten, lost an eye and donned[9] a black patch. It went on.

3   I recall not long before I left for college, two local Vietnam veterans—one from the Marines, one from the Army—arguing fiercely, nearly at blows about which outfit had done the most in

[1] came out of

[2] incapable of being separated

[3] developed or rose step by step (as on an escalator)

[4] attacker

[5] turned by force

[6] the notion that people must eventually die
[7] rash, reckless

[8] having to do with the city

[9] put on

[10]a low-ranking officer
appointed from
enlisted soldiers

[11]wealthy, well-to-do

[12]from the suburbs
(the residential area
surrounding a city)

[13]mental disorder
characterized by the
belief that one is being
persecuted

[14]beaten

[15]masculinity

[16]invasions, offenses

[17]comfortably settled

[18]abandoned, dilapidated

[19]raids, adventures

[20]ground, area

[21]put on, assumed

the war. The most killing, they meant. Not much later, I read a magazine article that set that dispute in a context. In the story, a non-commissioned officer[10]—a sergeant, I believe—said he would pass up any number of affluent,[11] suburban-born[12] recruits to get hardcore soldiers from the inner city. They jumped into the rice paddies with "their manhood on their sleeves," I believe he said. These two items—the veterans arguing and the sergeant's words—still characterize for me the circumstances in which black men in their teens and 20's kill one another with such frequency. With a touchy paranoia[13] born of living battered[14] lives, they are desperate to be real men. Killing is only machismo[15] taken to the extreme. Incursions[16] to be punished by death were many and minor, and they remain so: they include stepping on the wrong toe, literally; cheating in a drug deal; simply saying "I dare you" to someone holding a gun; crossing territorial lines in a gang dispute. My brother grew up to wear his manhood on his sleeve. And when he died, he was in that group— black, male and in its teens and early 20's—that is far and away the most likely to murder or be murdered.

I left the East Coast after college, spent the mid- and late-1970's in Chicago as a graduate student, taught for a time, then became a journalist. Within 10 years of leaving my hometown, I was overeducated and "upwardly mobile," ensconced[17] on a quiet, tree-lined street where voices raised in anger were scarcely ever heard. The telephone, like some grim umbilical, kept me connected to the old world of deaths, imprisonings and misfortune. I felt emotionally beaten up. Perhaps to connect myself, I added a psychological dimension to the physical distance I had already achieved. I rarely visited my hometown. I shut it out.

As I fled the past, so Blake embraced it. On Christmas of 1983, I traveled from Chicago to a black section of Roanoke, Va., where he then lived. The desolate[18] public housing projects, the hopeless, idle young men crashing against one another—these reminded me of the embittered town we'd grown up in. It was a place where once I would have been comfortable, or at least sure of myself. Now, hearing of my brother's forays[19] into crime, his scrapes with police and street thugs, I was scared, unsteady on foreign terrain.[20]

I saw that Blake's romance with the street life and the hustler image had flowered dangerously. One evening that late December, standing in some Roanoke dive among drug dealers and grim, hair-trigger losers, I told him I feared for his life. He had affected[21] the image of the tough he wanted to be. But behind the dark glasses and the swagger, I glimpsed the baby-faced toddler I'd once watched over. I nearly wept. I wanted desperately for him to live. The young think themselves immortal, and a dangerous light shone in his eyes as he spoke laughingly of making fools of the policemen who had raided his apartment looking for drugs. He cried out as I took his right hand. A line of stitches lay between the thumb and index finger. Kickback from a shogun, he explained, nothing serious. Gunplay had become part of his life.

7   I lacked the language simply to say: Thousands have lived this for you and died. I fought the urge to lift him bodily and shake him. This place and the way you are living smells of death to me, I said. Take some time away, I said. Let's go downtown tomorrow and buy a plane ticket anywhere, take a bus trip, anything to get away and cool things off. He took my alarm casually. We arranged to meet the following night—an appointment he would not keep. We embraced as though through glass. I drove away.

8   As I stood in my apartment in Chicago holding the receiver that evening in February 1984, I felt as though part of my soul had been cut away. I questioned myself then, and I still do. Did I not reach back soon or earnestly[22] enough for him? For weeks I awoke crying from a recurrent[23] dream in which I chased him, urgently trying to get him to read a document I had, as though reading it would protect him from what had happened in waking life. His eyes shining like black diamonds, he smiled and danced just beyond my grasp. When I reached for him, I caught only the space where he had been.

[22] sincerely

[23] repeated

Comprehension Questions

1. Brent Staples's brother was murdered by
    A. a rival gang member.
    B. a stranger.
    C. someone who had been a friend.
    D. the police.

2. Staples and his brother turned out differently because they were raised under different conditions. (T/F)

3. Staples uses the anecdote about the Vietnam War to illustrate that
    A. more blacks than whites fought in Vietnam.
    B. black soldiers were better than white soldiers.
    C. soldiers from the inner cities saw battle as an opportunity to prove themselves.
    D. there were a significant number of black casualties in the Vietnam War.

4. Staples's brother moved from Chester, Pennsylvania, to
    A. Chicago, Illinois.
    B. Richmond, Virginia.
    C. Roanoke, Virginia.
    D. New York City.

5. When Staples last saw his bother, his brother had been injured
    A. in a fist fight
    B. by kickback from a shotgun
    C. in a construction accident
    D. in a car accident

Discussion Questions

1. Describe the life Brent Staples and his brother knew when they were growing up.

2. Describe the "circumstances under which black men in their teens and 20's kill one another with such frequency."

3. How did Staples distance himself from his old neighborhood?

4. What did Staples try to do to save his brother?

5. Discuss the significance of Staples's dream about his brother.

Journal Topics

1. What, in your opinion, could or should Brent Staples (or someone in a similar situation) have done to save his brother?

2. Have you ever experienced a situation in which someone you knew was headed for trouble and you were unable to do anything about it? Describe the situation and your feelings.

1. Compare and contrast Brent Staples and his brother.

2. According to Staples, why are black males in their teens and early twenties "far and away the most likely to murder and be murdered"?

3. Describe the choices Staples made to escape the conditions of his youth and the different choices his younger brother made.

4. Describe a situation in which you felt helpless to save someone you loved who was headed for trouble. What conditions contributed to the person's difficulties?

5. Describe Staples's feelings toward his brother. Why was he unable to save the brother he loved?

Writing Topics

Special Topics

Introduction: The two-sentence introductory paragraph sets out the purpose of this article. The first sentence gives background and sets up the contrast with the second sentence, which states the thesis that Martin Luther King Jr.'s "achievements are misunderstood."

Related Reading: "Pilgrimage to Nonviolence" by Martin Luther King, Jr. (p. 490)

Martin Luther King

"Martin Luther King: He led a mass struggle for racial equality that doomed segregation and changed America forever."
Jack E. White[1]

[1] *Time* correspondent Jack E. White has covered civil rights issues for thirty years.

[2] badly

[3] limiting

[4] bonds

[5] the act of pretending to have virtuous intentions

[6] sneers

[7] contempt

[8] not different

[9] a system of laws that kept whites and blacks apart

[10] protested

[11] a metaphor for the post–World War II separation of the communist world of the Soviet Union and its allies from the United States and its allies

[12] a metaphor that refers to one of the primary crops (cotton) on which the slave economy of the South was based

[13] The Supreme Court ruled that segregated schools were unconstitutional in the case *Brown v. the Board of Education of Topeka, Kansas.*

[14] a woman who sews for a living

[15] intimidated

It is a testament to the greatness of Martin Luther King Jr. that nearly every major city in the U.S. has a street or school named after him. It is a measure of how sorely[2] his achievements are misunderstood that most of them are located in black neighborhoods.

Three decades after King was gunned down on a motel balcony in Memphis, Tenn., he is still regarded mainly as the black leader of a movement for black equality. That assessment, while accurate, is far too restrictive.[3] For all King did to free blacks from the yoke[4] of segregation, whites may owe him the greatest debt, for liberating them from the burden of America's centuries-old hypocrisy[5] about race. It is only because of King and the movement that he led that the U.S. can claim to be the leader of the "free world" without inviting smirks[6] of disdain[7] and disbelief. Had he and the blacks and whites who marched beside him failed, vast regions of the U.S. would have remained morally indistinguishable[8] from South Africa under apartheid,[9] with terrible consequences for America's standing among nations. How could America have convincingly inveighed[10] against the Iron Curtain[11] while an equally oppressive Cotton Curtain[12] remained draped across the South?

Even after the Supreme Court struck down segregation in 1954,[13] what the world now calls human-rights offenses were both law and custom in much of America. Before King and his movement, a tired and thoroughly respectable Negro seamstress[14] like Rosa Parks could be thrown into jail and fined simply because she refused to give up her seat on an Alabama bus so a white man could sit down. A six-year-old black girl like Ruby Bridges could be hectored[15] and spit on by a white New Orleans mob simply because she wanted to go to the same school as white children. A 14-year-old black boy like Emmett Till could be hunted down and murdered by a Mississippi gang simply because he had supposedly

1

2

3

made suggestive remarks to a white woman. Even highly educated blacks were routinely denied the right to vote or serve on juries. They could not eat at lunch counters, register in motels or use whites-only rest rooms; they could not buy or rent a home wherever they chose. In some rural enclaves[16] in the South, they were even compelled to get off the sidewalk and stand in the street if a Caucasian[17] walked by.

[16]parts, sections

4   The movement that King led swept all that away. Its victory was so complete that even though those outrages took place within the living memory of the baby boomers, they seem like ancient history. And though this revolution was the product of two centuries of agitation by thousands upon thousands of courageous men and women, King was its culmination.[18] It is impossible to think of the movement unfolding as it did without him at its helm.[19] He was, as the cliché has it, the right man at the right time.

[17]white person

[18]end point
[19]a place of control (from the word for a steering wheel on a ship)
[20]rhythms

5   To begin with, King was a preacher who spoke in biblical cadences[20] ideally suited to leading a stride toward freedom that found its inspiration in the Old Testament story of the Israelites and the New Testament gospel of Jesus Christ. Being a minister not only put King in touch with the spirit of the black masses but also gave him a base within the black church, then and now the strongest and most independent of black institutions.[21]

[21]fundamental organizations such as churches and schools

6   Moreover, King was a man of extraordinary physical courage whose belief in nonviolence never swerved. From the time he assumed leadership of the Montgomery, Ala., bus boycott in 1955 to his murder 13 years later, he faced hundreds of death threats. His home in Montgomery was bombed, with his wife and young children inside. He was hounded by J. Edgar Hoover's FBI, which bugged his telephone and hotel rooms, circulated salacious gossip[22] about him and even tried to force him into committing suicide after he won the Nobel Peace Prize in 1964. As King told the story, the defining moment of his life came during the early days of the bus boycott. A threatening telephone call at midnight alarmed him: "Nigger, we are tired of you and your mess now. And if you aren't out of this town in three days, we're going to blow your brains out and blow up your house." Shaken, King went to the kitchen to pray. "I could hear an inner voice saying to me, 'Martin Luther, stand up for righteousness. Stand up for justice. Stand up for truth. And lo I will be with you, even until the end of the world.'"

[22]unfounded hearsay about sex

7   In recent years, however, King's most quoted line—"I have a dream that my four little children will one day live in a nation where they will not be judged by the color of their skin but by the content of their character"—has been put to uses he would never have endorsed. It has become the slogan for opponents of affirmative action like California's Ward Connerly, who insist,

incredibly, that had King lived he would have been marching alongside them. Connerly even chose King's birthday last year to announce the creation of his nationwide crusade against "racial preferences."

Such would-be kidnappers of King's legacy have chosen a   8
highly selective interpretation of his message. They have filtered out his radicalism and sense of urgency. That most famous speech was studded with demands. "We have come to our nation's capital to cash a check," King admonished.[23] "When the architects of our Republic wrote the magnificent words of the Constitution and the Declaration of Independence, they were signing a promissory note[24] to which every American was to fall heir,"[25] King said. "Instead of honoring this sacred obligation, America has given the Negro people a bad check; a check which has come back marked 'insufficient funds.'" These were not the words of a cardboard saint advocating a Hallmark card-style version of brotherhood. They were the stinging phrases of a prophet, a man demanding justice not just in the hereafter, but in the here and now.

[23]scolded

[24]a note that promises something, an IOU

[25]become an inheritor

Comprehension Questions

1. Martin Luther King Jr. died in _____.

    A. Washington, D.C.

    B. Atlanta

    C. New York

    D. Memphis

2. Martin Luther King Jr. worked as a _____.

    A. lawyer

    B. politician

    C. preacher

    D. singer

3. According to the author, the strongest and most important black institution is the _____.

    A. church

    B. government

    C. family

    D. courts

4. What prestigious award did Martin Luther King win?

    A. Pulitzer Prize

    B. Freedom Award

    C. Nobel Peace Prize

    D. Academy Award

5. According to the author, if Martin Luther King Jr. were living today,

    A. he would support opponents of affirmative action.

    B. he would still demand justice for African Americans.

    C. he would be happy with the progress the nation has made.

    D. he would organize more protests worldwide.

Discussion Questions

1. What does the author mean when he writes, "It is a testament to the greatness of Martin Luther King Jr. that nearly every major city in the U.S. has a street or school named after him. It is a measure of how sorely his achievements are misunderstood that most of them are located in black neighborhoods?" In other words, why does having streets and schools named for him give evidence of King's greatness, and how does the fact that these streets and schools are in black neighborhoods show that Martin Luther King's achievements are misunderstood?

2. The author writes, "For all King did to free blacks from the yoke of segregation, whites may owe him the greatest debt, for liberating them from the burden of America's centuries-old hypocrisy about race." What does this statement mean?

3. Why was King "the right man at the right time" to make sure that the injustices of racism were not only judged unconstitutional but were effectively eliminated from much of national life?

4. Do you think that different races are treated equally in the region of the country where you live? Explain.

5. Is a leader like King necessary today? What issues would such a leader tackle in America today?

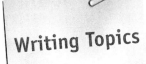

Writing Topics

1. Explain what gifts Martin Luther King Jr. possessed that enabled him to lead the movement for racial equality in America.

2. What leader today has some of the same qualities of leadership as King?

3. If King were alive today, what would he view as the greatest challenge to human rights in this country or the world?

4. Choose another leader in civil rights, human rights, or women's rights and explain this leader's accomplishments.

5. Narrate an event in your own life of a time when you had to stand up for what was right. Did you have conflicting emotions about doing what was right? How did you find the courage to overcome your fears? What did you learn about yourself in the process?

Appendix
Rules and Tools

Capitalization

Capitalize

- The first word of a sentence.
- Proper nouns (names of specific people, places, and things).
- Professional titles used with a name.
- The word *I*.
- Specific geographic features and proper place names.
- Names of cities, counties, states, regions, countries, continents, and planets.
- Proper names of institutions, businesses, and federal agencies.
- Proper names of buildings and historical monuments should be capitalized.
- Names of holidays.
- Names of specific school courses.
- Days and months.
- The first word, last word, and all important words in the titles of books, poems, articles, chapters, academic papers, songs, journals, and magazines.
- Names of eras or periods in history.
- Nationalities and languages.
- Abbreviations for agencies, organizations, trade names, and radio and television stations.
- The first word of a quoted sentence.

Do not capitalize

- Places that are not proper names.
- Directional words ending in *-ern* (northern, southern, eastern, western).
- Subject names that are not part of a course title.
- Names of seasons.
- Centuries or decades.
- Animal and plant names (unless they refer to a specific place or person).

Subject–Verb Agreement

	Singular	**Plural**
First person	I work	We work
Second person	You work	You work
Third person	He works	They work
	She works	Students work
	It works	Bill and Mary work.
	A student works	
	Everyone works	
	Mathematics is easy.	
	My family is home.	
	Either my father or my friends drive me.	
	Either my friends or my father drives me.	

- A third person singular subject (*a student, she, it*) takes a verb with an *-s* **ending.**
- **Single subject** begins with *s*, and the verb needs an *-s* **ending.**
- A plural subject (*students, they*) takes a verb with no *-s.*
- *Plural* doesn't begin with *s*, so the verb needs **no** *-s.*
- *I* and *you* take a verb with no ending.
- The subject is **never** found in a **prepositional phrase.**
- Most indefinite pronouns (*everyone, nothing*) are singular.
- **Collective nouns** (*family, class*) are usually singular and take a verb with an *-s* **ending.**
- **Fields of study** (*mathematics*) are singular subjects and take a verb with an *-s* **ending.**
- Some **subjects can be either singular or plural** (*a lot, most*) depending on the meaning of the sentence.

- **Compound subjects** (*Bill and Mary*) are plural and take a verb with no ending.
- When **subjects are joined by *or* or *nor*,** the verb agrees with the closest subject.
- A **gerund** (an *-ing* word used as a subject) is singular and takes a verb with an *-s* **ending**.
- Both verbs in a **compound verb** should agree with the subject.
- The subject usually comes **after** the verb when a sentence begins with *There* **or** *Here*.

Fragments

A **sentence fragment** is a group of words that

- Lacks a subject.
- Lacks a verb.
- Lacks both a subject and a verb.
- Includes a subject and a verb but does not express a complete thought.

Ways to correct fragments

- Add words such as subjects or verbs to make the fragment complete.
- Delete words such as subordinating conjunctions to make the fragment complete.
- Attach the fragment to a complete sentence.

Run-ons

- A **fused sentence** incorrectly joins or fuses two independent clauses together without any punctuation.
- A **comma splice** incorrectly joins or splices together two independent clauses with only a comma.
- To identify a run-on, first identify the subjects and the verbs in a word group that ends with a period. In a run-on, a second subject and verb can be separated from the first subject and verb to make two complete sentences. No run-on occurs if the word group cannot be divided into two complete thoughts.

Ways to correct run-ons

- Separate the independent clauses with a **period** into two complete sentences.
- Join the two independent clauses with a **coordinating conjunction** and a **comma**.

- Join the two independent clauses (sentences) with a **semicolon** and a **transition** and a **comma**.
- Join the two independent clauses (sentences) with a **semicolon**.
- Join the two clauses with a **subordinating conjunction**.

Commas

- Use commas between items in **dates** and **addresses**.
- Use commas to set off items in a **series**.
- In a compound sentence, use a comma between **two independent clauses** joined by a **coordinating conjunction**.
- Use a comma after an **introductory element**.
- Commas are used to separate **interrupters**.
- Use a comma after **certain small words** at the beginning of a sentence.
- Use commas to set off people's names or titles from the rest of the sentence when **directly addressing** them in writing.
- Use commas to set off **transitions** that interrupt the flow of the sentence.
- Use commas to set off an **appositive,** a word or group of words that defines or explains the word or phrase that comes before it.
- Use commas to separate information that is **nonrestrictive or nonessential** to the meaning of the sentence.

Apostrophes

Apostrophes are used

- To make contractions (*don't, there's, it's*).
- To show possession (*Maria's car, the players' coach, the people's choice*).
- To form plurals with some letters and numbers (*A's, 10's*).

Rules for showing possession

- To make a singular word possessive, add *'s.*
- If the owner is singular and ends in *s*, add an *'s.*
- To make a plural word that ends in *s* possessive, add an apostrophe after the final *s.*
- Some plural words do not end with an *s*. With irregular plural owners, add *'s.* (The most common irregular plurals are *children, women, men,* and *people.*)

Pronoun Agreement

- A pronoun must **agree in number** with its antecedent (the noun to which the pronoun refers). The student…he or she. The students…they.

- Because there is no single accepted solution to the problem of how to refer to an antecedent that may be male or female, it is best to consult with your instructors for their preferences.

- Pronoun agreement errors occur when the wrong pronoun is used. The most common error is the use of a plural pronoun with a singular antecedent. Incorrect: *The student…they.*

- With antecedents joined by *either…or* or *neither…nor*, the pronoun should agree with the nearest antecedent.

- Most indefinite pronoun antecedents (*everyone, something*) are singular and must take a singular pronoun.

- Some indefinite pronouns are plural (*many, few*) and take a plural pronoun.

- A few indefinite pronouns may be either singular or plural (*most, none*) depending on the noun or pronoun they refer to.

- Collective noun antecedents (*class, family, business*) are singular and must take a singular pronoun.

- Do not shift from singular subjects to plural subjects or vice versa within a paragraph.

- Do not shift from one person (*I, you, he, she, it*) to another person within a paragraph.

- Avoid using the second-person pronoun, *you*, in most academic writing because it is considered vague.

- When correcting pronoun errors, correct related errors like verb errors.

Pronoun Reference

A pronoun should clearly refer to one noun, called its **antecedent**.

Ambiguous Pronoun Reference

- If a sentence contains more than one noun, **avoid ambiguous pronoun reference** by using a pronoun that is close to and clearly refers to only one of the nouns.

Vague Reference

- The pronouns *it, this, that,* and *which* should refer to a single noun, not an entire idea.

Implied Reference

- Avoid using a pronoun for which no antecedent exists. The noun must be mentioned first before a pronoun can refer back to it.

Pronoun Case

- When a pronoun is used as a subject, use the **subjective case**.
- When a pronoun is used as an object, use the **objective case**.
- A pronoun may also serve as the object after a preposition. Use the objective case when a pronoun follows a preposition.
- In **comparisons** using *than* or *as*, complete the clause to find the correct pronoun.
- A pronoun in an **appositive** should use the same case as the noun it renames.

Who and *Whom*

- If pronoun functions as a subject, use *who* or *whose*. If the pronoun functions as an object, use *whom* or *whomever*.
- Use the objective case, *whom* or *whomever*, after a preposition since objects follow prepositions.
- In questions, if the pronoun functions as a subject, use *who* or *whoever*; if the pronoun functions as an object, use *whom* or *whomever*.

Semicolons and Colons

Semicolons

- Connect two independent clauses that are closely related.
- Join two sentences with a conjunctive adverb or a transitional expression.
- Separate items in a series when the series has internal punctuation.

Colons

- Are used after an independent clause that introduces a list
- Come after the words *as follows* and *the following* at the end of an independent clause.

Modifiers

Misplaced Modifiers

- Modifiers that modify the wrong word or words because of their placement are called **misplaced modifiers**. To avoid confusion, place the modifier as close as possible to the word it describes.

Limiting Modifiers

- **Limiting modifiers** usually come before the word or words they modify. Different placements of these modifiers change the meaning of the sentence.
- Don't place limiting modifiers in front of a verb unless they are intended to modify the verb.
- Generally, limiting modifiers are placed before the word or words they modify. However, if a modifier is placed between two words that it could describe, the sentence becomes unclear and is sometimes called a **squinting modifier**.
- In general, do not **split** parts of an **infinitive** (to plus the base form of the verb: *to be, to go, to dance, to think*) with a modifier.

Dangling Modifiers

- Some modifiers are incorrect because what they modify has been left out of the sentence. If a modifier has no word to describe, it is called a **dangling modifier**. Dangling modifiers can be corrected by **adding a subject** after the modifier or **rewriting the modifying phrase** to include a subject.
- Often, a dangling modifier occurs when a sentence begins with a verbal phrase: a present participial phrase (begins with a verb ending in *-ing*), a past participial phrase (begins with a past tense verb), an infinitive phrase (begins with *to* + verb).
- In a command sentence, a modifier may describe the implied subject (*you*). In this case, no dangling modifier occurs.

Parallelism

- Use the same part of speech to express items in pairs, series, and comparisons.
- To create parallel sentences, balance a word with a word, a phrase with a phrase, and a clause with a clause. Make sure the words, phrases, and clauses have similar grammatical structures.
- Use parallel constructions for words joined by coordinating conjunctions.
- Use parallel structure with correlative conjunctions.

Paragraph Writing Process Prompts

The following prompts will guide you in writing paragraphs. You may wish to consult it each time you write a paragraph until the process becomes second nature.

1. Understanding the assignment

   Assignment: _____

   Length: _____

   Due date: _____

   If necessary, use a narrowing tree or brainstorming to narrow your topic to a subject that interests you and that you can develop in a paragraph. You may find it helpful to use scratch paper.

   Narrowed topic: _____ _____

   _____

2. Determining the writing context:

   Decide on your purpose, audience, and tone. Then choose a tentative main idea.

   Purpose: _____

   Audience: _____

   Tone: _____

   Tentative main idea: _____

   _____

   _____

3. Generating ideas

   Generate ideas for your paper by brainstorming, free writing, listing, clustering, or dividing. You may find it helpful to use scratch paper. Come up with as many ideas as possible. Keep your purpose and audience in mind as you generate ideas to support your topic sentence.

4. Organizing ideas

   • Examine the ideas you have generated and revise your tentative topic sentence.

   • Select your strongest support ideas and place them in the map or outline template in the order you would like to use them. Do more brainstorming if you do not have enough supports to develop your topic sentence.

- Generate specific details for each of your supports.
- You may wish to state how each support relates to or proves the topic sentence.

Map Template

Topic Sentence:_____

Area of Support	**Specific Details**	**Relation to Topic Sentence**

1._____

_____

2._____

_____

3._____

_____

4._____

_____

5._____

_____

Outline Template

Topic sentence:_____

 I. Support #1 _____

  A. Specifics_____

  B. Relation _____

 II. Support #2 _____

  A. Specifics_____

  B. Relation _____

 III. Support #3 _____

  A. Specifics_____

  B. Relation _____

 IV. Support #4 _____

  A. Specifics_____

  B.Relation _____

5. Drafting

Write a draft of the paragraph by creating a sentence or sentences for each area of supports on your map or outline. Incorporate your specific details and, where appropriate, the relation to the topic sentence.

6. Revising

If possible, get feedback on your paragraph from peers or your instructor. If not, analyze the strengths and weaknesses of your paragraph using the Paragraph Revision Checklist on p. 62.

Paragraph Revision Checklist

1. **Form**

   Title: Are the major words (including the first and last words) capitalized?

   Does the title reveal the topic and slant of the paragraph?

   Does it catch the reader's attention?

   Is the first sentence indented?

   Does the paragraph have the required number of sentences?

   Does the paragraph have the required organizational pattern?

2. **Topic Sentence**

   Does the topic sentence fit the assignment?

   Is it appropriate for the intended audience and purpose?

   Is the main idea clear?

3. **Support**

   Is there enough support (three to five supports, depending on the assignment) to explain or prove your topic sentence?

   Does each support clearly relate to or develop the topic sentence?

   Are there enough specific details, facts, and examples to convince the reader?

   Are any supports repeated?

   Does anything in the paragraph not relate to the main idea?

   Is the relationship between support sentences clear?

   Are there clear transitions within and between sentences?

   Is the order of supports clear and logical?

Are the sentences varied in length and structure?

Is the vocabulary appropriate?

Is the language clear and precise used? (Are there strong verbs, specific nouns, colorful adjectives and adverbs?)

4. **Conclusion**

Does the conclusion tie together the paragraph?

Does it introduce any new ideas or arguments that might confuse the reader?

Directions: Read the paragraph carefully and answer the following questions as specifically as possible. Remember your goal is to help your peer improve his or her paragraph.

Peer Review Questionnaire: Paragraph

1. Is the topic sentence clear? Restate it in your own words.

2. Does the paragraph adequately explain or develop the topic sentence? List the areas of support used.

3. Does the order of supports seem logical?

4. Is there enough information or support to develop the topic sentence? What additional information or supporting ideas could the writer have included?

5. What did you like most about the paragraph?

6. What seemed most unclear about the paragraph?

7. Did you notice mechanical errors in the paragraph?

---

1. Understanding the assignment

Assignment: _____

Length: _____

Due date: _____

Essay Writing Process Prompts

If necessary, use a narrowing tree or brainstorming to narrow your topic to a subject that interests you and that you can develop in the length of paper you have been assigned. You may find it helpful to use scratch paper.

Narrowed topic: _____

_____

2. Determining the writing context

Decide on your purpose, audience, and tone. Then write a tentative thesis.

Purpose: _____

Audience: _____

Tone: _____

Tentative thesis: _____

3. Generating ideas

Generate ideas by brainstorming, freewriting, listing, clustering or dividing. You may find it helpful to use scratch paper. Come up with as many ideas as possible. Keep your purpose and audience in mind as you generate ideas to support your topic sentence.

4. Organizing ideas

- Examine the ideas you have generated and revise your tentative thesis to fit the ideas generated.
- Select the main ideas you will use to support your thesis. Remember that you will develop one main idea in each body paragraph of the essay.
- Generate additional ideas if you don't have enough main ideas to support your thesis.
- Using the Essay Outline Template below, write a tentative topic sentence for each body paragraph (next to each Roman numeral).
- Generate ideas to develop each body paragraph.
- Decide which supports to use and the order in which to present them. Add them to your outline.
- Revise your thesis statement to fit the ideas you will develop in the essay.
- Generate ideas for the introduction and conclusion after you have written a draft of the body paragraphs.

Essay Outline Template

(*Note:* Use as many main topics, support topics, and specific supports as necessary.)

    I. Introduction

    Thesis:_____

   II. Main topic _____

     A. Support topic _____

     B. Support topic _____

     C. Support topic _____

  III. Main topic _____

     A. Support topic _____

     B. Support topic _____

     C. Support topic _____

  IV. Main topic _____

     A. Support topic _____

     B. Support topic _____

     C. Support topic _____

   V. Conclusion _____

5. Drafting

Body

Write a draft for each of your body paragraphs, incorporating the information from your outline into your sentences. Focus on communicating your main ideas as clearly as possible.

Introduction

Use a technique such as brainstorming, freewriting, listing, clustering, or dividing to generate ideas for your introduction. How can you get your reader's attention? Can you think of a story or anecdote to dramatize the point of your essay? What background information does the reader need to understand your thesis?

Conclusion

Generate ideas for your conclusion. Can you refer back to something in your introduction to conclude your paper? Can you emphasize or restate the main points of your essay?

6. If possible, get feedback on your essay from peers or your instructor. If you cannot get feedback from someone else, analyze the strengths and weaknesses of your essay using the Essay Revision Checklist on page 82.

Essay Revision Checklist

1. **Introduction**

   Is the background information interesting? Does it engage the reader?

   Does it prepare the reader for the thesis?

   Does the introduction provide a logical progression toward the thesis?

   Does it focus on, provide background for, or lead into thesis?

   Is the introduction adequately developed?

   Thesis:

   Is the thesis a clear statement of the main idea of the essay?

   Does it fit the assignment?

2. **Body Paragraphs**

   Organization:

   If there is a blueprinted thesis, do the body paragraphs develop points in the same order as they are listed in the thesis?

   Even if the thesis is not a blueprint, do the body paragraphs follow a logical order?

   Is the relationship between paragraphs clear?

   Are appropriate transitions used between paragraphs?

   Topic Sentences:

   Is each topic sentence clear? Does it make one point that supports the thesis?

   Supports:

   Are there enough supports (three to five supports, depending on the assignment) to explain or prove the topic sentences?

   Does each support sentence clearly develop the topic sentence?

   Do any supports wander away from the topic?

   Are any supports repeated?

Is the relationship between support sentences clear?

Are there clear transitions between sentences?

Is there enough specific detail in each sentence to convince the reader?

Is the order of supports clear and logical?

Do the sentences vary in length and structure?

Is the vocabulary appropriate?

Is the language clear and precise? (Are there strong verbs, specific nouns, and colorful adjectives and adverbs?)

3. **Conclusion**

Does the conclusion summarize or tie together the essay?

Does it relate back to the hook or story used in the introduction?

Does it introduce any new ideas or arguments that would confuse the reader?

4. **Entire essay**

Does the essay make sense?

Does the essay develop in a logical order?

Does the essay adequately develop the thesis?

Does the essay deliver everything promised in the thesis?

Does the essay repeat itself?

Directions: Read the essay carefully and answer the following questions as specifically as possible. Remember your goal is to help your peer improve his/her paper. Wherever possible, provide suggestions for improvement.

Peer Review Questionnaire: Essay

1. Is the introduction well developed?_____

   Interesting?_____

2. Is the thesis clear?_____

   Restate it in your own words._____

   _____

   _____

3. For each body paragraph, indicate whether or not there is a clear topic sentence that supports the thesis. Restate the main idea in your own words.

   #1 _____

   #2 _____

   #3 _____

   #4 _____

4. Are body paragraphs well developed?_____

5. What additional information or supporting ideas could the writer have included?

   _____

   _____

   _____

   _____

6. Does the essay develop in a logical order?_____

7. Does the essay adequately develop the thesis?_____

8. What did you like most about the essay?

   _____

   _____

   _____

   _____

9. What seemed most unclear about the essay?

   _____

   _____

   _____

   _____

10. What mechanical errors did you notice in the essay?

   _____

   _____

   _____

   _____

If you are not sure about an error, take the time to look it up in *Writer's Resources.*

1. Check for run-ons and fragments. Is there one complete sentence between every two periods? (Identify the subject and the verb and make sure the word group expresses a complete thought.)

2. Check every verb. Do subjects and verbs agree and is proper verb tense used? Be sure to check the problem phrases such as *there is/there are* and pay attention to singular subjects such as *everyone.*

3. Use the dictionary or spell check to check for capitalization errors and misspellings. Remember the spell check will not catch errors with problem words such as *there/their.*

4. Get out your personal list of errors. Check your writing for any of these errors.

5. Check for apostrophes in contractions and possessives.

6. Check commas.

7. Be sensitive to pronouns in the writing. Do they agree with their antecedents and is the reference clear?

8. Look for any missing words or letters by reading the writing slowly from the last sentence to the first.

9. Once you have mastered these skills, check parallelism in pairs, series, and comparisons.

10. Check for dangling and misplaced modifiers.

11. Check semicolon and colon use.

ERROR LIST
KEEP A LIST OF ALL ERRORS YOU MAKE.

Your Writing Error	Correction	Explanation/ Type of Error
rec*ie*ved	rec*ei*ved	*i* before *e* spelling
When I took the course.	When I took the course, I got an A.	fragment
My grade *on* the class was	My grade *in* the class	preposition
She went thorough	She went *through*	homonym
the people *is*	the people *are*	subject-verb agreement
a person *have*	a person *has*	subject-verb agreement
use to go	*used* to go	spelling
you can buy	*a shopper* can buy	Don't use *you* (vague)
___	___	___
___	___	___
___	___	___
___	___	___
___	___	___
___	___	___
___	___	___
___	___	___
___	___	___
___	___	___
___	___	___
___	___	___
___	___	___
___	___	___
___	___	___

Index